Tears Before the Rain

TEARS BEFORE THE RAIN

An Oral History of the Fall of South Vietnam

LARRY ENGELMANN

New York   Oxford
OXFORD UNIVERSITY PRESS
1990

Oxford University Press

Oxford   New York   Toronto
Delhi   Bombay   Calcutta   Madras   Karachi
Petaling Jaya   Singapore   Hong Kong   Tokyo
Nairobi   Dar es Salaam   Cape Town
Melbourne   Auckland

and associated companies in
Berlin   Ibadan

Published by Oxford University Press, Inc.,
200 Madison Avenue, New York, New York 10016

Oxford is a registered trademark of Oxford University Press

Library of Congress Cataloging-in-Publication Data
Engelmann, Larry.
Tears before the rain : an oral history of
the fall of South Vietnam
Larry Engelmann.
p.   cm.   ISBN 0-19-505386-9
1. Vietnamese Conflict, 1961–1975—Personal narratives.
I. Title.   DS559.5.E45   1990   959.704′38—dc20
89–26629

9 8 7 6 5 4 3 2 1

Printed in the United States of America
on acid-free paper

For My Mother
Delores Barnett

I don't want my memories to be lost, like tears in the rain. So I will tell you my story. Then you can tell it to others. Maybe if enough people know what happened to Vietnam, then my memories will never be lost. Maybe then they will be like tears before the rain. So listen. This is very important. This is what I remember. This is what happened to me. These are my tears before the rain.

Duong Cang Son

Preface

During the last days of January in 1975 an unusually large swarm of bees descended on Saigon, the embattled capital of South Vietnam. The bees settled on two small apartment buildings. The terrified inhabitants of the buildings ran away. A few dauntless residents, however, soon returned to assail the swarm. They decided to use smoke to dislodge the bees.

But before the smoke was used, other people who had heard about the bees suggested that they had been sent to Saigon to convey a warning. The many seers and mystics of the city who were adept at deciphering fantastic and arcane phenomena announced that the arrival of the bees indicated that in a short time the Vietnamese people themselves would be like the bees. "And as we treat them," the mystics and seers said, "so will we in turn be treated."

The conviction that the bees were a sign gained popular acceptance quickly. No smoke was used to dislodge them. From around the city people came to gaze at them and to wonder. No one entered the buildings. And then, only a day after they had first appeared in Saigon, the bees departed. They fled to the southeast in the direction of Vung Tau and the South China Sea. And although no one could say for sure what was meant specifically by the revelation that the people of Vietnam would be like the bees, many people wondered and worried more than ever about the future.

Only a few days after the bees abandoned Saigon, another unusual swarm appeared; this time near Phan Rang, northeast of Saigon. A vast army of caterpillars materialized, seemingly out of nowhere, and migrated to the southwest, blanketing the roads and fields. At first cars and cyclists simply drove over them and people walked on them. They were nothing more than a nuisance. But once again the mystics cautioned that the caterpillars should be regarded as a divine omen and should not be harmed. "Soon we shall surely be like the caterpillars," they warned, "and as we treat them, so in turn will we be treated." Then, like the bees, the caterpillars disappeared.

By the time the bees and caterpillars had appeared, South Vietnam was engaged in the second year of what President Nguyen Van Thieu termed "the Third Indochina War." In that war the armed forces of South Vietnam continued to fight against the insurgent Viet Cong and their North Vietnamese allies. But missing from the conflict was the United States. More than a decade earlier President John F. Kennedy had talked about making power credible and defending freedom and had concluded that "Vietnam is the place" to do both. In 1973, however, the American people and their leaders had decided that Vietnam was not the place. No more Americans should die for Vietnam, they decreed.

And so, early in 1973, after more than four years of negotiation in Paris, the United States finally came to terms with North Vietnam and signed what was called "An Agreement on Ending the War and Restoring the Peace in Vietnam." South Vietnam signed the agreement only reluctantly and after prolonged pressure and threats of an aid cutoff from the United States. The agreement provided for the disengagement and withdrawal of American combat forces from South Vietnam and an exchange of all prisoners of war. It also provided joint commissions for monitoring the release of prisoners and the withdrawal of American and other non-Vietnamese troops from South Vietnam. A four-party international commission was charged with supervising the cease-fire that was expected to follow the signing of the Paris Agreement and investigating violations of it. Another joint military commission was established by the agreement to investigate the whereabouts of American MIAs (missing in action). The agreement also anticipated establishment of a council to facilitate the peaceful reunification of North and South Vietnam.

The only part of the treaty that was actually strictly adhered to was that requiring the withdrawal of American forces. On March 29, 1973, the last American combat troops withdrew from South Vietnam. The old MACV (Military Assistance Command, Vietnam) headquarters at Tan Son Nhut air base became the home of the American Defense Attaché Office (DAO), which was strictly limited to monitoring the flow, distribution, and use of American supplies to the South Vietnamese military. The DAO staff was forbidden to assume any military advisory role in South Vietnam.

In one of its most controversial clauses, the Paris Agreement allowed the North Vietnamese to maintain somewhere between 80,000 and 160,000 combat troops in South Vietnam. For that reason alone, many South Vietnamese recognized the agreement, not as a peace treaty, but as a death sentence for their nation. According to the agreement, the North Vietnamese troops could be maintained, but not expanded; they could be supplied and replaced, but not reinforced beyond their existing numbers. In order to assuage the misgivings and the fears of the South Vietnamese, who were asked to coexist peacefully with this North Vietnamese military presence, both President Richard M. Nixon and Henry Kissinger, who personally negotiated the agreement, assured the South Vietnamese that the United States would never stand aside and allow North Vietnam to violate the treaty and expand its presence within South Vietnam. In fact, they promised President Thieu that the United States would respond with decisive military force to any gross violations of the treaty by the North. The military might of America, they assured him, would protect the territorial integrity and political independence of our ally. Soon after he took office in the summer of 1974, President Gerald Ford reaffirmed America's commitment to South Vietnam and the Paris Agreement.

Yet, in the end, the pledges of the two American presidents proved empty. The passage of time brought new problems and new leadership to the United States. The Watergate scandal brought first the discrediting and then the resignation of President Nixon and a weakening of the executive branch of the government. For Vietnam this was ominous, since support for South Vietnam had been centered in the executive branch while opposition to support for South Vietnam was centered in the legislative branch. A war in the Middle East and an oil squeeze by OPEC (Organization of Petroleum Exporting Countries) brought rapidly rising prices and a concern for America's ability to maintain its commitments to allied nations in areas outside Southeast Asia.

And in Vietnam the war continued. The Paris Agreement produced no peace. It merely altered the complexion and numbers of the combatants. After the spring of 1973, the long war in Vietnam was almost exclusively limited to Vietnamese killing Vietnamese with America and the Communist bloc nations providing the necessary machinery and materiel of defense and death.

But rising prices, severe congressional budgetary reductions, corruption in Vietnam, the persistence of the "peace movement" in the United States, and the gradually intensifying conflict in Vietnam worked together to produce vital shortages in essential military supplies. Those shortages, in turn, brought uncertainty and fear to South Vietnamese soldiers and civilians alike. They believed, despite the assurances of Ambassador Graham Martin and his Embassy staff in Saigon, that the United States was about to abandon South Vietnam to the not-so-tender mercies of the North Vietnamese. America had at long last truly written off South Vietnam, they concluded.

In the first week of 1975, the North Vietnamese Army (NVA) gained control of Phuoc Long province. The seizure of the province was intended as a test. The North wished to see what the response of the United States might be to this flagrant violation of the Paris Agreement. There was no American response. America, in fact, seemed uninterested in what the North Vietnamese Army did or did not do in South Vitenam. There was little NVA action when, in the next month, an American congressional delegation visited the South to assess the military situation there and to advise Congress and the President on providing additional military and humanitarian aid. A few days after the congressional delegation departed, the North Vietnamese made their next move.

On March 10, 1975, the North Vietnamese Army launched what was to be its final major offensive against South Vietnam, assured that America had lost its will to fight or to finance the independence of South Vietnam. No longer fearful of American intervention, the North Vietnamese were certain that victory and the forceful unification of Vietnam was, after nearly thirty years of conflict, soon to be accomplished.

The North moved 100,000 fresh troops down the Ho Chi Minh Trail, a route now unthreatened by American B-52 raids that had been transformed from a series of bicycle paths zigzagging through the jungles of Laos, Cambodia and Vietnam, to a bustling highway and an accompanying oil pipeline leading to the heart of South Vietnam.

The town of Ban Me Thuot in the central highlands fell to the North in mid-March. A counterattack by the South Vietnamese fizzled.

On March 14, President Thieu made one of the most unfortunate military decisions in the long conflict in Vietnam. He ordered the secret redeployment of the Vietnamese forces in the central highlands to the coast along the South China Sea. The forces were then to regroup and prepare for a counterattack on Ban Me Thuot. But the attempted redeployment turned into a rout. The unannounced and unexplained movement of the army out of Pleiku and Kontum encouraged frightened speculation and rumors about what was really happening. Many soldiers and civilians concluded that there had been a secret agreement and that Vietnam was about to be partitioned once more between the North and the South, this time with the central highlands and the northernmost provinces of South Vietnam going to the Communists. The military withdrawal became "the Convoy of Tears" as tens of thousands of civilians joined in the frantic exodus from the highlands. They jammed the roads and disrupted the movement of military vehicles. Advance units of the North Vietnamese Army caught the convoy and destroyed much of it. There was no counterattack on Ban Me Thuot because the army that withdrew from the central highlands disintegrated before it reached the coast.

With the obliteration of the military forces of the highlands, President Thieu next sought to redeploy his forces in the northernmost section of South Vietnam. That effort, too, turned into a disaster, and the divisions in the region disintegrated. Masses of people and remnants of military units flowed along crowded highways toward the safety of cities further south—toward Nha Trang and Saigon, or east to the safety of a flotilla waiting to evacuate them by sea.

Now the social and military fabric of South Vietnam began to unravel rapidly in many places at the same time. The South suddenly began to lose the war faster than the North could win it. The military forces of the South seemed to be imploding toward Saigon. Cities and provinces were abandoned to the North without a fight. In some areas, desperate South

Vietnamese soldiers, frustrated by the cowardice and incompetence of their political and military leaders, turned their rage on South Vietnamese citizens in an ugly orgy of violence and murder. Victory for the armies of North Vietnam became, in many strategically important places, a mere matter of marching.

On March 29, the chaotic and desperate situation was recorded graphically by a CBS news crew that flew aboard a World Airways Boeing 727 to Danang, Vietnam's second largest city, to evacuate refugees. The plane was mobbed by soldiers who shot women and children and each other in a frenzied attempt to scramble aboard the aircraft and escape from the advancing North Vietnamese. As the plane took off with people clinging to the wheels, soldiers on the ground fired at it and a hand grenade blew up under one wing. The plane limped back into Saigon, and that evening a tape of the flight was shown on the *CBS Evening News*. American television viewers that Easter weekend saw the almost unbelievable horror of an army transformed into murderous rabble and a country thrashing about helplessly in the throes of a violent death.

In Saigon, American businesses, news bureaus, and government agencies began evacuating their employees and dependents. Commercial and military aircraft carried thousands of people to the Philippines, Thailand, Hong Kong, and the United States. But a special airlift to transport Vietnamese orphans from Saigon to the United States ended tragically on April 4 when a huge Air Force C-5A crashed soon after taking off, killing 135 of the orphans and escorts on board. For many Americans in Vietnam or watching the disintegration of Vietnam on television in the United States, the crash of the "Orphan Airlift" plane was particularly shocking since it involved a slaughter of helpless, innocent infants. The United States seemed incapable, at that moment, of guaranteeing that anyone—even infants—might escape unscathed from the frightening conflagration that was consuming the entire population of South Vietnam.

The collapse gained momentum. On April 21, under pressure from the United States as well as from members of his own government, President Thieu resigned after delivering a tearful speech on Vietnamese television, a speech in which he laid the blame for the collapse at the feet of the United States. A few days later he left the country. Vice President Tran Van Huong took control of the government.

As if to leave no doubt as to America's determination not to intervene again in Vietnam, on the evening of April 23, in a major address at Tulane University, President Gerald Ford announced that the war in Vietnam was "finished as far as America is concerned." The audience of students gave him a standing ovation.

On April 28 President Huong resigned and was succeeded by General Duong Van Minh. It was commonly—and incorrectly, it turned out—believed that Minh would be acceptable to the North Vietnamese and that he alone of all the political figures in the South could arrive at a negotiated settlement with the advancing North Vietnamese Army. But that, too, proved to be an illusion. Minh found that there was no one willing to make an agreement with him. He had nothing to offer the advancing divisions of the North but surrender. His most important act in his brief tenure as President was to make an unconditional surrender to the North Vietnamese.

On the morning of April 29, Operation Frequent Wind began. The exercise involved the evacuation of American and Vietnamese civilians and military personnel from Tan Son Nhut Airbase and from the American Embassy in Saigon to the Seventh Fleet in the South China Sea. The operation was completed early in the morning of April 30, a few hours before the surrender of the South. When the last Marines were airlifted from the roof of the American Embassy on the morning of April 30, they left behind more than four hundred Vietnamese waiting to be airlifted out of the compound. Throughout the previous day and night those same Vietnamese had been promised again and again that they would never be abandoned by the United States. They watched in silence as the last American helicopter left the roof of the Embassy. Even the final American promise to Vietnam had been broken.

Late in the morning of April 30, the Frequent Wind evacuees aboard the ships of the Seventh Fleet observed what appeared to be a massive swarm of bees darkening the sky and heading out over the South China Sea from the coast of Vietnam. As the mysterious swarm drew closer it was identified as hundreds of helicopters coming out from the coast and the Delta and other areas around Saigon, piloted by South Vietnamese airmen bringing out their families, relatives, and friends. So many helicopters attempted to land at once, crowding the decks of the American ships, that as soon as the choppers landed and emptied they were pushed into the sea. On the flight deck of the *Midway,* in order to protect the diminutive Vietnamese who landed and to prevent them from being blown over the side of the ship or struck by helicopter blades, the crewmen used pieces of rope, about ten feet long, to guide the Vietnamese to safety. The rope was handed to the refugees inside the helicopters, and then they held on to it and were led by an American across the flight deck and downstairs to a special processing center. From a short distance away, the groups of people clinging to the rope and walking quickly across the deck of the large carrier looked like large, multicolored caterpillars.

Fifteen years have passed since the collapse and surrender of South Vietnam. The victorious North Vietnamese have, since liberation, consolidated their power, revamped the economy of their nation, invaded and withdrawn from Cambodia, fought a war with China, opened Cam Ranh Bay to the Soviet fleet, changed the name of Saigon to Ho Chi Minh City, and transformed their homeland into one of the poorest nations in the world. For more than a decade, Vietnam has been hemorrhaging "boat people" who have risked their lives on the South China Sea in an effort to escape from the ruins of "liberation." When faced with forced repatriation, these same people vow that they would rather die than return to Vietnam.

And in the past fifteen years the vast multitude of Vietnamese who came to the United States and other nations as refugees have adapted to their new homelands. They have become citizens of other countries, and the hope of ever returning to Vietnam has gradually faded. The children of the refugees have grown up, attended universities and colleges, married and started their own families, and distinguished themselves in a wide range of careers. And they have become "Americanized."

America's Vietnam veterans have also, for the most part, become reintegrated into American civilian life. A striking memorial for those who were lost in the conflict in Vietnam has become the most-visited monument in the nation's capital. Films, books, and television programs have offered serious and sensational efforts to understand what really happened in Vietnam and what it means.

In the early spring of 1985 I began talking to American and South Vietnamese veterans about their experiences in the war and afterward. I continued my project for the next five years, visiting dozens of cities in the United States and traveling to Malaysia, Thailand, the Socialist Republic of Vietnam, and Hong Kong to interview victors and vanquished, children and adults, soldiers, civilians, and politicians, asking them what they remembered about the last days of the war in Vietnam and asking them about their lives since that fateful spring fifteen years ago.

What follows are the memories and opinions of many of the more than three hundred individuals I interviewed during the past five years. They told me, not simply about the spring of 1975, but also how they came to be involved with Vietnam at that time, how they saw the events of that spring unfold, how they have adjusted and remembered Vietnam in the past fifteen years, what they tell their children about Vietnam, and what they see in their dreams.

Contents

Part One

AMERICANS

What has occurred in this case, must ever recur in similar cases. Human-nature will not change. In any future great national trial, compared with the men of this, we shall have as weak, and as strong; as silly and as wise; as bad and good. Let us, therefore, study the incidents of this, as philosophy to learn wisdom from, and none of them as wrongs to be revenged.

Abraham Lincoln
November, 1864

I saw the battle corpses, myriads of them,
And the white skeletons of young men, I saw them,
I saw the debris and debris of all the slain soldiers of the war,
And I saw they were not as was thought,
They themselves were fully at rest, they suffered not,
The living remained and suffered, the mother suffered,
And the wife and the child and the musing comrade suffered,
And the armies that remained suffered.

Walt Whitman
"When Lilacs Last in the Dooryard Bloomed" (1866)

They were innocent. They thought we'd stay. But we were liberals and we didn't want a bad conscience.

Graham Greene
The Quiet American (1955)

CHAPTER I

Last Flight from Danang

Jan Wollett
"Why Are They Shooting at Us? We're the Good Guys"

I was supposed to get a wake-up call at my hotel in Saigon at five in the morning on March 29, 1975. I was to be the senior flight attendant on a flight up to Danang and back. I never got the call.

At six o'clock I got a call from Val Witherspoon, another one of the attendants on the flight. She asked me to be in the lobby in five minutes. So I jumped into my uniform and hurried downstairs. Mr. [Ed] Daly and Val were waiting for me. Bruce Dunning of CBS News was in the lobby, too. I told Bruce that we were flying up to Danang, and he said that there were rumors that the city had already fallen to the North Vietnamese. I said, "Well, I'm sure we wouldn't be going up there if it had fallen." Bruce then asked if he could come along on the flight, and Mr. Daly told him to be at Tan Son Nhut Airport in an hour. "You get there, then you're there," Daly said.

Bruce rounded up his cameraman, Mike Marriott, and his sound man, Mai Van Duc, and brought them out to the airport. We all boarded the aircraft—a World Airways Boeing 727. As the senior flight attendant I had been informed that we would be carrying one or two Vietnamese flight attendants as interpreters and that we would also be accompanied by guards for crowd control, since they had had some difficulty with crowds in Danang on the previous day. We were also supposed to be carrying soft drinks, orange juice, and sandwiches for the passengers.

Once we were on the plane I told Val and Atsako Okuba, the other flight attendants, to check and see what we had on board. Well, we discovered that the aircraft had not been catered. That was our first sign that there was something very strange going on. There were no soft drinks, no orange juice, and no sandwiches on board. And there were no Vietnamese flight attendants and no guards, either.

There was a discussion on board the plane about whether or not we should make the flight. Daly and the flight crew were on board by that time and so was Dunning and his CBS crew. Eventually, two officials from USAID came on board and assured us that everything was fine up at Danang and that we would not need the guards.

By that time it was already eight in the morning—much later than we had planned to take off. Mr. Daly decided that we would go up to Danang and pick up some refugees—women and children—and bring them out, even without the help of guards or interpreters.

The flight was very good. We took along with us a British newsman and another man from UPI [United Press International]. We chatted casually on the way up.

Then we started our descent into Danang. About twenty minutes behind us was another World Airways Boeing 727 flown by Don McDaniel, and behind him was another 727 flown by Dave Wanio. We figured that we would be on the ground for ten or fifteen minutes; we would load and take off; and then the next plane would land, and then the third. That way we could bring out three planeloads of people in less than an hour.

When we landed it was very strange, because we did not see a soul at first. Nobody. The entire airfield was deserted. And then, as we started to taxi, a massive swarm of people came up and out of bunkers. Thousands— and I mean literally thousands—started racing toward us. They were running, they were on motorcycles, they were in vans, they were in jeeps and cars and personnel carriers, they were on bicycles—they were coming out to us in anything they could find.

We had a plan. Mr. Daly and Joe Hrezo, a station chief for World Airways, would get off the plane first and line up people on the back air stair. I was to stay in the forward part of the plane, Atsako would stay in the middle, and Val would be in the aft.

We started a slow taxi. I was standing in the cockpit door looking out the front window. Then I realized that something really bizarre was going on. A group of people raced up next to the aircraft in a little truck. A man jumped off the truck and ran up in front of us. I was looking down at him as we were slowly taxiing, and he took out a pistol and started shooting at us. Suddenly, I had the fantastic feeling that I was in the middle of a John Wayne Western. And I thought, "Why are they shooting at us? We're the good guys."

We taxied past the man with the gun and slowed down further. I was now waiting for the first people to come on board. We were going to put them in seats, starting at the front of the aircraft and then keep going back, and fill up the seats in an orderly fashion.

Then the soldiers started coming on board. They were running. And they were just wild-eyed. About nine soldiers came on board and I seated them. Then a tenth came on and he wouldn't sit down. He was hysterical and he kept running up and down the aisle screaming in English, "TAKE OFF! TAKE OFF! TAKE OFF! THEY'RE ROCKETING THE FIELD!" He was just screaming it over and over again. And I grabbed him and I shouted, "Shut up and sit where I tell you to sit!" I pushed him into a seat.

Still, there were surprisingly few people getting on board the aircraft. So I thought I'd better go to the back and see what was happening. When I got to the back, I saw Mr. Daly at the bottom of the air stair and he was being mauled. His clothes were in tatters. And Joe Hrezo was gone. Val was trying to help Mr. Daly and was trying to pull people onto the air stair as the aircraft continued moving down the taxiway. At the bottom of the air stair were hundreds of people, all desperate and crazy and screaming and clawing at Val and Mr. Daly. You could see no end to those people. They were running to the air stair from every direction. I climbed down on the stair and tried to help.

Mr. Daly was at the very bottom of the air stair, waving a pistol in the air, trying to restore some kind of order. Val was helping people climb over the side of the stair onto the steps. A family of five was running a few feet from me, reaching out for help to get on board. It was a mother and a father and two little children and a baby in the mother's arms. I could see the fear in all of their faces as they ran and reached out for me. I reached back to grab the mother's hand, but before I could get it, a man running behind them shot all five of them, and they fell and were trampled by the crowd. The last I saw of them they were disappearing under people's feet. There were just several loud shots and they were gone—all five of them. And the man who shot them stepped on them to get closer to the air stair. He ran them down and jumped onto the air stair and ran up into the aircraft. Everything was so chaotic and insane, I remember thinking at that mad moment, "I'll deal with that later." And I just kept pulling people onto the stair.

I felt a woman pulling on me from the side of the stair. She was trying to get over the rail, and she grabbed my arm. I wanted to help her on, but I also had to worry about getting pulled off the stair. I turned and grabbed her arms and tried to pull her over the rail, but a man behind her grabbed her and jerked her out of my arms, and as she fell away he stepped on her back and her head to get up and over the railing. He used her as a stepping-stone. Mr. Daly saw that happen, and as the man swung his leg over the railing, Mr. Daly smashed him in the head with his pistol. I remember suddenly seeing a sheet of blood splash across everything, and I saw the man fall off and I saw people trample him, and I remember thinking, "Good." The man disappeared under the feet of the mob.

By that time people were streaming into the plane, so I ran back inside to see what was happening and to see if Atsako was getting them into their seats. She grabbed me and said, "Captain Healy needs you." So I went to the cockpit and knocked on the door. It was opened and Captain

Healy told me, "Joe Hrezo has been separated from the plane. When he's back on board, you let me know." I said "okay."

What had happened during all of this was that Joe and the British newsman had been pulled off the plane by the mob, and then they couldn't get back on. We lost both of them. Joe had run to the [control] tower and the guy operating the tower had let him in. Joe then called the plane, and Ken Healy said he would taxi over onto the taxiway. He told Joe to make a run for the plane when we came by. We would not be stopping at any time. The moment Joe was on board we were going to take off. Captain Healy told me, "When you know for sure that Joe's on board, just pound on the door."

I went to the back of the plane and told Val, "Val, watch the air stair and when you see Joe step on it, raise your arms in the air and I'll signal Ken."

While we waited to go by the tower, people kept getting on the aircraft. We were just shoving them into seats—five and six people in three seats. I remember asking as I directed them to the seats, "Where are the women and children? Where are the women and children?" It turned out that all of our first passengers were soldiers. Later we found that we had eleven women and children on board, but that was it. The rest were soldiers.

People on the aircraft were sitting in their seats totally in shock. And this one fool kept yelling over and over again, "TAKE OFF! TAKE OFF! TAKE OFF! TAKE OFF!"

As we taxied by the tower, Mr. Daly was still somewhere on the bottom of the air stair, pulling people on. A moment after we passed the tower, Val turned around and raised her arm in the air and I turned around and started to pound on the cockpit door. And as I did I heard the engines start to roar and we started to gain speed. And then this man who had been yelling for us to take off just started shrieking, "OH, NO! WE'RE TAKING OFF ON THE GRASS!"

We were taking off from the taxiway and Ken had gunned the engines to warn people to get out of the way or we would run over them. We were on the grass because the taxiway ended and the grass began and there was no way for us to get back on the runway at that point. We gained some speed and lifted off, and as we did, we hit a vehicle and then a fence pole, which did considerable damage to the wing. There was more damage to the aircraft from bullets and from a grenade that went off under one wing. But inside the aircraft we couldn't see the damage, so we didn't really know how bad the situation outside was. But Captain Healy was aware of it.

In any case, we were airborne. We had gotten out of Danang. I never really thought we would not make it out. You don't have time to think about things like that in the midst of so much confusion. But I discovered later that we almost didn't make it. We ended up with all that damage and with 358 people on board. We had sixty people in the cargo pits and we had people in the wheel wells. The plane was supposed to carry 133. Ken Healy later sent Boeing all of the statistics from our takeoff, and they ran them through their computer and told us that according to their figures our plane could not possibly have taken off. But we did. Ken sent Boeing a telegram later that said, "You build one hell of an aircraft."

As we took off I started counting passengers. I noticed a man sitting in the front seat who was very pale and who had been badly injured. His intestines were all hanging out. I took my hand and just shoved his intestines back inside and then I ripped a towel off somebody's neck and tied it around his waist to keep his intestines in. I grabbed the first-aid kit and found that it had been looted on the ground in Saigon. We had no medical equipment on board. None. There were no supplies of any kind anywhere on the aircraft.

When I was finished helping the guy in the front row I looked down the aisle and I saw a man crawling toward me. I recognized him right away. His whole head was caked with blood and there was blood all over his face. It was the man who had pulled the woman out of my arms—the man Mr. Daly hit with his pistol. The last time I had seen that woman she was just pulp and cotton on the ground. And the last time I had seen the man he was being trampled. But he had managed to get on board. And now he was crawling up the aisle toward me. That was the only moment I remember saying a prayer that day. I asked, "Oh, please God, don't have him come to me." And he crawled up to me. And he grabbed my pants leg and looked up at me and he just said, "Help."

So I grabbed somebody and pulled him out of a seat and I helped this man into the seat. His head was laid wide open, and I could see inside his head and it was just a bloody, pulpy mess. I had nothing to stop the bleeding with. I knew that if I didn't stop the bleeding he would die right there in my arms. A soldier next to the man had on a flak jacket. So I ripped open the flak jacket and grabbed the sawdust stuffing and pushed the sawdust into the man's wound to try to stop the flow of blood. I just kept packing the wound with sawdust. I am sure that the American Medical Association would have been shocked by what I did. But it worked. I ripped off another man's shirt and I tied it around the wounded man's head in order to keep the sawdust in and keep his head in one piece. He made it through the flight alive. He must have been very strong. He never even went into shock.

I then went to the back of the plane once more. I saw Val and Mr. Daly and Joe Hrezo working to free a man who was trapped in the aft air stair. The aft door could not be closed. The man stuck on the air stair had broken his leg. They finally got him loose and brought him inside the aircraft. Val and I tried to put together a splint for his leg. Joe then told me that the British news guy never made it back on the plane. He had stepped off onto the runway in Danang to film the crowd, and he was unable to get back on board in the panic. He was still in the tower back there, and Ken Healy promised him that an Air America chopper would come in and pick him up. Later that day it did, and he made it safely back to Cam Ranh Bay.

Val and Atsako and I just kept working and repairing the obvious damage to the people on the plane. That consumed most of our time. I guess we had been airborne for about an hour when I started looking at the passengers who weren't wounded. And I saw this horrible look on their faces. Finally, they had realized what they had just done. And then the questions started. "Will another plane come?" And we lied to them and assured them that "yes, there will be other planes." They realized that they had shot and killed their own people to get on board our aircraft. Now they were sorry. So we lied to them. We knew there would be no other flights to Danang. We were the last. The people left behind would not get out. In fact, Ken Healy had talked to Don McDaniel on the next 727 and told him to wait for us over Phan Rang, and he had radioed Dave Wanio and told him to go back to Saigon to prepare for an emergency landing. We had quite a bit of damage to the aircraft, and Ken was not sure that the landing gear would come down when we tried to land in Saigon. I knew what that would mean.

In the meantime it got incredibly hot inside the aircraft, even though the aft air stair was down and the door was wide open. With that number of people in the plane you just could not breathe. It was incredibly hot. We had Duc—who was the CBS sound man—keep announcing over the PA system in Vietnamese, "No smoking!" The passengers were not allowed to smoke at all because we could not have dealt with a fire, and we knew there would be one if some of them started smoking.

After working on the first-aid stuff for the passengers for a while, I noticed that there was nothing for these people to drink on the aircraft. But there was a drawer that had been full of ice and it had melted, and now the drawer was filled with cold water. I asked Bruce Dunning to rip up the galley curtains into little squares, about four or five inches square, and to soak them in the water. Then I took them and walked up and down the aisle passing out little wet pieces of galley curtain so people could mop their faces. They were all just sweating like crazy. I told Val and Atsako to do something to buck up the morale of these people. The shock of what they had done to their friends and comrades seemed to be destroying them slowly. They had left their families behind them on the ground. They had run over each other and shot each other to get on this plane. Now the panic was disappearing and the realization of the horror of what had happened—of what they had done—was starting to sink in. So we went around and talked to them and patted them on the shoulders and wiped their brows and their hands and tried as well as we could to comfort them.

I was dying of thirst myself by that time. And Mr. Daly came up to me and opened his shirt and showed me some Coke bottles. He said, "Go to the cockpit." I went up to the cockpit and sat down on the observer's seat, and Mr. Daly came in with the Cokes. He opened one and gave it to me. I remember putting the Coke to my mouth to drink, but everything went down my chin and onto the front of my uniform. I couldn't swallow. We passed that one Coke bottle around the cockpit. And once more Ken Healy told me about the damage to the aircraft. He said he was not sure about the nose gear on the plane coming down, and if it did come down, he was not sure that it would hold. He warned me to be ready for anything when we came down in Saigon.

I returned to the cabin to do whatever more I could do for the passengers. Then there was a startling moment when everyone on the plane suddenly looked over to our left and there was a great deal of excitement. We had finally arrived over Phan Rang, and Don McDaniel and his crew had been sitting up at 35,000 feet waiting for us. They finally saw this little dark dot way down below them, and they thought it might be us. And they came down to us. We looked out the window and there against the gorgeous blue sky and the big puffy white clouds was this beautiful red-and-white World 727. I know that there was suddenly a terrific feeling that went through the aircraft at that moment—and I know that it certainly went through me—a feeling that our sister ship had found us and that we were going to be safe because she was going to escort us home.

So Don flew his aircraft all around ours and assessed our damage. That's when he told Ken Healy, "It looks like you have a body hanging out the wheel well." Ken asked him about that. One person did get crushed as the wheels were retracting. But his death saved the other eight people in the wheel wells because his crushed body stopped the gears and did not let the wheels fully retract.

So by that time we knew that we were possibly going to have a problem with all of the wheels, and we knew also that the cargo doors were open and that the aft air stair was hanging down, and the back door was open, and the air flaps were shot and we would not have them to assist us in landing. We were in very serious trouble.

We continued on to Saigon. I said to Val at one point, "Come on, let's go into the lavatory and have a cigarette." So we went into the lavatory, and I told her all about the problems with the aircraft. During the landing I was going to be sitting in the front seat over the nose gear, and she was going to be sitting in the aft of the aircraft. I told her I did not know if we were going to make it. So I told her what I wanted her to tell my family if she made it and I did not. And she told me what she wanted me to tell her family if I made it and she didn't. I remember saying to her, "Just tell my family that it was okay. I didn't have any fear." I didn't cry and she didn't, either. You don't have time for emotions that are obviously there at a time like that. You keep them hidden.

So then it came to the final hour of the flight. I was again in the aft of the plane and I started walking forward, and there was this spontaneous movement. This man handed me his M-16. He didn't speak English and I didn't speak Vietnamese, and I was not quite sure what he wanted. But I knew he wanted me to take it. So I put that damned gun on my shoulder, and as I walked, people started handing me things. When I ended up at the cockpit I had a couple of M-16s hanging off my shoulders and a bandolier full of bullets and a handful of loose bullets. Some of the men handed me one or two bullets and some handed me more, and I had two pistols hanging on my little fingers. There I was, holding that little cache of bullets and weapons, and there was suddenly the most obvious feeling—that the war was over for these people. They didn't want their guns or their bullets or anything anymore. And it was so poignant. They were finished with it. Then, as I was walking toward the cockpit, this one fool put a hand grenade on top of the pile in my hands. I looked down and I thought to myself, "That's a hand grenade!" My instinct was to turn around and toss it out the back of the plane. But I was afraid it would hit the air stair and explode, and I thought then, "My God, what am I going to do with all this stuff?" So I made my way up to the cockpit and kicked on the door, and Charlie Stewart, our flight engineer, opened it. I can remember saying to him, "Charlie, take this thing!" I was so terrified of that hand grenade. I had never really been exposed to a hand grenade before. Charlie took it. Then he and Mike Marriot took electrical tape and started taping all the stuff. They taped the hand grenade and the bullets and whatever else I had carried in. If something went off they wanted to cushion the explosion as much as possible.

Then it came time to land in Saigon. I checked out Mike Marriott on the side by the galley door. I showed him how to open it in an emergency and how to inflate the emergency slide. Normally that would have been Atsako's seat, but she was a fairly new flight attendant and her English was not that good, and I wasn't sure at that point how she would perform in a real emergency. So I wanted a man sitting there.

I was sitting on the front jump seat with Bruce Dunning when Mr. Daly came out of the cockpit and asked Bruce to sit in the back of the aircraft. We wanted Bruce to put the film of the Danang landing in the back because we figured that if anything survived from the flight, that film would, and there was this strong feeling among all of us that the world should know what had happened to us that day.

Mr. Daly sat down on the front jump seat with me and asked me if I knew the condition of the aircraft, and I said I did, and then he asked me if I was afraid to die, and I said, "No, I'm not afraid to die." Then he put his arms around me and said, "Good girl. I'll buy you a drink if we make it to Saigon." And I said, "Mr. Daly, if we make it to Saigon I want you to buy me a case of beer." He laughed at that.

Then Mr. Daly said to me, "These people don't know that my gun is empty." He'd shot all of his bullets trying to maintain order on the air stair in Danang. And he said, "I'll hold it on them when we land and give you time to open the door and pop the slide." I said, "Fine."

So we started the long descent into Saigon. Of course we were coming in much faster than we should have, because we could not adjust the flaps or anything. And the front jump seat was right over the nose gear. I could feel it if it came down and if it didn't hold. I felt the main gear touch the ground, and I watched the airport go flying by. I kept waiting to feel the nose gear come down and touch the ground. Ken held the nose of the plane off the ground for so long—I don't know how he did it. All of a sudden I looked at the buildings flying by and we were running level and I knew then that the nose gear was down and that it was holding. I hadn't even felt it come down. That's how gently Ken put that 727 down in Saigon.

We raced along the runway because we couldn't stop real well. Thank God they had a 14,000-foot runway in Saigon. There were fire trucks racing along next to us. At the last minute we turned onto the taxiway. Then we stopped and had no visible sign of an emergency. I threw open the door, but I did not pop the emergency slide. Joe Hrezo was on the ground already. He'd run out the aft air stair. Joe and I both yelled at the same time, "We need an ambulance and stretchers." Then we waited for them to bring a stair up to the front door. The people inside stayed very calm. Duc told them over the PA to stay seated and not to move. Nobody moved. Finally we started getting people off. And I remember that one man lit a cigarette, and as he got to the front door, I told him that he couldn't have the cigarette because of the fuel. And he dropped it and stepped on it. I saw he was barefooted. And I thought, "Oh, my God, that must hurt." But he wasn't feeling anything anymore. Not many people on the plane were.

Most of our passengers were herded off to a side area. Stretchers were brought on board, and they carried out the man who had the bad wound in his head and the other man with his intestines hanging out. When everyone was off, we started to check out the inside of the aircraft. Val and I walked through it and started picking up guns and bullets and hand grenades left in the seats. I realized that there was far too much for us to carry out. And so I said to Val, "Never mind. Just leave this stuff. Somebody will come and take care of it."

Then Val and I got off. We were the last two people off the plane. We looked at the damage to the aircraft and we were really quite appalled at how torn up the metal was and at the bullet holes in the wings. And I said to Val at that time, "It's amazing that this plane could fly."

Val and I were picked up and taken to Flight Operations and then to the Caravelle Hotel. We were escorted to Mr. Daly's suite, where NBC was interviewing all of us. I was sitting on the couch drinking beer as they made their film. There was a room next door and a suite where there were several dozen reporters waiting for us. They all wanted an interview. I asked Mr. Daly, "What should we say about the flight?" And he said, "Just tell the truth."

Mr. Daly took us all out to dinner that evening. When we got back to the hotel I took a long shower. Then I lay down on the bed to sleep. But I couldn't sleep. I kept seeing the people from that morning in Danang. I saw the woman trampled to death, and I could see her clothes and the bloody pulp of her body. And I saw that family of five again, all shot in the back and falling. And the man crawling down the aisle to me. I realized that I was not going to sleep at all that night.

I got up and went over to the desk. I thought maybe I could write it all down. I tried writing. I got some of it. But it was really frustrating because it was too big for words. I don't know how to write it down like it really happened.

Time went by. I had lost my conception of time. All of a sudden the phone rang. I answered and the operator told me that I had an international call. I looked at the clock and realized it was seven in the morning. Then a woman came on the phone from a radio station in Los Angeles. She wanted to interview me. She had seen the CBS film of the flight from Danang on the news. So I told her what had happened. And at the end of the interview she said the dumbest thing I ever heard anybody say in my whole life. She said, "Miss Wollett, it sounds to me like you're still upset." I couldn't believe the naïveté of her remark. Many things went through my mind at that moment. But all I could say was, "Let's just put it this way. It's not the kind of thing you see every day."

Then she said, "Well, thank you, Miss Wollett. And by the way, have a happy Easter." Only then did I realize that it was Easter Sunday.

Joe Hrezo
"Just Glad to Be Alive"

I was a World Airways station manager at Clark [Air Force Base] in the Philippines in 1975. And I worked on any special projects that Ed Daly wanted. So when one of our 727s in Vietnam got shot up I got a call to contact the president of Philippine Airlines to try to charter his Sydney Hawker 125 jet. I guess Daly knew him pretty well. Daly wanted to charter the little jet to fly this spare part for the 727 down to Saigon. So I called and I talked to somebody in their executive offices, and they okayed the flight.

Then I had to go to the people at Clark airbase and get clearance for the plane to land at Clark. It got into Clark about eleven o'clock at night, and then I and a twenty-five-pound part flew to Saigon with the airplane. We got into Saigon at maybe two in the morning.

When I got there I guess they were already starting to use the 727s to ferry the people down from Danang. It was supposed to be orderly. So I went up on one flight one day—no problem. The next day I went up and we had the security guards along from the Embassy. We landed at Danang, taxied over to the Air America terminal, and the damned people started rushing the plane. We went in, swung the airplane around, dropped the ramp, and the two security guards went down, big, burly guys, and people started getting on. All of a sudden people started pushing, and it got to the point where the airplane was full and they wouldn't stop coming. The guards had a little Mace, and they used it. I think more of it got on us than on the people. The wind was blowing. Anyway, we got the people on and we left.

That night the people at the Embassy, when Daly told them he was going up the next day, started giving him a little flak.

Daly actually tried to get in to see the ambassador [Graham Martin] for about ten days, and I went with him when he finally got in. Daly hadn't shaved for about three days, and he was wearing a big cowboy hat. He got in there and the first thing he said was, "Now you can turn your goddamn tape recorders off!"

And the ambassador says, "Okay, we don't have any on." Then Daly says, "I can get in to see popes, heads of state, generals, with one or two days' notice. Why do you make me wait ten days to see you?" Daly was really mad. He told the ambassador Saigon was going to fall within two weeks, and the ambassador said, "No, it isn't."

Then Daly asked him just what the hell he was trying to do, because he should let the people know what's going on rather than trying to hide it all. And he said—I was kind of awed because here's Daly telling the goddamned ambassador off—"You're nothing but a used-car salesman."

Here I was, these two guys control all this stuff, and Daly's got all this money, and I'm just sitting there listening.

The ambassador wasn't really nasty. He was being a diplomat. But Daly was ranting and raving. I'll say the ambassador really was polite. But what could he say? I guess he was doing what he thought was best, but I don't know.

Anyway, we didn't get clearance to go up to Danang.

Daly said, "We're going anyway. We'll show them how to do it." He said we were going to take all three planes up and go in. "You and I are going to get off and organize this," he told me. But I think the Embassy told him not to go because it was not secure.

When you worked for Daly you didn't sleep very much at all. He liked to stay up late and get up early. And so early the next morning I got a wake-up call from somebody, I don't remember who. They said Daly was waiting for us. We had all the crews on five-minute standby. And when we saw Daly he just said, "Let's go."

So we went up.

I sat in the back with Daly and Bruce Dunning and Mike Marriott. Daly was sitting on the jump seat by the door, talking to them.

Daly said, "Well, we'll go up and go over to the Air America ramp. Joe, you and I will get off and we'll organize." What the hell could I say? "No"?

We got up there and landed, and the field was quiet. As soon as the airplane started slowing down, they just came from everywhere. And suddenly Daly says, "Okay I'm going up to tell Ken to lower the ramp and we'll get off."

Shit. We stop, the ramp goes down; I figure it's time to go. So I get off. And the next goddamned thing I know, the ramp is up and there goes the airplane.

After the ramp went back up, Ken Healy went down the runway, did a circle, and went back up the runway. That's when all the people started coming out. One guy was standing and shooting at the airplane and—I saw this—Ken just kind of swerved the airplane like he was going to run over him. I don't see how the guy didn't hit the airplane. I had a little .38 snubnose with me. But I figured if I started shooting at the guy, I'd have gotten the shit shot out of me, so I just kept my gun under my shirt.

One truck full of people came out racing next to the plane. I was alone on the ground watching all this. And I was scared shitless. These masses of people came racing by me—hundreds of them.

This one pickup truck or jeep full of people came—a guy sprayed it with an M-16 and the jeep flipped over and everybody went out of it. They had an A-37 trainer—tandem seat P-37—that was abandoned fully loaded right off the active runway. The pilot was trying to get that group of people.

So I walked over—trying to be as inconspicuous as I could—everybody was going to the airplane, so I was going to the tower. I didn't go after the plane because I knew I'd have never got on. There was no way Ken could have known where I was.

I'll tell you what, if I had been Ken Healy, I would have taken off right there; but he couldn't. On the active runway there were vehicles all over. There was no way. So Ken goes all the way down again, weaves his way down the active runway, makes another 180° turn at the far end. By this time I'm up at the tower, and the Vietnamese guys let me in. No trouble getting in. I got the captain on the radio and said, "Hey, Ken, how about if I get out to the taxiway by the Air America ramp?" He says, "Okay, just watch for me when I get to the ramp and make a circle. When I clear, try to get on the airplane."

Fortunately, somehow I got on the airplane. He had to kind of—he didn't stop, but the plane was going at almost a small crawl. I saw Daly back there beating people over the head with his gun and kicking them.

If there were people with me, around me, hanging onto me, I didn't feel them at that moment. All I wanted to do was get on the airplane. That's all I was thinking about. And I finally got on. And when I got on,

Ken started rolling. We took off with the ramp down. I was on about the second-from-the-bottom step, and Daly was on the next one above me when that airplane lifted off.

I know that as we started to roll, some guy was hanging onto me. Anyway, I know I kicked one off, but we weren't airborne yet. I wish we had been.

I saw Mike Marriott filming at the top of the air stair. And when I looked down the ships in Danang Harbor looked very small—like toys. I was scared shitless that whole time. There was a guy stuck in the air stair—it has retractable pivots, and somehow the guy had gotten wedged in there. Half of his body was inside the airplane, and his feet were out. I don't know how high we were when we finally managed to get him out and carry him up the steps.

Then we got up the stairs and tried to close the ramp, and we couldn't. It wouldn't stay closed. So I think we used my belt and Daly's belt to tie the handle to one of the braces. We went back to Saigon with the ramp that much from closing up tight with the airplane.

When I got inside the plane and saw the crowd, I couldn't believe it. There were four, five, or six people in every row of seats, and most of them were males.

I guess I was just happy I was back on the plane. The flight attendants were doing a great job. There were a lot of people who were pretty beat up, and they were trying to take care of them.

I went up and sat in the cockpit. And I told Ken, "Thanks." And he said, "I'm sure happy to see you."

When I went up to thank Ken, Daly was up there. He just couldn't believe all the people on the airplane. Most of them seemed to be soldiers. He was saying, "Look at all these goddamned soldiers. Look at all these guns. I hope no hand grenade goes." Hand grenades were rolling around on the floor.

Then Daly had people go around and start collecting all the weapons and bring them up to the cockpit. Pretty soon we had a cockpit full of weapons.

Ken was worried because we were losing fuel—and because of that I know he was going to try to get into Phan Rang. Then, when we got just to the point where we could start descending into Phan Rang, they told him the fuel was not secure there and they couldn't guarantee refueling. You had the "friendly" and "unfriendly," or "secure" and "not secure." In other words, the fuel in Phan Rang could be in enemy hands. They weren't sure.

So he says, "We're going into Saigon." And we went into Saigon.

We talked about the landing gear. They didn't know if it would hold when we landed because we went back with the gear down the whole way. We couldn't cycle the gear because a guy was in the wheel well.

But we landed okay. As soon as we landed I saw more troops than I had seen in some of the combat areas. They surrounded the plane.

I went out the back. We slipped our belts off the air stair and it went down by itself. And I carried one guy out, the guy that had been caught in the steps. His legs got pretty well beat up. I handed him to some of the soldiers waiting for us.

Everybody went back to Daly's hotel. Then later that night, up in the hotel restaurant, Daly was trying to talk and the newsmen in the back just kept talking. So he got up and said, "I'd like your attention please." He took out his pistol and slammed it down on the table and says, "I want to have your attention here or somebody's going to get shot."

It got very quiet. Some of the newsmen walked out then.

I tell you, Ed Daly was quite a character. A lot of people didn't like him, but he did what he wanted when he wanted, and he got things done. He wasn't afraid to say what he thought. He hurt a lot of feelings, but he never hurt anybody. As long as you stood your ground with him when you were right, he respected you for it.

And I'd do it all again with him, too. I really would.

Anyway, I felt glad to be alive that night—just glad to be alive. So, later I went across the street to a bar and found a girlfriend.

Mike Marriott
"In Deep Shit"

I was the cameraman on that last flight up to Danang. Bruce Dunning and Mai Van Duc and I got permission to go along with Ed Daly. When we asked him for permission to go along, he said, "Sure, the more the merrier."

When we came in for the landing in Danang, the twin runways were perfectly clear, and there was not a person near the runways or the taxiways or anything. And there seemed to be no one around the hangars. It It seemed contrary to every report we had heard that Danang was about to fall. We had expected to see panic in the streets and wild mobs. We could see the city of Danang, too, and the streets were quiet. So we landed.

We started to pull off the active runway onto the taxiway when suddenly, out of every hangar—and it was a huge airbase that had served most of the U.S. Air Force during the war—there must have been 20,000 people suddenly heading toward our aircraft. They were in jeeps, on motorcycles, in tanks and personnel carriers—in about every kind of vehicle known to mankind—and they were all coming toward us. We stopped between the two runways for a moment. My camera was running. We were all going to get off before we saw all those people. Then, all of a sudden, I got a gut feeling—it was one of those feelings you get when you're covering a war. And I said to myself: "Don't get off this plane.

Those people are panic-stricken. Anybody, no matter how small they are, if they panic, they're stronger than you are, Mike."

I went to the back air stair to take some pictures of what was happening. We were still moving around the airfield, and people were running up the ramp. They had come over the side of the ramp and bent it so that it was impossible to pull it up again. As I was filming they started shooting each other. They were shooting each other in the back to get closer to the aircraft. That's when I turned and said to Bruce, "We are in deep shit!"

We taxied all around the airport. Then Daly finally just made a decision. He said, "Let's get the hell out of here." At that moment we started to take off down the taxiway. We hit a vehicle as we started to lift off. Our left wheels clipped a jeep. I thought at first that maybe we were just taxiing, because I was still standing on the air stair. Then suddenly, I heard the engines wind up and I thought, "Oh, shit! And I'm still on the steps." I did not want to fall down those steps. And there were five Vietnamese below me on the steps. As the nose of the aircraft came up, because of the force and speed of the aircraft, the Vietnamese began to fall off. One guy managed to hang on for a while, but at about 600 feet he let go and just floated off—just like a skydiver. I watched him fly away. Incredible.

What was going through my head during this was, "I've got to survive this, and at the same time I've got to capture this on film. This is the start of the fall of a country. This country is gone. This is history, right here and right now. It has to be recorded as history, whatever I personally might be feeling about it."

I got off the air stair and filmed out the windows of the plane. I doubted all the way back—very strong doubts, I should say—that we would be able to land the plane. Ken Healy, our pilot, was unable to retract the landing gear, and they told us that there was a body hanging out of the wheel well. The wings and the flaps were damaged, and we were losing fuel all the time.

I sat in the galley most of the way back. I didn't have a seat. The soldiers on board had hand grenades and M-16s and .45s. I figured that in the event that we didn't crash, they might still hijack the aircraft—to another country. We were really concerned about that at the time. So we said to some of the men, "Look, these things might go off accidentally. Can you give them to us?" Duc and I went around and picked up some of the weapons and hand grenades. We used tape on the grenades to secure the pins; then we tossed them out the back of the aircraft.

We landed safely in Saigon. When there was trouble, the police always went for the camera crew. So we again expected them to go for us. We handed all of our film to Bruce Dunning, and he put it under his shirt when we got off. They didn't realize that there was a correspondent on board, and he got away with the film. It was something we did all the time—we made ourselves prominent with the camera, and they went for us, and the correspondent got away. The military police in Saigon detained us for a time—Duc and I. But Bruce just walked quietly away without acknowledging our existence. And he got the film out.

We won two awards for that film. The Overseas Press Club gave us one award and the National Press Photographers' Association gave us another.

Still today—and I would not describe them as nightmares, really—but still today, whenever I look at that footage or something that reminds me of Vietnam, I get an immediate, graphic flashback. Whenever I see something on Vietnam I get the flashback. It is crystal clear in my mind. I will never be able to forget it. Never. Not as long as I live.

CHAPTER **II**

The Orphans

Susan McDonald
"Just Pictures of Children"

I am a registered nurse. I graduated from Loretto Heights College in Denver in 1970 and then nursed for about three years in Kentucky. The war in Vietnam was on television every night. I watched the stories of what was happening in Vietnam, and I often saw shots of children. I was interested in caring for children and so I became interested in going to Vietnam and working there.

I wrote to several addresses to get information on working in Vietnam. One of the people I wrote to at that time was Rosemary Taylor, an Australian woman who had been working in Vietnam since 1968. Rosemary had become interested in abandoned children in Vietnam and in finding homes for them and caring for them. She had worked at Phu My in a home for the homeless, and she took care of the children there. Then she set up her own facility to care for orphans and abandoned children. She worked through the various Vietnamese agencies and the embassies in Vietnam to find homes for the children in many countries.

Rosemary answered my letter and indicated that I might be useful in working with the orphans. Air France let me have a ticket to Vietnam in exchange for an agreement that I would escort five children out of Vietnam when I returned. The date of my return was left open.

I had never been to Asia before. In fact, I had never been out of the United States. I went to New York and then I flew to Paris. I stayed in Paris for a few days with some friends and then flew on to Saigon.

I was not prepared for what I found when I arrived. I had grown up in the United States, which is a land of plenty; and my only acquaintance with something other than what we had in the United States was from television. And television just couldn't convey the truth of something that was outside the context of what I had experienced in the United States. I was just overwhelmed, at first, by the poverty. I remember seeing houses along the Saigon River and wondering if people actually lived in them. I think that later I saw things in a much different light. But my first impression was clearly one of thinking, "This is *really* a poor country." There were people living along the river, and the river was used as a sewer.

I lived right in Saigon and worked in a home called New Haven. It had once been a French villa and it had been made over into a home for children. There were two French nurses still working there when I arrived. They wanted to work with other refugees, so I was to take their place. They stayed only for about two weeks after I arrived. There were about fifty toddlers in the house. This was the second or third such house that Rosemary had opened. One of the houses was for toddlers and one was for older children. There was one for babies, also. Later on I took care of newborns in our house, too.

I loved the work. I don't think I ever felt a moment of homesickness, because the kids were always there, like a big family. Since they were toddlers there wasn't any language barrier—I could communicate with them just as with children of that age anywhere in the world.

One of my duties was to buy food for the house. I would buy stuff at the market and then use blenders to turn it into baby food. There weren't any American-supplied baby foods for us. I bought carrots and other vegetables and meat and put it all in the blenders. At first I also bought chicken for the children, thinking that since it was the cheapest meat I could buy in the United States, it would be the cheapest in Vietnam, too. But I found that chicken was really quite expensive. Fish and lobster were not as expensive. So I had to learn a few things about shopping and what was economical and what wasn't. People would give us food, too. One day someone gave us several cases of apricots, and so for several days we had apricots. And someone else gave us a case of jam, and that lasted for quite a while, too.

I got used to all of this and there weren't really any serious problems.

We drove down to towns in the Delta, to the different orphanges there. We took them supplies and medicines. In those orphanages there were many children who had lost one parent. The other parent had then put them in the orphanage to be cared for. We didn't deal with those children except to see that they were immunized, had clothing and whatever supplies we could offer. The expectation was that some day the mother or father would come and take them back. Those children, naturally, were not available for adoption. Any child, in fact, with any relatives—cousins or aunts or uncles—was not available for adoption. Our record-keeping was orderly. Since the children were abandoned, we didn't have problems with people taking children from the orphanage. In fact, information regarding abandoned children was published in newspapers in hopes of finding relatives.

For the most part, the American army was gone by that time. But Vietnam was still at war. It was an everyday sight to see jeeps and soldiers in the streets. There was also a curfew, and you could not go outside after 11:00 p.m. There was shelling at night. We could hear it. But in 1973 there was never any sense that the country was doomed, or that time was running out, or anything like that. I was there, in fact, with no definite term of stay, and I never thought about having to leave at some future date.

I really liked what I was doing, and I was treated very well by all of the Vietnamese. We hired all Vietnamese child-care workers. They were young Vietnamese women and they were called "Mother Care Nurses." We had one Mother Care Nurse for every five children in the house, unless a child was ill or needed special care. Then it was one nurse for one child.

We had a lot of children with cleft palates. They had been abandoned. I didn't know if the parents felt unable to cope with the disability or felt some superstition about them, or what. But we had many of them. Those children caught respiratory diseases very easily unless they were fed very slowly and carefully. They had a hard time swallowing, and we wanted to make sure that they didn't get any food in their lungs. So for those children there was one worker per child.

When the children with cleft palates were adopted abroad they had surgery to correct the problem. One of the reasons I decided I wanted to become a physician—I'm in medical school right now—was to help children with cleft palates. I'm hoping it will be easy enough to correct with surgical procedures and that it will make a difference in their lives.

We flew out the adopted orphans fairly frequently. That was difficult. I felt sad because they were leaving, but we knew a loving home was best for them. I'd take some of them to the planes. It was hard for the child-care workers, too, because they'd gotten quite attached to the children, especially the children who had been with us for many months.

People who wanted to adopt the orphans applied through an agency, and then a home study was done. Our agency was based in Boulder, Colorado, and they made sure that the family wanting to adopt one of our orphans was able to take care of a child from another country; and that the local community would be willing to accept that child, too. The United States, Australia, Sweden, Germany, Finland, France, Belgium, Canada, England, Italy, Switzerland, and Luxembourg, all accepted orphans from Vietnam.

Toward the end of 1974 a dramatic change started to take place. It was harder to get supplies, at first. And then the curfew got earlier and earlier. But nobody ever came to us and warned us that the end of the war was approaching. We were never told to prepare to close our facilities.

There was also trouble with getting orphans out of the country. The ministers in the government who worked with us seemed to change almost daily, and the new ministers didn't know the usual procedures. So we were working all the time with people we had not worked with previously—the people who had worked with us previously were all leaving the country. We had difficulties regarding the children leaving on a World Airways jet. Then we had trouble getting papers for them to leave on the U.S. Air Force Orphan Airlift after that—the C-5A. But finally we were able to get permission for the children who had passports to go on the flight. I think we put about 230 of our orphans on that C-5A.

Some of the children left for Australia about fifteen minutes before the C-5A left. I was at the nursery making sure the children were boarded on the proper flights. I did not go out to Tan Son Nhut—Rosemary did that. And then she came back to the nursery. I remember she told me when she came back from the airport that the C-5A was such a big plane. We had understood that the children would be going on Nightingale planes— which were medically supplied Army planes with cots. But the C-5A was a big cargo plane, and Rosemary was feeling some anxiety about that.

She had been back only for a few minutes when I got a telephone call from the Seventh-Day Adventist Hospital The woman on the other end of the line said, "Could you send some child care workers out here? Your children are being brought in wounded."

So we got in a taxi, an old yellow and blue Renault, and went out to the hospital. We didn't say a word on the way out; we had no idea what had happened. I was thinking at the time: "Was it hit by something? Did it crash? Was it just an aborted takeoff? What happened?"

When we got to the hospital they were just beginning to bring in the living and the dead. Every kind of conveyance you could think of was bringing them in—trucks, ambulances, jeeps, and cars. And there were sirens sounding all around.

It was probably the most shocking experience of my entire life. I had friends on board the plane who died when it crashed. Adults. And there were children that I had cared for on the flight and they had died, too. Just seeing their little injured bodies was like a scene out of a nightmare.

I couldn't identify many of the children. I couldn't tell who they were. I did unzip a body bag or two, but the sight was unbearable. So I stopped doing that. There had been secretaries from the Defense Attaché Office on board the plane, too, and some of them were dead. I went through the hospital wards to see if there were any survivors I could identify.

In the context of what was going on at the time in Vietnam, the crash was not so unusual. The women who worked for us would get a phone call, and then they would have to go out and identify the body of a husband or a son. And we saw many coffins. We saw them go by on trucks every day. So the crash fit in with everything else that was going on around us. If it had just been an isolated event in a country that was at peace, perhaps somehow it would have been different.

Some of the children from the nursery where I worked were among the living. One little girl I had cared for for a long time had sustained a skull facture and both of her hips were broken. I found her the next day in the hospital. She didn't know how injured she was. When I found her it made me happy, and the happiness blended in with the shock of the deaths. In the next days I found other children from our home who had survived the crash.

There were a lot of people at the hospital after the crash. There were people there from the Embassy and USAID, and they offered their cars to take the children back to the nurseries. We stayed at the hospital until it was past dark, identifying the children and helping them leave.

I don't know if I was in such good condition at the time to decide how the children were. When I found some of them I was just so glad that they were breathing. I gave attention to their outward injuries—cuts and things. But I wasn't really aware enough to do complete physicals on the survivors.

Many of the children left the next day on a chartered Pan Am flight. The children who were badly injured also eventually got out. Homes were found for them.

By the end of the first week in April, we were aware that the end was near. The Embassy was interested in getting U.S. citizens out of the country. But I just couldn't leave the children and go. There was no one to take over the task of operating the nurseries; no one to see that they got the food and supplies they really needed. And the child care workers weren't in a position to take on all the responsibilities.

So I stayed until I was sure that there was transportation out of the country for the children. I left on the twenty-sixth of April. Two days before, embassy personnel came by and said that there was a plane ready for us. We got ready to go, and they returned saying the flight was cancelled. The same thing happened on the twenty-fifth. But then on the twenty-sixth we did in fact leave with the children. And that was the end of the nurseries, too.

We left on a cargo plane, a C-141. We went to the airport on buses provided by the Embassy. I remember it was very hot that day. We tried to keep the children hydrated. I brought bottles to feed them with. I had very strong feelings at the time about leaving the Vietnamese people I had gotten to know and love. When I left the orphanage, the child care workers were still there—they stayed there until all the children had left. Some of the workers came as far as they could, and they helped us to board the plane. But then they stayed behind. They were very calm about what might happen to them later; they did not seem panicky at all at the time.

There were about 250 children with us when we left. They were from three of our nurseries. There were fourteen other adults on the flight, too. I sat on the floor in the back of the plane with the very small babies.

The doors on a C-141 are like a big clam shell. I had no fear when the doors started to close. We had boxes in the plane with maybe two children to a box. They needed a lot of attention, so I was thinking about the children. I remember some of my friends leaving the plane before the doors closed. Doreen Beckett, an Australian, left and returned to the orphanage. She stayed behind with Rosemary and with Ilse Ewald, from Germany. The three of them stayed to take care of the buildings and to see that the staff members were paid and that they had the letters of recommendation they might need in the future. So they were not on the plane with us, and I did not know what was going to happen to them. I was thinking about them when the doors closed. There were lots of feelings mixed up in me at that moment. Rosemary, Doreen, and Ilse finally left on the last day of April from the roof of the Embassy by helicopter.

I really loved Vietnam. I loved the friends I had worked with from many countries. Leaving that way was so abrupt—such an abrupt ending with all decisions made from the outside. I realized that this, suddenly, was the end of all the work that I had been doing. And I was not going to see many of my friends for a long, long time—if ever again. And I would not see Vietnam again for a long time.

We flew out to Clark Air Force Base in the Philippines. It was a big relief landing there. The clam shell doors opened and I could see a line of people that seemed to stretch forever and they were there to take care of the children. There was one person for each child and each baby on board. A doctor came to me and asked, "Who is the most ill here?" He wanted medical reports on the children. It had been so long since something like that had happened. I had forgotten what it was like. I had been in a country where children in the outlying orphanages were dying every day and where it was not uncommon for epidemics to strike the orphanages. And this doctor said, "Last night we almost lost *a* baby." I remember getting all choked up because they really cared about the children, and there was someone there to take care of the kids, and there were ambulances to take the sick ones to the hospital. The children who were in better condition were taken to a gymnasium and mattresses were put on the floor. There were concession-like stands with baby food in the building.

The first night we spent in the gymnasium. Everything was very well organized. Every day the military had sixty children leaving for the U.S. on C-141s with seats, and one escort for every two children.

I was in the Philippines for about seven days. When the last group of children left, I went with them.

Back in America it was a different world. There was a lawsuit in California—something about orphans who had been taken from panicky mothers in Vietnam. I felt very angry about that because it was untrue. Some people were saying that the children we brought out were kidnapped. And I found that very hard to deal with because I had seen how the orphanages were, and I knew how many orphans were left in Vietnam (over 24,000 in orphanages and over 150,000 cared for by Vietnamese families). In fact, there were women who, near the end, came to the gate of the orphanage to give us their children. But the administrator of our place, who was Vietnamese, talked to them and assured them that the Communists were not going to kill their children. And they were sent away.

It took me a long time to get my sensitivity back once I was in the United States again. I remember looking at sunsets or at a beautiful landscape or something really pretty and thinking, "Gosh, that's really beautiful." But I did not feel happiness and I did not feel sadness. I just felt a kind of numbing dullness.

My life changed dramatically after I left Vietnam. I took some of the children to Europe. I stayed with a family in England for a brief time, and I went to France and stayed in the home of a man who had lost his wife and two children in the C-5A crash. Then I visited Ilse in Germany and the children who had been adopted there and in Finland.

I remember being on a train somewhere in Europe at that time and seeing a farmer plowing a field, and I thought, "Not all countries are at war!" I had to keep reminding myself that the way it had been in Vietnam was not the way that it was everywhere else in the world.

But still I have dreams about the C-5A crash. In one dream a friend comes to me and says, "The plane crashed and the children were on it." Then I am at the crash site. In the dream I run toward the plane. There are little pieces of paper flying all over in the air. The air around the plane is filled with these little pieces of paper—like snowflakes. So, before I get to the plane I pick one of the pieces of paper out of the air. And on it is a picture of a child. Then, in the dream, I turn to the others at the crash site and I shout to them, "It's all right! There weren't any children on the plane. There were just pictures. Just pictures of children."

CHAPTER III

The Congressional Delegation

Pete McCloskey
"Boy, I'm Going to Give You the Whole Story"

The purpose of the congressional trip to Indochina in February of '75 was to look at the situation in Vietnam and Cambodia, because President Gerald Ford was asking Congress at that time for $222 million for Cambodia and $300 million for Vietnam. He encouraged us to go, saying, "We know about it and Congress doesn't." I went initially with Senator Dewey Bartlett. We were only there for a couple of days when six other members of Congress joined us: Bill Chappell, on the Armed Services Committee, was one, Bella Abzug was another, and John Flynt, Don Fraser, John Murtha, and Millicent Fenwick. And Phil Habib was there— Assistant Secretary of State for East Asian and Pacific Affairs. So there were eight of us from Congress on the trip and my recollection is that on the way home, when we tried to put down our impressions and views, we split about four to four, four hawks and four doves.

I had several things I wanted to do on that trip. One was to compare the situation in 1975 with what I had seen in 1970: the IV Corps situation down in the Delta, the III Corps area right outside Saigon, the II Corps area in either Pleiku or Kontum, and the I Corps in Danang. I wanted to see the order of battle—our lineup against the other side, the South against the North. I wanted to check the morale of the South Vietnamese, and I wanted to see the will to fight of the North Vietnamese.

The money that the President was asking for was for additional military support in Vietnam. The South Vietnamese army, as I recall, outnumbered the North Vietnamese, with something like 740,000 men under arms for the South. The North never had more than 450,000. The South had interior lines of communication. They were defending a fairly long area, but there were interior lines of communication. I recall, however, the statistic that the South was using thirteen times as much artillery as the North, which meant that much of this money was for artillery shells.

I'd been a second lieutenant in the Marine Corps in Korea. After that I stayed in the Marine Corps Reserve and had specialized in counterinsurgency. I was about the only member of Congress who went to Vietnam four times. In 1967 I was the first Republican elected as opposing the Vietnam War.

When I first ran for Congress they asked me what my position was on Vietnam, and I said I didn't think we ought to be there. I concluded it was the wrong place to fight; wrong terrain, wrong enemy. We just squandered American resources trying to fight such a war.

I thought it was inevitable that South Vietnam would fall when the United States got out. What I thought was essentially this: the division of Vietnam in 1954 had been an artificial division. Everybody thought the Vietnamese should be united. One of the things that impressed me the first time I went to Vietnam in 1967 was that all over Vietnam, in these little village, regional, and district offices, the map they used of Vietnam was of one Vietnam. The Southerners never conceded there was just a South Vietnam. Whenever you looked at the map of Vietnam, even in the South, it was the map of the whole country, not just this artificial division. Obviously every Vietnamese thought of his country as one country, so the question was, could the United States support an artificial division and create a new country? We did, and we called it "nation building."

When I went over there I was prepared to accept the possibility that we could create a new nation in South Vietnam if they had the will to fight. They had more people than the North. They had the interior lines of defense. If you looked at the order of battle there were thirteen North Vietnamese divisions and sixteen South Vietnamese divisions. There was an army, an air force, and a navy in the South. There wasn't in the North. We were giving all this money and aid and assistance. We were training them to use our weapons and methods. The whole question was, could the South Vietnamese will to fight overcome the will of the North Vietnamese?

The generals were telling us one thing about the quality of the South Vietnamese army, the lieutenants and the advisers who worked at the local level were telling us a completely different story. Sure, there were some crack South Vietnamese fighting units; the Marines, the paratroopers were good, tough, able. But the ordinary ARVN [Army of the Republic of Vietnam] didn't want to fight, didn't have a motivation to fight. The Popular Forces on the government side were people who were pressed into service, who really didn't hate the Vietcong that much. It was clear from the very beginning that there were leaks all through the establishment. Vietcong permeated the government forces. No Marine commander

I knew, from the first time I went there, to the end, would ever announce his plan of battle in any way that could be determined by the Vietnamese ally, because they knew it would leak.

But I would submit to you that Kissinger and everybody else knew, from about 1971 on that sooner or later the South Vietnamese were going to collapse. Now that doesn't in any way invalidate the South Vietnamese leader's saying, "If you goddamned Americans had fought this war like you fought in Europe, we could have prevailed. If you'd gone into North Vietnam and captured their cities and driven them into the underbrush." My argument to that was, sure, we could have done that. We could have destroyed the dikes in the Red River delta. We could have destroyed Hanoi. We could have carpet bombed and wiped out every city of more than a hundred people. But once we had done it and won, and once we had left the country, what was going to happen? The forces in the country were going to govern that had the faith of the people, or had the means of getting popular support.

Ky and Thieu and all of that set of guys from Diem on were always propped up with American assistance. None of them were popular figures in South Vietnam itself, as Ho Chi Minh was in the North.

Before I went on that trip I had gotten this information that these political prisoners, these journalists, had all been arrested and were being tortured. So I wanted to see them in their prison and talk to them. When I got there Ambassador Graham Martin, I think, felt that I was a challenge. So he had some briefings prepared for me. One was by the CIA [Central Intelligence Agency] station chief, Tom Polgar. Hell, what you look for in an intelligence officer in any branch of the service is a dispassionate appraisal of enemy capability—not intentions, but capability: what can they do? I could guess at what their intentions are, but enemy capability is the key. But Polgar gave us this line of crap that the enemy had no capability, that our people were so strong.

I left that briefing and went up to I Corps and I met the commanding general there, Ngo Quang Truong. It was my interview with him that led me to come back and say to Ford and Kissinger: "You can't win. They can break through whenever they choose to do so." Truong may remember this. I'd gone to see him personally because a friend told me he was the finest general of the Vietnamese Army. And he was.

Truong was sitting up at I Corps—bear in mind I Corps was five provinces on the coast, including the DMZ [Demilitarized Zone]. At one time we had something like five American divisions fighting in and around the area. The First Marine Division reinforced the First Air Cavalry, and God knows what else. My recollection is that, of maybe thirteen South Vietnamese divisions, Truong had maybe three lined up against maybe three North Vietnamese divisions, but right on the border. And he had just lost his crack outfit, because Thieu had gotten panicked, and pulled it south to defend against a coup in Saigon. And Truong—I'm a Marine

Corps colonel and I'm talking to a Vietnamese general, and I knew the terrain—told me "no way." He pointed to the map and told me, "If they want to commit a division here or here, I can't defend. I've got one division down here at Quang Ngai, I've got another one up here at Danang. I've got another at the DMZ. They have the capacity, if they want to commit the troops, to break through at any point in the area."

Well, they ultimately chose to make their breakthrough in II Corps. But as he pointed out, anywhere in his perimeter there was no way he could defend. Because they had the choice. It's one of those rules of war: you concentrate your strength where the enemy is weak.

The other thing—if you ever watched one of these South Vietnamese units you saw the officers in the rear. You saw the dependence on artillery fighting, the refusal to patrol aggressively—all of the things we'd been trying to teach them, when our guys left they went back to dig in and negotiate. I think there were a lot of private truces between Vietnamese units on both sides.

The other guy that impressed me was a guy who commanded III Corps: General Toan. I looked at the casualties and at the ratio of artillery ammunition he was using and the enemy was using. Graham Martin is telling me that without artillery we can't win. And this guy is showing me that he fired 9,600 rounds—and you know every enemy round that came in was numbered—the disparity made it clear that the South Vietnamese did not want to fight an aggressive infantry war.

So between what the guy said in III Corps and what the guy said in I Corps, there was no way, looking at the order of battle in the I and III Corps area, that those people could defend.

My feeling was that it was a lost cause, that the other $300 million wouldn't make any difference because there was no way to remedy what was there on the ground.

Martin made a real effort with me. He took me everywhere, ushered me into his private chambers, said, "Boy, I'm going to give you the whole story." He was the retired army colonel reliving his youth. Polgar had given us a line of shit. And Graham Martin had become demented. I really thought he was demented.

I don't know that anybody predicted the collapse of South Vietnam, but they could have because of the psychology of the thing. The thing that surprised me was the North Vietnamese pouring in their reserve divisions. Usually they didn't attack until they'd done the sand table exercise. They were very, very cautious. But they apparently knew that they had enough hidden strength in the South and enough discipline, because they poured in everything they had in 1975.

Then I requested a meeting with some journalists who had been imprisoned in Saigon. President Thieu was very kind and gave me a special dispensation to get into that prison and meet these young Vietnamese.

The prison was one of these deals with little tiny cells that we built for them. And the twenty journalists who had been arrested—including one woman, I think—were all in contiguous cells. And I said, "Look, we hear these rumors and I'd like to dispel the rumors." But in each case when we would talk with the prisoner, the Vietnamese prison guard would be there, ramrod-straight, and listen to the conversation.

I spoke with this girl and I think two to three of us went into this room with her, and when we left the room, the Vietnamese guy went out first, and somebody else was between me and him. So for just a brief instant I was out of his view and the interview had concluded. She took the opportunity to whisper to me. She said, "This isn't true. They beat us every day. They beat me very much." And she had told an entirely different story through the interpreter when they were there.

So my feeling was that the whole thing had been staged, that all the other prisoners we talked to had similarly been told, "When the congressmen come you will tell them this or that."

The girl was tired and crying, but she didn't have any outward signs of beating that I could tell. But as I say, she whispered to me, "They beat us."

My recollection is we divided either five to three or four to four as to whether we ought to vote for more aid. I said, nothing for South Vietnam because they are going to fall. I said we ought to get something for the Cambodians because if they fall there will be a massacre.

We went to Cambodia for a day. And I was appalled. What happened in Cambodia was entirely different from Vietnam.

Phil Habi was our escort. We landed at that airport at Phnom Penh, knowing it was shelled sporadically. I don't remember any shells landing while we were there, but just before some did, and just after. Even Bella Abzug was a little shook up to come landing into this airport with a lot of burned-out aircraft lying over on the fringes. They got us out and pushed us into cars and rushed us through the streets of Phnom Penh to the Embassy, where we did our first briefing. We knew we had to leave that night. All but a few of the embassy personnel had been evacuated.

We had two formal briefings. We had one by Lon Nol—this kind of funny little caricature walked in the room and sat down—we got his plea for help. But they told us that there were forty thousand Cambodian troops inside the perimeter around Phnom Penh, and the estimated strength of the Khmer Rouge outside the perimeter was sixty thousand. This was a nation of six million. And you wonder, if there's only that many and you've got all these superbly trained Cambodians equipped with all this materiel, why can't we hold them off?

So I said to the ambassador that I had had enough briefings and I wondered if I could go out and tour the front lines. I had a captain who was a military attaché with a jeep and we roared off to see the front lines. We went to the division headquarters first, and then we went to a regimental headquarters, and I asked to talk with a battalion commander or somebody in a company. At each headquarters I said, "I'd like to talk with some of your prisoners, the Khmer Rouge," and they'd say, "We haven't got any." Finally I got down to the battalion level, and these guys were dressed in these black camouflage uniforms and they were in a little pagoda. It was a company that had been pulled back to the rear but was scheduled to go back as soon as they were paid. I asked this major about prisoners, and he said, "We don't take prisoners. When we get a prisoner, we eat him."

The captain explained to me that when they kill a soldier, everybody takes his knife and cuts a piece of his flesh and eats it thinking he gets strength from the flesh of the enemy. I thought, Jesus Christ, what's going to happen when the perimeter falls? You've got two million people in there.

When I came back I said, "For Christ's sake, give these people enough money to last through the monsoon so they can disperse and get out of Phnom Penh," because when it fell, after the Khmer Rouge had been having all their prisoners eaten, I'd thought they'd massacre everybody in the city. That's why I came back and made that speech and practically got run out of Stanford and San Francisco. How could I be against the war and want to give money to Cambodia? "If we don't give money to Cambodia it's wholesale slaughter," I predicted. This was March. Cambodia fell about mid-April, as I remember. And there was a slaughter.

I came back and with Phil Habib held a press conference to say we thought they ought to give money to Cambodia, just to hold on through the monsoon season. I could not approve giving money to Vietnam. Habib pled with me and a guy from the Defense Department begged me to support the funds and I just couldn't do it. It was just a question of time with Vietnam. It was a lost cause.

But I made a written report and gave it to Gerald Ford when I came back that essentially was concurred in by at least three and maybe four members of the delegation. We concluded that we needed accurate intelligence. I believed the intelligence apparatus in Vietnam had become biased and was an advocate. Your intelligence officers are supposed to give you the bad news, not the good news. With this guy Polgar it was all good news. "We are winning and we're going to win."

I then met personally with Kissinger and Ford in the Oval Office. I remember Ford turning to Kissinger and asking if there was any chance that I was right. Kissinger said, "No way. Vietnam can hold out for years." He said they had good morale and good fighting ability, and they were well trained, and all they needed was that money for supplies and equipment and replacement parts and so on.

My impression was that President Ford believed him and didn't accept what I said.

I gave my report to the President in early March. The North Vietnamese attacked in the central highlands within a week. And then the

South came apart. I said something like this was going to happen and it was just a question of time. Then they attacked and the newspapers were filled with the news for the next six weeks from Cambodia and Vietnam.

I don't have any quarrel at all with the South Vietnamese. I'd be very bitter toward everybody if I were them, particularly toward those of us who were coming over and making a judgment as to whether they ought to get another twenty or fifty million dollars. But the question to ask them is, How could they delude themselves as to the fighting quality of their own people? How could they collapse around Saigon?

I think what we did in Vietnam was a disaster and a tragedy, and I thought when we got to the point at which we backed out and were unwilling to die on the ground but kept dropping bombs, it was an outrage. If the South Vietnamese had been able to make it on their own, more power to them. The fact that they were not able to make it on their own is not necessarily the fault of anybody but their own generals.

CHAPTER **IV**

American Embassy

Wolf Lehmann
"This Is the Last Message from Embassy Saigon"

There was mounting concern in the Embassy during late 1974 after the fall of Phuoc Long. The signs kept mounting and the intelligence kept getting harder and harder that the North Vietnamese would start a major offensive in early 1975, which they did.

One of the events in the sequence is the Soviet military mission visit to Hanoi. About ten days before Christmas of 1974, a large Soviet military mission headed by the Deputy Defense Minister, General Victor Kulikov (who subsequently became the Warsaw Pact commander for Soviet forces in Europe) visited Hanoi, ostensibly for Vietnamese Army Day. They stayed for a week. Although our intelligence on it was spotty, it was quite evident that the main purpose of that mission was to put the final touches on whatever arrangements existed between Hanoi and Moscow for Soviet resupply of ammunition, tanks, and guns. The Chinese were already backing off. But things had not deteriorated to the point that they did later on.

The attack on Ban Me Thuot in March came as a real surprise. That was a very well concealed operation. The NVA [North Vietnamese Army] had built up their forces on the Ho Chi Minh Trail. We knew and the Vietnamese knew, in general, about the buildup and kept some track of it. But the actual attack on Ban Me Thuot, its timing, its vigor, came as a surprise. More thought was given to attacks on Pleiku and Kontum than on Ban Me Thuot.

Early in the year that congressional delegation came to Saigon. You're going to get some more colorful reactions to it. Phil Habib was accompanying them. The first of the congressmen arrived on Monday, February

24. That was McCloskey and Senator Bartlett. What resulted was kind of of circus at the airport as the American press mobbed them and accused me of having tried to keep the congressmen away from the press, which wasn't true, just because the South Vietnamese wouldn't let the press go out on the tarmac to the steps at the airplane, but rather brought the congressmen to the VIP lounge where the press was.

The rest of them arrived a couple of days later. Ten o'clock on February 27, the entire delegation arrived, including such luminaries as Bella Abzug, Millicent Fenwick, and Congressman Don Fraser of Minnesota. The leader was Congressman John Flynt from Georgia. They stayed there in Vietnam and made a side trip to Cambodia, and the whole group left on the evening of March 2, Sunday. Ambassador Martin was going back with the group at that time.

I know that McCloskey, like some of the rest of them, took things seriously. And of course for some of the others, notably Fraser and Abzug, the whole visit was nothing but a simple occasion to try and whip up anti-Vietnam feelings in the United States. Some of their assistants showed up early to arrange contrived meetings with so-called dissidents, and Abzug took every possible occasion she could simply to embarrass both the South Vietnamese and us, the American Embassy, as much as she could. I had quite a run-in with McCloskey myself at my house because part of the program the evening before their departure was an occasion for the whole group to meet with as many nonofficial Americans in the area as possible, the Voluntary Relief Agency people, business people, and others. I invited them all to my house, and the evening broke up with a terrible argument between me and McCloskey because McCloskey kept talking about—like the rest of them—all these terrible alleged human rights violations by the South Vietnamese because they wanted to lock up people who were trying to bomb them. That's a human rights violation, you see. And so we got into a terrific argument, McCloskey and I, and he threatened to subpoena me and get me up in front of his committee and I told him, Well, go ahead, just do that. I never heard from him. He's a very erratic type. Blows hot and cold.

The whole thing started with good intentions in a last ditch-effort in Washington to see if they couldn't mount some better congressional support for providing the Vietnamese some official support. It backfired. When you have a delegation loaded with people like Fraser and Abzug who were totally dedicated to destroying South Vietnam, then you don't have a chance.

I had never met Abzug before and I hope never to meet her again. She wasn't civil. She's a left-wing ideologue, always has been. To her the Left can do nothing wrong, and Communists are better than the alternative. Somehow, I've never been able to figure these people out, but she is one of those.

The big thing for many of them was to visit the prisons where these alleged "political" prisoners were being held by the "repressive, corrupt Thieu regime." Never mind that the North Vietnamese were trying to take over the whole country; you've got to go and visit the so-called political prisoners.

We prevailed upon the Vietnamese to let them do this. I was embarrassed about it, but I insisted, please let them go ahead and do this. And of course, those so-called political prisoners, who were Viet Cong agents, naturally, we prevailed upon the Vietnamese to allow these people to talk privately with the committee. I'm not going to say that no Vietnamese ever beat up somebody in jail, like New York cops do. I'm not going to say that. But the notion that there was widespread torture is nonsense.

Martin went back to Washington with them and I was in charge then for the rest of the month. Again, the North Vietnamese, knowing everything that goes on that we do, had ceased any heavy military operations just before the congressional delegation arrived. And they resumed them again on about the seventh, eighth of March. They kept very quiet while that group was there.

Thieu met in Cam Ranh Bay with General Phu on Friday, March 14, at which time the decision was made to abandon the central highlands. I had an appointment to see Thieu at nine o'clock Saturday morning, March 15, to give him a message either from Ambassador Martin or the President (I've forgotten which) I'd been asked to convey. And we discussed the situation at the time. He did not directly tell me at that time of the decision he had made, but he hinted at it. He hinted that he didn't think the situation in the central highlands was tenable, and that struck me and I went right back to the office. I no sooner got to the office than I got a call from Moncrieff Spear up in Nha Trang confirming to me that the decision had been made to abandon Pleiku and Kontum. Just a little bit later, Polgar, the CIA station chief, came in, and he'd gotten the same word that a decision had been made.

In light of that, everything came together for me. I then gave orders to Spear up in Nha Trang to proceed immediately with evacuating all the Americans and the Vietnamese employees we had up in Kontum and Pleiku, and I told George Jacobson to go ahead and arrange necessary air transport—give us priority with Air America. That done, I sent off a telegram to the State Department that I had given those orders and that it would be completed by nightfall.

The retreat from the central highlands turned out to be a disaster for several reasons. One was no planning and very short notice. Make that decision on Friday and do it right away. And you know that Route 7B was in terrible shape. That's the second reason. And also military credit has to go to the other side; the North Vietnamese were extremely effectively organized. We're not talking about a guerrilla war, we're talking about a main force war. They were mobile. Their communications were superb. They found out very quickly what was going on. They could react fast and make a shambles of the attempt to extract forces from Pleiku and Kontum.

I discussed the decision with Thieu in more detail on the following Thursday, March 20, at four-fifty in the afternoon. He gave me his rationale for it at the time. And at that time, incidentally, he quite clearly conveyed to me that it would be followed by further decisions in MR 1 [Military Region 1]. He was very distressed that the withdrawal from Kontum and Pleiku had gone very badly. Very upset and distressed about it. I don't blame him. Any withdrawal operation is a difficult military operation to begin with.

We foresaw doom. Obviously it now became more and more doubtful that the country could survive.

Thieu didn't solicit our advice on that kind of strategic decision and I don't blame him. He was beginning to sense he was being let down; we were cutting our aid and economic assistance. We had gone through this damned agony with the congressional delegation that had insulted him, in fact, left and right, and in Vietnamese. He saw no other choice but to resurrect this old option, which was an earlier option, to give up part of the country. He had been advised at one time some years earlier by an Australian, Ted Serong, to consider that as an option.

I was in contact with Washington all the time through the regular channels as the situation deteriorated. We took our people out of Hue first, and initially had them go back in for the day from Danang, just because we wanted to keep a presence as long as the Vietnamese were there. I wouldn't let them stay overnight as things got bad. But they'd come back in on a helicopter the next day from Danang to their offices, until we finally had to take them out because Hue was falling.

On March 27 in the evening we knew all control was lost at the Danang airport. I went to see the Prime Minister at 6:15 at the JGS [Joint General Staff] compound to talk to him about getting hold of General Ngo Quang Truong to see if he couldn't organize enough military force up there in Danang to get control of that air field again. While I was there, he got a radio link to General Truong, and they talked about it. It was in Vietnamese and I didn't follow it, but the essence of it was, the Prime Minister told me, that Truong would try. That was the evening of Thursday, March 27.

I went back to work at the Embassy until late at night. I got a couple hours' sleep. At three o'clock the next morning, General Weyand and Ambassador Martin came in and I was out at the airport to meet them. That whole day on Friday the twenty-eighth we were having the final pullout from Danang. That's the time at one point I lost Al Francis [U.S. consul general in Danang]. I couldn't get hold of him. A couple of his people who were aboard a boat didn't know where he was. We then found out he was aboard a Vietnamese navy ship, and I finally got a radio link to one of his people on a barge to tell them to get off and get out of there and not worry about Francis.

So we were bringing refugees out of Danang. And Ed Daly in the beginning brought some refugees out of Danang, although he made a great big nuisance of himself. In fact, he wasn't sober a good part of the time. I think everybody knows that. And he waved guns around. For a few days he operated within the framework of others and that was all right. I had been in constant close touch with Al Francis in Danang as this thing was deteriorating more and more, and it reached a point where all control was lost over the airfield at Danang. It was just overrun with people. You couldn't bring airplanes in any more. And it was at this point that Daly engaged in that disastrous thing without any clearance or authorization—taking off with an airplane, going into Danang. They managed to land all right. They had people on board that they got out, but they killed people going down that runway.

The Vietnamese called me from the airport, furious, and told me that he had taken off for Danang without clearance. I got hold of Francis. I was still able to get hold of him in Danang. He had three planes taking off. And I remember Francis saying, "Oh, shit." He knew that the field wasn't workable any more and at that time was desperately trying to get whatever he had left down to the port, the boats, and the barges.

I don't have any problem with Mr. Daly and World Air as long as they were operating within the framework. If they were donating airplanes, that was fine. But that particular action was irresponsible, utterly irresponsible, and should have never taken place.

The baby-lift operation was something different, you know. The baby-lift operation was started as an organized thing and we were all for it; in fact we began, we say it now, we didn't admit it then, we began to use the baby-lift operation to some extent to begin evacuating our women. Then came the C-5A crash. Talk about dark moments in my life—this was one of the saddest.

We had people on that. It was April 4. We said all these children needed escorts. They didn't need that many, but we used it, because we didn't want to talk about evacuation. Of course then the C-5A on the fourth takes off and there's a terrible accident, which is also a story in itself. I got word in a phone call that the accident had happened, that they were using every available Air America helicopter to recover people. We had to think immediately not only about the people, but about the political repercussions of the accident. When one of these things happened again, we didn't want an Air Force General back in Washington saying it could only happen because of some enemy action or sabotage—and that is exactly what was said. If you had this word get out, it would add to the panic in the city. And our first word was that it was neither one of those, which turned out to be true later on.

What happened was either structural failure or a human failure, and

I'm not prepared to say which. One of those rear doors hadn't been latched properly, flew off, damaged the stabilizer of the airplane so that the pilot could hardly maneuver the plane. He did an extraordinary job crash-landing it as he did in those paddies. But the result of it was that all the people on the lower deck were dead. The ones in the upper deck survived. But we couldn't take the business that this was sabotage or enemy action. It wasn't.

So I was on the telephone with the White House staff to knock off this nonsense. The Air Force couldn't dream that one of its favorite toys, the C-5A, could possibly have a structural problem or that it could be a human failure or crew failure.

Well, we were able to contain that rather quickly. We got this guy to shut up, you see. We said that there was going to be an investigation, but that there was no indication that this was hostile action. It wasn't. So we got it under control.

On March 26, I sent a message to Washington saying that I wanted immediate authority and I wanted it in Saigon, nowhere else, to ship out as I saw fit some families, dependents, and household goods. It was never answered. Authority of this kind involving commitments of money is something that Washington is very reluctant to grant anybody in the field. There were some bureaucratic questions being raised and the thing was never resolved. But anyway I asked as early as that.

I date the actual evacuation with the beginning of the baby-lift because we were using it for that purpose. So contrary to what a lot of people said, we began evacuation the beginning of April, reducing people even in late March.

That brings up another point, you see. You can't just bring foreigners into the United States by flying them in, as you know. And as a matter of fact, we didn't actually get any formal authority to send any Vietnamese to the United States until the twenty-fifth of April.

We had been doing some of this anyway—to Guam, to Subic. Subic was a problem because it happens not to be United States territory; it happens to be the Philippines, and the Filipinos don't like other people shipping foreigners into their country. And we were doing so. And we were doing it to Guam without knowing what we were going to do next, because we didn't get any formal authority until the twenty-fifth of April, and then we got authority to ship up to 35,000 Vietnamese into the United States. We brought 135,000.

Beginning on the fourth of April, we were trying to cut down the number of Americans. Insofar as it was Embassy people, U.S. Government people, and dependents, we had the control; we could tell them to get out. But we had a hell of a lot of Americans in the country after all these years, thousands of them who were not government employees—contractors, private business people, retirees. A lot of these folks, including contractors and retirees, had acquired Vietnamese families, except they acquired Vietnamese families without the benefit of law. So you have a common-law wife and children of that particular union, with a mother and a father and cousins and brothers and sisters, and if you consider that the average Vietnamese family has seven children, you can see what you get into. We had a terrible time. We had no authority to ship these people anywhere, but they wouldn't go without the whole family. So we found ways and means (and they were frankly of questionable legality) to try and do some of this.

The categories of Vietnamese at risk were virtually endless. First of all, direct employees—and there we had to start with the ones that were in most sensitive positions. There were some at the Defense Attaché Office and some of those we took out very early, as a matter of fact.

Then you have government officials and military people particularly close to us. You have relatives of Americans. You have people like the labor leaders. So we divided the responsibility for this among various parts of the mission. The Defense Attaché was responsible for at least getting the remaining military people out. The Labor Attaché would worry about the labor people. That's how we had the thing divided. It's not true we had no plan. We missed people; yeah, that's perfectly true. But there was a plan and there was a system. But again, we had no authority to ship.

Then you had the other situation. You can't have Vietnamese citizens leave the country without permission of the Vietnamese government. And we are trying to do several things. We are trying to keep a Vietnamese government functioning and in authority as long as possible, knowing that we're facing the end. You've got to keep order. You've got to prevent chaos.

So while we were in fact evacuating people, we kept yelling that we were not conducting an evacuation. Martin and the rest of us did things like keep all our pictures hanging on the walls, because the moment you start packing—"Oh, the Deputy Ambassador is packing up!" spreads like a wildfire—that's how we left all our personal things behind. God knows who's got them now. I hope the servants. We were flying people out on C-130s and commercial aircraft, and every time somebody back here in Washington would say "evacuation" I would get on the damn phone and yell at them to stop talking about it.

The channels to Washington were working sometimes, and sometimes they weren't, and if I had to get something done immediately I would grab the phone and call the White House staff. For example, suddenly in April the FAA [Federal Aviation Agency] types in Honolulu decide without a word to anyone to declare publicly that Tan Son Nhut is no longer safe for commercial aircraft. Well, at the very same time, I'm holding Pan Am's feet to the fire to keep flying in and out so we could keep using the commercial aircraft. So this decision had to be reversed, and there was no point in going to the State Department, which would be in a meeting the next day. I went to the White House and said, "You give those bastards an order to immediately rescind that thing." I got it done within four hours.

On things of this kind you had to move very fast. The channels were working but we were in such a tight situation I sometimes bypassed the channels.

We didn't have a timetable. Our overall evacuation plan called for everything: first priority, use the commercial airlift as long as possible; second: use military fixed-wing aircraft as long as you can; and only in the end do you go to Option Four in the evacuation plan—Operation Frequent Wind, which was the helicopter lift. We did that, basically. And we kept flying C-130s back and forth to Guam and Subic Bay.

The C-130s went out full, but the commercial aircraft would way overbook, even more than normal. But then the people wouldn't show up, a lot of the Vietnamese, because they couldn't get the exit permits or they'd changed their minds. That's how you often had airplanes going out not loaded when they should have been loaded. But when you add it all up, we still got 135,000 people out. Of those, about half we took out in commercial aircraft, in military fixed-wing aircraft, and in the helicopters, and a small number of barges in the Saigon River. The other half came out because we facilitated their leaving, mostly by boat, but we didn't physically take them. We picked them up with the fleet outside. But that's the bottom line.

We got out every single American in that country (and a lot of foreigners, incidentally) in addition to the Vietnamese we took out. Some of them had left early on, but those that remained we took out the last day. We took out every American except for those who didn't want to go.

Now therein is also a bit of a story. Among those Americans we took out were seven prison inmates who were serving sentences in Vietnamese prisons for various crimes, including rape and murder. The Vietnamese turned them over to us, our Consulate people, a few days before. Six of them reported to evacuation points and were taken out and I guess roam this country now. One decided he was going to stay there and disappear. He's not the only one—a fellow who was up North comes to mind who stayed voluntarily. He was one of the American Friends Service Committee and they'd been sort of loyal friends of the North Vietnamese, and this fellow was to be evacuated and he jumped over the wall and disappeared to await his friends. He came out about half a year later. I remember an article in *Newsweek* saying that he discovered to his great amazement that he was dealing with Communists. I always thought that was funny.

The danger of the South Vietnamese military turning on us was always a possibility. This was certainly a major consideration of this government. Much of what we did that we were so heavily criticized for was due to the fact that we had to keep Vietnamese authority functioning somehow. We didn't have any force in the country. We had no way to make our will prevail. We had to keep Vietnamese authority cooperative with us and we had to prevent civilian panic that would have made a shambles of any evacuation. And finally, we were very much concerned about some of the military leadership saying, "if we're going to go down you Americans are going to go down with us. And we're going to stop you."

In fact, we had some very hard intelligence on at least one senior military officer in command of the necessary units who had that in mind. And the prospect of having this whole thing end in that kind of a confrontation came very close in some ways. That was just too horrible to contemplate. It was this kind of consideration that governed everything that we did, that made things look rather disorderly, much more disorderly than they really were. Of course, that never occurred to some of the critics of this operation.

On about the twenty-fifth and twenty-sixth, Friday and Saturday, we had kind of a lull on the battle. There seemed to be kind of a stop to North Vietnamese offensive operations. I was trying to figure out just what this was, because there were two possibilities. Was this a strictly military thing, a certain amount of regrouping and reorganization? which in the end I think it was. But there was of course the possibility that maybe they would halt just short of the city and would go for some sort of coalition government, which they said they wanted to—as a pure political gimmick.

Now, contrary to a lot of things that had been said, coalition was not something I was in any way hoping for. In fact, I was hoping it would not be the case. If Hanoi had done that, there would have been a big outcry in this country about supporting this new coalition government, which would simply be nothing more than a façade.

So frankly I was hoping they never would do that. I was hoping the North would smash into Saigon with tanks and artillery and motorized infantry as they did, so at least it would be clear what really happened. Some people accused the Embassy of deluding itself that this would happen. We were prepared in planning, in case the coalition government was formed, that we would perhaps leave a small staff behind, probably with myself in charge and a half-dozen other people. But those were people who were the last ones to go anyway. This had nothing whatsoever to do with the evacuation.

I think we will never quite know whether the North really considered a coalition or not until we get to the archives in Hanoi, and I'm not going to be around and probably neither are you when we do that. But I think, looking back on it, it was pretty much a military decision that caused that lull on Friday and Saturday, and Sunday even was kind of quiet. And all through the weekend we were continuing the C-130 flights, moving people out. Then on Sunday afternoon at about six o'clock, there was the air attack on the flight line at Tan Son Nhut airfield.

I was in my office working at about six o'clock, when I was notified by one of the people in the Embassy compound who were loading buses of Vietnamese evacuees being processed for movement out to the airfield, that there was a holdup out there because some of the guards had refused to get on the buses, because they were tired and wanted to eat. Would I please come over and straighten this out?

So I left my office and went down across to the swimming pool area where the processing was taking place to see what the hell the problem was and straighten it out. Just as I get there, the air strike starts out at Tan Son Nhut. In fact, I could see the planes making their bomb runs over the roofs. And anti-aircraft fire starts, including the gunners over at the Palace grounds—at God knows what, because they weren't anywhere near the planes. And there was consternation among the crowd, and some of the Marines got a little bit excited and were very concerned, rightly so, about people's safety, and they herded everybody into the restaurant and tried to herd me in, too. They were very concerned about my safety as the deputy. It was all very touching. But some of this was a little over done. I'm a veteran of a war. I've been shot at during the Second World War by the greatest experts in the business. But in any event I knew there was something happening at Tan Son Nhut that would moot the business of sending more people out there until we found out what was going on. So I went back to my office, and on the way back—and this is the famous story about the tree—you've heard that story—on my way back I passed this big tamarind tree, a beautiful thing, in the courtyard, and I saw one of our Seabees chopping at that thing with an ax. Now we always knew we had to take the tree down if we were going to operate helicopters from the courtyard. But the tree was also visible from the street. So I came in back of the Chancery building and told the security officer there to have this guy knock it off. "Bring him some power saws and equipment to do this, but don't do it until you get the word, because we don't want panic."

This tree was not a symbol of Graham Martin. I don't think he even knew about this. I went back up to my office. I forgot about the tree. I knew we had to take the tree down if we were going to operate. I also knew we were not going to start helicopter lifts that night. We knew what the military situation was. I heard later somebody during the night cut a little bit more into it. That was all right. I didn't care. The next morning it was still standing. And when we made the decision to go for the helicopter lift, one of the first things I said to the administrative officer was, "Now tell them to take down the tree." The tree was taken down hours before the first helicopter could arrive.

The helicopter-lift operation out of the Embassy courtyard was a difficult one because there were walls. It was a tough job for the pilots to get up over them.

Anyway, we immediately got on this thing, finding out what was going on at Tan Son Nhut. Yes, it was the DAO [Defense Attaché Office], of course, who were on the scene, and we did find out that there had been an air strike that had done quite a bit of damage to the flight line and that we could not continue any C-130 operations that evening.

Ambassador Martin and I both remained in the Embassy, I guess until about midnight that night, working. At about that time, he and I decided that we had better go home and try to get a few hours' sleep. The staff were operating all night, wrapping up their final plans for bus routes to pick up people the next day in case we went to the helicopter lift. The buses belonged to USAID [U.S. Agency for International Development]. Some of the drivers were American Embassy officers. They didn't know how to drive very well, that's true. But they did a great job.

So we decided since we'd have so many life-and-death decisions to make the next day, we'd better get some sleep while the staff wrapped up the final details. I didn't get back actually until about two o'clock, I guess, to my house. And I couldn't really go to sleep very much. Dozed off for a while. Then I heard loud explosions at about four or a little after in the Tan Son Nhut area. And sure enough, fifteen minutes later, I got the telephone call that there had been a rocket attack on the Defense Attaché compound and two Marines were killed in a direct hit.

So a little after that, about 5:30 or so, I went back to the Chancery and, as daylight broke, everybody assembled. Then, of course, the ambassador drove out to Tan Son Nhut to talk with General Smith [Homer Smith, the Defense Attaché] and to look at the situation out there to make a decision whether we could resume C-130 flights or had to go to Option Four.

Graham Martin wanted to have a personal look before making that final decision. And when he came back he got on the telephone with Washington, and that's when the decision was made.

I got the word he was on the phone with Washington. In fact one of our staff people was in with him on his other phone with Washington. The staff person came out of his office and into mine and said, "This is it!"

I went into Martin's office and said, "I've just been told that this is it. We are going to go for Option Four, Frequent Wind, the helicopter evacuation." And he said, "Yes." I immediately went out, because we had the senior staff assembled outside the office. I told them that this was it, and they fanned out to do their thing.

The original plan of Option Four was that the first helicopters from the fleet would bring in additional Marines to secure the two evacuation sites: Tan Son Nhut Defense Attaché Office and the Embassy compound itself. They were supposed to come in one hour after the word "Go": H-plus One. That did not happen. Unfortunately, they were about three hours late, which I found out later was the result of a mixup out in the fleet. The Marines who were scheduled to come in were on some ships, and the helicopters were on yet another, and cross loading was necessary to get the thing together.

The three-hour delay created a problem. On that final evacuation, the first priority was to evacuate the people of the Defense Attaché compound, everybody out there. And Priority Two was the Embassy Chancery itself—the main Embassy buildings—several buildings and a swimming pool.

Now into the night already, the suggestion was made by General Richard Carey in a phone conversation with me, that we perhaps might stop the helicopter lift for the rest of the night and then resume at first light. We said no to that. We said we cannot stop, we've got to keep going. So the decision was made to keep going.

Meanwhile, of course, the whole situation around the Embassy is getting more and more tenuous. There are masses of people surrounding it all through the night. We finally got in an additional platoon or so of Marines flown into the compound to help out the Marine guards in the Embassy, just to secure our Embassy compound, because people were trying to come over the walls. It was very, very touchy.

The DAO operation was closed down after they got everybody out, and from then on the lift went out only from the Embassy for the people who remained. About midnight or a little after we got definite word about the limited number of additional sorties we would have from the fleet. We were told there would be thirteen more sorties and that was it, except for extracting the Marine force.

That wasn't quite enough sorties, considering the number of people we had in the Embassy compound, mostly Vietnamese and some Koreans. There were not many Americans left. We had an exchange on that issue but were told flatly that that was it—thirteen more missions and then no more, other than to extract the Marines. So we sent our final message, and the message read, "PLAN TO CLOSE MISSION AT ABOUT 0430 30 APRIL LOCAL TIME. DUE TO NECESSITY TO DESTROY COMMO GEAR THIS IS THE LAST MESSAGE FROM EMBASSY SAIGON." We sent that message manually and then the communicator took the sledgehammer and did whatever else he does to destroy the communications gear. And he was evacuated. We were not out of total communication then, however, because the Marines who were loading the helicopters had backpack radios and had communication with the fleet. It was over that network that at about four o'clock we received the peremptory order that the White House has now directed that the Ambassador and remaining staff should leave on the next helicopter. We didn't quite do that, but at a little before five o'clock the time had come for everybody to leave.

I sort of took a last look at the courtyard, and talked to the Marine major down there. We still had about 250 Vietnamese and some Koreans, also. And the Marine major and I agreed that it would take just three more sorties from the big helicopters to get those people out. But those we were not going to have. That was due to the delay at the beginning of the operation. That is how those people—and it's not 400 or 500 as some are saying, it was about 250—were left behind.

Now there was a good number of Koreans among those, and they were later recovered and repatriated through the help of the Japanese. They maintained an office in Saigon. They stayed there. So I don't feel too bad about that. But I do feel bad about leaving people; but it was, as I say, due to that delay. The fuss that's been made out of it and some other things obscures the fact that what we did leave behind in Vietnam was nineteen million people. That's the real story. The U.S. left behind nineteen million people.

At about five o'clock in the morning we went up to the roof, the Ambassador and I and the remaining senior staff people, and a helicopter put down on the roof. The lighter helicopters were landing on the roof—the heavier ones in the courtyard. As the helicopter put down, Ambassador Martin, accompanied by Tom Polgar and George Jacobson, started moving toward the helicopter and the rest of us followed. The crew chief had his helicopter already loaded and he knew he had his man, so he waved the rest of us back. And that chopper took off. There was another one hovering nearby, and he came down. I just sat there with about six of the remaining staff members in the stairwell saying to myself, "Now the Ambassador has left, I'm back in charge and maybe I'll change my mind about it." A last attempt at humor. I had hardly had any sleep in four days. The other chopper put down, and the very capable young Marine major who was running that operation was using the chopper communications to coordinate the extraction plan for the Marines with the fleet, which was the last act. So we just sat there for about twenty minutes, and we took off about 5:20 in the morning. That ended the official presence in Vietnam, and the only thing that the Marines could do then was extract themselves, which they did in the next couple of hours.

On the way out, there was some weather forming so you could see lightning and some thunderstorms approaching. We could see the lights of the North Vietnamese convoys approaching the city. Some of the fleet fighter planes could be seen off in the distance still covering the rest of us.

The chopper was packed with the rest of the staff and remaining civilian guards, mission warden guards, and it was utterly silent except for the rotors of the engine. I don't think I said a word on the way out and I don't think anybody else did. The prevailing emotion was tremendous sadness.

Lacy Wright
"Hope Springs Eternal"

I grew up in the Midwest—Springfield, Illinois. After college I studied in
Rome for two and a half years to become a priest. Then I quit. I went
back and taught high school for a year in Chicago. I took the Foreign
Service exam during that time and then went to the University of Chicago for a year in their masters program in international relations. I did
not finish that because I went into the Foreign Service at the beginning
of 1968. In those days, anybody who could walk and chew gum who went
into Foreign Service was sent to Vietnam.

In those days, I would say for most of us who went in the Foreign
Service, being sent to Vietnam was a bitter blow. In fact, I would say
that most of the people coming in at that time with me were against the
war with more or less a passion. Besides that, people were just plain
scared. You knew there was a war going on and you didn't want to die
young. Nonetheless, most of us were sent to Vietnam.

After that, an incredible transformation occurred: most of us who went
to Vietnam ended up liking it. In fact, many people who went to Vietnam, including myself, went back again and did so willingly.

We learned Vietnamese at the Foreign Service Institute in Washington.
There was a ten-month course in Vietnamese, and although my Vietnamese was not as good as that of some others, it was all right. In spite of
all you hear about Americans not understanding the country and so on,
and of course there's much truth in that, a very large number of Foreign
Service officers and others did speak Vietnamese and spoke it very well.
That could not be said of the French or certainly of any other foreign
group in Vietnam.

At the Foreign Service Institute there were not only people from the
Foreign Service, although they were the most numerous, there were also
army officers—majors and lieutenant colonels, usually—as well as people
from other agencies. And I think it's generally true to say that the army
officers almost all (at least that we studied with) were too old to learn
Vietnamese. They were in their forties. And almost none of them did.
Not all of the Foreign Service officers learned Vietnamese, which is a
difficult language; but a large number of them did, and a large number
of them, after they went to Vietnam, went out and worked in the provinces and so really did perfect their Vietnamese.

I arrived in Vietnam in March of 1969 after spending a year learning
Vietnamese and going through orientation.

I would say a number of things, some of them nobler than others, combined to make people like Vietnam. First of all, I think that even people
who went there without much sympathy for the South Vietnamese government, when they came into contact with the people and worked with

them and worked with local officials, did develop sympathy for them, and started identifying with them and started wishing them well, hoping they would win.

They also became more familiar with the tactics of the other side and saw that there was a big difference between the Communist side and this side, for all its flaws. All of us saw that the South Vietnamese regime had a great number of flaws, but nonetheless I think we all developed a sympathy.

Second, you could kind of live an adventurous life on the cheap. Most of us civilians lived comfortable and fairly safe lives. That wasn't always true. Some people were in dangerous areas, particularly people who lived in the provinces. But for most of us I think that there was just enough danger to make life interesting but not enough to be a real danger. So there was a sense of excitement. You were at the center of what was certainly the most interesting and controversial activity of that era. And there were lots of women. You were in a time and place where the normal restraints were off. That of course has a perennial appeal.

So there were some good things and some bad things—or less noble things.

One of the interesting stories I like to tell is, in 1973, when the Paris Peace Agreements were signed, the State Department decided to send a lot of Foreign Service officers back to Vietnam. When they did this, they felt they had to think up a lot of incentives to get people to go back. They had uprooted a lot of us and sent us to Vietnam once over a lot of objections and certainly turmoil, and here they were about to do the same thing again. So they sat down and devised this package. First, you only had to go for six months. This was to monitor the observance of the peace accords. Then you got 25 percent more than your salary. During your six-month stint you could take a trip home, or go anywhere else at equivalent cost. Since you were on the other side of the world, that meant you could go anywhere in the world you wanted.

And then, after offering you all those incentives, they also said, if chosen, you've got to go. It's not optional. What they found out when they promulgated this, was that everybody wanted to go back. In fact, they had people calling up the personnel department and saying, "Hey, how come I'm not on the list to go back to Vietnam?"

I was there on my first tour for a year and a half. Those were the years in which a lot of progress was made in pacification. Pacification had two aspects—getting rid of the Communists, and making life better for people, and there really was a lot of progress in both areas. And that progress, I guess in broad terms, started after the failed Tet offensive in 1968, and continued for several years. So much so, that in large parts of the Delta one was very safe.

For example, there were sixteen provinces in the Delta, and I was in every one of them. There was no enemy activity. And it was like this in large parts of the Delta and became progressively safer. At first, when I returned, my attitude was a kind of naïve optimism. Everyone was so delighted that the war was over, or at least that there was this hiatus, this new possibility for peace, despite the fact it was clear that the peace agreement was not perfect. I guess hope springs eternal, and we were hopeful that somehow this would be made to work.

At that point there were still a lot of Americans there. It was after that that we started to pull out in really large numbers. So at that point, there was still all the prosperity there was before. It was from then on that things started to go downhill and they really started to have severe economic, military supply, and morale problems.

At the beginning of '73 I was out in the province in the central Delta called Chuong Thien for a month or two. Then I went up to Can Tho, which is the capital of the Delta and also the capital of the military region, and at that point we established in the Delta, as well as in other military regions, a Consulate General. So I was one of about sixteen Foreign Service officers who worked under the consul general in Can Tho.

At the end of six months, when a lot of other people went back, I stayed and I became the head of the political section in the Consulate General, and the number-two person, the deputy consul general. At that point the new consul general was Wolf Lehmann, who eventually became the deputy chief of mission at the Embassy.

In the Delta, the situation was actually getting worse. In spring of '74, our consulate did an analysis of the military situation. It was a long one, and it was very pessimistic. We had a lot of facts and figures in there about desertions, lack of supplies, and morale, which was going down. There were clear signs that after having gone quite well in the Delta in 1973, in the spring of '74 things were starting to go downhill.

Also that at this same time Cambodia was in the process of being taken over by the Khmer Rouge, and we were a bit on the fringes of that. One of the little-known and fascinating features of that period is that there were a number of Cambodian refugees fleeing the Khmer Rouge, and I guess the war in general, who were coming down into South Vietnam, into Kien Giang province, and being put up there. And one of the officers at our Consulate General did several long and very perceptive reports on the basis of talks with these refugees. What came out of them clearly was that the Khmer Rouge, who eventually took over Cambodia and were responsible for killing a couple of million Cambodians, were even at that point doing what they later became famous for doing. They were killing people in the areas they took over in a very very brutal way. And this was being documented as early as 1974.

But the situation didn't get much publicity. I think we did publicize it from Washington to a certain degree, but I also remember that people like Sidney Schanberg of the *New York Times* dismissed these reports as American propaganda. And I think that, generally speaking, people not totally averse to seeing the other side take over were of the view that this was just more American slanting of the news, or outright propaganda.

I left the Delta in September of 1974. I was the deputy chief of the internal unit in the political section. Our job was to follow internal Vietnamese politics.

As to the visit of the congressional delegation in early 1975, I mostly briefed them in my area of specialty. They did not come to me to ask how Thieu was doing, or whether he should stay in power, or anything like that, but rather to talk about the role of the political parties and the role of different political figures, such as the famous Father Thanh who headed the anticorruption group.

The whole question of repression and political prisoners was not new. It existed and was of some concern. I would say also, however, that the focus at that point was not on that, but rather on the survival of the country. Now this is important in human terms, especially if you're the guy in jail. But where it's important in political terms was that these congressional delegations were coming out to make some hard judgments about the Thieu regime and whether the U.S. ought to continue to support it.

People like Don Fraser had very liberal sentiments and they were looking for signs that the Thieu government was corrupt or wasn't corrupt. I think again, probably they made the same mistake that we Americans tended to make all through the war; to focus on the sins of the Thieu regime. There were such sins, but to fail to properly balance it against the characteristics that were much more obnoxious on the other side, or to think sufficiently about what would happen if the other side took over, is inexcusable.

During that time Ambassador Martin was in the U.S., and the debacle in the central highlands occurred while he was gone. As I understand it, he was being very optimistic back in Washington—unwarrantedly so, possibly because he wasn't on the spot and didn't see what was happening Of course, this is an interesting subject—the role of Ambassador Martin and the way he tried to keep things together.

Needless to say, when you are in a situation like this, you have to be extremely careful of what you say. And Ambassador Martin was. He was regarded as a bellwether. What he did had symbolic importance. So I think before you analyze or criticize him you've got to look at his activities in that light. And when you do, you'll see he had to be optimistic. Once Ambassador Martin started going around being pessismistic, then it was really all over.

Also to be said is that Ambassador Martin did explain our involvement in Vietnam, what we were there for, and why we needed to hold on, probably in better and more cogent terms than anybody else did or could. I heard him do that a few times, and he was very impressive.

I think where the Ambassador didn't do as well as he could and should have was in his relations with the press. I'm not saying the press never did anything wrong; in fact, I think they did a lot wrong. But Ambassador Martin antagonized them. He made people who were already antagonistic toward him and toward our involvement even more antagonistic. I think that could have been handled a lot better. I don't know if it would have affected the final outcome. It might not, but it certainly didn't do us any good.

It was hard, often, with Martin to tell how much he believed when he was saying things for public consumption and had to put the best face on things. I'm not sure anybody knows. And now we know that one of the things that was in his mind was the hope that there could be a negotiated, face-saving settlement that would not be much more than a disguised defeat. It would at least allow the city to be evacuated and the people to leave the country who needed to. We also know now that that was a forlorn hope. But it was one of the things in his mind when he was trying very hard to hold things together.

There were many small operations in early April designed to get certain people out of the country without much notice. My job, given to me by Ambassador Martin, was to assist in getting out the Vietnamese relatives of Americans. We had a number of Foreign Service officers married to Vietnamese, whose families lived in Saigon or elsewhere in the country. Many of those people were bombarding the State Department with requests to help their families. Needless to say, those people would have been very much at risk.

During those last ten days or so we were so incredibly busy doing this, operating from different safe houses, that I would just go home at night dead. One of my great regrets is that I never wrote anything down, but at the end of the day I'd be so exhausted that I just couldn't do anything. That continued all the way up until the last day.

On April 29 I woke up early because of the noise of the airport being bombed. I was then living about a half block from the Embassy, so I got up and went there, not knowing that this was the last day. Once I got there it soon became clear that this was the last day and we were pulling out all the stops.

That morning several of us were calling around to all of the Vietnamese in our pipeline who were supposed to come to the Embassy or one of the safe houses. Everything was absolutely quiet on the streets because there was a twenty-four-hour curfew in effect, and there was not a soul moving. I left the embassy, and got into a car, and went over to the safe house we'd used the previous day to get the list of names I'd left there, thinking we would be back the next day. I wanted to get that list so it didn't fall into the wrong hands. I went and came back with no problem.

Up in the asmbassador's suite of offices a little bit later, Alan Carter was wondering—he had a couple of Americans as well as a large number of Vietnamese over in the USIA [United States Information Agency] compound—how he was going to get them out, at least the two Americans. I told him I would be glad to go get them. I drove over there and got them and came back. Still no problem. The streets were deserted. In fact, we were kind of milling around that morning. About eight o'clock or so a Protestant minister, an Englishman, appeared at the gate of our embassy, looking in. He said, "What's the situation like?" I said, "It's getting bad, you'd better come in here. There's going to be an evacuation. This place is going to be jumping pretty soon." He said, "Oh, I don't want to be any trouble." I said again, "You'd really better get in here." So he did and he was taken out by helicopter. He was one of the self-effacing guys—here you are in the middle of this tremendous maelstrom and this guy says, "I don't want to be any problem."

At about noon, I guess, we had to go out and start picking people up and bringing them in. At this point there swings into operation an idea which turned out to be a godsend: using barges to take Vietnamese down the river. This was the idea of a couple of guys, one of whom was Mel Chatman, who came up with it a week or two before, when everybody thought it a kind of harebrained idea, but in the absence of any inertia to the contrary they went ahead and made the preparations and had the barges waiting.

So from noon until I stopped at about 3:30, I was going with a friend, Joe McBride, in minivans, and bringing people to the barges. I'll never forget the first trip that I made with my van, which was packed to the gills. First of all, we had to find the barge. That wasn't so easy. We had to cross a bridge and by that time people were starting to come out and the city was really turning frenetic. I didn't think we were going to make it across that bridge. It was starting to be a big traffic jam. If we made it I figured it would probaly be the last trip.

However, what happened, or so I was told, was that somebody came from the Embassy with a fistful of money, gave it to a policeman directing traffic, to stand there and direct traffic. Pretty soon things were moving again. I went back again and again to the house for more people. It was really a heartrending experience because we had a lot of people coming that day to the house, and of course all of them desperate to leave and all of them knowing that it was all over. You could see the helicopters overhead and it was clear that there were more people at this house than Joe and I were going to be able to take. I'll never forget the last run I made. People were desperately trying to get aboard the vans and I had to get almost violent to keep order. I'll never forget one man, an old man, who voluntarily stood aside and helped me calm people down, and he himself didn't try to get on the bus. He said, "Don't worry, he'll be back," I think knowing full well that I wasn't going to be back. And he was right. I was told by the Embassy that it was the last run and to come in.

Later that evening, while I was in the Embassy, I got a phone call from a guy in the city—he seemed to be on a street somewhere. And he said they told him to meet at such and such a place and nobody ever came.

He was on the street, not at a safe house. I said the only thing he could do was go down to the barges.

But you see, by then, everybody was afraid to go out. It was the old story—as long as you were with an American you felt a lot safer, and felt that you were going to get through. People were afraid to go down just on their own. Who knows what might happen? But I tried to convince this guy that that was his chance and that it was a good chance.

I left the Embassy at about nine or ten on the night of the twenty-ninth. I could pretty much have left when I wanted. Helicopters were coming in and anybody who wanted to and was ready could just go up to the roof. So about nine I figured well, why not now? There was no reason to stay any longer.

One of the things I'll never forget was that after we left and the helicopter circled out over the city you could look out to the west and see Long Binh Base burning. A huge, huge fire. Long Binh was one of our largest bases in Vietnam. I guess that watching it be consumed by fire summed everything up for me. Everything that we had tried to do was going up, literally, in flames. And also, of course, you had to think of all the people you were leaving behind, which was a tremendous number.

Today I remember all the people we left behind. I think about how vindictive the other side has been. It does seem there was not a bloodbath like there was in Cambodia; nonetheless, there were plenty of people killed, and after all this time there are still people in re-education camps who have been there for years.

During the Vietnam War nobody ever left Vietnam in a boat. During all of what the world thought were horrible years of war, nobody tried to escape from Vietnam. Since 1975, a million and a half people have left. They are still leaving. Twenty-five thousand people a year are still leaving Vietnam by boat, not to mention three thousand or so per year who escape by land by coming across Cambodia.

Since the end of the war, in watching what the Communists have done in Vietnam and Cambodia, most people now recognize that when our government said we were fighting a bunch of really nasty guys, that turned out to be the case.

Ambassador Graham Martin
"Walking Around with My Head in a Basket"

Vietnam was probably not worth another American life by 1975. We should never have gone in with American soldiers. I opposed that. I re-sisted sending in advisers when I was ambassador to Thailand. I did fight a long-drawn-out four-year battle with Robert McNamara to keep the war from spreading into Thailand, as Defense wanted very much to do. We had the same sort of insurgency in the Northeast that they had in the beginning in Indochina, and I kept insisting that I didn't see any white faces on the other side; we want to support the government and we surely should, but no Americans in combat or any combat advisers, even. I wouldn't let them go below the battalion level. And there is a guy who I think is still broadcasting—Paul Harvey—somewhere in the Midwest, and he said one day that there was an ambassador in Thailand "who has sense enough maybe to be ambassador to Johnson Island, which is a thousand feet long and fifty feet wide, but not anything bigger." And the reason for that is that I wouldn't let the Americans even carry sidearms on the bases out there. That's true. I was sticking my neck out because all we needed was one ambush and my throat would have been publicly cut from ear to ear. But we eventually broke the back of the insurgency. We didn't have any My Lai massacres either. I was successful.

But McNamara and the military got their way in Vietnam. And once they went in there with combat troops you didn't want to see it fail totally. By 1975 there was still something very important at stake out there—our word. Were we going to keep our word and our commitments?

The attack on Ban Me Thuot and Thieu's decision to withdraw from the central highlands came as a complete surprise to me. This was at the stage when President Thieu made up his mind that we were leaking information through certain people to the American press or the peace activists and then back to the Vietnamese on the other side. I don't know who convinced him of this. But throughout all of this he didn't tell us anything. And as far as the intelligence network telling us what the North Vietnamese were doing, they never were all that good.

I was in Washington at the time trying to get aid for the South Vietnamese. And I told the policy-makers back in February, when I came back with the Congressional delegation: you'd better prepare for refugees, you'd better prepare the setup, you better get the authority, and so forth. But they didn't do any goddamned thing about any of that.

In my last meeting with Henry Kissinger in Washington in March of 1975 at the State Department, he told me, "You gotta get back out there because the American people have gotta have somebody to blame."

This is a fact. We've always done that, and we always will. Then I told him, "Remember, the one thing you've got going out there is the fact I am the only guy involved in this whole business who has absolutely no pressure to make some goddamned fool decision to avoid criticism. There is absolutely no way that I am not going to be held responsible for the fall of Saigon. From beginning to end, it's going to be me. So I am not interested in doing anything except what makes sense right now to get the Americans out alive and as many of our Vietnamese friends, to whom we have committed ourselves, as we can. And I'm going to do that, and I'm not going to be pushed until you relieve me." So I went back out to Vietnam.

I never really had any great attachment to the Vietnamese, North or

South. I don't particularly like any of them. I love the Thai. I think
they're the most marvelous people in the world. I like most Chinese, but
I don't like the Khmer particularly and I don't like the Lao or Malay. I
like the Indonesians.

I lost a nephew, killed in Vietnam way back in the beginning. But the
only resentment I ever had about that was toward the U.S. Marine Corps
because they never got around to putting armor plate on the bottom of
helicopters, before they put them into combat with 50-caliber machine
guns on the ground.

So my commitment to the Vietnamese had nothing to do with my
nephew or an affection for the Vietnamese themselves. It was that we
had given our word. And when you don't keep your word you pay enormous consequences for it all over the bloody world.

One of the first people who came to see me when I got back was Ed
Daly of World Airways. When he came in he was wearing a couple of
guns, and I told him he had to leave them outside. When he hesitated I
told the Marines to go out and take his guns away from him. Then he
took his guns off. He came in and sat down, and said, "You know, the
Vietnamese tell me if I try to take off out there to go up to Danang,
they're gonna shoot me down. What are you going to do about that?"
And I said, "Applaud them! Who the hell do you think you are? I mean
you don't know your ass from a hole in the ground, you don't know what
this whole thing is about." We didn't have any other conversations after
that and he didn't come back to the Embassy any more.

I sent Harry Summers back up to Hanoi in April. We had this liaison
flight to Hanoi, carrying the Camp Davis people from the Joint Military
Commission. Admiral Geyler didn't want that to go, but I insisted that
we go up to Hanoi. Why? Well, nobody out there but me and my deputy,
Wolf Lehmann, knew about the Brezhnev-and-Kissinger business to Hanoi and the fact we had, according to Leonid Brezhnev, until the third of
May to get out. That was an agreement.

I said to Kissinger that I wanted about two weeks and he said that they
had communicated with Hanoi and that that was acceptable. I counted
on all of this—with Murphy's law in mind. You always count on Murphy's law—if something can go wrong, it will. They said the plane might
get shot down. Nevertheless, I wanted it to go. So we took the people
from Camp Davis; Summers took them up to Hanoi and sat down and
talked with the Vietnamese. We wanted to tell the Vietnamese that we
were carrying out our part of the Kissinger-Brezhnev bargain. They were
to leave us alone. I was counting on May 1, not May 3. I didn't want to
go any further than that.

I sent a cable a week or so before the end, when Washington was beginning to get very upset. And I said that "the only thing we've got going
out here is my coolness, my calmness, my ability to judge the situation.
We really don't have anything else. Now I don't have anything to lose,

because I am already walking around with my head in a basket." That's the truth.

President Thieu resigned on April 21. I did not persuade him to leave the country after that. Actually, Thieu's successor called me up and said that Thieu was still there in the Presidential Palace and it was hard for him to turn loose, which was a very polite way of saying that Thieu was still seeing his generals. And would I help get him out? And I said I would if he asked me to. Then about fifteen minutes later, Thieu called me on the phone and asked if I could get him out of the country. Now I have another problem. Do you use the U.S. military to do this, and risk going back to the Joint General Staff and risk it getting to the North Vietnamese and getting the plane shot down? So I got the military to bring down by plane, an old four-engine plane they kept up at Nakhon Phanom. So they sent it down to Saigon, and then—I think it was a mistake probably—I got Polgar instead of the military. The military knew the plane was coming in but they didn't know whether I was going on it or what. But I hoped they wouldn't know that Thieu was even going to board the plane until he was actually on it. I mean our American military, let alone the Vietnamese military. So I asked Polgar to use Frank Snepp to drive from the military compound just a little way over to where the plane was parked and I put them on the plane. Before that, Charlie Timmes and I rode alone, just he and I in his little Volkswagen, out to see Nguyen Cao Ky. Timmes had an appointment with Ky, and I said, "Well, I'll go along." It was a sort of hairy ride because downtown was already getting a little edgy. We drove out there and into the compound at Tan Son Nhut and they were surprised to see me. So the whole point of that trip was to talk about a bloody coup that wouldn't have served any purpose on God's green earth at that stage except bolstering Ky's ego. So I just talked around the subject with Ky. He may have inferred from this that his timing wasn't right or something, but I just wanted to put that idea down, and I got other people to work on him and told them not to pay any attention to him.

If anybody out there ever sort of totally knew what the hell they were doing, I did. I didn't know exactly at the very end what everybody else was doing. One guy who gave me trouble was a very good friend of mine, in fact, and I still like him very much, Erich von Marbod.

He came out from the Department of Defense and he got the South Vietnamese Air Force to fly some of their F-5s over to Thailand. That was against my instructions. In a way it didn't matter all that much. In a way it mattered very greatly indeed. Because I had asked Kissinger to pick up some time for us; I said I wanted about two weeks. We were trying to get all the American defense contractor people out, and we didn't know where all of them were, and we weren't about to leave without them. To round those people up we needed to keep some Americans there. We couldn't draw down precipitously without pulling the plug. So von Marbod persuaded General Tran Van Minh to fly all these planes over to Thailand, and that was a great mistake. It caused great consternation among the Thais. The men who went over had not been told that they would not be allowed to go back to their families. In order to calm them down, they were also drugged in Thailand. And these were the same people who rebelled when they got them to Guam. It was my fault. I should have sent von Marbod out two days before. Just as I should have sent Polgar out. He didn't know what the hell was going on. He really didn't deserve to run intelligence there. He tried to make an end run with Malcolm Browne of the *Times* and his Hungarian friends on the International Control Commission, and both William Colby and Kissinger came back and told me about it. And I told Polgar I'd cut off his balls and stuff one in each ear if he did something like that again. That's what Jim Kean heard me say to him on the elevator.

I have little to regret except not getting rid of Polgar and von Marbod earlier. But that didn't really make all that bloody difference. The greatest difference, we found out later, when we read the wires of the North Vietnamese generals, was that they thought that in flying those planes to Thailand we were breaking our word to them. This was something we said we were just not going to get into—taking out military equipment. We just wanted to be left alone and for them to let us leave in our own sort of order, but they rocketed the airport the next day, and they killed some of the Marine guard that was out there.

Because of that, I finally called for the helicopter lift, and that's when things really began to come apart.

After the rocketing I went out to Tan Son Nhut. I had retired as Air Force colonel after thirty-some years. I was commissioned in 1936, and know a great deal about what flies and what doesn't fly. I was deputy chief of staff for the Pacific Division during World War II, in addition to having the duties of chief of Army intelligence. When I do things I sort of work at it and I know what the hell I'm doing. Out at Tan Son Nhut on the morning of April 29, they were telling me they couldn't land the planes. That didn't make any bloody sense. I went out there to see and it still didn't make any bloody sense. You could have taken a jeep and cleared the runway of the debris in thirty minutes. But the panic had already set in with the Vietnamese military. They had already pulled out the top command; there was no one left to command the post on Tan Son Nhut, and there was no way we could have brought in transport planes without them being mobbed. You see, we no longer had the protection—as we had had up to that time—of the Vietnamese troops, as we evacuated the people we chose in specific order, with the promise that in the end we would evacuate them.

The helicopters landed, not at Tan Son Nhut, but at the DAO compound, because there was security there. There was a defense system at the DAO compound, but we could not guarantee security for fixed-wing at Tan Son Nhut itself.

Then I told everybody—and I told the fleet people and Washington did insist on this—I told the Vietnamese, a lot of them, "we can't guarantee to get you all out by airplane, but if you people can get out by boat we'll be around there to pick you up." Well, I kept the fleet out there for three bloody days and we were fully loaded, and the chief medical officer finally told me that if we waited any longer we ran the risk of an epidemic and we couldn't load any more on. That's when we finally left.

I had also ordered two planes coming from Clark to sit down at Vung Tau and pick up the families of the Vietnamese marines. And Admiral Geyler wouldn't permit that. I overrode him and they set the two planes down and we picked up those people in fifteen minutes and took them to Clark. From that time on out, the Marines belonged to me. They were going to provide cover down there in case we wanted to evacuate anything over the beach. Well, CINCPAC [Commander in Chief, Pacific] wouldn't have anything at all to do with evacuating over the beach. They wouldn't even let us have any landing reconnaissance flights in the weeks before, but we went ahead with them anyway. But that was just the kind of thing I had to deal with.

The tamarind tree story is absolute nonsense. It was absolute nonsense to have it cut down. This tamarind tree had no symbolic significance at all. But I was trying to maintain a surface calm in Saigon. What I did not need was a repetition of Nha Trang and Danang, for God's sake, and there was no point in cutting down this tree to make room for the helicopters to come in. And I just said, "Leave it alone!" It's just that simple. When we need it to come down, we can dispose of it in ten minutes. And in the end that is exactly what happened. But we didn't want to do something that would manifest to the city that we were caving in and running. All that was needed to have Saigon tumble was that belief that we were absolutely bugging out.

The tree was not at all a symbol of the American presence. But in one way, though, Jim Kean is right to say that it was. It was just physical evidence of our moving out. My saving it had nothing at all to do with anything as abstruse as its being a symbol of our commitment. I was trying to keep the lid on.

At the very end we did have one of those inescapable things, for which Secretary of Defense James Schlesinger still deserves a black mark. At that time he was just stupid—parts of him always were.

We had a guy named Stuart Herrington. He worked under Colonel Madison; he was helping to load people out in the yard. He didn't really know anything about anything other than loading. But he was a guy who would always volunteer an answer whether he knew it or not. So when these pilots were coming in, they were asking me how many additional people we had. Herrington was telling these pilots, "You got 2,000 or 2,500 more." And Admiral Noel Gayler who was out there with the fleet was just absolutely sitting on pins and needles, because he feared he was going to be the man in charge of a disaster, and so he was putting enormous pressure on us to "evacuate the Americans! Evacuate the Americans! Evacuate the Americans! And just come the hell out of there and just leave everybody else." Now this I refused to do. Brent Scowcroft had promised me fifty more of those big helicopters. We had taken the Vietnamese and the Koreans to whom we had made a promise, we carefully counted them and brought them across the wall into the inner compound. We had no intention of bringing the people we had left in the outer compound. We were going to bring these other people out—some of them were cabinet ministers and so on. But this Herrington message went to the pilot, to the admiral, to CINCPAC, and then back to Schlesinger in the Situation Room in the Pentagon. Schlesinger was being pushed by the Joint Chiefs to get it over with. "Martin's always going to have 2,000 more, no matter what we do; you'll have 2,000 more until the very end," they were saying. Actually we very carefully calculated the whole bloody business, taking out ninety at a time, and with what Scowcroft had promised me—well, God knows if you can't count on the President's National Security Adviser, who the hell do you count on? Then suddenly we got this message that everything was off! "The next helicopter is coming; please come out." That was because of Herrington. And then Herrington wrote a book, you know, and he became a great hero.

I had the same trouble with the Embassy security chief, who was responsible for evacuating all of the Vietnamese police. I held two boats over on the river for the police and then he wanted to take them out early. I got word back from some of my friends still left on the Vietnamese General Staff that if they pulled the police out of Saigon they had no way of maintaining order in the city. And so I told him not to do this until about three in the afternoon. He was very upset, like everybody else. They wanted to do their own thing. So he held until three in the afternoon and we got everybody over to the boats, and loaded them up with their families and evacuated them.

I don't really have much complaint about the operation because the President and Kissinger stayed with me until the very end. I am not saying it was totally perfect or anything, but looking back on it, I am entitled to ask, "Who would have done what particular thing differently under the circumstances?"

I was aware what an important historical moment it was when I left the Embassy. Sure. But even before that, I said all of this back in Washington: "We have a choice here. What's going to come after me? It's the fact that all over the world, people are going to push that extra step further than they would have pushed before. We've got to keep our word."

On the helicopter going out, I was thinking we had gotten away with it, really. We had gone through all of this and we had gotten out every American. My primary responsibility was getting out the Americans. We had gotten all of the Vietnamese we could. We should have gotten out more. We could have brought out those last 400. But there is bound to be that kind of confusion and what-not anyway.

I think the Americans have a right to be proud of the evacuation. I have absolutely nothing for which I apologize at all.

I did take the blame for Vietnam. That's why I took so long getting up on the Hill, letting it all sort of settle down a bit, and letting everybody come up with their own bloody excuses, and they did.

Anyway, I had fun. I never worried about getting fired. I always figured if I got fired I'd go back to the typewriter.

The pressures of the peace people on the educational system and the blindness of the don't-do-anything-that's-going-to-be-arguable-or-be-attacked school of thought have tended to be predominant in our educational system, so the textbook publishers have either ignored Vietnam or treated it so blandly that nobody can have any real understanding of it. It's funny because in a way it's been a good thing. I do speak to students now and then, and I find that most of them are not only sort of ignorant of it, but completely innocent of it, and are therefore quite capable of approaching the subject from a totally objective point of view, and that makes them about the only group in the country who really do. When something totally reasonable is laid out in front of them, they get angry that they've been denied all knowledge of this and have read only part of it, really.

Historians will eventually dig it all out. They will perhaps treat me very kindly, perhaps more kindly than I should be treated. But there is a hell of a story there that is yet to be told.

CHAPTER **V**

Central Intelligence Agency

Thomas Polgar
"We Were a Defeated Army"

It was easy to read North Vietnam's intentions because the North Vietnamese did not keep their intentions secret. They kept briefing their own cadre in astonishing detail about what they were going to do. It was a little bit like Hitler and *Mein Kampf*. They kept saying what they were going to do but we kept not believing them. And our national policy was simply not responsive to the intelligence we were gathering.

For example, we started to get reports from Hanoi in the fall of 1974 stating that now that Nixon was gone we have a different ball game, and we are going to have some tests in the military sphere. I took that very, very seriously. Starting in October 1974, when we got the plan for 1975, I remember I drove up to Bien Hoa to talk with my base chief in whose area this particular plan was acquired. And we came to the conclusion that the language in this document was terribly similar to the COSVN [Central Office for South Vietnam] 90 directive that came out a couple of months before the 1972 offensive.

One day I had an opportunity to ask Kissinger what he thought of our intelligence. Not speaking of Vietnam, but generally. He was getting this big flow of intelligence from CIA world-wide at the time. What did he think of the value of it? And he thought for a moment and then he said, "Well, when it supports my policy, it's very useful." And I think this is the heart of the problem. It is that American policy is not formulated in response to what the intelligence shows. We first formulate the policy, and then we try to find the intelligence to support it.

The three principal collectors of intelligence in Vietnam were Military Intelligence, the National Security Agency, and the CIA. We never had a situation where the DAO–DIA [Defense Attaché Office–Defense Intelligence Agency] would say something entirely different from everyone else. And we coordinated very closely with Bill LeGro, who was the intelligence chief for DAO throughout most of the period after the Paris Agreement. The problem was that American policy was based on the premise that the Vietnam War was finished. The American forces were out that there was no way whatever that President Ford was going to risk his re-election chances by reintroducing American forces into Vietnam.

In 1974 we were not delivering supplies on time to the South Vietnamese. We were falling behind on our obligations. And I reported at that time that when the South Vietnamese lost their faith in American support, they would collapse. And I put the emphasis more on their faith—their morale—than on the actual level of logistical support.

Five things happened in 1973 that Vietnam had nothing to do with but that affected it very badly. The first was the Arab-Israel war, which diverted Defense Department attention and vital military supplies from Vietnam. The ensuing oil embargo and meteoric rise in crude oil prices had a most damaging impact on the South Vietnamese economy. The newly renewed vulnerability of the U.S. to foreign pressure produced a strong psychological reaction against continuing expensive foreign commitments. The overthrow of Salvador Allende by a military coup in Chile infuriated liberal and leftist opinion, which worked off its frustration against South Vietnam. Congress, increasingly disgusted with Watergate-related disclosures, punished Nixon where it could, including in spheres related to Vietnam.

And I think Thieu knew very well that without the U.S. he could not survive. I knew his nephew, Hoang Duc Nha, very well. And Nha understood that a lot better, having spent four years in college in the U.S. He appreciated much more the mercurial nature of American politics and the ups and downs as a result of purely domestic pressures that really have nothing to do with the foreign issues but that had an impact on foreign relations. But how could a man like Thieu appreciate how Congress works when he worked with his own parliament, which was always subservient?

When Phuoc Long fell in early 1975 it was not important militarily, but it was terribly important as a symbol of America's refusal to carry out this "massive and brutal retaliation" that Nixon had promised Thieu. The North was testing the water there, and the temperature kept getting more and more favorable and they kept getting in deeper and deeper.

Then the congressional delegation came out to Vietnam. I thought the performance of Fraser and Abzug in that delegation was inexcusable. Abzug came into the room and asked, "Which one of you is Polgar?" I identified myself, and she said, "Well, I've been warned against you."

There was a South Vietnamese student leader who was in prison

who had become a bit of a *cause célèbre* in the U.S. Abzug at first said
he was dead and that the South Vietnamese had killed him. I said, "No,
the South Vietnamese don't do that. They can locate anybody who's in
prison." She said, "Well, locate this one." And we located him and he
was in a jail up in MR 3, in Tuy Hoa. So she said she wanted to interview him, and it was too far to go by car. It had to be by helicopter.
And the only time she could possibly see him was on a Sunday morning,
which would have been an inconvenience for everybody, but all right.
We arranged for the helicopter and arranged access to the jail, and once
it was all arranged she just said, "Well, I'm no longer interested." She
never went to see him.

Millicent Fenwick, who was on that trip, didn't have much sympathy
for the Vietnamese war, but she behaved very properly. She went through
the motions of listening to the briefings. But Abzug was terrible, and
so was Fraser. For example, President Thieu invited the delegation to
dinner and those two simply failed to show up. They didn't cancel or
anything; just failed to show up. They came to the prime minister's
reception, which was before the president's dinner, but they didn't attend the president's dinner. The ambassador invited the whole delegation to dinner the first night they were in Saigon. Everybody except
Abzug showed up. And I was really disappointed because I had arranged
to sit next to her!

I don't think anybody can say that the attack was expected on Ban
Me Thuot on the fifth of March, but everybody in his right mind expected that there was going to be a major North Vietnamese attack in
the central highlands. We knew how they would first cut the roads,
which they did, how they would move these various divisions in, which
they did, and incidentally that intelligence was never accepted by Washington. It wasn't accepted because—well, we are getting here into an
area of sources and methods which I'm not sure I can talk about—but
the fact of the matter is, the Washington intelligence did not share the
information that was coming out of Vietnam, both from the DAO and
the CIA, that there would be a major offensive in the central highlands
in 1975. They refused to believe it.

The South Vietnamese had no strategical concept of their own beyond
putting a regiment here and a regiment there to defend. The reinforced
regiment that was in Ban Me Thuot was insufficient to cope with the
situation. They were also very unlucky.

These forces were very good for local peace-keeping and were very
good auxiliaries when you were on the offensive. But these were not
troops that were trained or equipped to fight main force units reinforced
with armor.

After the fall of Ban Me Thuot, Thieu met with General Pham Van
Phu at the Cam Ranh Bay conference and called for a withdrawal from
the central highlands. That meeting was held, I believe, on a Friday.

Phu put the process in the works on Saturday. I got my first word of it Saturday morning. I chased Charles Timmes out to the JGS—the Joint General Staff—to tell him, "I don't know what the hell is going on." I sent my other top-level assistant to see General Dang Van Quang, Thieu's security adviser, and to ask Quang what was going on in MR 2. Quang reported, "You know, the situation isn't good. We don't seem to be able to reopen roads and we are very worried about the situation and will have to shift some troops around, but nothing is going on in MR 2." Quang apparently didn't know Phu was evacuating. Timmes went out to JGS and he couldn't find General Cao Van Vien, chairman of the JGS, and on the whole it was a rather Saturday-type of atmosphere out there. But he found General Tran Dinh Tho, who was chief of operations, and he asked him what was happening in MR 2. And Tho said, "Nothing is happening that you don't already know." The JGS apparently had no idea that Phu was evacuating. I got my report directly from Pleiku. Wolf Lehmann was on some errand and Joe Bennett, the political officer, was at the dentist. So I called up the consul general in MR 2, Moncrieff Spear, and said, "You better get your people out of Pleiku because I understand they are evacuating." And he said, "You're crazy." He's sitting in Nha Trang, on the coast. I said, "No, I have reason to believe this is happening." And he said, "Are you ordering me to evacuate Pleiku?" And I said, "Now you know I can't do that. But I can conclude that it would be a smart thing to do."

The point I'm making here is that what General Phu did that morning, whatever his previous merits might have been, was totally uncoordinated. He didn't even tell the consul general, whom he was obligated to tell—he was the principal representative of the U.S. in MR 2. Quang didn't know about it. I mean, had there been something going on, Quang would have looked like a busy man that morning but he was just killing time. And Tho, the chief of operations, didn't know.

What happened, in my judgment, is that Phu initiated a course of action having misunderstood what President Thieu had in mind, and without knowing anything about how difficult it actually was to do. The fact is that there is no such thing as a successful evacuation. Every evacuation becomes a tremendous fiasco sooner or later.

Then the North Vietnamese caught up with Phu's evacuation. North Vietnamese tanks were able to come up a side road and meet the column at Phu Bon. And there was a slaughter.

Before the Cam Ranh conference I was on record with Washington as saying that the game was over. I remember talking to one of my closest contacts in this context (I will not mention his name), and he told me that South Vietnam could not digest the loss of Ban Me Thuot and the loss of the highlands, which he thought was the inevitable consequence of the loss of Ban Me Thuot. He was a general officer.

At that point nothing was happening in MR 1. Then disaster there.

Thieu made the decision to withdraw both the Marines and the Airborne from MR 1. And that of course pulled the rug out from under any plans of General Ngo Quang Truong to make a stand there. And then, as it turned out, the Marine division was lost and totally useless, because first they were ordered to retreat and then they were ordered to turn around and go back, and that was just an impossible military move. So in fact the Marine division lost part of its equipment because it was impossible to extricate the equipment from the refugee stream. By this time, of course, Thieu, awash in the ocean, is grasping for straws. But it made no difference what he did at that point. The game was over.

I firmly believed that the moment the Vietnamese got the impression that we were going to run, everything would collapse. I completely agreed with Martin on that point.

The ambassador had left the country with the congressional delegation. He felt that he could lobby some of the congressmen, and then he was going to testify to Congress. When he was in Washington, a medical condition that required immediate surgery was detected and this delayed his return. And because no one wanted a great production of the fact that he needed surgery, Martin went down to North Carolina. The State Department didn't even know how to get hold of him—he was a very secretive man. He returned at the end of March, just prior to the fall of Danang and the C-5A crash.

When the orphans were sent out on the C-5A, that was strictly a public relations proposition. Mr. Dan, who was a medical doctor, deputy prime minister, and minister of health, felt that they had to do something about the orphans. And Ambassador Martin and some of his advisers felt that having all these orphans arrive in the U.S. *en masse* would generate public sympathy, a big human-interest story. At the same time the Defense Attaché Office had a lot of female employees, and they were already almost ready for evacuation, but you couldn't give people travel orders because the U.S. was not officially ready for evacuation. And who's going to pay for their air transport from Vietnam? The U.S.? So I thought, well, I could put them on this empty military plane and designate them as escorts for the orphans, and it won't involve any transfer of cash. My wife went out as an orphan escort, but she happened to go out on a civilian plane—Cathay Pacific—just about the same day that this C-5A crashed.

I had two CIA doctors on my staff, and when the plane crashed they took the bodies, all these little babies, to the Seventh-Day Adventist Hospital in Saigon. One of my doctors had the presence of mind to take along a camera and took a lot of pictures. When I showed the pictures to the ambassador, the ambassador considered for a long time whether or not to have them published. But he made the conclusion that these terrible pictures, all of them very clear and in beautiful, living color, showing these mangled bodies of women and children, instead of generating sympathy, would have a bad effect on morale. That's precisely what was happening in DAO at the time, so they were not published.

A couple of days before Thieu's resignation, one of the senior Hungarian officers with the ICCS [International Commission of Control and Supervision] came to me and said, "Look, you must be a realist. You must know that this war is lost." I said, "Okay. I admit the war is lost." And he said, "Every lost war must have political consequences." I said, "I agree with you." He said, "These political consequences are obviously going to be bitter. But there is no interest in the side which I represent"—and he left unsaid whom he represented, "to unduly humiliate the United States. Maybe something can be worked out—not to change the outcome of the war, that's finished, but to permit an ending which would not be"—again, to use his words—"unduly humiliating to the United States."

I asked, "What have you got in mind?" "Well," he said, "you know we are out at Tan Son Nhut talking to our North Vietnamese colleagues. We have people in Hanoi. I have the impression that perhaps something could be worked out along the following lines. Thieu must resign. The United States must pledge nonintervention in South Vietnamese affairs beyond the maintenance of a normal Embassy structure. And in South Vietnam the government created must consist of people that the North Vietnamese find acceptable. These are the essential problems."

I said, "Well, thank you very much. I will naturally report our conversation. I will discuss it with the ambassador so we can get it back to Washington. And I will be back to you. And while we are awaiting the answer from Washington, would you be kind enough to talk to your friends again and find out who might be some of the people that they would consider acceptable in the government?"

A couple of days later, Thieu resigned. I went back to my Hungarian friend and I said, "Look, I have delivered on your first point. We still don't have a definitive answer. Have you got any suggestion as to people's names?"

And he said, "Well, as a matter of fact, I do. But I am very poor on Vietnamese names, so I wrote them all down." He got out a little notebook and started reading me some names, all of whom registered with me. I said, "That's very interesting. I will of course follow up on our previous conversation and I'll get back to you." But he said, "I have an additional word from my colleagues here and they tell me that when they said you must move fast, they meant within a matter of days, not weeks."

The ambassador was very favorably inclined. He thought that this was something that we could do something with. But we got a very negative reaction from Kissinger, who did not want to have any negotiations.

Then on the twenty-sixth or the twenty-seventh of April we saw each other again, and the Hungarian said, "Well, I think it's now too late." I'm telling you this because I can't emphasize in strong enough terms that there never was any deal and we never did anything that the other side had asked us to do, because in fact Thieu resigned for reasons totally different from this, except that I pretended to them that we had something to do with it.

It was on a Monday that Thieu resigned, the twenty-first of April. The ambassador didn't talk Thieu into resigning, but by the nineteenth of April, when the ambassador talked to the president, it was perfectly obvious that Thieu had lost the confidence of everybody, that everybody felt that he was in the way of any kind of settlement, of any kind of decent cease-fire; that you simply couldn't do anything with Thieu around.

One day the ambassador called me to his office and said he had just come from seeing President Huong, and the president was very uncomfortable with the continuing presence of Thieu in the country. Huong thought that Thieu's presence diluted his authority and that he, Huong, was paralyzed in trying to do something as long as Thieu was there. He urgently turned to Ambassador Martin because the U.S. alone was in a position to do something about this. And getting President Thieu out of the country must be done in total secrecy. Well, Ambassador Martin, very logically, when he hears "total secrecy" thinks of the CIA, and so he told me this and said, "Can you do it?" I said, "Yes, I can do it, Mr. Ambassador. But under conditions. You leave me alone. You give me the task and let me do it but let's not have a committee approach on this." This must have been about the twenty-fourth.

Things went very fast after that. I knew where I could get the right airplane. I used General Timmes as the principal point of contact. By this time Thieu was staying out at his villa at the Joint General Staff compound. The senior Vietnamese generals had a villa compound at Tan Son Nhut. We agreed on a plan of action. We had a couple of things to worry about. We had to worry about public opinion; we also had to worry about some undisciplined South Vietnamese military interference, some junior officer taking it into his head to make history. We also had to worry about the police blocks all along the road leading to Tan Son Nhut that had nothing to do with Thieu, but they were always there, so we cooked up a story that we were going to a party at the JGS compound. We got a couple of standard black American sedans, including the ambassador's car, my car, my deputy's car; enough to carry ten or twelve people, drivers, Timmes, and myself, plus luggage. We specified that everybody could carry only one piece of luggage. And we made arrangements that everybody was going to meet at the prime minister's house, Prime Minister Khiem, because first, it was the biggest house, and second, less attention would be paid to him than to Thieu. We agreed to fly a plane to Taiwan, where Thieu's brother was ambassador, so he could make a deal with the Taiwan authorities to let everybody in. And Prime Minister Khiem was a former ambassador to Taiwan, so he had his own connections. In picking Taiwan as a destination, I was also influenced by the fact that this was a DC-6 plane and this was about as far as it could go without refueling.

So I picked what I considered my best, most reliable, and steadiest people as drivers. Obviously, I didn't want to use any Vietnamese drivers in this. Frank Snepp was one of the drivers. Timmes was one of the passengers because his rank prevented him from driving a car, and my rank prevented me from driving a car. Then I arranged to get a police colonel who was also a military colonel and I said, "I want a guy with a commanding presence," just in case there were any questions from the guards. I didn't think there would be, because when people saw four American sedans driven by Americans they'd say "this is a big deal"; when they recognized the ambassador's car they'd say "the ambassador's coming to a meeting here." So, sure enough, we never had any trouble, but I had this police/army colonel just in case. We didn't know who Thieu was going to bring. We knew that Thieu himself was going to go and that Khiem was going to go, but we didn't know who the others were going to be. So we brought along a lot of blind documentation and Charlie Timmes was filling them out by hand, writing in people's names on the documents, which we took and gave to the plane's captain and said, "When you arrive in Taiwan we are going to notify U.S. military authorities, and you have to ask to speak to the senior U.S. military officer and give him this envelope, which has all the documentation."

In the meantime another car took the ambassador directly to the plane because he wanted to say goodbye to Thieu. I said to the ambassador, "I don't want to drive with you around town. That's an additional risk." So I think in fact we changed cars. Everything worked like a Swiss watch, as was usually the case when we decided to run an operation on our own. We delivered everybody safely to the aircraft, loaded them on, and they took off.

I rode with the prime minister. I didn't ride with Thieu. I think General Timmes rode with Thieu. It was very subdued; no crying. The families had already gone. In fact, I was surprised. I was surprised because of all the people who were closely associated with Thieu, the only one he took with him on the flight was the prime minister, Khiem, which was particularly funny because for a couple of years before you could hear in any Saigon coffee house rumors about how Thieu and Khiem had parted ways; one was going to throw the other out, and so forth. Of course, I never credited such talk because I had a very good relationship with the prime minister and I always considered him a loyal servant of Thieu. There were a total of fourteen people that night for the flight, all of them men.

I was concerned that an unpleasant incident could happen if somebody knew that Thieu was in the motorcade. But I figured that the Vietnamese know the difference between the four important-looking American Embassy vehicles and Thieu's normal method of moving around town, which was in an old Mercedes. It was after dark and I thought interference with four American vehicles very unlikely. The lead vehicle was the ambassador's armored Chevrolet Caprice, in which I rode. But I had this police colonel with me. My biggest problem was, what happens if a police blockade asks people to identify themselves and turns their floodlights on us? Because at that point they would recognize Thieu and the prime minister. But as it happened, when the four important-looking cars came to the police block, everybody came to attention and saluted; that's what I expected would happen. I once brought out a very important defector from East Berlin in a big car like that, figuring that when the Soviets see this car they will salute. And they did.

Thieu didn't take any gold out with him that night. That story is just bullshit. Nobody in his right mind packs gold so that it is loose in a suitcase, for gosh sake. I mean, I've had a Vietnamese friend who took out gold and I know this gold was packed very tightly and surrounded with all kinds of clothing and rubber bands and tape. Nobody wants to hear coins rattling around in a bag.

In fact the Vietnamese gold reserve stayed in the country and was still there when the North Vietnamese Army arrived. The Vietnamese National Bank had the gold reserve and this was valued at eighteen to twenty million dollars. But in fact it was worth a lot more, because for reasons of their own, the gold price was fixed at thirty-five dollars to the ounce, which was the price at which the Vietnamese got it before Nixon devalued the dollar in 1971. But by 1975 gold was about $170 to the ounce. Now here we were in a period when South Vietnam's credit around the world was nonexistent, and Congress was slowing up the aid requests or denying them altogether. And, as usual, Ambassador Martin came up with a hot idea. He thought that South Vietnam should send its gold to the United States Federal Reserve and pledge this gold as a collateral against arms purchases on credit. Well, Thieu accepted the idea. The Swiss Air Freight trade carrier, Basel Air, happened to have a plane in Saigon. The South Vietnamese asked Basel Air to take the gold as a regular commercial consignment. And the Swiss thought about it for a day or two and said, no, they would not take it, for insurance reasons. They said there's no way they could get insurance to cover $70 million dollars of gold coming out of Saigon. So then they went to the U.S. Air Force. It was discussed at the National Security Council. The U.S. Air Force can easily take out a ton and a half of gold, but you cannot get commercial insurance if it goes on a military plane, period.

So then the hot potato was passed into the lap of the State Department lawyers. All this time the gold is sitting in the National Bank in Saigon. How can we get insurance for this shipment if it goes by military plane? Now this is a kind of topic that can keep lawyers busy for many a day. In the meantime, Thieu resigned, and we got a new crew in, and Huong at first said, well, let's ship it, but the next day he says let's not ship it. Huong finally concluded that it was best to keep the gold in Saigon because the situation was changed since Ambassador Martin first talked about it, and even if they got more American military aid with the help of the gold, it couldn't arrive in time to do any good. And they would look better if they kept the gold in the country. So the gold stayed.

The last big international cocktail party I went to in Saigon was that night. It was held at the residence of the Polish ambassador and the occasion was to introduce the newly arrived head of the Polish political section of the Saigon diplomatic corps. Everybody was there. All the ambassadors were invited who were still in Saigon, and the newly arrived Pole said he was very anxious to meet me. He said obviously we were in a changing situation, and he would like to have my views on the situation. We made a luncheon date for a week from that day. That would have been on the first of May. I fully expected to be there on the first of May to meet my Polish colleague, among other things.

Ambassador Martin was not much of a partygoer, but he said that night because of the nervousness of the city, "I am going to go to the party, too, but let's go in separate cars." So I went back to the office to file a cable—I wrote the cable before and then just radioed in saying a code word that my deputy and I agreed on. All in a day's work, that's how I felt about sending Thieu out.

On the day we left Saigon I was about as depressed as you can get without suffering a collapse.

The final act opened on Monday. Monday evening was bad. Duong Van Minh got inaugurated on that night, and just as he was giving his acceptance speech, this tremendous storm broke over Saigon. And it rained heavily. It was a little early because we were not yet in the rainy season. Then came the converted planes—you know, the American planes with the fifty-gallon extra gasoline tanks, flown by pilots under North Vietnamese control—and they bombed Tan Son Nhut. At that point we were all still in the office, although it was maybe about seven o'clock, because there wasn't all that much to do in Saigon by that time, in the evening. Second, because of the time difference: I think it was exactly twelve hours. When it was evening in Saigon, it was just morning in Washington. So we wanted to get out the maximum amount of message traffic to keep Washington informed as they opened for business.

There we were, all still in the office, when we heard all this shooting and took a dive under the desks and tables, and I remember I was in the room of the chief reports officer. The reports officers are the people who prepare the intelligence reports which then go out in telegraphic form. But we pride ourselves that these things, even in an emergency, must be properly edited and in good English, you know, like a good newspaper. And there we are under the tables—I'll never forget this—there was an attractive young lady reports officer there and she reached up and brought down her typewriter and she started typing: *To Washington from Saigon, situation report as of 1900 hours local. Explosions of unknown origin rocked downtown. While it's still going on around us, nobody knows what's happening.*

Pretty soon it was established what was happening. We properly took it as the North Vietnamese answer to Minh's inauguration speech. He said he's going to fight on, and says all kinds of stupidity that he wouldn't have said a month ago. I think it was a real illustration of the Peter Principle. Everybody rises to the level of his incompetence.

Despite the raid, everything in Saigon was functioning beautifully that last week. Electricity, the telephone, and the food supply was okay, except for maybe a shortage of lettuce.

I went to bed late that night, only to be awakened around 4:30 by the sound of explosions again. And this sounded like pretty heavy incoming stuff. I called my duty officer at the Embassy—a CIA duty officer. The CIA had separate duty officers at the Embassy. The Embassy duty officer had to be on call, and of course we had Marines there all the time. But we always had two officers who were physically present in the Embassy at all times. Not on call, but there. So I figured he was the logical person to call. And I said, "What do you know?" And he said he didn't know much at that point, but that artillery was hitting Tan Son Nhut, the Marines had gone up on the roof, and from the roof they could see fires burning, and that he was in touch with his counterpart at the DAO but it was too dark yet, they didn't know anything definitive. But the first thing was that the damage was considerable. And that two Marines had been killed.

So I said, "All right, it sounds pretty bad to me. It's a good thing you're on duty." He happened to be our chief finance officer. I said, "Prepare departure envelopes." Departure envelopes were envelopes with some instructions or maybe telephone numbers of American embassies and other places in East Asia. And in each departure envelope was supposed to be stuffed $1,500 in American currency and some other currencies we had on hand. Everybody is supposed to get one of those envelopes, and somehow he will make his way out, if he gets separated, to somewhere safe. I told him I would come to the Embassy.

In fact, I was the first officer there. By then the Marines had more reports from the DAO. And based on those I felt the Embassy should be mobilized. I called the ambassador and I said, "I'm terribly sorry to call you at this time in the morning"—he couldn't have been sleeping for more than three hours—"but I really think you ought to come in." Well, he said he would. Meanwhile, we had a system where you call one man and he's supposed to call four people, and those people are supposed to call four people, and so on. So we put that system into motion. The ambassador was in very bad shape that morning. I mean physically. He had an extreme case of bronchitis, which once we got to the warship we found out was bronchial pneumonia. He was very hoarse and could hardly talk. He was mentally 100 percent alert. When Kissinger called us, Martin couldn't make himself understood over the scrambled telephone, so he would whisper something and I would repeat it to Kissinger.

The ambassador went out to Tan Son Nhut because, being Graham Martin, you know, he only had a couple of Air Force generals at the airfield, but he wouldn't accept their version of whether or not you could land planes. He had to see for himself.

When the morning started, the pilots with the Seventh Fleet were ready, the helicopters were fueled, and everything was set to go. Then that morning at around 8:30 or close to that, we got the word that we were not going to evacuate. That we were going to reduce the size of the Embassy; that we were going to keep an Embassy in Saigon; that the Embassy was going to number about 180 people and fifty of those 180 should be CIA. But that the CIA in that group should assume the responsibility for all Embassy communications. And other Embassy section chiefs would get their orders—economic section, eight people; political section, sixteen people; medical people, finance section, administrative section—from Washington. Presumably from Kissinger to the ambassador. I've never seen it in writing but I got my instructions delivered to me orally by the ambassador that morning. So I went back to my office, called a meeting of my senior people, and at this point I still had over 200 CIA people on the premises. I said, "Fellows, we have to reduce to fifty and we've got to have a bigger than normal slice for communications to handle Embassy traffic. Now let's figure out which fifty people we want. Start with me." This is not a simple matter because, unlike naval officers, CIA officers are not interchangeable. People have different specialties. One is a reports officer, one is an operations officer, one is an analyst. I've got to have a mixture of linguistic talent. I've got to keep some Vietnamese speakers. I've got to keep a couple of Polish speakers to deal with the Poles at the ICCS. I wouldn't have any problem with Hungarian speakers because we didn't have any other than myself. So for a couple of hours I was out of circulation, working on this. I had to consider whose tour was about up anyway, because if a man is supposed to go home the first of May, I'm not going to keep him. Even if he's supposed to go home on the first of July, I'm not going to keep him. And we had people's family situations to consider, since we might have been in a bad situation, like we were in Hanoi in 1954 when we had an American consulate up there and the people were kept incommunicado for a couple of months, although not as hostages. They were effectively locked up in the compound but nobody bothered them.

The same word went to the fleet, too, that the Embassy was staying. There was this commander of the fleet, Admiral Noel Gayler. He was not a

political analyst. He said, "Well, the Embassy's staying. Pilots, go back
to bed." The gasoline was taken out of the helicopters, because you don't
store aircraft on a ship with gasoline in them. They got taken off the
flight deck and put down below.

This was nine o'clock in the morning. Or maybe a little later. So then
the order finally came at 11:30 that we were in fact going to evacuate
everybody. I didn't know when the order went to this Admiral. Ambassador Martin got it at about 11:30. Brent Scowcroft must have notified
the Pentagon, presumably, but this is nighttime in Washington, and
maybe the guy who was supposed to get it was out. I don't know when
the admiral got it. But I talked to him on the ship later and I asked,
"What happened?" He said, "Nothing happened. The moment I got
the order there was going to be an evacuation, I ordered the planes
fueled. I ordered up the pilots, but then we got this request that there
must be a Marine security force landed in Saigon to help with the evacuation. Well, the Marines don't happen to be on the 'copter carrier. So
we had to start ferrying these Marines from all the different ships to
where they can get into the choppers. All this takes time."

If you ask me was I surprised by what happened, I wasn't surprised.
I have a very skeptical opinion of the American military's ability to
operate on short notice. It's a very bureaucratic setup. Now you would
have thought that, given everything that had happened in Saigon in
the previous twenty-four hours, the Marines would have been near the
choppers, not spread out over the ocean in different ships.

Another thing happened that was perhaps not foreseeable. Once the
word got around in Saigon that the Americans were leaving, such a mass
of people formed around the Embassy that surface travel around the
Embassy became impossible. So having convoys of buses leaving the Embassy and ferrying people out to DAO was out of the question, because,
had we opened the gates wide enough to let the buses out, these people
would have just stormed the Embassy.

We had to start to destroy files long before that morning. In CIA we
had a very good rule that anything that is in the field must have a
duplicate in the U.S. So at any time a CIA station loses all its files, it's
not more than a small inconvenience. So we destroyed all files and in
the last hours that we had there we went through offices very methodi-
cally destroying anything that would suggest that certain Vietnamese
had a close relationship with us.

As for the famous tamarind tree, in all the meetings I attended in the
Embassy, I never heard any discussion about the tamarind tree coming
down. I felt very sentimental about that tamarind tree because it was
proof of absolute rank in the Embassy. There was a parking space under
the tree, which meant that your car was in the shade all day instead of
sitting out and getting to furnacelike temperatures. So having a parking
space under the tamarind tree was a proof of rank in the Embassy. But

seriously, in connection with the evacuation, never once have I heard anybody say anything about it. It was perfectly obvious that if we were going to land large helicopters in the Embassy parking lot, the tree that stood in the middle of the parking lot had to come down.

Once the ambassador had left the Embassy the next morning, there was no point in my staying there. And my communicators couldn't leave as long as I was there. And my deputy and a couple of others said they wouldn't leave as long as I was there. You try to send people out in reverse order of essentiality. When I say that they were not essential at that point, this is not derogatory. I mean, obviously, certain people's jobs ended before other people's jobs. Really, at that point we could send most of our reports officers home because they didn't have anything more to do. I could send everybody home whose responsibility was MR 1, 2, or 3. They had nothing else to do. I would still have my people in the Delta, because I didn't know what was going to happen in the Delta. I would send the administrative people home. I didn't need a personnel officer any more.

And that is how we decided who left and when. It went very smoothly. We never felt that there was any risk of being overrun. Absolutely not.

Perhaps the last big incident that happened concerning myself and my people was when we lifted these Vietnamese across the wall. At that point the Embassy was surrounded, literally, by tens of thousands of people, and it was very difficult even to approach the Embassy because of the masses there. But we had some people on the outside that we desperately felt we needed to evacuate, such as the chief of communications intelligence and the deputy chief of special police, which was in fact the political police. We had the wife and children of a lieutenant general in charge of psychological warfare. We had the defense minister, Tran Van Don, in the group. We had the chief of protocol and his family—all outside the Embassy. How are we going to get them evacuated?

I was able to communicate with them. Don managed to load on a helicopter off the roof of an apartment building that was not a designated helicopter site (and that's a story, too). I had with me a couple of pretty determined and brawny types with whom I was able to get on the Embassy fence and we physically were lifting these people across. And we had a couple of military officers in the crowd with whom we had a deal that, if they pick out of the crowd the people that we want, then in the end we will lift them in and they can go, too. We were able to move people through the city of Saigon all day by making deals with police officers and saying, "Put your families in among these people and when we safely put them on the plane or bus, then we are going to take you, too."

Our arrangements with the police were friendlier because we knew these people and we trusted them, and they trusted us. It was very funny that on that last day some of the people were escorted to their evacuation points in convoys run by these white motorbikes of the presidential security force.

In the Embassy courtyard, we had our Embassy sedans, and we faced them toward the center of the parking lot when it got dark, and they ran their engines and turned on their headlights and as long as there was gasoline, or as long as the battery held out, they had lights there.

Then we got word to go, and the ambassador was finally told, "You must be on this plane." But the first word we got was that we were going to go on a chopper in the parking lot, so we all went downstairs and found out that was wrong. They changed their plan and said, "No, it's going to be from the roof after all."

I didn't have a great emotional attachment to Vietnam like some of my colleagues who really fell in love with the country. But in the end, seeing how it ended, I thought that we really did a miserable job for these people and they would have been much better off if we had never gone there in the first place.

It was really quite dark when we left. Out toward Tan Son Nhut you could see a few fires, but basically the city was its normal nighttime self. The street lights were on, the traffic lights were working. It was a very eerie thing, and this was what was so strange about those last days. I'm not speaking only of the last night, but any of the last weeks in Saigon. They were so unreal because everything appeared to be so normal. It wasn't like the long siege of Warsaw, you know. A day before the collapse you could still go to restaurants and get a very nice meal and a good wine.

Nobody fired at us on the way out. And that's another thing. The North Vietnamese are a rational people. They are not like Shiite Muslims. And the last thing in the world they wanted to do was to create an incident that would provide a peg for American intervention. Because if they had killed the ambassador that would have been maybe a little too much, even for Congress.

Our reception on the *Blue Ridge* showed the American military at its worst. They started out by searching everybody. I think the ambassador was the only one who was not searched. And in normal peacetime I far outranked the admiral commanding the ship.

Nobody objected, though. We were tired. We were pretty placid. And we were a defeated army.

CHAPTER **VI**

Defense Attaché Office

Henry Hicks
"I'm Trying to Come to Work and They're Trying to Shoot Me"

I sent my family out of Saigon on April 24. I thought when the emergency was over they would come back. I never really believed the country would fall—even at the very end. But I sent my family out anyway. I think I felt at that time like the old guy who had been an atheist all his life. When he was dying he called his friend and asked to see a preacher. And when his friend asked him why he wanted to see a preacher, he said, "Because I could be wrong." I didn't think the country would fall, but I thought I could be wrong. And if I was wrong I didn't want my family to pay for it.

General Homer Smith put me in charge of evacuating the DAO personnel. And everything went all right until the night of April 28. We were just grinding away, flying people out, when all of a sudden here come these goddamned airplanes and they bomb us. They were flown by former South Vietnamese Air Force pilots who had defected to the goddamned North, and they bombed our airstrip to stop our planes from landing. And then that night—the same night—they sent in some rockets.

About 2:00 a.m. on the twenty-ninth I decided to go home for a while and sleep. I drove through the city and it was pitch black. There wasn't a light on in the place. Then the next morning I woke up and drove my car back to Tan Son Nhut and the goddamned Vietnamese guards started shooting warning shots at me as I approached the gates. So I drove back home and telephoned the DAO to find out what the hell was going on out there. And they told me that all I had to do was park my car and then walk to the gate. Then there would be no problem, they said. So I drove back out there and I parked my car and I started walking to the gate and those goddamned guards started shooting at me again. They were not trying to kill me, remember. They were just trying to scare me. I got about 200 yards away from them and they were still shooting, so I turned around and left a second time. I got in my car and drove home again and called the DAO. I said, "Your goddamned men out there haven't gotten the word yet. What in the hell is happening? I'm trying to come to work and they're trying to shoot me." This time they told me to go down to 191 Cong Ly Street. I thought when I got there somebody would take me to work. Well, I got there and was directed up to the roof. And a helicopter landed there—an Air America helicopter. Then he just waited there. He waited there for three goddamned hours! So I called the DAO and asked them why the guy couldn't take me out to Tan Son Nhut. And they said, "Well, he's got orders to wait for some other people." So we waited. And more people showed up. Then finally the pilot said, "All right. Let's go." There were so many goddamned people in that helicopter that he couldn't take off. So he had to make some people get out. When he finally took off, he didn't head for Tan Son Nhut, he headed out toward Vung Tau.

He swung out low over the city and I was looking down. I could hear gunshots, but they sounded like firecrackers. I saw some kids playing in a schoolyard as we flew out over the city. Everything looked pretty peaceful. But I felt absolute chagrin as we were going out. Absolute disgust. I just could not believe that we were going to let the Communists win.

We passed over Vung Tau and headed out over the South China Sea. I was looking out the window as we were going out, and all of a sudden I saw the fleet. It looked like something out of World War II pictures— the gathering of the fleet. We approached the *Blue Ridge* but were waved off on our first pass. Then we came in a second time and landed.

The next day they had helicopters landing on the *Blue Ridge* and after they landed they just pushed them over the side into the sea. It was the damnedest sight you ever saw.

On the *Blue Ridge* the press had their own special room. And they did their thing. But I didn't socialize with them. In fact, I had gotten along well with the press until 1968 and the Tet offensive. After that it dawned on me that they were calling Tet a great victory for the Communists. And I knew damn well that it wasn't, and so did they. I thought then, "What in the hell are they saying?" Then I saw some photographs, obviously staged, that they had taken after Tet. Photographs that were meant to pull at your heartstrings. Then I saw more staged photographs, and I started to think that there was nothing that they wouldn't stage. Nothing at all.

At first, early in the war, we set up briefings for the press so they could get any information they needed for their stories. Well, pretty soon they

were calling those briefings "the five-o-clock follies." It was always a goddamned game with them. Really, I never felt that it was anybody's duty
to make sure that the press got good stories so they could sell newspapers
and make profits and pay dividends to their stockholders. That's what
they do. They're a business. But they act as though they're a very special
group.

The television people were the worst. The goddamned television people never told the truth. They never even looked for it. I never understood what the hell they were after in Vietnam. But it sure as hell wasn't
the truth.

Becky Martin
"The Light at the End of the Tunnel Has Just Been Shut Off"

In 1974 I was working in Washington for the Department of Defense.
I found the job somewhat boring and I wanted to see the world. So
one day I just went over and I signed up for all the open government
positions I could qualify for, in twenty different countries. I just signed
up indiscriminately. Two weeks later Vietnam popped up and they called
me.

Well, the war was over; "peace with honor" and all that jazz was in
the past, I thought. So I had no misgivings at the time. And I would
have gone anywhere. I thought it would be great.

They gave me two weeks to report from the date of notification. I
needed to get a passport and make moving arrangements. But they took
care of it. The only thing that bothered me prior to my arrival was that
the flight from Guam into Manila was full—a Pan Am 747. And that
plane emptied in Manila. I mean *emptied.* I looked around, and I was
the only Caucasian aboard the flight other than the attendants, and I
saw four to six Vietnamese military types in their uniforms. That was
it. On a 747! And as we took off from Manila, some hostess came over
to me and said, "Why are you going to Saigon?" I said, "I have a job
there." And she said, "You're kidding." And I said, "No. How many
flights do you make a week?" And she said, "We have to go in twice a
week." I said, "Do you take any more people than this?" She said no.

Pan Am had the mail contract. They went in nearly empty. That was
my first inkling that I may have made a mistake. It was obvious to me
that an awful lot of people knew something that I didn't.

I went out as an intelligence aide, and once I got into that I didn't
like it. So I got into administrative functions and worked in the Current
Intelligence Section of the Defense Attaché Office.

When the war was over, supposedly, there were many enclaves that
were left to the Viet Cong and North Vietnamese throughout South
Vietnam. I didn't know that. And in the first briefing I ever went to,

an order-of-battle briefing of what was going on in the country, the first
map that went up on the wall was a map of Military Region 1. I saw
these red and blue symbols and at that time the symbols really didn't
mean that much to me. I didn't know what they meant, but the color
scheme was easy to catch on to. And I noticed that most of the colors
were red. I thought, "Gee, that's unusual. Red usually is the bad guys.
They're not usually the good guys."

Then the MR 2 map went up on the board. Cripes, something's wrong.
There are fewer red and more blues. And I turned to Captain Stu Herrington sitting next to me, nudged him—I'd only met him once before—
and said, "Who's red and who's blue?" And he said, "Red's the bad
guy." And I thought, "Oh, shit!"

Then MR 3 went up. Well, we had more blues. But not many more.
I thought, "What have I done? I've got to be out of my mind to be here."
Peace with honor? What a joke. My God, we left half the country to the
Vietcong.

After that briefing, Jim Wink asked me, "What'd you think?" I said,
"Jim, this place ain't going to make it. It's half gone already." He said,
"Oh, no, no," and I said, "Yes, yes, yes. There's no way in hell they can
pull this out." And they got into a big discussion, he and Jimmy Harris
and somebody else. They said, "Oh, no, they're going to be fine. We're
going to provide them with logistical support that they need to make it.
We're their allies . . ." and blah, blah, blah. I backed off. It was never
a subject I harped on.

That evening Stu Herrington came by my apartment. He said, "You
seemed a little upset by today's briefing." And I said, "Right." And he
said, "Well, I thought I'd come down and talk to you and try to put
things in perspective." So I invited him in and he tried to put things
in perspective for me, militarily. In other words, all the symbols didn't
mean we were going to be overrun any second.

Another thing that really bothered me the first three months in country was that there were an awful lot of young people on the streets.
They would lie about their age, draft-dodgers, have fake cards made
up. There was still quite a bit of desertion. The war was not a popular
thing. It had claimed so many lives and been fought for so many years.
I felt the will of the people just wasn't there.

I think Vietnam was a terrible waste. Honest to God. We spent so
much in manpower, which was our greatest loss, and so much money,
so many years fighting something that should have been over with in
a very short period of time. But it was so political, and the politicians
never permitted the army to do what they should have done—just go in
and win it.

We had a MISTA (Monthly Intelligence Summary and Threat Analysis) the morning after Nixon resigned. General John Murray, the defense

attaché at that time, was devastated with emotion. He said, "Gentlemen, the light at the end of the tunnel has just been shut off."

The Communists had never been able to key in on Tricky Dicky, really. He was an unknown to them. He didn't think like other Occidentals think. As a prime example, when Kissinger was at the peace talks in Paris, things weren't going very well with Le Duc Tho. And all of a sudden Hanoi was bombed. They would not agree to the terms, and Richard Nixon turned around and unleashed firepower. The North Vietnamese went back to the table in a very short period of time. And we had the making of peace with honor. But that bombing hit them very hard. It just didn't hit them in Hanoi, in logistic grids and depots, not only in North Vietnam but in South Vietnam, the northern part.

Then Nixon resigned. That bothered me. Where we were, things would be printed in the press about Watergate, but we weren't consumed with it. We didn't have it thrown at us in our TV news. We didn't have a news station. We only had the one English-language paper, and Watergate was not of paramount importance to them. In fact, if you talk to most people who lived overseas at that time, they'll tell you that most foreigners do not understand the big deal about Watergate. They don't understand the way Americans crucify themselves over something that's ho-hum to them.

So the Nixon resignation changed things for us. We started winding down. We spent two or three months microfiching documents and destroyed everything we microfiched as soon as the film came back and it was good. We shredded and burned everything. Our security officer would have a heart attack every time he came through, because he would see such volumes of paper. And all that stuff had to be destroyed. We just couldn't leave things behind. The consensus was to get it down to a manageable size, when and if there's a need.

Still, I never really felt that Vietnam would fall apart, until Danang fell. That for me was very symbolic. I saw the reports by the DAO personnel up there. Collection and Liaison had representatives there, and we saw their reports and their accounts of what was happening. Suddenly, here they come! Fourteen or fifteen divisions!

We had another MISTA on April 4, and that morning a colonel came into the office and said, "We're going to have our first evacuation; it's going to start today." Earlier we had made up a priority list of who would leave when—the least essential individuals were to go out first. He said the people on the first list were to go that day—April 4. I knew that included my message man and one of the secretaries. It also included three junior analysts from our office. And I said, "Since we have the MISTA, why don't we go ahead and just keep everybody? We're going to be here for a while and they can go out on one of the later flights." He says, "Gee, I was thinking the same thing." I said, "Great." He came back later and said, "Colonel LeGro agreed. We'll leave everybody in place."

And so our office, the current intelligence section, was the only one that didn't lose anybody on the fourth of April because that was our big production day.

But they went ahead with the evacuation that day. They decided to evacuate a large number of Vietnamese children. And they thought, "What a beautiful way to cut down on personnel and go ahead and evacuate mostly women from the DAO." So they let the women know that morning after they had come to work. They were called to a meeting center and told they were going to leave, and they were given time to go home and pack (I think two bags is what they could take with them), and that arrangements would be made to send their effects on later. So most of the women did return to the pickup point and were taken by buses from the DAO over to the air base and loaded on. A couple of the women did not want to go who were supposed to go. Some other women felt they had commitments to some Vietnamese families and they didn't think they should go without making an effort to get them out. They didn't come back to work until the next day.

We were at work late in the afternoon and one of the guys from security came in and said, "The C-5A crashed returning to Tan Son Nhut." They said they wanted people to help with the off-loading of helicopters that were going to be flown into Tan Son Nhut. So we all went out and piled into a pickup truck and went over to the airport and stood there and waited for helicopters. Not very many came in.

A few dead came in at first, but most were survivors, initially. And most of the survivors were children. The C-5A is a triple-decker plane. Most of the kids were on the upper level and they survived, but they had burns. I think the thing that just shocked me or intrigued me was that all the kids seemed to have injuries. You could see where the skin had burned, and they had wet themselves or excreted, but none of them cried. They just lay there like limp dolls. I would have expected them to be just screaming their lungs out, but they made no sound at all—nothing, no response.

My friends from the DAO were all dead. It was like losing my family. I had a feeling they were dead even before, when one helicopter came in and they off-loaded the youngsters. So many people rushed to help, and I stood there and I watched. And I thought, "They're all gone." A numbness crept from the back of my head and spread to my whole brain. I was just so overwhelmed at the sense of loss. Something chemically happened to my body to enable me to cope with it. I had never experienced this numbness before.

Another helicopter came in very quickly, and it had a lot more children on it. I went out and helped transfer them from the helicopters to the ambulance. Then I saw they had a woman's body, and it was Barbara, a gal that worked in the office. Her daughter survived, sitting right next to her. Barbara's nose and mouth were filled with mud. Other than that, there wasn't a mark on her. And they said later that she had died of fright. She had had a heart attack. Another helicopter came in and it had the body of a crew member on it. His head was bashed in. He must have died instantly. They had twelve body bags on the next helicopter, and when I saw that I just turned around and left.

I always believe in celebrating family holidays, wherever you are. You always have a lot of people in and you do it right. Set the table and sit down and don't eat off paper plates, a little bit more like home. So I always went all out to have American-style holidays. Easter had just been celebrated that Sunday, and all the women who came to my Easter dinner were dead within the week.

That night we went back to the office and tried to find out who was on the plane (at that time there was not a consolidated list). There was another Becky Martin on the plane. She was from Texas. She worked in the Air Force division. One of the guys in security asked me, "Do you want me to call your parents?" I said, "Can we get out?" He said, "I don't know." They really shut down communications at that point because they didn't want calls going out to families and they didn't want calls coming in. They wanted to control it until they got a handle on who was on the plane and sent out official notification. You don't want somebody calling and giving out, "Yes, I'm sorry, your mother's dead." And your mother may not be dead.

One of the guys in security called my folks and got my mother on the line and told her, "Mrs. Martin, there's been a very serious accident here, a plane crash, but your daughter is safe. She was not on the plane." And they cut him off. He didn't get a chance to say my name might be on the list because there was another Becky Martin on the plane.

My father had friends in Thailand and evidently knew someone in Saigon, and they called me at the office, and got back to my parents and said, "She really is okay." Someone from California had sent the list to them, so they were really uptight. My mother still didn't believe I was okay until she talked to me about a week and a half later.

After the accident I packed up some of my friends' belongings and went through their papers, making inventory lists of everything they had. This was supposedly done for all the crash victims so that later, if the belongings didn't get out of country in time, the families could be compensated. There was a lot of jewelry, a lot of expensive things, and mementos and picture albums. It was tough, but in a way it helped me, also. I felt that somehow they were with me.

I had a dream about a month before the accident. All of us were in a room and it looked something like our office. It was a huge room, very long and wide, and the desks faced in different directions. And we had a music system in the office. It was great. We used to listen to Monday night football on Tuesday morning. But we had the music system on and all the desks were turned upside down, the drawers had been opened, papers were taken out, and everything was empty. And I was sitting there and some of the people, Anne Reynolds and Joan Prey and others, came whipping through the office. Joan had access to the bank area where we were, and she came in and said, "Come on, let's go." I said, "Well not yet. We're not supposed to go yet. It's not time for us to go." She said, "Okay, I'll see you later." I said, "All right." And she went out. I got a call from Ann and the others and they said, "Come on over, we're all going to meet over at such-and-such a place." And I didn't know where that was. In my dream it was raining like crazy and the door was flapping back and forth in the wind. I heard a Vietnamese talking, a Vietcong, and I got worried and I wondered, "Where are they? They were all supposed to be here and now there's nobody here but me!" And as the Vietcong opened the door, I woke up.

It bothered me, and the next day I went to Anne's place for a drink. I gave her hell and I said, "You turkeys left me." And she said, "What do you mean?" I told her about my dream. She said, "No, we wouldn't ever leave you, Becky." But they did. They all left. It was a weird dream and it haunted me for a couple of days, and then I just kind of shoved it aside.

Two days after the crash some of us went to a security meeting down at the Embassy. They presented their plans for the evacuation of Americans from Saigon. They showed us a couple of buildings they had plans to land helicopters on top of, and fly people out. They also had plans for third-party nationals to be admitted to these buildings so they could also be evacuated. Some of the helicopters would only hold three or four passengers at a time, and that's not very many people when you get a panicky situation. They thought the North Vietnamese would let us leave. Why tear up a city that you can take whole, intact? But what if the South Vietnamese panicked and wanted out, where are they going to go? They're going to go for American helicopters! And we're supposed to maintain crowd control, and we don't speak the language!

When my office heard what the Embassy plan was for evacuating—I won't tell you what they said. You can't print it. We couldn't believe it. I just sat there dumbfounded, thinking, This man's in a position of responsibility? Elementary school kids would have seen holes in the plan. If people had ever come to the gates, forget it. Who were you going to let in?

At that point I thought I'd better write somebody, get my affairs in order. I didn't have a will. So I sat down and wrote a letter to my father and got a power of attorney—talk about ignorant, I got a blank power of attorney. I wrote the letter to him and said, "In case I don't come home by the end of May, do this with my car, do this with my savings account, do this with my belongings." I just made a list of the things

I wanted him to do, and I took it down and I had Stu address it, because I was afraid my mother would open it if she saw my handwriting. And we put "personal" on it. My mother never opens my father's mail, but I felt she was in such a turmoil that if she saw my handwriting it wouldn't make any difference if it was addressed to him or not, she would open it.

My mother opened it. My God, she had a fit. Because it was from Saigon she was sure it pertained to me, and my father was not there to open it and she was.

Sending that off was like having a weight lifted off my shoulders. Doug Dearth said later that day, "What are you grinning about?" I said, "I've taken care of everything." He said, "What do you mean?" I said, "You know, in case we're a little late getting out of here, I've taken care of all my affairs." He said, "What did you do, send a will home?" I said, "Of course not. I sent a power of attorney." He said, "A power of attorney, Becky, is no damn good if you're dead." I said, "Well, it's too late now. Things will be okay."

We started sending people out, then, section by section. As a supervisor I was the last one in my section to leave. We left in pretty much an orderly manner. Because of the accesses we had, when we were told to get out, we got out.

I went over to Tan Son Nhut to leave the night Thieu resigned, April 21. I was up all night waiting in a staging area. They had C-130s coming in around the clock. All you had to do to take anybody out with you was to go over and tell them, "My name is such and such, I work for so-and-so, I've got X number of people I'm taking out," and they'd give you a card, and that was it. Then your name and number went on a list and when they got to you, you got on a plane. The C-130s were taking about a hundred people at a time. Just around the clock. And that had gone on for a couple of days.

I didn't leave Vietnam until the next morning, daylight. We were bused over, were body-searched and baggage-searched by Air Force security cops—Americans. They had also brought in a contingent of Marines to beef up security around the perimeter. The largest staging area was over by the DAO swimming pool, a bowling alley and gymnasium. It was just totally packed. You just waited your time to get on and go.

We were getting on the plane and a couple of Vietnamese fighter pilots went by, taxiing to take off in jet fighters, and we gave them a thumbs-up signal, keeping up the front, everything was fine. We were trying to make them think even then the Americans were not leaving! But the city knew better. It was never officially admitted that Americans were evacuating.

The plane was packed. The engine was loud. It was cold. I think I counted five Caucasians on the plane. The rest were Vietnamese and there were a hundred on each plane. Family units. After we got out over the water for a distance I cried.

We landed at Clark in the Philippines and then I tried to get a flight out. I finally got on a plane escorting Vietnamese children back. It turned out that some of them had survived the C-5A crash. The plane was a converted C-141. It had the passenger seats facing the tail and toward the tail end of the plane and they had a bunk arrangement, baskets for the kids so that they were safe.

I said I'd escort the children. I thought this was ironic. But I went ahead and did it. I didn't think any more about it, though. Too much had happened. Too many people had died.

They strap the children to you when you land on those planes so that if there's any kind of an accident or anything, the child doesn't go flying.

I held a baby. Well, he wasn't a baby. He looked like a baby. He must have been three but he looked like he was maybe one. He was so emaciated. And I had two other children, sisters. They were afraid the whole way home.

Diane Gunsul
"Drinking Champagne and Watching the War"

In the late 1960s I was really active in the antiwar movement in Washington. I did a lot of campaigning on the Hill against the war. I was in most of the demonstration marches. I never thought we should have American ground troops there. A lot of people believed the way I did, that we shouldn't send our guys over there to be killed in a civil war. That doesn't mean we are rooting for the Communists.

On March 29, 1973, the message came out of Vietnam that all the ground troops were leaving. And they were looking for civilians to go in to help with the advisory groups. Since I had been so strongly against the war, I said to myself, "Well, what keeps getting thrown in my face is, 'You've never been there, you don't know what it's like.'" So I said, "The hell with it, I'll go see what it's like." I applied for a job. There were twenty-five applicants for my job and I got it. I went over there on April 2. The troops were out as of the twenty-ninth. And I literally walked into an office in Bien Hoa where somebody, an American military man, had gotten up and walked out of that office and left his cigar in the ashtray. Everything was just like he was coming back. People just picked up their duffle bags and left. It was eerie.

I worked in what was called a logistics center. We built up from twenty-five people to a hundred civilians. General Richard Baughn was one of my bosses, but they were all downtown. We had a colonel in charge out at Bien Hoa, who had never worked with civilians before, obviously. He couldn't understand us.

The first six months I lived in Saigon and went out to Bien Hoa every day on a bus. But we kept getting cut off by the VC [Vietcong]. It got a little hairy if you missed the bus going back to Saigon and you went back on a later one. You couldn't travel after dark. We'd helicopter out. Finally, I just moved out to Bien Hoa itself. We lived in the Franz Blau apartment house, which was once a brothel.

I met my second husband in Vietnam. I met him on a bus in Saigon my first day there, in fact. But we both worked at Bien Hoa.

When I first went there I was a management assistant, very low rank, GS-7.* I made a 9 promotion there and I became administrative officer. But in Bien Hoa there were so few people that you did a lot of different things. So I had the evacuation disaster-preparedness plan; I had the security operation; I had the administrative paperwork stuff that you do when you come over on temporary duty. I was the protocol officer, so you meet a lot of people and go around.

The Vietnamese, I found, are a very warm, open people. More so than the Chinese, I found, or the Japanese. They aren't at all like the Japanese. We would talk a lot about the war, and how it affected almost every family that I knew there. I'd been in their homes. In fact my husband was a godfather to one of the children that was born while I was there, a Vietnamese lieutenant's. They had been at war their whole lives, so it was normal to them. It was a very unreal atmosphere.

When Phuoc Long fell in early 1975 there was a lot of wonderment rather than fear. "Is this the beginning of the real end?" or, "Are they going to be able to stop it?" Then they [the South] withdrew from the central highlands and the refugees started marching. I think that's when we had our very first feeling of doom.

We asked things like, "Are they going to be able to recover?" I still didn't think it was going for good. I didn't think it was going until April, after I had been evacuated out of Bien Hoa.

In early April a message came in from the Department of Defense: "Send out all American women immediately"—that's about what it said. I saw the message and I was just furious. The colonel looked at it and sent a message back: "I don't have any American women. I have logisticians, I have administrative officers. You tell me what skills you don't want in this country." He had ten women working with him still at Bien Hoa.

And they sent back another message that said, "Whoops."

He then made a list of all the people that were still in Bien Hoa, in priority order. And some were women who were sent out as nonessential. Some women who were considered essential, such as myself, stayed behind. It was officially not an evacuation yet.

What they did at first, they asked for volunteers, American women to take babies out, which was a way around evacuation itself. Now one of our people, Selma Thompson, had already been so spooked by the rock-

---

* GS—General Schedule. A pay grade is by number. 7 is entry level; a 10 represents the civilian equivalent of Captain in the military.

ets and mortars at Bien Hoa that she wouldn't go there any more. She was in Saigon when that request went out from the embassy. They had less than twenty-four hours to get ready.

The women at Bien Hoa who were still working there never got that message. We never even knew that there was a C-5A baby lift going out. But since Selma was living in Saigon and had already been spooked and wouldn't go to Bien Hoa, she did go on that plane. And that's the only reason she was on it. She was already terrified of being in country and wouldn't come out to Bien Hoa at all.

So she left on the C-5A on April 4. When we heard it went down, there was absolute shock. I could have been on it, easily. We stayed up all night waiting for the reports to come in. Someone finally called us in Bien Hoa from Saigon and told us that Selma had survived the crash and had been evacuated out. That was our first experience with the so-called evacuation.

I left Bien Hoa for good about the tenth of April. My colonel came out and said, "Okay, I'm sending everybody"—he had the list and he would go up the list each day and say who was leaving. And it got to where there were only four or five people left. My husband stayed longer.

It was about ten o'clock in the morning when I went out. We went by van, regular U.S. Government van. There were about four or five of us and we went through all the different checkpoints and roadblocks between Bien Hoa and Saigon.

I hadn't been on that road in months, because when I went into Saigon we went by helicopter. We had a shuttle service set up. I was amazed at all this concertina wire stretched across the road at checkpoints. When I had been coming out by bus there had been no checkpoints.

It was the first time I had felt in danger of friendlies. They knew we were bugging out from Bien Hoa. It was obvious, even though we each only had one small bag with us. Everything else was left behind. That was the first time I was afraid that friendlies would kill us. The Americans are bugging out again. To the very end people were saying to me, "When are the B-52s coming back?" They did not believe that the Americans would not come back with bombers when it got that close.

One of the things we were doing was getting our employees out of the country. They really didn't have to come and ask. We were asking them if they wanted to go out. And some people did not want to go.

I went down to the American consulate with a Vietnamese man who worked for me who had done his time in the Vietnamese military and been discharged. He wanted to leave with his wife and two children. After his wife and children left the country as my husband's wife and kids, I went down and signed a statement saying that this man was my common-law husband. We didn't go out with our "spouses." We would go down and swear that he or she was a common-law wife or husband

and that we wanted them out, although we were not declared nonessential yet.

I carried a letter that said I was a nonessential person. It was blank, and all I had to do was fill in the date when I felt I needed to go. We all had to have papers to get out.

My husband took out three women as his "wives" at different times. The American consulate knew we were lying through our teeth. The consulate had to abide by the Vietnamese government regulation that said that these people could not have exit permits. And the only way we could get these people out if they weren't actually employees was to swear we were married to them. I remember being just mortified going down there to swear that I had a common-law husband. And of course he would only call me "Miss Diane." That was my name. So I told this guy, "Don't call me 'Miss Diane' in front of the consul." So of course the consul asked him something, and I would answer. I would say, "This is my husband and I need to send him out." "Let me see the marriage license." I said, "Well we never formalized it, we've been living together." "How long have you been living together?" I said, "Well, almost a year and a half now."

He looked at me; he grinned. He knew damn well I was lying. And then he asked my "husband," and my husband turned to me and said, "Miss Diane . . ." and I said, "Don't call me Miss Diane." It was hilarious. The Vietnamese military, three different ones, that we worked with asked my husband to take their families out. They did not ask for themselves. I wasn't asked. It was a pride thing that none of them asked to be taken out by me. Of the three wives that my husband took out, all three husbands showed up within the month, on boats, in Guam. Because we worked in the refugee camps on Guam, we did get to see them reunited.

The husband that I took out did get to the Philippines and then to Guam and was reunited with his wife and children and now lives in San Diego.

We did this for those who had worked with us. They were scared. And rightly so. One of the people we did not take out, who did not ask to go out, a lieutenant who wanted to stay with his family—he had a young baby—was in a re-education camp for seven years and was brutally beaten. We get letters and we've had word from some other people.

There was that feeling toward the end that if you had any association with Americans you were going to be slaughtered by the Communists. It was a fear that was rampant.

I didn't know what to believe. I thought they would probably kill a lot of the military. I didn't think there was much so-called honor of conquering heroes in the Orient as there is in the Western world. There is much more bloodshed. I did not know if they would slaughter them or just make life miserable. And what they did was make their life miserable, mainly.

Everybody at that time carried weapons, but being a pacifist, I wouldn't. And everybody was carrying briefcases with weapons, and finally they carried them in holsters. They were issuing weapons and asked me which one I would like. And I said, "I don't want one." And they said, "What would you do if the VC came through that bunker door pointing a gun at you?" And I said, "Well, I would probably die." And they couldn't believe that. I said, "I made up my mind when I volunteered to stay in Saigon, being single"—my second husband wasn't my husband yet—with no children, no dependents, no debts, nothing, that I was prepared to stay and die if I had to. I wasn't looking forward to it, thank you, but I had come to terms with it. And this Marine colonel looked at me and he said, "That won't happen." I said, "What do you mean?" He said, "I would kill you first."

I said, "Whose side are you on?" He said he would not let an American woman be captured by the VC. I said, "I'll tell you what, let me be captured, and say for a couple years they'll torture me and all this wonderful stuff and then you can come in and rescue me and we'll write a book, make a movie, and make a million dollars." I was treating it as a joke. He didn't think it was funny. He said, "I will not let an American woman be captured by these people." He was a neat guy, but I'll never forget his saying that.

My husband-to-be was declared nonessential and went out before I did. When he went out and I was still there, I sent letters to my three brothers explaining why I was staying behind, saying that I felt it was necessary and if I died I was prepared for it. I had made out a will, done everything I could possibly do. I still hoped I could get out.

We wanted to get as many Americans out as we could but also to get all the Americans' friends out. I felt that if I could get as many more people out as possible that had helped us, get them out to a better life, that it would be worth it to me. The only time I had ever had that feeling before was when John Kennedy was killed. I had the feeling that if they could have killed me instead of him, I would have done it. And the march on the White House when we invaded Cambodia in the spring of 1970, since that was not a legal demonstration, we felt that we might get fired upon and killed at the White House. But we felt so strongly about the illegality of going into the Parrot's Beak in Cambodia that we went to the demonstration. So there were three times when I felt and believed something strongly enough that I was willing to die for it. I'm not looking forward to death, but sometimes you feel "this is right."

When I was in the bunker at the DAO I had a male secretary working for me who had a wife and two children, and I told him to leave. And

Admiral Owen Oberg said, "But he's the guy who's sending our messages." And I said, "He has a wife and two children. He needs to get out of this country. I'm single and I don't have any of those things. I'll type these things we need to have typed."

It was pretty much up to me as to when I wanted to go out. They kept very few people behind. Everybody was carrying around a blank form that said, "This person   " then left a blank and you put your name in, is declared "Nonessential" on such-and-such a date. And you just filled that in and went over to the airplane where people were lining up and said, "Okay, I want to go out."

I left on the night of the twenty-eighth of April, I believe. It was about one in the morning. The flashes (coded messages) were coming in, of course, that's why I was there. I had the crypto clearance and I was there to change the communications daily code. We had the tie-in to Washington and even though I was not a communications officer, I was dealing a lot with the communications line. I did pick up the top-secret flashes that were coming in. And reading those, I knew what was going on, and it got to a point where I said, "Okay, I think it's time." I knew it wasn't going to last much longer.

I was so exhausted that I knew I wasn't doing any good. My husband-to-be had already gone and I just knew by the traffic that was coming in that there wasn't much longer and I did not want to go out to the fleet. The admirals went out to the fleet every night. And Admiral Oberg said to me, one day—they were closing in around the compound at the time, getting closer, and we could hear a lot of gunfire, a lot of fighting—"Why don't you come along? We'll take you out to the ship each night." And I said, "Admiral, how long have you been at sea?" He said something like seven or nine months. And I said, "How long since you've been in port?" And he said so many months, and I said, "I think I'll take my chances with the VC!"

There was a lot of humor in the Evacuation Control Center, because there's so much tension there. You're calling in the planes. You're trying to coordinate the evacuation. You have to do something to relieve the tension.

One time Admiral Oberg sent me downtown in the midst of all this in a black government car with mirrored windows. I know a lot about artwork and we talked a lot about art in the bunker, and he wanted to buy something typically Vietnamese—a painting, or artifact of some sort to take back as a memento of the country to someone who had lost a son in Vietnam. He told me the price range, and he sent me downtown with a Vietnamese driver. And I went to downtown Saigon, out to Tu Do street where all the art shops were, and I could not believe how normal everything was. There was no panic. It was a little bit quieter, but it was very eerie, almost like a Fellini movie. To think of what was going on at Tan Son Nhut, trying to get people out, and the almost frantic tense atmosphere, and then to go into Saigon proper and it was like everything's normal.

Then I thought, "What should they be doing, running around in a frenzy? Of course not." I went into an art shop and spent a couple hours going through things until I found something that I thought was typically Vietnamese. Then I got into this big black limo and went back to Tan Son Nhut. It was very eerie. I was afraid going into Saigon in that car. I was afraid if they knew there was an American inside there and they knew that we were bugging out. . . .

So on the night I left I went over and got on a bus that took us to the plane. And I remember the airplane seemed to continue rolling as we were boarding and we combat-loaded. I'm sure it stopped, but in my mind it was on the ground like two minutes. It wasn't a frantic boarding but it was very swift. As you came off the bus it was "Move! Move! Move!" as they made us move fast and get into those cargo straps. You sat on the floor and hung onto the cargo straps. It was very quiet, eerie. And it was very fast. And I remember the American crew guys standing at the windows of the aircraft with some sort of flare gun in their hands.

They were startled to see an American woman, I remember that. They looked at me like, "Who are you?" It was strange for them, because everybody else on it was Vietnamese. We had so few Americans left there. There were some women who came out by helicopter later. But only a very few.

I was so tired and so exhausted I don't think I was thinking at all at the time. The only thing I remember I was hoping we wouldn't get hit on the way to Clark. That was the only thing that was worrying me, because they were firing at planes as we took off. We don't know if it was friendlies or VC. There were stories going around that the friendlies were firing at the airplanes going off. It got a little bitter. It got a lot bitter.

I knew then that I was leaving a country that I fell in love with. It's a beautiful country. I was sad to know that the people had lost their war and that they would probably regret it. I still think they could have won their war if we'd just stayed the hell out of it. Eventually freedom is going to win over there. They have a taste of it. And eventually, I truly believe, places that are oppressed, no matter what type of regime it is, will win their freedom back.

I went to the Philippines. The airfield had been closed but we landed there anyway. We off-loaded but were not allowed off the tarmac. I sat in a chair, and when I woke up, I was the only one left; all the Vietnamese were gone. I asked where they were and they said they had taken them on to Guam. They had not awakened me and I had not heard anybody leave. I was in a hangar in some big chairs that the officers wives' club had set up. And I remember standing up and saying, "Where are my Vietnamese?" "Oh, well, we loaded them on to Guam because Ferdinand Marcos has closed the country to them." When they told me that my Vietnamese were gone, I don't know what else they said to me, but I was so tired and so exhausted that I started to cry. Luckily the Americans left me alone.

They wanted to send me to Guam but I told them I had a Philippine visa—I'd picked it up in Saigon when I first arrived. A colonel came over and said, "I can't believe that." And I showed him I had both a red passport and a tourist passport, and he just could not believe it. He said, "I will take you over to VOQ [Visiting Officers' Quarters] myself and get you a room." I went to sleep there and when I woke up the war was over.

I got up and went downstairs and saw *Stars and Stripes* and the headline said something like "Saigon Falls." When I read that, it was almost a feeling of relief—it's over. When I knew the country had fallen, it was over. There was closure. There is a psychological need for closure in most relationships and I think I needed that, because I had a very close relationship with that country.

Then I went over to our logistics center people and said, "Next time you call Guam, tell Roy—my husband-to-be—that I'm here." Well, they didn't tell him, and it took me three days to get a flight. And he thought I was still in Saigon. But then when I got to Guam they asked people who had been in Vietnam to volunteer for work in the refugee camp. Although we didn't want to—we wanted to go on—they really needed people badly because there were lots of folks coming in and they were still processing so many people. So we volunteered.

We stayed there one month. Then we took two weeks in Hawaii to unwind and came back to California.

If you ask people today, you'll find that most Americans don't know when the war in Vietnam ended and they don't know that there were no American ground troops in Vietnam when Saigon fell. They don't understand that Americans left in '73, civilians went in after that. We had a joke out there: It took the military ten years to lose the war. It only took the civilians two. It's a sick joke, but. . . .

For two years I couldn't talk about Vietnam. You're supposed to make out a report when you come back of all the things you lost and the government reimburses you, like ten cents on the dollar. I left a lot of furniture, my clothing, and all my personal papers and pictures, which weren't supposed to be left. It took me a year and eleven months before I could sit down and do that form.

When you come back to the U.S. you feel like an absolute idiot because when you hear a backfire or something you dive for the ground. The military have that experience. You get over that in a year or two. Then you think about the people and how they are doing. It's a big chunk out of your life, a very important part. I talk to the people back here about it but it's sometimes like I'm an alien. They're interested but they have no conception of what I've been through.

And as I'm talking to you right now, I'm shaking. Every time I talk about these things I get, not nervous, but very emotional. The whole experience was deeply emotional.

I do think that my memory and accounting of that time are colored by the fact that I met my husband in Vietnam, so I have a different view of the country. I loved it, because I was very happy there. I think if someone had not made that type of attachment there they would probably look at it through different eyes. And I had a very happy marriage.

Those are normally the things that I remember and talk about, the fun parts. Like going to Vung Tau with my husand and sitting on the beach drinking champagne and watching the war, watching these huge clouds of black smoke coming up around the peninsula where there's been bombing and saying, "I don't believe this is true. Here we are sitting on the most beautiful beach in the world watching a war and drinking champagne."

CHAPTER **VII**

Joint Military Team

Stuart Herrington
"Khong Ai Se Bi Bo Lai! Dung Lo!"

I was optimistic when I returned to Vietnam in August 1972. By the time the cease-fire was signed I was less optimistic. I became pretty sure that the country was probably going to fall when I heard about the resignation of Nixon. When Nixon walked out on the eighth of August '74, I had my radio in my office in Saigon listening to it and that, for me, that was pivotal. My confidence in the South Vietnamese being able to prevail and survive ultimately was badly shaken. But the event that caused me to begin to mail my possessions home and write my parents and tell them "I'm coming home and it'll be before next August probably," and to write to the Pentagon and start looking for an assignment, was the fall of Phuoc Long in early 1975. That was the event that caused me to move my wife and kids out of the Delta into Saigon where I could reach out and grab them.

On a day-to-day basis in the DAO, we were living and breathing on everything the Congress said or didn't say, or did or didn't do on the aid requests. And there was nothing but a nonstop series of rebuffs by that time. General John Murray, the Defense Attaché, had left disenchanted and had shared his disenchantment with me. He was bitter. And Murray's departure and his bitterness made a deep impression on me. I happened into his office right after he had a shouting contest with someone who had reprimanded him over the phone from DOD [Department of Defense] about his interview on "blood for bullets," with a reporter from the *New York Times.* He talked to me about the interview, and said, "I just told him if I get one more phone call about that I'll give a press conference in Hawaii and tell the whole goddamned story."

My visit to Hanoi for the JMT [Joint Military Team] on April 11 was
my last. Harry Summers went after that. Anyway, there was no doubt that
the North Vietnamese were saying, loud and clear, "We're going to let
you guys leave, take your people with you. There'll be no bloodbath.
There's been enough blood shed. We need the people of South Vietnam's
support to rebuild the country." But the most loud-and-clear message was
that the North Vietnamese had no intention of interfering with our departure.

And they wanted the U.S. JMT delegation to stay—they wanted the
Paris Agreement to remain valid because in their judgment the Paris
Agreement contained commitments by the United States to participate in
healing the wounds of war—paying money under Article XXI. They de-
sired to reinforce that although the cease-fire itself may have broken down
because Thieu had violated it, that in no way meant that we couldn't accomplish anything on Article VIII(b), the missing-in-action location. They
felt the Paris Agreement was the legal instrument to get aid from the
United States.

So they had told me and Harry Summers, and anyone else who would
listen, that the U.S. delegation, regardless of how the situation on the
ground was to work out, should remain in Saigon. We would be safe
there.

I was sending my possessions out because I felt everyone was leaving.
Only in the last four weeks did we begin to get the idea that the U.S.
JMT delegation might stay. Colonel John Madison comunicated with Dr.
Roger Shields and they told him, "We think we've heard clearly that they
want us to stay and we need guidance on that issue." And we were told
to be prepared to stay. And we thought we were to stay right up through
the time when we arrived at the Embassy on the morning of the twenty-
ninth.

When we left Tan Son Nhut on that last morning we had medicine, we
had radios, we had food. We had our own little three-vehicle convoy with
everything packed into it, and we had even tried to recruit a communications guy to stay with us. For a while there, it appeared that the national
leadership wanted us to stay, that this was symbolic that the United States
was prepared to do business on the MIA question. And so like good soldiers we were ready to do that, although speaking for myself I was not too
sanguine or warm about being in Saigon after the Americans had pulled
out. We laughed about that—we were going to lock ourselves in a room in
the Embassy and pray for the arrival of the North Vietnamese Army. Let's
face it, we were walking out on the South Vietnamese. They weren't
happy.

Around one o'clock in the morning on the twenty-eighth of April, Colonel Summers, Colonel Madison, and I were over by the DAO swimming
pool where we were putting people on buses and taking them out to the

flight line for evacuation. I went over to the office to get a couple hours' sleep on a couch. I was driving a Land Rover type vehicle and I went through Post Two where the Marines were, right at the edge of the street by the compound. Marine corporals Darwin Judge and Charles McMahon were on duty. I paused and said, "How are things going, guys?" "Fine, sir. No sweat." The two of them were in their flak vests. I went into the office and I crashed on Colonel Madison's couch. I had a radio that had the Embassy Marine net; all the Marines were on it, the guard posts were all linked, and I was monitoring. And at four that morning when the rockets came in, one of them hit right across the street, hit the general's house. Another one hit right were Judge and McMahon were standing, and others hit all around the trailer park.

The impact of the 122mm rocket was so great that the whole DAO building just rocked. I remember there was a flag in the stand behind Colonel Madison's desk, and it fell down. Immediately I heard a couple voices screaming over the radio that we took a hit at the gym, we got casualties at the gym. And then another voice that there were casualties at Post Two. I ran out of the office. I ran to the dispensary and broke the door down. Marines who had been in the building were all in the concrete bunkers outside the door of DAO headquarters. The barrage was continuing. I yelled down, "Any of you guys a medic?" "Yes, sir." I got the Marine and told him where the medicine was, and told him to get in a vehicle and get over to the gym, because the last time I saw this gym there were about four hundred people in it. In my mind's eye, if a rocket had hit that gym there was a mess for sure.

Then I ran over to Post Two. The ambulance was parked there, and Sergeant Kevin Maloney was there and an ambulance was just pulling away. Maloney was standing there like this, like a guard, just standing there. I asked him, "What are you doing?" He said, "I'm Sergeant Maloney, squad leader, manning the post. My two men are dead." And a rocket came in and landed right across the street, ferocious. They are a terror weapon. And we both jumpd into the ditch and I said, "Maloney, old man, this is a better place to man the post if you're gonna man this post. Man it from here."

At that point in time the 122mm rockets were hitting, then the artillery started up. And it started coming in big-time. Hundred-and-thirty-millimeter stuff. And it was walking its way right down the street, across the street. It was observed fire you could tell, because the short rounds were landing right across the street from us, uncomfortably close. There was shrapnel flinging against the chain link fence behind us.

I didn't have a helmet on. My helmet was back in BOQ [Bachelor Officers' Quarters]. I had a soft hat. I crawled over to a helmet that was lying there on the ground and put it on, and crawled back to where Maloney was. It was not healthy at that moment to stand up. I was lying there waiting for a chance to get the hell out, but it was a pretty heavy barrage, and it was obvious the way the rounds were landing you were playing Russian roulette if you stood up and started moving around. So we lay there. This was Maloney's post, and until he was relieved he was going to man it. Fires were bursting across the street on the Tan Son Nhut ramp. There were explosions. Maloney saw a figure starting to cross the street about fifty, sixty, feet to our left, pointed, didn't know who it was. Maloney and I jumped up—he had his M-16 and I had a .45, and intercepted them. It turned out to be two of the security guards, Vietnamese who worked for the American contractor, World-Wide Security. They had been over at the Air America terminal doing security duties. Maloney halted them. I recognized them. They told me in Vietnamese that they had to get out of there because the artillery fire was awfully accurate and too dangerous over there.

Some aircraft took off during the barrage. At least one AC-119 went up. One spotter plane went up. Both were shot down by heat-seeking missiles. And thousands of people saw that.

I remember Air America Hueys flying around, but for sure an AC-119 and an old L-19 birddog took off and they were both shot down. Within sight of the city of Saigon.

We went back to the little ditch for a while. By that time it had started to get light out. Maloney and I got up. The barrage had subsided. We walked around. We recovered parts of bodies that had been blown around. A boot with a foot in it. A piece of a rifle, the bolt and receiver group of a M-16 rifle with the serial number on it, which was important because it established identity. No dog tags. Pieces of flesh that were in the chain link fence.

I found out later that rounds had hit in the handball courts of the DAO and the wooden walls of the handball courts absorbed all the shrapnel. I think they had one or two wounded over there (lightly), and that's about it. The rest of the rounds caused more fear than they did damage. Judge and McMahon happened to be in the wrong place at the wrong time.

I went into the command center to bring the rifle to Marine Colonel Slade and I ran into Homer Smith's wife Joan as I walked into the building, and she screamed when she saw me. Just a huge scream and I couldn't figure out why, and she just kept pointing. I took the helmet off and it was crimson with blood. So I went into the men's room and scrubbed it off. There was a hole about that big right through the side of the helmet. Just like somebody took a can opener and put a hole in it.

It was Judge's helmet that I had picked up and put on. I wore it throughout the evacuation. I wore it to Bangkok. I mailed it to the States and I wrote a letter to the U.S. Marine Corps and told them what it was and how I came upon it, and I felt it was something that the Marine Corps ought to have. It had his name written on it, and a big hole in it.

I sent it to the Marine Corps for their museum and I never heard a word about it. I suspect some son of a bitch probably purloined it. I probably should have kept it. I debated sending it to the young man's family and then I said, "Don't do that, Herrington, that would be too much for them to take. Some dads would like to have their son's helmet, other dads might not be able to take it. Don't get in the middle of the Marine Corps casualty reps and the family."

After I went in to the command center, I got the map—because I wasn't just lying there, I was figuring out what direction the rounds were coming from, laying it down on the ground. I drew an arrow, and the back azimuth of that arrow was where the rounds were coming from. So I went in and plotted the location of the artillery in the command center in case somebody was going to try and drop some bombs on them. I was told that Colonel Madison and Colonel Harry Summers were looking for me and that we had orders to report to the Embassy.

I linked up with Madison and Summers about seven in the morning. We had breakfast in Madison's office. Because I cooked it. We weren't sure when we were going to get another meal, or what was going to happen. We decided that there was a lot of food there and we damn well ought to eat. I cooked bacon and eggs, opened a bottle of champagne we had—that sounds sick, but I remember I did that. That could be made to look really—it was a fatalistic, "Well now what?" It was obvious that the end was near. We were on hold, for the moment, about going to the Embassy. We were told, "Time, you'll be told. Stay where we can get in touch." So we got the word to proceed to the Embassy.

We were ready for a hectic drive because, given what was going on, we felt that all roads were going to lead to Tan Son Nhut. There was going to be a massive migration of Vietnamese towards Tan Son Nhut and as Americans out on the streets at that stage of the game, that there was always the possibility of an incident. So we had two or three vehicles. I was driving the Land Rover, Madison and Summers were in the black Ford sedan. And when we headed out the gate, it was, "Stay close to one another. Jesus, I'll feel better when we get there."

It was just chaos in the streets and there was a very good chance of being victimized by disaffected ARVN troops. We didn't think of the NVA. There was some disorder right outside the gate, to the point we actually had to go off the road into a ditch and around an obstacle. I can't quite remember what the devil it was, but I remember I was first in Land Rover, and I made it. I watched in my rear-view mirror and crossed my fingers and hoped that Madison and Summers would make it the same— and they did. As we went towards the Embassy you could see swirling groups of people and what appeared to be lots of uncertainty. There were columns of smoke to our rear coming up from Tan Son Nhut and, you know, I had the feeling it was good to get out when we got out because the gates of Tan Son Nhut were going to be pretty hairy later on.

We drove into the Embassy.

Inside the Embassy, the Marines had a lieutenant on the roof with a radio that was supposed to be calling the birds in, and he fell off the chopper pad about fifteen feet to the roof of the Embassy and landed on his head and had to be medevaced out to the fleet. The flights coming into the Embassy were only sporadic and we didn't know why. People were worried about not getting out. The Marines didn't have good radio contact with DAO. They could talk to their helicopters, apparently, but they couldn't talk to DAO.

When we found that out, it was very late in the afternoon. It was dark out. And we were astounded. Colonel Madison said, "Jesus Christ, that's the dumbest thing I ever heard of."

So I went in and got hold of this guy and I said, "Hey, we have a real stupid situation here. Don't you know the frequency of the evacuation control center, the ECC out at Tan Son Nhut?" So he told me the frequency and I went out to the vans where we had radios. I got a radio out, put a long antenna on it, put it on the frequency, and I called out to DAO and used the call sign of Embassy Marine.

It turns out the guys at DAO don't know what's happening at the Embassy. When they heard this voice in the night calling, "Embassy Marine calling DAO," someone came back, and I said, "What's going on? We're waiting for helicopters that are never coming." He said "What's the situation there?" and I said, "The situation is we got a couple thousand people and where are the helicopters?" And the guy told me to wait.

Here we were about five miles apart and there was no communication. This is about eight in the evening of the twenty-ninth. We found out that the DAO evacuation was proceeding apace without any big problems, and that priority was the pull at DAO and that around midnight when the DAO pull was complete, priority of birds would shift to us. We needed to hold tight.

Then around midnight almost all flights just stopped at the Embassy. If we knew that ahead of time, we could have planned on it. To plan on it meant we could tell the people. As it was, there was nothing happening, and all these people were thinking that they were being left behind and there was a terrible control problem of these people. They were afraid they were being abandoned. So we went around and told everybody, "The word is we're all going out. The helicopters are going to be coming. Don't worry, the evacuation is not ended. Above all, I'm here with you, and my government is not going to leave me, so relax. As long as I'm here, I'm going on the last helicopter when all of you go. And you can just please cooperate by getting in line, get in family groups, and stop shoving and stop pushing."

It was dark and there was confusion. There was this tremendous pushing and shoving going on, almost approaching panic. A young Vietnamese interpreter came up and whispered in my ear that the people doing the pushing were Korean, they don't understand what we are saying; they were pushing and shoving. So then in English I asked if there was a Korean officer present, with this bullhorn I had. Then this Korean naval officer, attaché guy, came up with his wife, and I said, "You have to help me. You have got to control your people."

There were probably forty or fifty of them, men and women, secretaries from the Korean Embassy. The ambassador, his secretary, the army attaché, the naval attaché, some of their families as well. Quite a contingent. See, we didn't know that.

The Korean ambassador, his secretary, and the army attaché all got out, finally, but they tried to bring their suitcases on the helicopter and I caught them doing that. We had told everyone, you have got to take your suitcases and throw them away. "Go in your suitcases, get out any valuables, letters, papers, but suitcases can't go. The choppers will only take people, not luggage." And all the Vietnamese stoically and obediently did it. We told them they could have a Pan Am–type bag or attaché case. I was controlling access to the chopper, and when this one Korean arrived with this suitcase I yanked the suitcase out of his hand and threw it in the bushes. Second guy tried it, I yanked that suitcase and threw it in the bushes. And the third was a woman who had a suitcase she was dragging, and I yanked it out of her hands and threw it in the bushes. She screamed at me like a banshee and crawled after it on all fours and retrieved it and tried to get on the helicopter again. And I ripped it away from her a second time and threw it over in the bushes and told her to get on the chopper. And she ran back and got it again. She grabed hold of that suitcase by the handle and would not let it go and I finally took my M-16 and I beat her across the forearms with the butt of the M-16 about three times saying unprintable things, until she screamed in pain and let it go, and I threw her, literally grabed her by the body and threw her into the chopper and the chopper went up. That was the last chopper that left with civilians.

I later learned that she was the ambassador's private secretary. She had bruises all over her forearms. And Harry Summers later told this South Korean officer, "You need to explain to her that if Captain Herrington hadn't shoved her on that helicopter, she would be in a Hanoi prison right now, and that he got her out. If he had let her stay with that bag, she would still be there with that bag." The bag contained gold and jewelry. And it was damned heavy. Apparently it had all the valuables collected from all of the Koreans. Harry did legion work in telling this guy to convince her that she should decriminalize me because I saved her rear end.

I was doubtful a week or two before the country fell, as to my ability to walk out with my personal honor. I was extremely worried and told my folks that the way we had mishandled this whole thing over the years, there was no reason to expect that it would be handled with class at the end. I was extremely worried that we were going to be made to abandon our people, our employees, their families, my friends. As an American, even though I was charged with responsibility for getting all kinds of Vietnamese out who had a reason to want to get out, I really feared that in the end that somebody was going to say, "Let's save Americans and to hell with everyone else." I was worried about that from the beginning. There weren't a lot of Americans who were worried about the Vietnamese at that stage of the game, but I was, and so were Colonel Madison and Harry Summers.

But that night in the Embassy, the helicopters were coming in as fast as we could throw people on them. Between, say, midnight and three in the morning (3:30 when that last one came), Colonel Madison had made a very strong statement to Wolfgang Lehmann, the deputy chief of mission, who was really in charge. In my opinion and in the opinion of a lot of other people, Ambassador Martin was too ill at that stage of the game. He did come out and survey the situation personally with his security guard, but he was shaky, and the contact we had with anybody in authority was primarily with Lehmann. And Lehmann was a cool cucumber. When Lehmann came out and said, "You know this thing's going to wind up, Washington's impatient," or words to that effect, Madison said, "Look, we've done a head count here, we have 420 more people and we need a few more helicopters." And Lehmann said, "Okay, you'll get what you need." By then we definitely had control of the situation. We had the refugees in groups, ready to throw them on a bird. Throughout the night when a bird came in, we had a group of fifty here, and a group of fifty there, and if it was a big bird, a CH-53, we threw them all on. Ninety folks went on those birds. If it was a smaller bird, a CH-46, then half went. By the time Lehmann came down to survey the situation, Madison told him how many people we had left and how many helicopters we needed, and Lehmann said, "Okay, I'll arrange it." And it was then that it all broke down.

We had people in the stairwell going up to the roof of the Embassy. You couldn't get them all out just using one landing zone on the parking lot here, so we had choppers landing up on the roof. And we had fed a couple hundred of these Vietnamese up that stairwell like toothpaste through a tube. They were going off in the CH-46s from the roof. Even though they had told us that the chopper pad wouldn't hold the weight of the '46, we had to do it.

And then word came as we go into the final push that we're only going to use one pad; get all the Vietnamese out of the stairwell, and put them all outside so we have everybody out there. First Lehmann came out and told Madison, "I think that things are winding up," and Madison said, "No way, we have 420 people, and it's do-able, and we made commitments to them." Madison was hard-nosed about it. Lehmann said, "Okay, I'll arrange it."

So when Lehmann walked out of that parking lot, Madison thought we had the assurances of the guy who was running the show that everybody was going to get out, and he told me to go and tell everybody that. I did.

I told all the Vietnamese, "Khong ai se bi bo lai! Dung lo!" ("Nobody's going to be left behind! Don't worry!") I said it over and over again. And I believed it. Madison believed it. Summers believed it. And all of a sudden there were no birds.

Then Kean came walking over to Madison and I saw them in earnest conversation. It was dark out, but we had floodlights and automobile headlights, so they were illuminated. And Madison was arguing with Kean and telling him, "I've got the helicopters promised to me and I'll just take this up with the ambassador." And Kean said to Madison, "Presidential order, and I'm not going to risk my men any more. And Madison said, "Well, I'll just take this up with the ambassador if I have to." And Kean said, "You can't, he just left." And he pointed to a CH-46 that had just taken off from the roof, which apparently was Lady Ace Zero Nine piloted by Gerry Berry. That was 4:47 in the morning.

Madison was just crushed. He called Harry Summers and me over and we had a little conversation. "Shit, now what do we do?" And Madison said, "The Marines are pulling out. It's a Presidential order. We're losers." And Madison made the tough call, and he said, "Stu, you go stay with the Vietnamese. Give Harry and me and the others time to get in and get our stuff together and get it to the roof. Then come up to the roof."

There were still Marines out on the wall. The Vietnamese who were left, 420 of them, were by that time all down in the parking lot. They were sitting in ranks. The ranks were right behind the cars that were running with their headlights on. I was sitting on the trunk deck of one of the cars with a radio. At that point I wasn't talking to anybody, because once the Embassy closed at midnight they destroyed all their communications. That radio was nothing, but it looked like I was talking to helicopters. I told the Vietnamese, "Don't worry, there's a big helicopter coming and we're all going." That was a hard thing to tell them because at that time I knew better, so I was stalling.

I sat there for fifteen minutes, and I came very, very close to saying, "Screw it all." I debated holding myself hostage and saying, "I'm not going until you send the choppers." And I realized that the Marines were leaving, that they would never let the choppers in a landing zone that wasn't secure, that I would be detained and then repatriated. My Army career would be ruined because I disobeyed a Presidential order, and it was obvious to me that however sick I was about it, I could not get those people out. "Don't be a fool, you'll never get these people out. You have a wife and kids, you have an Army career. You won't get them out. So what good will it do you? You'll accomplish nothing." That all went through my head.

There were families there with kids. I remember very clearly the Vietnamese firemen were there in their yellow coats. I'll never forget the firemen. And there was a German priest who spoke some Vietnamese, who'd helped out. But there were these firemen. And I remember the firemen because I asked them earlier if they wanted to go and they said, "No, we have to stay. If there's a chopper crash we can work the equipment." They wanted me to take their families out so they would be free to work. So I took their families and put them all on a bird about mid-afternoon.

So I stayed there. And you know a bird came in and landed on the roof and took off, and I realized there was a whole other plan. Madison didn't say how long I should stay down here. I thought, "Geez, was I supposed to be on that one." It was dark and I was looking for some sign. Could I see them up there? And finally after fifteen or twenty minutes, during which time I was pretending to talk to helicopters who weren't there, I looked at the Vietnamese closest to me, and I said, "I gotta take a leak." And the Vietnamese closest to me laughed, and I sneaked into the bushes like I was going to go to the bathroom.

There was a house there and there were shrubberies around the house, and I just walked into the shrubbery and I beat it around the house and out of their sight, and I went in the back door of the Embassy.

Earlier in the day—there was the plaque, it was a piece of history, and I had permission to take it. I got a navy chief, a retired Navy guy who was the Embassy engineer, and he found me a crowbar and the two of us pried this thing off—the plaque's very big, very heavy. We put it on the floor right inside the door, leaning against the wall. I was going to take it with me when I went.

Inscribed on the plaque were the words, "In memory of the brave Americans who died defending this Embassy during the Tet Offensive, 1968," and then it listed the MPs and the 101st Airborne, the Marines, and the U.S. Military Police who died. There were five guys who died and their names were on it. I just didn't think it should be left behind. But when I came through the lobby and it was lying there, I was so upset and so angry at being ordered to leave, that I thought, "After what those guys did here, to have died right here where I'm standing and for me to have to dishonor—they died to defend this Embassy and now I'm running away from it with the Communists outside the gates of the city, and leaving those people out there, they'd roll over in their graves." And I just said, "To hell with the plaque." And I left it there.

I ran up to the second floor. I ran into the ambassador's office suite. It was empty. I ran four or five more steps, peeked into Martin's office. It was in order as if he were ready to hold a meeting. I ran back to the stairwell, checked the political-military office to see if our stuff was there. Everything looked like it was gone. I ran up to the top of the steps and Gunnery Sergeant Pace and Bill Bell were there. Madison and Summers and Bill Herron were gone.

Bell and Pace and I got on a CH-46. Bell was exhausted. He was at the end of his rope, because he literally crawled up the ramp of the '46. I got on. One Marine came waltzing out of the darkness and got on with us. And that '46 took off with a total of me, Bell, Pace, and one Marine. Four Americans!

That was the sickening part of it. It could have carried forty-five more people. I looked down out the back ramp, and you could see the people waiting down there and the street lights of Saigon, and the Embassy. There was dead silence in the chopper.

I was sickened, naturally. I never in my life felt worse, never will feel worse than at that moment walking away from those people.

After the bird took off and got some altitude they closed the cargo ramp door. I remember when the bird ascended, it banked, and there was the Embassy, the parking lot, the street lights. And the silence. Quiet streets, no traffic, no crowds, no nothing. Looked like the curfew was being obeyed.

Madison sought out Jim Bolton on the U.S.S. *Okinawa* when we got there. And I saw Bolton but I was not privy to the conversation that Madison had. They came to me, Summers and Madison, and told me that they talked to Bolton. See, we were mad. We were damn, damn angry because we had, in our judgment, been forced to betray the Vietnamese. We had lied, albeit unwittingly, to the Vietnamese. We had left those poor people behind. There wasn't a one of us who was not alienated by that.

A guy was on the *Okinawa* from the *Cleveland Press* and he interviewed Summers and then me. And Summers asked the guy, "Do you know what you just saw" And the reporter said, "The fall of Saigon." And Summers said, "You saw betrayal of the worst order."

The guy interviewed me about what happened in the Embassy because I was the last to leave. And I remember I just couldn't stop crying as he interviewed me. Every time I thought about leaving those people, I just couldn't talk about it without crying. I was so ashamed and felt so bad that those people had been left behind.

Later I flew to Subic Bay and then to Thailand. No sooner had I gotten to Thailand than I was summoned back to Subic Bay. The purpose was a Joint Chiefs of Staff investigating commission on the evacuation. I was summoned there (Madison and Summers had been called to Hawaii, I guess) to report on what had happened, and I was the only officer left who was an eyewitness to the Embassy events. And the big mystery, the big X-factor, was the Embassy. There had been no plans for any big evacuation out of the Embassy. The Embassy plan was a very simple plan. Several hundred, max, would be bused out to Tan Son Nhut and some fifty, sixty, or so, the ambassador and his inner circle, would be Air America'd off the roof of the Embassy. And the buses were there as part of the plan to take several hundred, max, out to Tan Son Nhut. So when the Embassy became the focus of a major helicopter extraction, that happened by circumstance. And because it was not planned for, they didn't even know about it. There was no communication after a certain hour between the Embassy and the DAO apparently, and no one knew what was going on in the Embassy.

To the very end, all the people who were out with General Smith, who were at the DAO, the people who were out on the ship, at CINCPAC, and the Thailand headquarters—nobody knew what the hell was going on there. So I was called to testify before a Joint Chiefs of Staff board that was dispatched to Subic to interview the Marines. And I did. The difficulty was that the Marines, when they briefed the board, briefed a picture of the overall operation of Frequent Wind.

I don't necessarily believe there was any deliberate attempt to misrepresent what happened, although there are cynics who say the Marines are embellishing the facts again because the Marines want to look like they were the first to fight and the last to fight alone. I don't necessarily believe that, although I believed it at the time.

The Marines came to the Embassy off the fleet, with, first of all, word that they had two guys KIA [killed in action] already. There was no secret about the fact that Saigon was surrounded by sixteen divisions and under heavy artillery fire, which meant they were within twenty, thirty kilometers, at least. And there was no secret about the fact that the North Vietnamese could and would enter Saigon. The enemy had brought surface-to-air missiles [SAMs] down the same tubes, down Route One from North Vietnam, from the Khe Sanh area. This was the intelligence estimate. So when the Marines came in, they knew they were a small Marine force that could be under fire by the entire North Vietnamese army. And then two guys get killed, and there's rocket fire, artillery fire.

We know that there were North Vietnamese attacks against Saigon on the morning of the thirtieth. That a column came in from the direction of Tan Son Nhut. Another column came in from the Newport Bridge, from the North. And there was a pincer of at least a three-column thrust against the city of Saigon, with the objectives being JGS headquarters, the National Police compound, and the Presidential Palace.

But the Marines in Subic created the impression that we got out by a cat's whisker and there was a lot of hostile fire and resistance to the evacuation. They gave the impression that the Embassy was hot. I sat through these briefings at Subic. I was the missing link to put the whole picture together. The Marines were about thirty strong in the conference room. General Carey was there, and they briefed him. I had a problem. I'm hearing them tell about the Embassy, and it doesn't bear any resemblance to what I saw and lived through. And I wrote a note to General Cleveland who was the head of this commission. I said, "I got a problem. I'm supposed to get up and brief on the Embassy, and I'm going to contradict all these Marines." And General Cleveland, before they broke for lunch, said, "I understand you have a problem, Captain Herrington."

I said, "Yes, sir. If that's the Embassy that they described, then I don't know where I was, because it wasn't that way at all." He said, "Well, that's why you're here. I want you to tell it like it is. Maybe you better stay here over the lunch hour and get your act together." And I said, "Yes, sir." So I stayed over the lunch hour and I drew a big butcher-paper map of the Embassy compound, the pool, the wall, the walls of the Embassy, the whole bit. And I briefed. And it was a tough briefing to give, because the Marines bristled right away.

I told them the Embassy evacuation had taken place unopposed. That there was no hostile fire at the Embassy. We were not under small-arms fire, machine gun fire, artillery fire, any kind of fire, and that the end at the Embassy was premature—that we could not understand it, that it was not a clean sweep. The Marines had briefed that the evacuation was completed at the Embassy and this was all one great big success. If Kean had been there, Kean could have told them that it wasn't a big success. I don't know how he depicts it or what his memory of it is, but see, Kean wasn't there. The Marines who briefed clearly weren't there at the Embassy. They were briefing what they understood, based on what helicopter pilots were telling them over the radio.

So I finished my briefing. General Carey took exception to what I said, and I said, "Sir, the only thing I can tell you is, I have briefed you. The collective, confirmed, cross-checked memories of a Marine Corps gunnery sergeant, an Army E-7, an Army E-8, an Army O-6, an Army O-5, and myself. Between the six of us we probably have twenty-five or thirty years' combat experience. If the Embassy evacuation was opposed, then why did not a single Marine fire a single round? The first rule of engagement is to return fire. Since we commanded the heights, no one fired. There was a lot of—the Marine pilots for example, mistook the toxic fumes from the CIA crypto-destruct devices that were destroying radios on the roof, they took that to mean the Embassy was under a gas attack, and that went out over the air. And fire on the roof of the Embassy, which was documents being destroyed, translated into "The Embassy's on fire." Every time a shot was fired around the Embassy out in the city of Saigon, the Marines— a squad-size element of Marines—would come crashing across the Embassy compound screaming, "Penetration of the north wall," "Penetration of the south wall." And repeatedly during the course of night, Marines came crashing from one side of the Embassy wall to the other, screaming that there was a penetration here or there. And there wasn't. What you had was frightened young Marines who had two guys killed, who'd heard about that. The pucker factor was there. And they were a problem. But as far as the Embassy coming under attack, or that the Embassy evacuation was happening under combat conditions: No!

So I briefed it that way, and I told them about the four hundred and twenty people who were left behind. I had the distinct impression that the Marines didn't like my briefing one bit. I believe that they told the picture as it came through the fog of war, as they heard it from the chopper pilots. And there was a lot of misconstruing of events on the ground. The overall impression they left was that we barely got out of there and that NVA tanks were knocking at the door.

And you know, it didn't happen that way.

I have visited the Vietnam memorial several times. The first time I was there I looked for the names of people I'd known in Vietnam. I looked for Judge and McMahon's names. I was not deeply moved by the Vietnam memorial. Unlike a lot of guys who have trouble handling their experiences in Vietnam and the memorial triggers for them another fit of depression and melancholy, or shame or remorse, that did not happen to me. I thought it was a dignified memorial, that basically didn't turn me emotionally one way or another.

I can't get excited about the architecture itself one way or the other. It's a wall. I don't see where it's either a stunning architectural idea, or something offensive. I see it as a wall with a bunch of names on it, and I don't see what the controversy was all about, myself. I think that it makes a statement because when you see fifty-eight-thousand names carved all in one spot, it gives one the idea of the enormity of the human sacrifice. But I didn't have a problem handling it. Even though I spent a lot of time in Vietnam and I have a lot of reasons to feel pretty terrible about what happened, I'm also lucky because I'm one of the vast silent majority of Vietnam veterans who handles it well.

I believe strongly that the picture of the average Vietnam veteran that has been foisted on the American people is a picture of a very small percentage of the Vietnam veterans who run around in old field jackets, unshaven and scruffy, blaming all of their failures in life on the Vietnam war, and that's not the typical Vietnam vet. The typical Vietnam vet is a pretty well-adjusted, healthy guy who is in his mid-forties and pretty successful either in business or some other pursuit.

And I do not accept the notion that the average Vietnam vet is like the vet that you see in the tiger cage outside the Vietnam memorial trying to convince people there are still live prisoners. I find myself to be a lot healthier as a result of the Vietnam War in many ways, because of the perspective that it imparted to my overall philosophy of life. And I think there are a lot more of us than there are of the kind that wear field jackets and jungle hats and embrace one another tearfully every Memorial Day.

I don't mean to be uncharitable about that, but I'm sorry, the collection of veterans who are the most visible to the American people, that picture of the veteran population is as cloudy and as inaccurate as the picture of the war and what happened. I shouldn't be surprised that the picture of the Vietnam veteran has been distorted by the American media. The whole war, the reality of the war was distorted.

CHAPTER VIII

Military Sealift Command

Harold J. Murphy
"We Were Their Saviors"

Around 1975 I got the urge to go to sea again. It just comes over you once in a while. If you have any family or friends who've been to sea, you understand. I started when I was very young and it was almost impossible to quit. All the time you're ashore you're thinking about going back to sea.

I went to New York and they had a ship, the *Greenville Victory,* with a carpenter's job open, and they told me that the third mate was going to leave the ship at some point and I would relieve him. So I sailed on the *Greenville Victory* as carpenter. We loaded ammo in Port Chicago on the West coast and we took a load to Cam Ranh Bay and Danang.

The Vietnamese didn't really know how bad it was, I'm sure. And I don't think we did, either. We knew that it was bad and that they couldn't last too much longer. But I don't think anybody knew that they were going to break out as quickly as they did.

We went to Cam Ranh Bay first and then Danang. In Danang it was a very tense situation. You knew something was going to happen. They had swimmers in the water trying to plant mines on ships and there were boxes of concussion grenades every fifty feet along the deck and we'd chuck them overboard once in a while in case there were any swimmers in the water.

We went back to Thailand to load military cargo and return to the United States. But as soon as we arrived there, this thing broke loose, so we were sent back to Vietnam. That was on Easter Sunday in late March. We were sent to Danang and told to rescue survivors.

We were aware of what was going on in Vietnam. The United States had pulled out a year or two before. I was aware that they were in deep trouble and that we had really done them a bad turn. I felt really guilty about that.

When we arrived off the coast, the Communists were moving down so fast that Danang was already gone. We made several attempts down the coast to get into various ports, but we couldn't get in because one after another they had fallen to the Communists. One or two places that we went into, there were people there, but there were no landing craft or boats to bring them out. They were on the beach and we couldn't load them.

The first place we got into was Cam Ranh, and there we started to load at the docks and it was utter chaos. So we left the dock and went out at anchor, and they came out in small boats and we loaded them from boats. They lived on these boats, you know, and some of them came out with all their belongings. Of course we couldn't take anything except the people, some foodstuff and their little 50cc Honda bikes. We let them take those— I don't know how many of them.

There were civilians, women, children, and Vietnamese army personnel, obviously on the run, whom we tried to disarm because we didn't want all those weapons on the ship. We did the best we could. But you had to be there to see this. This was really chaos. We loaded them in cargo nets, put the booms over the side and loaded them like cargo, and they just clung to each other trying to get aboard. And some came up the gangway.

At any rate, we disarmed as many as we could. We had a whole room full of rifles and grenades and weapons, but we didn't get them all.

We loaded about ten thousand people. This is a Victory ship, remember; it is about a five-hundred-foot, nine- or ten-thousand-ton ammunition ship with five cargo holds. We just loaded them like cargo. They were everywhere. Even the lifeboats were full of people.

We tried to keep them out of the main interior of the ship, the crew's quarters, but they were in there, too. We fed them what we could, but there were too many of them. We just did what we could for them. We all felt, at least I did, that maybe in some little way we could atone for the lousy things we did to them—because we did, really. We shouldn't have gone there in the first place, maybe, but once we were there we should have done what was right, and we didn't. We just left and said, "Here, now you do it." They were incapable of doing it.

We had no food or water for them or sanitary facilities. Mind you now, ten thousand people. You can imagine what happened. At any rate, we had no food. They brought rice with them, and the ship could make about fifteen tons of fresh water a day with the evaporator, and they were using thirty.

So we set up the fire hoses and turned the fire pumps on so they bathe at least in salt water and wash the excrement off the decks. It was real bad.

Ammunition ship holds are lined with wood battens to prevent sweat from damaging the ammo, anti-sparking and everything else. They were ripping the wood down off the lining of the hold and building fires so they could cook their rice. Of course they started quite a few fires. Some of the fires got out of control and we had to put them out. So we cut oil drums in half eventually—fifty-gallon drums. We gave them tools to cut the wood properly and put it in these fifty-gallon drums and cook their rice over those and not start any fires on the ship.

The entrance to Cam Ranh Bay is surrounded by high cliffs fortified with 105mm howitzers, and we didn't know if they'd start firing them at us. But luckily, about the time we had as many people aboard as we could handle, we were hit by a very heavy rain squall. Visibility fell to practically zero and we got out under cover of that.

The fleet was offshore. It had orders not to come any closer than thirty miles, so they lay offshore, but we were naturally in radio contact with them and under their command as a Navy ship. We were civilian crew, but a Navy ship.

We were told to take them to an island called Phu Quoc, offshore near the border between Vietnam and Cambodia. I think it took us two or three days. When we arrived there, we anchored and planned to discharge the people there and then go back and see if we could help some others.

Well, they refused to get off the ship.

The landing craft that were supposed to disembark them didn't show up. So we lay there at anchor for a day or so. They got very uneasy, and they finally sent a delegation up to the wheelhouse. This is why Captain Ray Iacobacci says he was lucky he got out alive, I think. The delegation was a Catholic priest and other people who were representing the people on board. And their demands were that we leave the area immediately. They would not go ashore. They said that, number one, Phu Quoc was a former penal colony, which they didn't like the sound of. And second, they would be trapped there if the Communists did come. There was no way off this island and they were dead meat if they stayed.

Then they said they had enough weapons and explosives in the hold to destroy the ship and they would do exactly that if we didn't leave immediately. They had a Gulf Oil road map with them, and we asked them where they wanted to go, and they pointed to Vung Tau, the port at the mouth of the river that leads up to Saigon. So the ultimate decision was, "Let's get the hell out of here."

I sympathized with them. I don't blame them. I'd do that, too. Captain Iacobacci said, "What am I going to do?" I said, "What the hell. Haul the anchor and get the hell out of here." It's simple. I think everybody understood what they were saying. There was no escape from there.

You know I didn't really feel my life was in danger at all during that time. But also I didn't doubt that they'd sink the ship. I had no doubt that they meant exactly what they said.

They never threatened an individual crew member. Oh, no. We were their saviors.

We left Phu Quoc and we returned to Vung Tau. I forget the total length of time they were on board the ship, but it was at least five days, and we were really without food or water for them, to speak of.

We returned to Vung Tau and finally discharged them. Landing craft came out and took them off. We went up the river, then, to Saigon to get the ship cleaned. It was beyond description.

During all of this operation we lost one person. Some of them had come out on a barge, and one little boy fell down between the ship and the barge and didn't come up. That was the only fatality we had. Actually we were ahead of the game, because I think two were born on board.

We were in Vung Tau when the country fell. We watched the choppers go overhead from the Embassy. We knew it was all over. Then chaos broke out again. Thousands of boats came out. Small boats, big boats, all kinds of boats. And we loaded people from the boats with our cargo nets mostly. And when they left their boats they would poke a hole in the fuel tank and set it on fire so the Communists wouldn't get it. The whole place was full of burning boats. Those boats had been the people's homes. And now it was sad to see people burning their homes.

What those people went through—I think a lot of American people would go crazy. They set fire to their homes with all their possessions. They couldn't bring anything with them.

We had to move every so often because they crowded around, so many thousands of them that we couldn't work. We had to back away a mile or so and start over again. We did that several times. I think we sank one boat with our propellor in the course of backing up. It was total confusion. We continued to load people on into dark until we were full. And then we took that load to Subic Bay in the Philippines.

We had no problems. We confiscated as many weapons as we could. Some we kept on board, and thousands were thrown overboard.

The people wanted to get out of there, so they cooperated with us. Everybody on the ship that could do anything did it. Whether it was down on the gangway handing up babies or whatever it was. There were a lot of kids, a lot of babies, handed up from man to man up the gangway.

The crew was involved in this thing one hundred percent. This was more than just a job loading ammunition. These people were in big trouble. Their lives were on the line. We were the only hope they had to get out of there. They were American sympathizers, or in the eyes of the North Vietnamese they were the enemy, they were collaborators. We were the enemy of the Communists and these people had cooperated with us and that was their death warrant right there.

There were no deaths on the way to Subic. And we added one baby boy to the number of refugees during the trip.

When we had been back in Saigon there were a couple of relief organizations that showed up with tons of food. We were stocked with food for the second pickup. We were much better prepared for the second go-around. We made firepots to cook the rice on up on tripod legs and on the fantails, back aft. We didn't know what we were going into the first time. All we knew was, Go in and see if you can rescue some refugees.

The refugees were all very friendly, considering what they'd gone through and were going through, they were wonderful people. And there were so many of them. They were everywhere. For me to walk from midship to the bow I had to go through all these people. They would move aside to make a path for me so I could walk through. Every square inch of space was filled with people.

There was an island in Subic Bay that they used as a staging area. They took them all to the island, and I guess tried to ascertain names and identification and make some kind of a record of what was going on, and they had us stand by. We stood by there a month or two in Subic in case we were needed to transport them to Guam, which was going to be the main staging area. But we were never used for that. I think most of them were flown to Guam. But we stayed for the time until they were sure they didn't need us.

I think we did a good job. We got eighteen thousand of them out of there. I wish we could have gotten more.

After Subic Bay we went to Mobile, Alabama, and we had a big reception in Mobile. You had the mayor and the whole town, and the band and all that good stuff, you know. We've all got a piece of paper that says thanks for a good job, which is nice.

You can talk about it afterwards and try to find reasons for what you did, but actually there's the thing to do and you just do it. Maybe later on you think about it. "There these people are, let's get them out of here"—It's that simple. You are so full of adrenaline at the time that you don't really think about it. Seamen are a funny lot, you know. They do the job when the job has to be done. They are good people, the best people I ever knew in my life. They just do the job. These are merchant seamen, not military personnel. Professional sailors that do the job of ten. The ships that we sailed on, a ship like that, the *Greenville Victory*, was a ten-thousand-ton ship with a crew of about thirty-eight men. If it had been a Navy ship it would have had a crew of three hundred and fifty. We are professional seamen and I was always proud of that.

I never ran into any of the people I brought out at that time. I've often wished that I had a name of somebody that was on that ship that I could meet—one of the Vietnamese that got out of there on the *Greenville Victory* and made it here. I read an article in the paper not long ago about the Vietnamese community on the West Coast and how successful they had become, some of them. They are industrious people, great people; they work hard, don't want welfare, want to work and send their children to school. One of them, I think, graduated top of his class at one of the military academies, I read recently. That kind of thing doesn't surprise me. It surprises some of the rednecks that these people can do it. But the Vietnamese are very intelligent people and they are industrious.

I spent a lot of time in the Far East and I think that probably that experience in Vietnam really showed me what those people are made of.

My children are thirty-seven, thirty-five, thirty-three, and a stepson who's fifteen. After I was back here I told them I thought that we had abandoned those people and nobody asked me if I thought we should pull out and leave those people. Nobody asked anybody anything. You don't have any say in what happens; then you have to regret it. I felt very strongly when I was there that—you could almost see it in their eyes— "Why did you abandon us? Why did the Americans leave us?" But not with animosity. It was like a kid would look at his father, "Why did you hit me?"

But they were wonderful, those people. I love them. I wish we had gotten them all out of there. Or better yet, I wish it wouldn't have been necessary to get them out of there. It shouldn't have been necessary.

Clinton J. Harriman, Jr.
"Well, Darling, At Least We'll All Die Together"

I started working for the Military Sealift Command in 1967. I had been in the industry for years, with private companies that went under, so I was working as a harbor pilot down in the Virgin Islands and I just wanted to get out to Vietnam. I had been down to the Far East several times, but never Vietnam. It was right about the time of the big Tet offensive. As a matter of fact, when I got there it was just going good.

So I got to Vietnam the first time in 1968. I was the first officer on the *Robinson*. I later became captain of her. We took mostly ammunition between the United States and Vietnam. I made several trips down there.

I got married in Vietnam. My wife's name is Tran Thi Tat. The wedding was one of those presided over by a village chief and they put it in the family book. It doesn't really mean shit later on. It's legal over there. But we had to get remarried when we got back to the U.S. My daughter, Thu Hong, which means "Morning Rose," was born December 10, 1970. Our boy's name is Minh, and his father was Tat's first husband. Our youngest boy, who was born in the U.S., is named Chin Si, which means "War Hero."

I was in the U.S. when things started coming apart in the spring of 1975 and I tried to get back out there because of my wife and the boy and the girl. And I couldn't get back out. I was stuck in New York. I knew the whole goddamn thing was going to be ringing down pretty fast. So I got hold of the port captain and practically begged him to get out there on the *Greenville Victory* because it was the only ship that we had going that I could have gotten on.

But then in March as I was leaving my house, I slipped on a piece of ice and broke my leg. But I went anyway. I could still walk, but it was real painful.

Then the thing started swelling up so bad that I had to go see a Navy doctor. So he said, "You're not fit for duty." I said, "Bullshit, I got to make this trip." And he said, "Well, I can't let you go." I said, "I got to go." I told him the reason why. So he said, "Well, Jesus Christ, you going to be okay?" I said, "Well, yeah, I'm the medical officer on the ship, for Christ's sake." So he let me go.

When I got to the ship, I got on Captain Ray Iacobacci's back and he carried me up the gangway onto the *Greenville Victory*. I couldn't do a goddamned thing for a week, though.

We had a full load of ammunition and we took it up to Cat Lai. We then went to Danang and Cam Ranh Bay, finished discharging at Cam Ranh, and then we went to Thailand and sat there. Jesus Christ, around eleven o'clock one night the captain was on board practically by himself because that's a hell of a liberty town, and the next thing you know he's tearing all over town in a cab trying to find guys because we got the word we're going up to Vietnam to start the evacuation.

I had an apartment in Saigon and a house in the country in the outskirts of Tay Ninh, which is up the line a ways. My wife is a country girl. She always stayed in the country when I was out at sea.

Things were starting to go nip-and-tuck and we were down in Vung Tau at anchor, and I said to Ray, "This is my only frigging chance to get them out." So he said, "Okay, Harry, you go ahead."

The excuse was going to be for me to get this cast taken off. I was on my feet fourteen, sixteen hours a day, and the cast was getting mushy and the leg was swelling.

I went down to the Seventh-Day Adventist hospital. My wife was with me and they took off this goddamned cast. The guy said, "I'm not going to let you out of this hospital unless you can walk across this room. I said, "Jesus Christ, I don't think I can make it." But I did anyway.

So now Captain Iacobacci and the ship left to go up north to do this other operation, and I'm down in Saigon. And the whole shit is now coming down. We had a nice little apartment on the other side of the river, one of the small branches of the Saigon river, and my wife was saying, "Well, it's going to be okay," and so on. Well I knew it was not going to be okay. So I went to a friend, a Colonel Vong, a hell of a guy, and he offered to put us up at Newport. He was commander of the base there. He had a big beautiful home. And we did stay there one night, but then all his relatives started arriving, his ancient mother, and all his sisters and aunts and so on. It's amazing, Vietnamese people, it doesn't make any difference whether they're from the aristocracy or the peasantry, they think nothing of fifteen people sleeping in the same room. But I said to myself, "My God, I'm sort of an appendage here and he's being extremely kind. I'm going to go in the town and stay in a hotel." We went to the Majestic and got this great big suite and this leg of mine now looked like an umbrella stand. I was waiting for the ship to come back, and saying to myself, "God damn, I'm going to be cut off here." These people coming down from the north were traveling so fast they couldn't keep up with their own gasoline, you know. My wife's mother had been through the Japanese and the French and this and that, and she always thought this was just an offshoot from a little war that's going on, you know. But I knew it was going to be the goddamned end. And the end of life as they knew it over there, as a matter of fact. So I had a friend who was a Brit. He headed up some little steamship company, and he arranged for this car, it was about a 1939 or '40 Renault. A great-looking car with a very old driver.

We drove to meet the *Greenville Victory* when it came back down to Vung Tau. On the way out the roads were getting more and more clogged as we went. And the last five or six miles we were maybe doing fifteen miles an hour. We got up there finally to this gate and there were abandoned pigs, and baskets, Lambrettas lying on their sides, and I could see the ship down there in the harbor. Then this little goddamned pimply-faced soldier, when we got to this barricade, stuck his rifle in the bloody window next to the driver. My wife and child and I are sitting in the back. And he said, "Get out and walk." Well, Jesus Christ, I couldn't. So I said to my wife, taking a chance he didn't speak English, I said, "Tell the driver to turn this goddamned car around, we're going back to Saigon." The Vietnamese speak softer than the Irish, and she leaned over and spoke so softly that I couldn't hear. This old man who was extremely nervous about the entire situation, wheeled this car around and just missed a truck by an extra coat of paint, and zip, back down the road we went.

There was nothing on the road. It was a beautiful road built by the Americans. It was like a four-lane highway with a divider and traffic going south one way and north the other way. And you saw all these people on bicycles and motor scooters and Lambrettas, little cars and trucks, all bumper-to-bumper going the other way, we were wheeling down this gosh-darn road, no problem. We got about, I would say, twenty miles down that road, and I could see some guys putting up a barricade on the road of 55-gallon drums. And it was at that point that I said to myself, "Here we are."

The old man started slowing down. I had, in the car on the floor, a box of hand grenades, a .45 automatic, and a .38 special, which I still have. And I had four or five boxes of .45 ammunition, plus two or three boxes of .38 special ammunition. So I said to my wife, "You tell this old guy"—and I don't like fast driving, believe me, I don't like fast driving at all, but that day you couldn't get the car to go fast enough to suit me— "You tell this old guy to step on his goddamn accelerator, because we're going to get past these frigging barrels. I'm not going to be stuck out here on this goddamn place."

He said to her, "Well, look, they're setting up a barricade, what can I do?" I said, "Tell him if he doesn't go through it I'll put a goddamned bullet in his head." And at that point he put it to the floor. And we went tearing down that road. And these guys were down off the slope of the road getting rocks to fill the barrels up with, and if you hit one of them, you're dead in the water. Well, he went tooling through there like Grant took Richmond, and he just hit one of those barrels a tiny bit and the thing went flying off in the air. By this time they had scrambled up on the edge and they each took two or three shots at the car. We were going around a bend at the time and I suppose they were getting their sights adjusted or maybe they weren't good marksmen, but we weren't hit.

So then the driver said, "Look, I'm going to tell you something right now, it looks like they're cutting off the road. When I was a young man I used to work in a rubber plantation that's not too far from here and there's an old country road that if we start slowing down now we can make a left-hand turn and take it."

So you say to yourself, "Am I being led into a goddamned trap or what?" But these guys were not fucking around up there on the main road, so I told him to do it. He darts off down this little bumpy road and we came out on a little tar road, which was built back probably in the '20s, a regular tar road with a real high crown.

He went putzing down this road. We could look up out of the right-hand side windows and see the main highway. We did see two helicopters land there and they were not friendly.

Now I don't give a shit what some historian of this war will tell you, but I was there in that car and I know what I saw. I saw uniformed North Vietnamese soldiers with AK-47s getting out of helicopters.

I said to my wife, "We could all get it right here on this road any minute." And I was saying to myself, "Screw it, if we do, I'm going to take a couple of them with me, I think." And she had the goddamned courage to say, "Well, darling, at least we'll all die together." And that gave me great courage. I don't even know if she knew what she was saying, but it came out pretty good.

So we went buzzing down the road, sort of following the river, and then we darted off into the jungle for a while. After about eighty miles we came out to this gate with a sentry box and with a real nasty little bastard of a soldier there. And in many many cases they didn't like to see a Vietnamese female with a white guy. We had papers with her picture and my picture and all that, intent to wed. Colonel Vong's signature was on her pass, plus the fact that we had a state pass, and Colonel Vong's signature brought this guy to attention, I'll tell you. So we went in through the gate, and I still didn't know where I was.

Well, we were back at the encampment and it was entirely deserted. And I saw the Seamen's Club, which was a huge, beautiful place. At this point my leg was so frigging sore I thought it was going to fall off. And my wife said, "The old man would like to have some cold soda." So I said, "Jesus Christ, woman, get him one."

She started to go in and got to the second swinging glass door and she looked in and came back out and said, "I'm afraid to go in there." I said, "Why?" She said, "Nobody there." So I grabbed a pistol and hobbled in. This was a big place, and you could have heard a pin drop in there. Now the guy who used to run this place was as tight as the bark on a tree. I said, "I'm going to get one free drink out of this place one way or another." The bar was way down the other end and I walked down there, and Jesus Christ, there was money in the cash register and everything. And not a bloody soul—not a waitress, not a waiter, not a cook, nothing.

So I went behind the bar and poured myself a nice great big vodka and I threw that down. Of course your adrenaline is running so high at a point like that, throwing down a vodka doesn't do anything, it burns that up. Then I poured myself another one and I got this old man a Seven-Up, came hobbling back out of there, and gave it to him. And my wife says, "Give him some money." Well I had about six hundred bucks in my pocket, but it's going through my mind, how I'm going to get out through Thailand with a woman and a little girl with only six hundred bucks?

So I said, "Do you think twenty would be enough?" And she said, "Twenty is fine." So I laid twenty on the old man, and he got back in the Renault and turned on the key and that was it. That frigging engine just froze up. Hundred and sixty miles at that speed and probably ran out of oil about a hundred miles back.

The last time I saw that old man he was walking out through the main gates sipping on his Seven-Up. I don't know what happened to him.

But I still had $580 and two pistols—one pistol, one revolver—that's always very comforting.

This point was kind of like the lull before the storm. I telephoned Bill Ryder who was right there on the base. As a matter of fact, it was only about a hundred yards down to Ryder's, and I said to my wife, "Let's walk down there."

The MSC [Military Sealift Command] offices were full of these absolutely delicious young Vietnamese girls who worked for them. And they didn't want to stay, because anybody who worked for the Americans, they were going to get fucked without getting kissed. Believe me, it was a choppy time in there.

Ryder, who was a Kings Point guy, hell of a wonderful guy, put me on the *Pioneer Contender*. There was some captain on there from Staten Island, Captain Flink. Ryder was up to his ass in alligators in this office, radio messages coming and going and all these little girls biting their fingernails and what-not, and all in their best *ao dais*.

So this big car, a Buick or something like that, with a woman driver, took us down to the U.S. Lines ship, *Pioneer Contender*. So I went aboard the longest goddamned gangway in the world, I thought, with this frigging leg which was now the size of a sewer pipe. And got up there and my wife always had our girl dressed in American clothes, I used to bring clothes over from the States. This one day, my God, she was wearing a pair of Chinese pajamas. She looked white; but of all the frigging things to dress her in that day, that was the wrong thing.

Well, anyway, I went aboard, and this guy Flink, he's sitting behind his goddamned regular U.S. Lines desk, and I said, "Bill Ryder sent me down here, for you to take me down the river with my daughter." My wife is on the pier. Now she's got to find the boy. I told her to wait with the driver until I gave her a wave. I was afraid of having no car, because just getting to the goddamed Captain's room, believe me, was like climbing the Matterhorn, the condition my leg was in.

Well, you know, here we are, two goddamned Americans; Saigon's about ready to fall, and this pompous ass sitting behind this desk says, "Well, I'll have to wait, I can't take you as a passenger." I said, "For Christ's sake, you're not going to leave us here on the goddamn pier, are you?" And he said, "Well, hey, look, we have rules here in this company."

You know, when they went into Chapter Seven not long ago, I said, "It's on account of pricks like you they went into Chapter Seven." I couldn't believe this guy's attitude.

I went out on his deck and I yelled down to the driver, "Can you get Ryder down here?" And she said, "No, no, no, too busy." I said, "Wait for me."

Now I got to go back up to the office. They heard some shots going off, and the driver, she took off with my wife.

I didn't walk to the office. There happened to be a Vietnamese soldier with a motorbike, so my daughter got in back of him and I rode side-saddle. And we went up to Bill's office. Ryder's still there with the girls chewing their fingernails. Bill said, "What the hell are you doing here?" I said, "This frigging guy doesn't want to take me down the river." He says, "God damn his ass." So he breaks out of there, we get another car, go back down to the ship, back up the gangway to the captain's quarters, and Bill says, "Look, you're to take him down the river with his child." And Flink said, "Well, you know"—MSC was keeping U.S. Lines alive—

Bill Ryder says, "I'm going to tell you something right now. If you don't want to do it, you're off hire." Off hire means you don't get any money for this ship—at about $27,000 a day. Well this caught this guy's attention, because his days as a sailing captain were going to be all over. He says, "Well, in that case . . ." and they swung the goddamn booms in and they got some kind of orders within a matter of half an hour or so, and down the river we went to Vung Tau.

Now this guy Flink is pissing his pants. They must have been doing six, seven knots. Captain Iacobacci sent a lifeboat out to pick me up, and they were just barely keeping abreast of this bastard. Three quarters of the way down the gangway this black ex-Marine in the lifeboat, James McGee, Jr., says, "Don't worry about it, Mr. Harriman, just throw her to me, I'll catch her." And I took that little four-year-old girl and threw her down there like a bag of grain, a good long drop, too, like fifteen, eighteen feet. And he caught her just like a basketball.

My wife went back up to the country to get the boy. Colonel Vong arranged for that. Then they got cut off. She walked about twenty-three miles through the frigging jungle carrying a suitcase in one hand and leading this little kid by the other. She just barely made it out. If it wasn't for Colonel Vong she would not have gotten out.

She got down there just as the thing fell on its face. She got a ride up, and some rides back, but she spent a lot of time walking through rubber plantations, coconut plantations, and shit like that.

She came back into Saigon. She was the only goddamned female that had a pass to get into that base. The only Vietnamese female, besides the ones who worked there. But she had this personal document that looked like the Diet of Worms, about the size of the Declaration of Independence, with Colonel Vong's signature on it. She could get in anywhere with that pass, because he was the big law there.

At least I had my daughter at that point. We went to the Philippines on the *Greenville Victory*.

My wife and boy came out on the *Boo Heung Pioneer*. That was the last ship out.

I remember when we were sitting off the coast a black guy dressed in a suit came on board the ship looking for the ambassador's dog. Really! We'd just picked up 11,000 refugees and Martin's second secretary, or whoever the hell he was, was going from ship to ship in some kind of a good-looking barge looking for the Ambassador's dog!

We went back into the Philippines, and there was guy by the name of Captain Ruebasmen. I'd seen him first when he was a lieutenant commander in the beginning of the war, or when I first went up there. I knew he was somebody big with MSC, but he was over in, I think, Japan. So I'm sitting up in the Officer's Club in the Philippines in Subic Bay at the Naval Base, and this guy walked up to me and said, "By the way, your wife is out on East LeGrande. She just came in on the *Boo Heung*

Pioneer." Then of course I knew she'd picked Minh up. Bill Ryder was very helpful in getting her aboard the *Boo Heung Pioneer,* and so was Colonel Vong. As a matter of fact, she slept in the owner's cabin.

It was late at night, about 10:30. He said, "You can have my launch in the morning and take a run out there and see her." So that was fine. And I went zipping out there in the morning and she was gone. They'd taken her down to Guam. But at least I knew she was on her way to the U.S.

The next thing I know, she turned up in a refugee camp in Indiantown Gap in Pennsylvania. I called her and said, "Don't move!"

I'll tell you one thing, the house we built on the outskirts of Tay Ninh was a really divine home. It was a beautiful place. And when all these Communists refer to Vietnam now as the "People's Republic" and "the People's this," and "the People's that," its all bullshit. Those people in the goddamn hierarchy of any Communist government live better than the fucking czars or anybody else ever did live. This beautiful home we had outside of Tay Ninh. You know where my wife's mother and her brother and sister were living now? Well, now they're living in a toolshed. And who do you think is living in the house? The Communist province chief is living in our fucking house. They just changed the buttons on the hats, is all. They took the Russian double eagle off, put on a red star, and moved right into the fucking palace.

But we're all safe and happy here. The oldest boy—well, my wife had been married to a Vietnamese guy who got killed during the war and when I met her the boy was about the size of a loaf of bread, a little, little kid—he never knew any other father except me. I didn't tell him until he was fifteen, because one time I said when he's about seventeen or so he's going to look in the mirror and realize I'm not his real father. He's very oriental-looking, but he's a real great kid, just like he's my own kid. And we have two of our own.

My sleep is not disturbed at all by war memories. I was one of the very few survivors off one ship that went down off the coast of Brazil in World War II. And I won't say I wasn't scared, but the only thing that bothered me was the first week or two I was home was when the telephone rang. To me it sounded like a general alarm. But I got over that in a couple of weeks. And I went in to get the *Mayaguez* out in 1975, too. But that's another story.

If I had to do it all over again, I'd do it in a minute. In fact, nothing would give me greater pleasure in the whole goddamned world than to walk into my goddamned house in Tay Ninh and blow that Communist provincial chief's ass away.

CHAPTER IX

Marines

Major Jim Kean
"There Has to Be a Better Way"

I had gone through the Amphibious Warfare School [AWS] as part of my intermediate level training. I had been in Quantico, Virginia, teaching at the Basic School for Marine Officers when a quota came up for the school. It was my time to go. Interestingly enough, Oliver North taught at the Basic School as well and we went to AWS at the same time. When I finished the school in the summer of 1973, because I was available on the one hand and because I had learned to speak Chinese and my undergraduate degree from Berkeley had been in Asian studies, the Monitor Shop at the Headquarters, U.S. Marine Corps, called me and said there was a billet open in Hong Kong. "Would you like to go to Hong Kong?" they asked me.

I said I would swim!

It was an accompanied tour, one of the few times that I was ever going to have the opportunity to take my family with me overseas. The Marines traditionally send their people overseas unaccompanied. I became executive officer for Company C, Marine Security Guard Battalion, Hong Kong. The commanding officer, Major Don Evans, was due for rotation in a year, and I was given the chance to succeed him. I was soon after promoted to major and qualified by rank to hold the billet.

My responsibility at the time included the Marine Security Guard from the Indian subcontinent all the way to Peking, Tokyo, and down to Wellington. There were twenty-three embassies and various consulates in the region. I split up the travel during the first year with my commanding officer. It gave me a chance to grow into the office of commanding officer.

As CO of the unit, I traveled on a regular basis to each of the embassies and consulates. They had to be inspected every six months. And there were other times when I had to go out to solve an immediate problem. Some kid had gotten into trouble, usually over a woman, and I had to take care of the problem. Well, that travel and experience gave me a much broader perspective as to what was actually happening in Asia. I got a feel for what the Indians felt about what was happening and what the Japanese and the Koreans were thinking.

When I went into a post, because of my clearances, I got to talk to political affairs officers, CIA people, and State Department people. It was just an amazing education. That was when I became really sensitive about Vietnam.

Then the roll-up came in Vietnam. It was so sudden. I guess there were plenty of educated people who said that it was a long time coming and that it had finally happened. But it seemed so sudden to me. First there was the NVA attack in March of 1975 on Ban Me Thuot. Then the withdrawal of the South Vietnamese Army from the central highlands. It was just like a tidal wave after that. A tidal wave of North Vietnamese troops and armor. The South Vietnamese regulars pulled out of the central highlands at precisely the time the North Vietnamese had decided to make a concerted effort to move in there. And suddenly everything just fell apart.

Once people started to run, they just kept on running. Units dissolved, and the poor guys who were committed, the guys who were going to die on their howitzers, literally did that. Or they became so isolated they were lost. Some of them are still up there fighting to this day—lost.

If you had traveled at that time in Southeast Asia you would have seen some curious things; and I'll give you an example. Laos was under joint occupation prior to the fall of Cambodia and the rollback in Vietnam. There were Pathet Lao in the capital as well as government forces, walking on opposite sides of the street. Well, about the time the trouble started in Vietnam and Cambodia, there was an increase in tension in Laos. It looked like we were approaching a confrontation. The Pathet Lao in Vientiane began to be replaced slowly, man-for-man, by regular hardcore North Vietnamese soldiers dressed in Pathet Lao uniforms. The Pathet Lao were initially guerrilla-type forces and not hardened military. Then all of a sudden we started to see traditional well-trained and well-disciplined soldiers in there, and the people knew that the handwriting was on the wall.

Then Cambodia crumbled.

I was in Washington, D.C., in the spring of 1975. I had gone back to Washington for a conference. Then a message came in to Marine Security Guard Battalion Headquarters. It was an operational-immediate message saying that there was trouble. It looked like they were going to have to evacuate Phnom Penh. My battalion commander gave me the information. And I told him, "Well, with your consent, I'm going to get my butt back there." I went back to Bangkok.

Actually Phnom Penh—Operation Eagle Pull—was a piece of cake. First, because the American ambassador, John Gunther Dean, was virtually a Marine general in mufti. He had the mission there down to 200 or less key types and there was a single field where a Battalion Landing Team (BLT) could set down and put up a quick perimeter, throw everybody on the helicopters, and leave. The old man came out with the American flag neatly folded. It was just like a textbook exercise. Phnom Penh was reachable by the fleet. A Battalion Landing Team went in, secured the area, extracted the people, and bundled them all up in a very tidy military operation. That is exactly what happened. I kept five of the Marines from Phnom Penh in Bangkok and I made arrangements for further reassignment of the other Marines who came out. Then I went home to Hong Kong. But dramatic events continued to unfold. It suddenly looked like all over the map in South Vietnam the pressure points were starting to blow. The alarms were sounding. I watched the situation build up near Danang as we were getting information back. And as soon as I was able to obtain permission from Battalion Command in Washington, I went into Vietnam again.

I arrived there on April 19, I traveled in civilian clothes. All of the Marines working for the Department of State wore civilian clothes when they were off duty or when they traveled.

It was not chaotic, really. I think what I saw was a real ominous tension. All of a sudden people were dusting off plans that had been written in 1973 for emergency evacuation, and they were looking at them and saying, "Oh, Jesus, this is bullshit; now what do we do?" And about that time CINCPAC—Admiral Noel Gayler—began to send people in to assist. General Richard Carey as the Marine brigade commander came in and looked around. And the Air Force communications people came in and looked around. They concluded that they would have to put something together soon if they were going to move many people out of there.

At that time I was Commander of Company C, Marine Security Guard Battalion, and Regional Marine Officer, Department of State, Far East. In Vietnam I had the responsibility for administering the Marine security guard in Danang, Nha Trang, Can Tho, Bien Hoa, and Saigon, all as part of my overall responsibility with the State Department. The Danang and Nha Trang people came to Saigon when those cities fell to the NVA. And several of those people had a rough experience coming down. They got evacuated out of country immediately. There were a few others whose experience had not been so bad. But essentially everybody from Danang and Nha Trang went out of country. The Bien Hoa people, once they pulled back to Saigon, I kept around.

Remember now, those guards were generally young Marines. And young Marines reserve the right to bitch about absolutely everything. This was probably the most exciting thing that had ever happened in their lives. And if you scratched the surface you would probably get them to admit it. "Oh, boy. It's exciting. It's scary, but I'm sure glad I'm here." I do not mean to be facetious about this. I think that it is absolutely true. But after it was all over, there were some very strong reactions. Some of the experiences those kids went through were just incredible. And in the end the experiences left some deep scars. But we only found that out a long time after the fact. At the time there was so much tension and excitement and they kept control. God knows what they experienced and what they saw—children and babies crushed, and people killing each other and getting trampled in the panic, and things like that.

I was the commander, but I couldn't see everything that went on. I mean some kids might have specific tragedies where lovers were left behind, or close friends. And there was no hope of ever seeing them alive again. Things like that happened all the time. And unless they came to me and told me about it, I didn't know it had happened. In some cases I could do something. I sent some kids over the wall of the Embassy to retrieve some people. And typically they would come back and with a smile and salute and say, "We got 'em, Major. Thanks." And after that, you know, I wrote them up for a little award, and by and large I put down everything I thought that they probably did so that they could get a piece of ribbon on their chest for it. But if the true story were known, they might have rated a much higher medal. It was just one of those impossible things.

In my opinion Ambassador Graham Martin, who was almost literally dragged into that job in Saigon, was committed to doing what he felt was the very best for the United States and for our ally, South Vietnam. He's a tough old son of a bitch, really. And he was committed to having the U.S. stay there and honor its commitment to the South Vietnamese people. There is no question in my mind today about that. Because he was a tremendous force and had a monumental ego he probably erred on the side of thinking that by the singular force of his personality and the fact that he was so damned tough he would see this thing through in spite of all the lesser lights around him and in Washington. He might be the subject of criticism then and today, but remember, he was the guy in charge, and anytime you've got a guy who takes the reins and tries to run with them and does his best job, I have a real hard time sitting in judgment on him later. I felt that Martin was committed to keeping us there as long as possible, and he probably did not want to do anything that would precipitate a rush that might make it look like we were going to pull out of there without warning. He was trying to avoid disaster. And quite frankly, up until about five days before we actually left, he was successful because things were relatively orderly and calm. But then all hell broke loose. There were a lot of people who were making plans. But how can you possibly cope with moving large numbers of people around in a short period of time with seventeen enemy divisions squeezing in on you? How do you even anticipate gridlock in the city streets? Well, you do the very best you can. And they laid out a plan for military and Air America helicopter lifts off the rooftops and putting as many people on the buses as they could to reduce the congestion of vehicles in the streets. But, you know, I'm sure that if you went to Washington and you looked at Civil Defense manuals for what happens in the event of a nuclear attack on Washington, it probably has bus-driver assignments to drive people out of town. That's how unrealistic plans can be.

And the plans that were done earlier were available, too. They had been written by people who had no comprehension of what might happen. So once the big boys started coming into town and they saw what was needed, then the real plans were made. They said we were going to need specific communications systems, and they addressed all of the major issues that they were likely to confront. Yet, even with all of that, in the end it was makeshift. And when I say makeshift, it was. You know, you put enough helicopters in, you have the ships in the South China Sea, you've got Marines, and you've got all these communications capabilities, and yet when push came to shove, they ended up using hand signals and yelling, "Hey, Roy!"

During the evacuation, I talked to General Carey out on the *Blue Ridge* through the helicopter crew chief's headset. Each time a bird would come into the zone, I would run up to the crew chief and he would give me his microphone, and I would talk to the general on the ship.

Now all along, in the planning phase, there had been a discussion of two lifts of CH-46s off the roof of the Embassy. They would be for the ambassador and the final party. The way they figured it, they would handle about twenty people per bird. So we would be taking probably somewhere between twenty and forty people out of the Embassy. Everybody else in the Embassy and the city would be ferried over to Tan Son Nhut, and then at some convenient time everything would be turned off and the ambassador himself would depart.

By the last few days of April, we were on duty twenty-four hours a day. I had arranged with Master Gunnery Sergeant J. J. Valdez to have the Marines who went off duty to stay at the Embassy and not go back to the Marine house. They brought their gear into the Embassy grounds and were sleeping on cots in the building by the swimming pool. We anticipated that things were going to get worse and then all of a sudden they would go to hell in a handbasket. So I was there day in and day out, and I was in touch with Marvin Garrett, the Mission Warden, so I knew what he was thinking. We were lining up our ducks. We were conducting meetings among ourselves, the Marines, to figure out what we were going to do and what our options were if we had to button up the building; if we had to bring our people inside the building and keep other people outside the building, how we were going to get off the building, and things of that nature—details.

In the Embassy itself, the Embassy detachment under Valdez was there and additional people who had come in from Bien Hoa. Gunnery Sergeant R. W. Schlager and a couple of other young Marines who had been out at the Bien Hoa post were now part of the Embassy detachment. The security for the DAO was made up essentially of people from the Army, the Air Force, and some other people. Well, during the week they said they needed some additional help in the form of trained security-guard-type people. So they had asked Wolf Lehmann, the deputy chief of mission, for some assistance, and, initially, I told Valdez to just tell them "No." But later on it looked like they were really going to need them, and I went up to see Lehmann myself, and I said that I did not think it was a good idea. And I was told then, "No, it is going to happen." He said they had to have—I think the number was sixteen, to assist in manning security on the fences. So I called the DAO and talked to a Marine colonel and a Marine major who were already out there, and I said to them, "Look, if these kids are sent out there, can you look after them? Can you make sure that when they start making up the helicopter teams, when it comes time to get the hell out of there, that my Marines will be part of it? Because I know for a fact that there is no way in hell we are going to be able to get across town if this thing blows, you know. We are just trying to best-guess everything."

They said they would take care of the kids I sent over there. So, under Lehmann's orders I had to send a senior staff NCO [noncommissioned officer], a marine gunnery sergeant named Martin and fifteen other young Marines. And we took those Marines who were relatively new to the post and with the sprinkling of people who had been around and didn't mind going out there. They understood that they would probably leave from there. Lance Corporal Darwin Judge and Corporal Charles McMahon were in that group. Judge and McMahon! Judge and McMahon were brand-new. They had just checked into the detachment and they had not been broken in to any formal routine at the Embassy, so it just made sense to put them out there with that group.

It was a little after 4:00 a.m. on the morning of the twenty-ninth of April. The approaching NVA started to shell Tan Son Nhut. Some of their rockets fell on the DAO compound. Then I got the news that there were Marine casualties out at the DAO. I remember the phone call distinctly. We were using just a regular Saigon telephone to call back and forth to get information. I talked to one of the Marine NCOs, and then I talked to an Army colonel, and I ended up talking to everybody out there that I could get on the line. The mission warden told me that two of my kids had been killed—Judge and McMahon—killed instantly by a direct hit, and that he had gone out to the scene to see to the picking up of the remains. He told me that there were really no bodies left. There was a charred stump and some other body pieces. He put them all in body bags. The bags had then been marked, put in the mission warden ambulance, and taken to the Seventh-Day Adventist Hospital. That was the standard operating procedure for any deaths that occurred. So I was satisfied that everything had gone by the book. I was trying to satisfy myself so that the messages could be released to the United States and the families could be notified, and that there would not be any error in the report. I was planning on talking to a responsible officer who had seen the incident and could tell me the cause, because there was no way in hell that I was going to leave the Embassy and look the scene over for myself. The South Vietnamese had moved some numbers of aircraft from Bien Hoa air base. They moved them down to Tan Son Nhut and, of course, those aircraft became the target of the North Vietnamese who were coming in. When they set up their artillery out in the Bien Hoa area, having gotten that close, they started shooting at the aircraft at Tan Son Nhut. The Defense Attaché Office compound out there was on the gun target line, and if there were any errors in trajectory—and there were bound to be some longs or shorts in the shooting—the shorts were going to fall right on the DAO compound. I quite frankly don't think that the North Vietnamese intended to hit within the DAO compound. They were really just shooting at the South Vietnamese aircraft.

It was my responsibility to be able to land the helicopters. I had looked at several sites outside the Embassy walls and had written them all off. Inside the Embassy grounds I came to the conclusion that we had to get rid of a large tree that blocked access to helicopters landing. Ambassador Martin had spoken to me personally and told me that if I laid one finger on that tree that I would be in very big trouble. It became a symbol. There were a lot of jokes about that tree, let me tell you. Someone actually strung a rope around the tree and tied a fire axe to it with a little sign that read, "Feeling frustrated? Take a whack."

Well, I kept my eye on that tree, because as long as it stood there we could not land helicopters safely. I can't remember the precise time when the decision was made to cut it down. It was late afternoon, probably before three o'clock, when Martin finally acquiseced and said, "All right, go ahead and take the tree down." Then we worked pretty quickly. There was a combination of mission warden people, Seabees, Marines, and even some newsmen who worked together to bring it down—Aussie and New Zealand newsmen. And they had that damned tree down and cut up and out of the way and the shavings all cleaned up and the place hosed down in almost no time at all. And when they finished with that, I told the Marines and Seabees to go out and find me some luminous paint because we wanted to make a big luminous H, thinking that if we had to land helicopters there soon, then there was no way we were going to get everybody out of there before dark. So we were under the gun to have things done by five that afternoon.

I knew that time was starting to run out. But I was still feeling calm. And I asked the ambassador to let his feelings be known that ultimately they were going to have to divert a regular schedule of birds out of the DAO and over to us to get things moving, because we could not take everyone out by just using the rooftop landing zone. We were going to have to bring the big birds in there to move bodies.

Well, shortly after the birds started to fly into Tan Son Nhut, I was talking to Colonel A. M. Gray who was in charge out there, and he knew we had a problem with crowd control. He agreed to send me some additional Marines. I think there were about a hundred young Marines from Colonel George Slade's BLT 2/4 who arrived to help us at the Embassy.

Beginning with a shelling back on the night of the twenty-eighth, the Vietnamese declared martial law at night. And the fear started to grow and gradually turned to panic. The Vietnamese began to gather outside the Embassy. And I started to get real concerned. By the afternoon of the twenty-ninth, my guess was that we had as many as ten thousand people outside the Embassy, and perhaps 160 Marine guards to secure the perimeter. There were not enough Marines to man those walls and to keep people from coming over into the Embassy. The walls were pretty substantial, but once the people made up their minds to come over, then there was no way in hell we could hold them back. We put our men on the walls to ensure that the people outside couldn't just jump or climb over. We didn't know, after all, who was coming in. And we knew for a fact that (this was generally known by all the Marines) the people outside were merely Vietnamese wanting to go to America. But in those groups there were also some real troublemakers, and there might be some assassination squads and some guys with demolition materials or something like that. We were getting those warnings from the Vietnamese military through the CIA all afternoon.

The ambassador wanted to drive his limousine outside the gate and around to his quarters, and he asked me (in fact this was filmed by a news crew on the scene) to open the gates. I responded, "Well, sir, I'll try." And so Gunnery Sergeant Schlager and a couple of young Marines and I tried to break open the gate, and there was just no way in hell that we could do it. So I went back to Martin and told him, "Sir, with all due respect, there is no way in hell that you are going to drive that car out of here. I recommend that you move back upstairs." Well, at that he was fuming. He got out of his car, he was livid, and he slammed the door. Then he walked away. And I said to Valdez, "I think after this I'll be demoted to PFC [Private, First Class]." But later in the afternoon, Martin came looking for me, and when he found me he touched me on my shoulder and said, "You're doing a good job." He was like that. There was a tremendous amount of pressure.

So, I'll be goddamned if he didn't just walk over to his house with his personal guard unit. We threw a group together and went out the back gate over by the French Embassy and walked down the street to the quarters. The Marines went in there and they used thermite grenades to destroy everything in the safe. There was a jeep in the garage at the house, and we set it up so that we could make a run from the house to the Embassy and bring Martin back in. And when he came back, we knew that it was just a matter of time before he would leave the country.

There was a two-way door built behind the recreation compound dining facility that went right into the French Embassy. I think that Martin's original plan was to go in there if everything came apart and wait to present his credentials. I think that he planned to stay in the country. But the plan was changed as the hours passed.

During the course of the afternoon and evening we knew that there were still a lot of people outside the Embassy that we had to get in. And we could not open the gates. So if there was someone out there that we wanted to bring in, then we'd go and we put a bunch of people on the wall, reach down, grab him by the collar and the hair, and just yank him up and over the wall, poor bastard. To the Marines it was like moving meat. It was absolute chaos. I heard stories all afternoon about what was happening out there along the wall, strange things. Sad things. One Marine was handed a paper bag filled with uncut gems. He handed it back. It belonged to a wealthy Chinese businessman who just wanted to get his family out of the country before it was too late.

We had chained and locked the gates. And we had Marines manning them. We were not going to open those gates under any circumstances because the press of people, once the gates were cracked, would swing them wide open, and there was no way to stop the flood that would pour in.

All of the time I was very conscious of exactly what we were doing. We were running. Some of the young Marines, of course, looked at it another way. As far as they were concerned, the Americans were still involved in that war, and that was that. Maybe a lot of people felt that way, but really, officially, in '73 we were done. It was now time for us to go, and if we had to get out, this was maybe the only way we were going to do it. It was either that or stay and refight the whole damned war. There was also the distinct possibility that the NVA would come marching right in. I mean, hell, they had seventeen divisions approaching Saigon. Seventeen divisions! I think, though, that the way the North Vietnamese had come down and formed themselves around the city, they were sort of inviting us to leave. They literally created corridors for the helicopters to come in and go out without there being any hostilities. They did not want to mix it up with the Americans, that seemed clear. The danger, of course, lay in the fact that any time you have troops in contact with troops at the small-unit level, you cannot always control everything that goes on. If and when they started to exchange fire with U.S. troops, then you had a whole new ball game. Then we were back in the war.

And, of course, the Seventh Fleet had about nine thousand Marines who were confined in an instantaneous alert for the past forty-eight hours. They had been locked up aboard ship and they were all armed to the teeth and pissed off.

There was some difficulty during the afternoon for the birds gaining access to the LZ [Landing Zone]. The fact that nobody got hurt is a testament to the professionalism of all of the people who were flying. They did a marvelous job. They were getting shot at by a bunch of knuckle-heads—you know there were looters and all kinds of people who had stolen weapons. We called them cowboys. You could tell exactly where they were once twilight came because then you could see the tracers, and I would tell a helicopter pilot coming in, "They're firing at you." And he'd reply, "We know, we know." Several of the helicopters had bullet holes in them. They were just sitting ducks. If the cowboys were in a building across the street from the front of the Embassy, if we saw fire coming from that area, then we got the word out to the Vietnamese national policemen, who then made an attempt to go in there and clean out the jerk who was doing the shooting.

The helicopter pilots had other serious problems. They had about a seventy-foot vertical descent to get into the Embassy. They had to come over, hover, and then descend seventy feet into this hole, and there wasn't that much room. Had we lost one helicopter, it would have been all over, believe me.

They loaded the birds up with as many people as they could take. Then, instead of doing what they call a "translational" maneuver, where you get the bird off the ground and then lean it forward, they had to go straight up. There was no room for a translational. They literally had to go straight up seventy feet. I recall one helicopter distinctly, the one that Ken Kashiwahara of ABC was on. Oh, hell, it tried to take off and it couldn't, and they got some people off and it tried again and it couldn't, and they took more people off, and finally we got enough off so it could lift off. We asked the pilot to take the underpowered son-of-a-bitch and park it.

While the evacuation was going on, I heard stories about high Vietnamese military officials running. But I didn't actually see any of it myself. Marines called me and told me that they had seen a high-ranking Vietnamese get in a C-141 out at Tan Son Nhut, buckle up and leave. In the mayhem out there it was not unusual to see some people just cut and run. We knew that our mission was just to be firemen. We were to stay there until the bitter end. We stayed and watched an awful lot of people run.

It got to be noisy, too, with all the people and the birds coming in and out. And it got to be somewhat disorderly, too. I would say it was less orderly than JFK [Airport] in New York and more orderly than, say, a Peruvian soccer match.

All afternoon and night there was a working assumption that everyone inside the Embassy grounds would go. It was never announced, I don't think, or there was never any official announcement. But you know even Marine pilots can't fly forever. They have to run out of gas at some time. They have to rest and sleep some time. But we believed that everybody was going to get out. So that kept the place relatively calm.

But there was always the potential for panic. There were always frantic people, naturally. We got as many people on a lift as we could and then we would count to see how many we had left, and those left behind were always a little nervous. But we just kept right on working. And in that way, by concentrating on the job at hand, we kept the panic factor to a minimum.

My job was sort of communications control. I had one of those Motorola walkie-talkies, so I was in contact with all the Marines. I had to go up to the LZ on the roof of the Embassy. I guided some of the birds in and out. The pilots would spot me, and I would guide them in. I could see what was going on up on the roof and I could see the walls from there. It made sense to me to be very visible and at the center of things—to take charge. And that's just what I did throughout the day and night. I had a bad ankle, too, and I recall that the damned thing swelled up almost to the point where I couldn't walk any more.

To get any instructions from Martin himself, I had to find him. There came times during the night when I was convinced that I'd better get the word from the old man himself so I would know what the hell was happening—what the plan was. I would run up the stairwell or the elevator to his office and then speak with him. Either that, or I'd go up on the roof and get on the headset and talk to the ship and then come all the way back down. That's what I seemed to be doing most of the time, running back and forth. One time I got on the elevator with Valdez, and the old man—Martin—was on there with Tom Polgar, the CIA station chief. Polgar had made a misstatement of some sort, and Martin apparently learned of it and didn't like it. I remember distinctly how mad Martin was. Martin told him, "If I ever hear you say anything like that again you are going to spend the rest of your career in Antarctica." All the time Valdez and I were trying very hard to be invisible.

Martin was vigorous at the time. But remember that for seventy hours or more he had had little rest, and he was not a young man and it was taking its toll. We were really making it up as we went along. But things sort of fell into place. As night fell and there was still a crowd inside the Embassy grounds I realized that we were going to need lights and the standing lights in the Embassy were not going to work. So we got the mission warden vehicles that were still in there and we swung them around into a semicircle and we made sure that they had gasoline. Then we started the engines and let them idle and left the lights on. We checked with the helicopter pilots when they came in and asked them, "Can you see okay?" And they responded, "Yeah."

But then late in the night it got critical. We learned that there was going to be a limit imposed. Then we had to run around counting people to see who was going to get out and who was not going to get out. It was grim.

The problem was always leakage. There was no way in hell Martin could ever give an accurate assessment of the numbers. I think we probably ended up taking 2,500 people out of the Embassy. And any time during the night the number of people inside the Embassy grounds seemed to remain steady.

Early in the evening there was a pause in the flights in conjunction with making the decision to fly after dark. All along during the day they assumed that no birds were going to fly after 5:00 P.M. But then they made the decision that they would fly after dark. Then they had to decide how long after dark they were going to fly. I was told later that General Lou Wilson, who would soon be Commandant of the Marine Corps but who at the time was Commanding General of the Fleet Marine Corps, Pacific, had directed that the birds would continue to fly as long as there were people in the Embassy and the DAO. They continued to fly, and then there was a second lull. It was at that time that we got word that the President of the United States had directed that there would be only twenty more lifts.

It happened like this. A corporal up on the roof with a machine gun called me and said, "I got the ambassador's bird up here." And I said back, "Hold it there. I need some instructions." And then I went up to the roof.

A bird was in the zone waiting to take Martin and his party out. The bird was instructed specifically to pick up the ambassador. The ambassador had not yet come up to the LZ. So I got on the crew chief's headset and I spoke to General Carey himself and Carey told me that the President of the United States had directed that the ambassador would now leave. And the only flights that would be flown after that would be for—and I remember the term because it seemed so funny to me at the time—"U.S. and amphibious personnel." Carey was repeating to me what the word from on high was. I explained to Carey what my situation was. "My Marines are on the wall and there's the front door of the Embassy, and between the Marines and the front door of the Embassy there are some four hundred people who are still waiting to be evacuated." I don't remember my exact words, but I said very carefully, "I want you to understand clearly that when I pull the Marines back to the Embassy those people will be left behind!" And I wanted that clearly understood because I did not want to be the person who was responsible for leaving all those people behind. I was quite prepared to take them out, and I knew that his orders did not include those people. I knew that my transmission was being broadcast in the war room on the ship over the loudspeaker and that the people who were in the command central on the U.S.S. *Blue Ridge* were listening to it. And Carey understood that. He repeated his order: "I want you to understand that the President of the United States directs."

I said, "Yes, sir."

During the time the ambassador was waiting, I had the young Marine corporal out on the roof with his machine gun holding the helicopter. I told him I didn't want that bird to leave until this was all resolved. Then I went and told the ambassador's group what my orders were. That's when Ken Moorefield made his historic statement to the ambassador: "It's time to go." Martin looked over at me for a moment. He didn't say anything, and he didn't show any emotion. He just looked tired. He knew that this sad moment would be coming sooner or later. Suddenly, it had arrived. Then he went upstairs and got into the bird and left Vietnam. He was carrying the American flag with him.

I left the office and went downstairs. Colonel John Madison of the Army, who had been a member of the Joint Military Team set up under the Paris Agreement, came over to me and I had to tell him that there were no more flights for the civilians and that it was time to go. There was a real hassle at that moment. Madison wanted all the civilians to get out. I told him there was no way. He said he would refuse to leave unless we took those 400 people with us. I told him that I had my orders. I told him we could sort all this out on the boat. But right now it was just time to go. And at that moment Madison's number-two man bolted for a helicopter. He wanted to make sure that he was going to be on one of the flights out. Madison just looked at me in grim dismay. He didn't know what to do. Then he threw up his hands, turned around, and left. There were many good people left behind in those 400 within the Embassy grounds. And I still feel bad about that.

Over in the recreational area on the other side of the wall by the swimming pool there was a cash-sales liquor outlet. Several South Korean diplomats had broken in there. They had a little too much to drink and they fell asleep. And when they woke up, the evacuation had ended. So when they came out of their alcoholic stupor, it was the Korean equivalent of "Ohhhh, fuck! The helicopters have gone without us!"

There were other people drinking during the evacuation, too. A lot of them were drinking but weren't drunk. In the Embassy itself they had set up a bar on the third floor. A lot of the principals got shitfaced during that night. I mean their whole lives were coming apart, right there, in the course of a couple of hours. Quite frankly, that's why I was dealing directly with Martin. I knew that he at least was lucid, even if tired, and

I didn't want to be talking to anybody that wasn't the man himself, particularly somebody who was shitfaced.

Near the end of the evacuation I was really surprised to find a woman in the Embassy. I referred to her affectionately as "Hilda the Milkmaid," because she was big-titted, handy, and strong. She was just great. I think she was a secretary to one of the CIA guys and she was one of those gals who can take charge of a PTA meeting or anything else. She saw the kids and how hard they were working, and she decided to help out, without even being asked. She was running around passing out hot coffee, and asking where else she might be of use. She stopped me one time and made me feel good, because she just grabbed my arms for a moment and said, "You're doing one hell of a job. Can I get you a cup of coffee?" And all I could say was, "Thank you."

After the ambassador and his party left, we had to get all the other Americans out. The arrangement down in the parking lot was that, on command, we would give a signal, I think that it was a red star cluster—that's a hand-held flare. And word went out along the wall to all the Marine NCOs that when the signal was given, people would begin to back towards the doors and form a large semicircle in front of the Embassy; realizing, of course, that once we backed away from the wall the people were going to come over the walls, and also realizing that the people inside the compound were going to freak out because it would occur to them that they were in fact going to be left behind, despite promises throughout the night to the contrary.

So I put people inside the great big mahogany doors of the Embassy, and I told them that as the Marines backed towards them they would have their eyes on the crowd, and that the people inside the door were to reach out and grab these kids and haul them in by the scruff of the neck, yanking them in as fast as possible. Ultimately, I thought, there was going to be a big donnybrook in front of the Embassy door. I wanted to execute the maneuver with as little violence as possible.

That's exactly how it all happened—the red star cluster and the withdrawal. We got down to the point where we thought, "My God, we're only thirty seconds away from pulling this thing off without a fight."

But at that moment, all hell broke lose. The crowd outside realized what was happening. They realized they were going to be abandoned by the United States, and they panicked. Then a great big Seabee chief petty officer in civilian clothes came up. And there was a huge timber that was used to bar the doors of the Embassy when they were closed. Well, he got that thing and he put it behind himself, across the small of his back, wrapped his arms down around it, and started swinging around in a circle. If you got hit with that, you were down for sure. So people stayed back as he spun back and forth. In the meantime, inside, guys were grabbing Marines and all the others and jerking them inside.

I got everybody inside the doors, secured them, and then we pulled down the motor-operated chain-link drop behind the mahogany doors. And it stuck halfway down. So we said, "Oh, to hell with it," and left it like that.

We sent the two elevators up to the sixth floor and froze them there by cutting the power so that they couldn't be used by anybody else. Then we all scrambled up the stairwells to the sixth floor. There were grill gates on the second and fourth floors, and we closed and secured them. There were about sixty of us at the time, and everybody proceeded in a relatively orderly manner to the top of the sixth floor. Then we proceeded along that long hallway from the sixth floor out to the rooftop itself. There was a short climb from the rooftop to the LZ, up some metal ladderworks. We were sending out twenty people per helicopter until we got down to the final eleven.

When there were eleven of us left on the roof, we were the last U.S. ground forces in Vietnam.

And we were all dog-tired. We had been up for seventy-two hours. Some of the kids sat down and stared off into space. The anxiety level was high, believe me. The people who were in the building were terrified—absolutely terrified. They wanted to get out of the country. And they had to get up on the roof to do it and we wouldn't let them. We knew there were people in the building, but we didn't know who was just a terrified civilian and who was a bad guy. Trouble could start at any moment.

Remember, these were young Marines. This would always be their Vietnam experience; this was the time, this was the day they would always remember. And as I looked around at them, I thought, "My God, I came into this mess in '66. But they hardly even know what this is all about. What will they think about this somewhere down the line?"

When the chopper didn't come back to pick us up right away, and as the time passed, some of my kids leaned back and rested. And then they slept.

Daylight came.

We were all curious as to what was going on in Saigon. When we looked out over the city in that early morning light we could see evidence of what had taken place during the night. There had been a lot of looting and trashing and there was still a hell of a lot of activity. We saw trash all over the damned place. In some areas fires were burning and there was smoke billowing up. We lay on the roof and watched, those of us who didn't sleep. I never had it confirmed because there was no way to confirm it, but a cavalcade of cars—and I assumed it was Big Minh, the new President of South Vietnam—came right up the main drag, right in front of the Embassy, with a national police escort, and the men fired at looters just to clear the way so Minh could get through to the National Palace. I think that was him trying to get into position to greet the North Vietnamese Army and to surrender his country.

It was all pretty exciting to us, lying up there. We were watching history being made and we were at the same time part of history. I remember it made a distinct impression in my mind, watching it all. Because we were the last Americans seeing this.

We could see the flashes in the distance of the NVA guns. I had the opportunity to think for two hours. And that's what we were doing, all eleven of us. We were looking back at it and talking about what our experiences had been, and just thinking, "My, God, what a mess." It was very likely, we realized, that we eleven represented the last of the American military involvement in Vietnam.

There were some regrets and some bitterness expressed in that time. That was among the others, however. That was not my feeling, because I felt it was, finally, the best thing. And I thought it was sad. And I recall distinctly feeling much as a fireman might after he does his work all night on a multi-alarm fire. What you end up with is deep melancholy. You are damned glad the fire is out. But you look at all the waste and you can't help but be moved by it.

After we had talked quietly for a time, I did something kind of funny. There was a big satellite dish antenna up there. And out of frustration, I walked over to it. I had a forty-five-caliber pistol and I emptied it into that damned dish.

We put tear gas in the stairwells to discourage people from coming up. We were afraid they might rush out and grab onto the helicopter, trying to leave with us, if they got up to the top.

Steven Bauer at the time had an important job. He was a corporal. He was one of the smaller guys and he fit nicely into a tight spot at the end of the hallway. There was a fire door on each end, and one fire door on the interior side had a fire window in it, one of those small square windows with glass with metal inside. That was smashed out, and people were trying to come through it and push it. Bauer sat in there with some Mace, and anybody that came up to the window he'd give them a little squirt of Mace just to discourage them. We had that whole hallway filled with these big old fire extinguishers and so on to block people from coming through, and Bauer just stayed in there. He acted as our final deterrent.

Then one guy came up the outside of the building to try to get on the roof with us. He got conked on the head and that discouraged him enough. I think that he got almost to the top before someone saw him and dropped something over the side onto him and knocked him off the side of the building.

Towards the end of the night, when the sun started coming up, nobody knew we were up there except for those people who were still hanging around in the hall and in the ladder wells. It was very uncomfortable for them to do that because they would have had to have a damp cloth just to be able to breathe with all the tear gas in there.

I knew how much ammunition we had and how many weapons, if we had to make a last stand if an assault by the North Vietnamese began.

Thoughts like that were going through my mind. But it did not do much good wasting a whole lot of time on them because I just had to deal with the situation at hand.

But I want to emphasize the fact that I felt that the North Vietnamese were doing everything that they could from a command position to allow us to get the hell out of there in an orderly fashion. My concern was not so much the North Vietnamese firing on us at all, but that we would have to fight to avoid capture and that it was no longer technically our war.

We stayed away from the edge and we just sort of sat around. Somebody had a jug and was passing it around—Bobby Frain, I think. We were trying to lie low and wait for that helicopter to come and get us the hell out of there.

Then just before 8:00 a.m. I saw the bird coming to get us. I saw him coming off in the distance, one unescorted CH-46 coming from the east out of the sunrise, heading for us. I saw him before I could hear him. I told the others to get ready. He finally landed about 7:58 or 7:59.

We started to get on the helicopter. I think some of us realized that this was a final, historic moment. We were the last American troops to leave Vietnam. At first everybody ran to the helicopter. Then there were just three of us left on the roof—Bauer and Valdez and I. Bauer had been sitting the furthest away so he was the last one to reach the helicopter. But then, as I recall it, Valdez paused at the tail of the helicopter to snap a picture. In fact, I think he snapped two pictures real quick as everybody got on the helicopter. We were all damned glad just to get out.

As the pilot prepared to lift off, we got a little whiff of tear gas. The pilot himself got some of the gas. None of us had gas masks. The gas was wafting up from the stairwells and it got caught in the down draft and started swirling around and came inside the bird. By that time the pilot just wanted to hurry and get the hell out of there.

We were all quiet once we got inside, just glad to be leaving. Nobody said anything for a moment as we sat there. Then this young kid, Bobby Frain, who was a sergeant, spotted a PRC-25 radio on the floor. It wasn't hooked up or anything. But Bobby Frain picked up the handset as if it were working and acted like someone was talking to him on the radio. The rest of us were just sitting there thinking, "Oh, boy, we are going to get the hell out of here at last." But then Frain yelled over the sound of the chopper, "Hey, Major, they want to know what kind of pizza you want in Manila!" I believe that those were the last words spoken by an American Marine as we left Vietnam for good. We all laughed at Frain's joke. It broke the tension. We laughed because it was a funny statement and because we were so damned happy to be going home at last.

After the bird lifted off he headed for the sea. The Seventh Fleet was down off the Bassac River at that time, the southernmost part of the Mekong Delta. We headed directly for the fleet. As a matter of fact, the helicopter crew had only taken enough fuel on the bird to get in and out of

Saigon. They didn't fill up. We had fuel warning lights on both tanks going back to the *Okinawa*. I became concerned. I saw the first red light come on and the pilot and the copilot started paying attention to it. And then the second light came on, and I said, "Jesus, wouldn't it be something if we ran out of gas before we got home?"

But then we saw the fleet. It was a clear morning. Once we saw the ships we also saw evidence of the remains of a lot of helicopters in the water around them. It was just a zoo out there around the fleet. There were lines on the flight deck of the *Okinawa* where people were being processed and weapons were being taken away and thrown over the side.

I'll bet between the eleven Marines in my group there were at least thirty-six weapons. Some of these kids looked like Pancho Villa when we got on the *Okinawa*. I personally had a .45 pistol, a nine millimeter automatic pistol, and an M-16. The other kids had weapons they had picked up on the roof of the Embassy, to keep as souvenirs. They had some little AR-15's with the collapsible stock, a chromium-plated .32 pistol, Czech machine pistols—every kind of weapon imaginable. You know, as soon as we stepped on board the *Okinawa,* they disarmed us completely and threw all of our weapons over the side. It was pretty sad. But Marines do that all the time. It's the only way, you know, and I guess we forgot about that when we picked up the weapons. Disarming everyone who arrives on board is the only way to make sure that there are no accidental discharges.

We saw the Vietnamese coming out in their helicopters trying to land on the decks of the ships. But I was too tired to stay and watch that. As soon as I went through processing I went and fell into the sack and went to sleep for six hours. Then they woke me up and told me that General Carey wanted to see me over on the *Blue Ridge,* immediately. So I got on the helicopter and they flew me over, but by the time I landed on the *Blue Ridge* there had already been a helicopter before us trying to land on the front end of the ship. It"s not an aircraft carrier, remember. And that Vietnamese bird knocked out some antennas and almost did more serious damage. But they were desperate to get out. They were all around in the air.

When it was all over I was never sure whether or not I was going to get an award or a good kick in the ass for using the tear gas. Ultimately, they gave me a medal, a Bronze Star for meritorious achievement for my part in it all. When I got back to Hong Kong, Bob Lewis and I, my executive officer, sat down, and we prepared, I believe, forty-two awards. These covered Phnom Penh, Nha Trang, Danang, Can Tho, Bien Hoa, and Saigon. After all the reports were in about who did what and what happened, I sat down and I started grinding them out. I know how the system works when it comes to awards and I was concerned that each and every kid who did something get noticed for it in some way. So I did the best I could. In some cases I had good, complete information. And in a few cases I had to fabricate the information—one citation would read a lot like another citation. But I knew that a kid was there and I knew that he had been part of the action and he had done something, so I just talked around it. And I then took them to the consul general and had him sign them in Hong Kong so that the State Department principal was signing the recommendation. That way nobody at Headquarters, Marine Corps, could dismiss it out of hand. As it turned out, I think, each and every person who had something submitted on them got an award. Most of them were downgraded. But somebody got either a Navy Achievement Medal or a Navy Commendation Medal, and it amazed me to find out after the fact how many of those Marines stayed in the Marine Corps. Steven Bauer, for example. The last time I saw him he was still in the Corps and was a gunnery sergeant. Those guys all had a little of what Napoleon's men had. Napoleon remarked about the brave deeds that men will do for a piece of ribbon. And it was amazing to me how many of those guys actually continued to make the Marine Corps a career after that.

We had a helluva drunk in Manila, but the eleven of us never got together again. There was no talk, that I can recall, of a reunion.

I myself stayed in the Corps until July of '83. But, then, I had always been a careerist. I think the evacuation of Saigon would just have to be the most memorable part of my long Marine career.

I was sensitive at that time as to what it all meant. That is the first time that the United States ever truly had to cut and run and admit that we had run out of energy. I remember I said, "Uh-oh. The United States has just had its wedding night. Now where do we go from here?"

I visited the Vietnam memorial. I thought it was beautiful with the names, just the names, inscribed on that black marble. And I felt that maybe when people saw it and read some of the names it would achieve its intended effect.

Apart from the Marine Corps, I am not a joiner. The war was just something that I was involved in because, quite frankly, it was my nature to get into whatever is going on. It was the thing that was happening at that point in my life. I wanted very badly to be a part of it. And it was a major event. It gave me a chance to try to share the experience of my father in World War II.

Every now and then I'll stop and think about something from Vietnam—a face that I saw, a voice that I heard, or a sound or a smell, under different circumstances—and it all comes back. I'll remember one little moment or event. But I never had any of the trauma associated with experiences in the war.

You know, I'll see a picture or hear something on the news, and I'll be back there again. I can think of a dozen examples like that. I'll remember when I saw some absolutely beautiful child, or I'll smell an odor like burning diesel fuel. Or I'll remember when I was out on patrol.

I remember one event in particular, when we were out on patrol. We came across this old mamasan, a little old lady. She had a festering thumb and it was gangrenous. The corpsman washed it and cut away a lot of the dead flesh and did it up with bacitracin ointment. He put this compacted gauze around it and bandaged it all up nicely. When we found her she had it wrapped up, literally, in cow shit with a banana leaf around it. And the corpsman, who spoke a little bit of Vietnamese, and one of the interpreters told her to go see the doctor because if she didn't keep it clean the gangrene was already there and she was going to lose it—or maybe even lose her life, if it spread.

Anyway, that was the message we imparted. We weren't going to surgically remove her thumb out in the field. But we thought we could help her a lot and perhaps save her life.

So, three days later we came through the same village and she waved to us and offered us some fresh coffee. And when she gave us the coffee we saw that she had thrown away what we had given her and had her thumb covered with cow shit and wrapped in a banana leaf again. So that little old lady, who looked to be about 126 but was probably about forty, if that, she was going to die. We were not going to change anything. I was struck by that sort of thing—that sort of revelation. Another time we were out on patrol going through a paddy and a Phantom flew over, real low. And we heard him and looked up and there was a ten-million-dollar aircraft that represented to the people working in this particular paddy something that was simply incomprehensible. I tell you it must have been like a bomber flying over New Guinea in World War II. These people working with a water buffalo and living in huts look up and see that Phantom, and how can they understand what it is or what it is there for? It is incomprehensible to them. All they do know for sure is that it is upsetting their way of life.

I remember seeing all of those people look up at the Phantom for a moment and then go back to work. Those kinds of melancholy moments come back to me again and again.

I'll tell you, those memories are important to me because they are the bottom line. Any time I get caught up in a question like American involvement in Central America I think about those things, because those were real experiences for me. And I say at those times, "Now we can't go down there with our yuppie ideals and solve all of their problems, because we don't have the answers." It could very well be that the best thing that we can do is to stay home, and stay the hell out of it. Except if we want to offer them some economic aid, or support the peace process. We must remember that any time economic conditions in a country polarize between "haves" and "have nots" there is a potential for real trouble. No man worth his salt will stand idly by for long and watch his family starve.

But the very worst thing we could do is to take all of our half-assed military solutions down there and thrust them on somebody who doesn't need them. And that is why I gave up totally on the idea of a military solution.

Believe me, there is no military solution to anything. I think that you must have the capability to defend yourself, but the system today seems to be totally out of control. I am a real peacenik right now. Especially when it comes to the military budgeting process. It's become unbelievable.

The honest-to-God truth is that I won't consider myself very much of a success as a father if my sons or daughters end up as saber-rattlers. I really believe that. I want them to do something constructive—be a good carpenter, build a good wall, write a good book. But I don't want them to make a career in the military.

I don't have any use for guns any more. I wouldn't have one in my house, really. And I am not really crazy about it when my kids go through the catalogue and look at BB guns or look at guns in sporting goods stores. I bite my lip when that happens. I just want to deep-six all that crap.

You know Ronald Reagan is the same age as my father. And I didn't see my father for four years in World War II while Reagan was in Hollywood. But I don't get nasty about that. Reagan at least raised his hand and volunteered to do something. But I do get absolutely furious about some of those war wimps who were around him. All those assholes who were never in the military, those fat old men who sit around and decide that they are going to play macho. And they roll up their sleeves and run off at the mouth and then send nineteen-year-old boys off to die. Always the nineteen-year-olds. That's the tragedy.

And so a President needs to be counseled when he starts listening to the jingoists and starts rattling his saber. He has to remember that there is a whole generation out there now that has grown up and they don't know anything about Vietnam. They are susceptible to all of this Rambo crap. And all you have to do is give them an opportunity and then with all that hot blood they'll go out and fight. And then they'll die. They won't die in Vietnam. That's been done. They'll die in some other place far away.

War is a waste. That's it. I saw it. I survived it. And I can see it still in my mind today. And I know for sure that there has to be a better way.

Sergeant Kevin Maloney
"A Mouthful of Ashes"

Until January 22, 1975, I was assigned to the American Embassy in Warsaw. Then I was transferred to Saigon. Out of the frying pan and into the fire.

I had left Washington the preceding October and gone to Europe for a few weeks. In addition to the regular training that an embassy guard gets, I was trained as a bodyguard. Then I'd served in London and Frankfurt and then Warsaw. I was in Warsaw only ten weeks before they asked me to volunteer to go to Saigon.

I wore strictly civilian clothes in Saigon, and I was Ambassador Martin's bodyguard until the twenty-eighth of April.

When I arrived in January I assumed I would be there a year. But then the "big party" started.

Saigon was secure when I arrived. As a matter of fact, I get a kick out of it when I think about it. The regional security officer told me there wasn't a VC within sixty miles of Saigon.

Saigon was, nevertheless, an armed camp. They had more security there than probably any embassy has ever had. There was an Embassy detachment, and across town at the ambassador's home six of us had the job of protecting the ambassador.

My job was strictly to protect the ambassador. At the ambassador's house we had a communications center and I manned that center. During the later stages there I would help out with communications between the White House and the ambassador. We had several folks from NSC [National Security Council] who would come in and I happened to be there when they did their planning.

The first time I met the ambassador I thought he was the gardener. He was an old fellow walking around with an old set of khaki pants on, loose shirt, just puttering around the yard there. I didn't know who he was. He didn't look like an ambassador to me. But I was introduced to him the day after I got there. He's an impressive man, a gentleman. And a real tough nut. He was in his seventies and kept longer hours than I did.

The ambassador was a stalwart to the end. And he did not want the perception that Americans were leaving. The idea was that it would cause a panic. So we pretty much kept things looking like business as usual.

The evacuation was probably one of the most significant events of my life. On the twenty-eighth of April, I'd been relieved from duty for my own misconduct. I drank too much, and I got to be a problem. As a matter of fact, Major Kean recommended me for court martial. Major Kean said if I did a good job out there, and it reflected, he'd lose the paperwork. When I got back to the States, I got nonjudicial punishment. I was fined and transferred.

I was the sergeant and I was put in charge of several of the men who were guarding the DAO compound. Corporal Charles McMahon and Corporal Darwin Judge were two of the people in my section.

They had only been there two weeks. I hadn't known them long—I'm talking a day. Those two guys were buddies. We couldn't pry them apart, I guess. They arrived at the same time and they stuck together. They were kidding Judge when I got there because he was picking up McMahon's Boston accent.

I took over there just about the time the Vietnamese A-37s attacked. We pumped out a few rounds at them with rifles and pistols.

After the planes left and things quieted down again, we talked. I'm sure you've heard that there are no atheists in foxholes. In fact, Judge was a Christian and he told everybody about his beliefs. He had talked to the rest of the guys in the unit before I joined it out there at Tan Son Nhut. He talked to me about it. I knew he was right and I agreed with him. I had heard it all before. It was my time to make a decision. Well, I became a believer that day. Right there and from that time on my life has been significantly different.

My experience that morning was just as a fellow coming to himself and realizing that the way he has lived his life was awful—I had been in the Marine Corps for four years and I had lived the John Wayne image, the hard drinking, hard loving type of Marine, that stuff that we all grew up on on Saturday morning. It left me kind of empty. There wasn't a whole lot left of me, and that's probably why the drinking was such a devastating thing to me. Just kind of burned out, nothing left. And all the good things that I joined the Marine Corps for, turned out to be just a mouthful of ashes.

Everything was kind of a swirl then. I'd done real well in the Marine Corps. I'd gone from private to sergeant in a very short period of time. I was very successful at it. If I hadn't run into this problem in Saigon I might have been the youngest sergeant major in the Marine Corps.

I posted the guard that night when those two boys were killed.

It was about a quarter to four in the morning. They took the first rocket that came in. I guess it was a 122-millimeter rocket that killed them. I found the motor later. It knocked me out of bed. I was in the building adjacent to where it came in. There was another kid out there with them, too. They were at the corner and he was at a gate. His name was Holmes. He got hit in the head. I got out there and grabbed a rifle. There was small-arms fire going around—turns out it was Judge's ammo belt cooking off in a pile of burning Hondas, so it sounded like machine-gun fire outside the gate.

The rocket looked like it hit eighteen inches from McMahon and Jude. So it hit them almost dead on. You can't aim a rocket that well. It looked like McMahon got the majority of the blast. He was totally dismembered; trunk over here, a hand here, a head there. Judge was in pretty good shape, I thought at first. I got to him and thought he might still be alive. I dragged him away from the fire. But he was dead. Stu Herrington picked up Judge's helmet when he got out there.

That morning things started really rolling. The Vietnamese Air Force tried to evacuate their planes. The C-130s were hit by rocket fire and burned in place. Their crews came back in and we were all ducking shells. You could hear the 130-millimeter artillery going over our heads and slamming into the fuel dump. I saw one C-119 gunship get off and then get shot down.

I guess I was a fatalist at that time and believed if it came, it came, and if it didn't, it didn't. If my number was up, that was it. I don't know if I believe that any more, but at the time I did. I was kind of hard-boiled. And if I was afraid, I wouldn't admit it to myself.

Major Tony Woods was the guy responsible for getting most of the Americans out of Saigon during the evacuation. He and I drove through town with the buses and picked up most of the folks at the hotels, a lot of the press folks. He got a Bronze Star for his action there.

Woods and I grabbed a jeep and started checking out some of the South Vietnamese roadblocks in Saigon. We'd drive up to them and see what they would do, and some of those guys would get pretty hostile. We took our share of being shot at there without doing too much in return. Later on, he and I got separated from Woods in a firefight. He went one way, I went the other.

That was right outside Tan Son Nhut. They made a big deal at the time about us getting out of there without firing a shot—well, I'm telling you what, the people who were saying those things weren't in Saigon.

The ARVN didn't hit us. But some of them did try to. There was a lot of shooting going on in the air, too. Some of the buses got shot up.

Woods and I escorted the buses until we got separated. I was in downtown Saigon and I got a bunch of South Vietnamese in a deuce-and-a-half pick-up [truck] behind us and wouldn't leave and they were all armed. So I went around the block and came up behind them, and wound up looking down the barrel of a half a dozen carbines. The buses moved on to the Embassy, those folks got out there, and as soon as we could get away from the South Vietnamese, I went to the Embassy, too.

I climbed over the wall to get in. I had a camouflage South Vietnamese uniform on. It made it easier to move through town. And I was armed with an M-16 and a .38. That was late in the day, after they had gotten rid of the tree and the helicopters were landing.

I just took up a position at the Combined Recreation Area [CRA] gate for a couple hours until we abandoned the CRA compound there. I guess I was the last one out. Our perimeter was shrinking. I guess a couple of other guys and I went through all the rooms in the Embassy one at a time to get everybody out. Then up onto the roof.

I left on a helicopter just about when the sun was coming up. There were only Marines on the helicopter. We threw away our helmets and flak jackets just so we could squeeze a couple more guys in.

By that time I was so tired I was ready to drop. I remember the helicopter ride out of there, but what I was thinking at the time, I couldn't tell you.

I did look down on Saigon when we went out. I sure did. The sun had just come up. We flew out over the docks and then out over the river, and I remember seeing tracers coming up from probably South Vietnamese shooting in the air, or anti-aircraft guns. We crossed the coast, and that's the last I remember until we landed on the *Okinawa*.

In general I thought it was an incredible loss. And I was there to witness the end of it. I think we turned our backs on those folks. I don't buy that peace-with-honor stuff. We shagged out of there and left them to the North Vietnamese. And you know how kind they are.

I was only twenty-two years old then. It was a turning point for me. I do think about it a lot, still. I may forget a lot of other things in my life, but I won't forget that. Even though it was a tragic experience, I got the brass ring as far as life goes when we left. My life—1975 was the worst year of my life as far as things going against me there, but in retrospect it was a turning point in my life and it led to better things since then.

There was a part of me that died out there, but a part of me that came up out of the ashes, too. It's been a long struggle, but I am doing better now. I found something a lot better in Jesus Christ.

CHAPTER **X**

POW

Dennis Chambers
"Are We Winning the War? Tell Us the Truth"

In August of 1967 I was shot down on my hundred-and-first mission near Dong Hoi, just north of the Demilitarized Zone. I was the copilot on an F-4C. Both the pilot and I survived the crash and spent the next five and a half years in a Communist prison in Hanoi—the "Hanoi Hilton." Before I was shot down I had become disillusioned with the way we were fighting the war. What we were trying to do was absolutely correct. But we were going about accomplishing our goals in the wrong way.

I was stationed in Cam Ranh Bay. I arrived there in March 1967, and after flying my first missions I wrote to my congressman and asked him, "What are we doing here?" We were making a big mistake. Anybody could see that. After I arrived in Cam Ranh I was told that none of us were supposed to go into the town. We couldn't cross the bridge into town because the people there weren't friendly. Not friendly? Cam Ranh Bay? My God. Those people were supposed to be our friends—our allies. And if they weren't friendly, then what was going on?

Then we were bombing things. Wildly bombing everything. We never wasted our bombs by dropping them in the sea. On the way back from a mission, if we had bombs, we'd find something to drop them on. Guys would find something, anything, and bomb it. And I heard stories about army troops who would shoot people because they didn't like the way they looked. There seemed to be no control. And that was in 1967. It got worse later. There was not enough control of the men by the officers. We had so many people there and it was not even a declared war. We would go out and drop our bombs, and I would ask, "Where do we go and what do we do?" And the answer always came back, "We don't know."

Then they tied our hands and told us that there were certain stupid things that we couldn't do. If we spotted a MIG [Soviet fighter plane] we had to identify it as a MIG positively before we shot it down. Do you know what that does to your chances of coming out alive? A MIG can do a lot of things that an F-4C or an F-105 or the F-111 cannot do. So your risk of losing your life while trying to identify the make of an enemy aircraft is fairly high. Then we were not allowed to shoot any boat larger than fifty feet or any boat smaller than twenty feet. So, of course, the Vietcong put everything in little boats and went up and down the rivers safely. So I was bitter about all of that.

And we lied like mad over there. Our airplane count was half of what we said it was. We were losing planes steadily. I was there five months and I was the thirteenth plane to disappear out of Cam Ranh. And the only time that our losses showed up on the statistics is when someone saw the plane go down. If they didn't see you go down, then you didn't go down. It was crazy.

In the camps in Hanoi the American prisoners survived for different reasons. Love and Christianity kept some of the men going. Hatred kept me alive. Hatred for Lyndon Johnson. Hatred for Richard Nixon. Hatred for the war. Hatred for the North Vietnamese. I built up enough hatred to keep me alive.

With my hatred came deep cynicism. When we got out in 1973, they put us on a C-141 to fly out of Hanoi to the Philippines. By that time I had no faith in anything. Especially not in the word of the Communists. I believed that they would never let us out alive. So when we left Hanoi I believed that they would shoot us down. I kept waiting for it to happen. I thought maybe there was a bomb on board or a MIG or a SAM would come at us. I thought to myself, "This is not going to happen. This is too good to be true."

On the plane coming out of Hanoi there was a group of doctors and nurses and some escorts to care for us. And we all asked them the same question: "Are we winning the war? Tell us the truth." And an American officer on board told us, "Absolutely. We basically won the war. They were defeated. The B-52s took care of them and we won." And when we heard that we were all just ecstatic. All of our time in prison had been worth it. There were no sweeter words than, "We finished it." That is what we were told.

Then we got home and found out that we hadn't finished it, and we hadn't won, and we hadn't been told the truth.

When Saigon fell I was living in a home in the Santa Cruz Mountains in California. I didn't watch television, but I read the paper every day and I listened to the news on the radio. As I heard and read about what was happening over there I had this tragic I-told-you-so attitude. What was happening was just the last of so many tragic mistakes over the years.

At the end of April when I started hearing about the refugees and all of those poor people trying to get out, I just felt sick. All of the people who did work for us over there got screwed. We left so many of them behind. American promises meant nothing anymore. Now our word isn't worth shit in Asia. What we should have done, without doubt, is to guarantee the safety of our friends. But the public was so anti-Vietnam. And the politicians were so anti-Vietnam. And that was ironic. If they had been anti-Vietnam earlier, all of that wouldn't have happened. I blame our entire country for leaving those people behind in Vietnam. No one stood up and was counted, no one protested when we abandoned our friends. There were people there who busted their asses for us. And we left them there.

What we should have done was simple. We should have set up a no-man's zone and told the Communists, "If you cross this line, we'll kill you." They understand that. Then we should have taken all of our friends out. We should have said, "Stay away, Russia; stay away, China; we'll be out in six months. If the North Vietnamese interfere with us, we'll wipe Hanoi off the goddamned map."

We should have gone to full red alert. We should have defined what we were going to do and then brought in Russian and Chinese observers just to prove that we were not going back in. We were getting out and we were taking our friends with us. We should have opened up refugee camps here in the United States as a temporary relocation facility for our friends. They did it fast enough during World War II when they turned on the Japanese-Americans. We could certainly have done it as fast in 1975 for our friends.

But we didn't do that. We didn't because we no longer had any balls to do it. We blew it. There was nobody with guts anymore making decisions. Nobody wanted to take chances.

We waited too long. We should not have ended up on the roof of the goddamned American Embassy. Just a strong word from us could have ended the panic. But nobody spoke up. And the goddamned Communists were laughing at us. We got our ankles kicked by a bunch of midgets. Hopefully, we learned something from it.

In Vietnam I lost my ability to love. I can't love any more. And I can't kill anything. I don't hunt and I don't fish and I don't love. When I got home people called me a hero. But I wasn't a hero. I didn't volunteer to sit in a prison camp for five and a half years. I volunteered to fight for my country. I volunteered to fight for freedom. I volunteered to fly an airplane.

I felt, when it all came apart in 1975, that my time in Vietnam had been wasted. I don't have nightmares or bad dreams about it today. I just don't think about Vietnam. I just don't think about it at all.

CHAPTER XI

Washington, D.C.

Robert Hartmann, Counselor to President Gerald Ford
"A War That Is Finished as Far as America Is Concerned"

The Tulane University speech on April 23, 1975, came at a time when the South Vietnamese were crumbling and we were drawing our people down into Saigon. The only issue at the time was protecting the allies who were still with us and getting our people out as safely as possible. The decision to get out was made before this speech. But the timing of this hinged on the fact that if we just suddenly announced that we were pulling out, there was every reason to believe that the South Vietnamese might turn on us and try to prevent us from getting out. They still had control of the airport and the roads around Saigon.

We were in a holding position. The President [Ford] had previously gone to the Congress and asked them for more money, which was basically money that would prop up the South Vietnamese government so we could get an orderly withdrawal, but the Congress didn't see it our way and didn't give us the money. This was after General Fred Weyand went out and came back, and his assessment was rather bleak. He said in order just to hold any part of South Vietnam, even Saigon, we would have to put in more support. Not troops, but air support from carriers committed to the thing, and that would be a rather big commitment, which the Congress and the country would not have supported. And probably it would delay the inevitable outcome. We weren't willing to start the whole thing over again. So at this point it was simply a matter of *how* we were going to get out, not *if* we were going to get out.

In our early discussions about this speech the President had said to me that he wanted to focus on the future and not on the past. Presumably the kids at Tulane would be less hysterical about the war than other campuses, but this anti-Vietnam contagion was all over the campuses in the country. Rather than to chew over the past and to try to justify the war, though, he wanted to talk about what this generaion was going to be able to do in the future. He wanted to put the war behind us. And he said to me conversationally, "I don't know why we have to spend so much time worrying about a war that's over as far as we're concerned." And I said, "Well, then why don't you just say that?" We were looking for a basic theme for his speech.

Ford said, "Well, I don't think Henry [Kissinger] would like it." And I said, "Well, what do you care whether Henry likes it or not? You're the President, and if that's the way you feel, say it. Sometime at some point it has to be said, and you're the one that has to say it, so why not now?" And he said, "Well, I'll think about it, but you go ahead and see what you can put on paper. Now don't tell anybody about it."

Obviously, he kind of liked the idea. But he wanted to try it out on Henry and others in the military first and see what the reaction would be.

Milton Friedman really wrote the speech, and then I went over it. And at first we left out the section about the war being over. The rest of the speech dealt with the limitless opportunities for young people on college campuses who could do positive things rather than just protest. There was nothing more to protest, we wrote, so they should get on with the business of making a better world.

We had a custom of circulating these speeches around the White House to the people who had some interest in them and also to those who needed to have some advance notion of what the President was going to say, so they wouldn't be taken by surprise and would be able to have some reaction when they were asked about it. And the people we circulated it to varied from time to time depending on the nature of the speech and the subject matter of the speech. But there was always a certain small group we circulated it to, and they would make notes on the copy and we would accommodate them if we could, and if I didn't like what they wanted to change, I would take it in to the President and let him decide. These were all cabinet-level top White House staff. And they usually included people dealing with foreign policy and the military—the Secretary of State and the National Security people in the White House, which for practical purposes was the same thing. Kissinger was Secretary of State at the time, and Brent Scowcroft was the National Security Advisor. He and Kissinger had worked together a long time and their thoughts were similar. Scowcroft was aware of what he didn't have to show Kissinger and what he had better show Kissinger.

This particular speech sailed through without any accretions because it was really just a commencement address, nothing for anybody to raise their eyebrows about. Milt had the speech done and redone after everybody commented on it, and we set off on the airplane for New Orleans. We had given the speech to the press people and the President went over it and edited it on the plane. He always made a few changes himself. While we were on the plane Milt and I worked out this one paragraph of the speech that declared that Vietnam was "a war that's over as far as America is concerned." And the President okayed that real quick, and I knew just where we were going to stick it in and we did. Now the statement had not been in the copy that had circulated initially, but it was in the text that was passed out just before he made the speech. It was put in there so innocuously that the traveling press didn't think it was as sensational as it turned out to be. If you read that in the middle of a long text, as the press did, you wouldn't see it as a very sensational statement in the context of the time. Everybody knew we were getting out of Vietnam.

It was a very warm crowd, and they gave the President a good warm welcome and some applause here and there when he spoke. At first he made a couple of jokes about football or something. And then when he got to this line about Vietnam he said, "Today America can regain the sense of pride that existed before Vietnam. But it cannot be achieved by refighting a war that is finished as far as America is concerned." Well, he didn't even finish the sentence before the cheering began. And the place just erupted. The kids jumped up and down and were whooping and hollering, and it took the press by surprise because they hadn't underlined that in their text. And so everything else he said was lost. That was the story. He quieted them down and then they whooped it up some more. It was almost like a national convention crowd. I wasn't really surprised. I think I was surprised by the intensity of it, but I wasn't surprised that the kids picked it up. That was just what they were waiting to hear somebody say.

The President was delighted by the way it had gone over, and he was highly elated by the success of this trip. Presidents do like to hear the rafters ring. Then somebody sent word up to the President's cabin that the press would like to talk to him on the flight back to Washington. Ron Nessen passed the word up and I said, "Wait a minute. There is no way you can top this. And I wouldn't do it if I were you. Let this thing stand and talk to them tomorrow because there's no way to make it any better." But the President brushed this all aside and said he was going to go back and he was more than a match for the press anyway. Most presidents think they are, and most of the time they are. So he went back to the press section of the plane and I tagged along with him. They started asking him questions and one of them was, in effect, "Did you realize or did you mean what you said, and did you know nobody's ever said that before?" And he said, "Yes, there has to be an end to these things sometime and even though things didn't turn out as well as I hoped, this was the end."

Then somebody asked, "Did Kissinger approve of this speech?" And he said, "No!" Presidents never like to have it suggested that other people tell them what to say or not to say, particularly Kissinger, who was prone to do that.

So that is when we really got in trouble. And I interrupted him and said, "Mr. President, we did circulate this speech as we always do to those who normally see the speeches in advance, and I believe that General Scowcroft signed off on it. And we assume from that that it had the approval of the foreign policy people." I think Kissinger was out of town when we circulated the speech. But that was just a coincidence. And besides, the line hadn't been in the first draft.

The President reacted to my words as if to say, "Keep your mouth shut while I'm having a press conference. I don't need to be coached."

The next morning, back in the White House, my phone rang and it was President Ford. He said, "Bob, Secretary Kissinger is here"—and he had kind of a chuckle in his voice since he knew he would be and I knew he would be—"and would you mind coming in and bringing Milt Friedman with you?" Now Milt Friedman was sleeping late this day, and I had the office right down the hall in the West Wing. I said, "Mr. President, I'll be right in." So then I got hold of Paul Theiss, who was the editor of the speechwriting department. He didn't really have much to do with this circus, but I wanted some company. And I wanted a witness with me.

Kissinger didn't intimidate me. After all, I knew who the guilty party was in this, but I wasn't about to say so. So if Kissinger was going to be mad at somebody, preferably it should be Friedman or maybe me, but I wasn't going to betray the President to him.

So Theiss came running over and we went into the Oval Office. Kissinger was pacing up and down on the rug in front of the President's desk. And Ford said, "Bob, the Secretary is concerned about something in our speech yesterday that he said he had no advance knowledge of." I said, "Well, we circulated it to General Scowcroft, and we didn't know for sure whether he'd seen it or not, but his initials are just as good as anybody's in this room." And the President knew and I knew that this line wasn't in there at the time. But Kissinger didn't know that. I said, "Of course, you made some minor changes on the airplane, as you always do." And then Henry ranted and raved and said, "This has got to stop. I can't hold my head up in front of all these ambassadors with a major statement like this and I don't know about it. I've just lost face." So when he got through, the President looked over at me and said, "Well I think it's an unfortunate misunderstanding; the system slipped up somehow. Just be sure, Bob, that this never happens again."

So I said, "Yes, sir!" and Paul said, "Yes, sir!" and we looked properly cowed and repentant and the meeting broke up.

Kissinger was in a fine temper. He was inclined to blame Friedman, who had done the basic speech, for sneaking this line in at the last min-

ute. If I remember it right, he pounded on the President's desk and de-
nounced Friedman. He didn't denounce me on this occasion—he'd tried
that several times before.

President Ford directed the final evacuation plan at 1:00 p.m., Washington time, on April 28. That is when they finally told Martin, who was
resisting the idea of hauling down the flag, to do it and get out. I was in
the White House during the evacuation. It was very tense, the last days.
The Americans were all crowded into the Embassy, and the crowd outside was pounding at the gate, and they just had a few Marines in there,
which wasn't enough really if the mob had gotten out of control. The
mob wasn't hostile, they just wanted to get out of the country, too.

Ford became disenchanted with the war way back when Johnson was
president. He had always been in favor of a massive offensive and ending
it in a month. But the Vietnam War was lost before Ford became president. His main concern about Vietnam became getting us out in a reasonably acceptable way.

In the end there was some satisfaction that we got them all out with
only two Marine casualties.

There was a concern after this that we would be considered an un-
reliable ally. However, our European allies had been whooping and hollering for us to get out of there. And we paid attention to them.

The process of getting out of Vietnam was all bound up also with the
move on the larger board of normalizing relations with China. The
Chinese wanted us to get out of Vietnam, since then there would be no
excuse for the Russians to be messing around there. We fought half that
war out there with the mistaken impression that the Russians and the
Chinese were enthusiastically supporting North Vietnam. But the fact
was that the Russians were supporting the North Vietnamese, and the
Chinese were just making some little gestures of support. The Chinese
didn't want the Russians down there. But now the Russians are still there
and the Chinese are still worried about it.

Thomas Moorer
"For Christ's Sake, Stop! Stop! Stop!"

When Congress passed the Cooper–Church Amendment in 1971, I guess
it was, and forbade U.S. air action in Southeast Asia, I said at the time
that I thought Saigon would fall as soon as we left or within a short time
after we left. Go back to the Vietnamization program where the idea was
to let the South Vietnamese do the fighting and withdraw U.S. troops.
That came from what was previously the Nixon doctrine, which he announced when he visited with Thieu on Midway Island, that we were
going to provide air assistance and supplies but ground fighting would be
done by local forces. Consequently, we considered that additional air

action, particularly offensive air action, would be required to keep the North Vietnamese at bay after the U.S. forces left. There was always, then, the assumption that we would augment the South Vietnamese air capabilities against the North Vietnamese should they try to come in. Then the Congress cut that out entirely. And that was the end, since there was no longer a deterrent to the North Vietnamese.

Congress had just gone crazy, led by Frank Church and his assault on everything. But anybody who knew anything about the military system knew darn well that if you left the North Vietnamese under complete sanctuary in their own country and left them free to focus their entire effort on South Vietnam without any opposition from the United States or any sophisticated air opposition, the end was just a matter of time.

Congress, in their zeal to bring this war to an end, reflected the impatience of the American people. One thing the American people can't stand is long wars. Whatever it takes in lives and money, get it over with. And we tackle every problem like that. I don't care what it is. We think we can cure it and forget it. We don't have the patience that the Orientals do.

It's crazy. Most of the problems we have are self-inflicted. Sometimes I just think we're nuts. And we do this over and over again.

For instance, I'll tell you the kinds of things we had to deal with at the very beginning. I was probably more involved in it than anybody at the high level. When the North Vietnamese started putting in their SAM missiles, I asked permission from Washington to attack them, because I could have prevented them from setting up any missiles if I had been allowed to attack them at the outset. Of course, you know they built the big missile-assembly building inside Hanoi and there was always a ten-mile circle we couldn't come inside of. And this fellow McNaughton who handled those kinds of things for McNamara says, "Well, they're not going to shoot at you, they're trying to deter you. If they ever shoot at you we'll let you attack them." Of course the first thing they did was shoot down airplanes and kill pilots. We could have prevented that.

Let me tell you about that mining in Haiphong Harbor, because I'm the world's expert on that, I think, because I was so heavily involved in World War II. I went over and laid mines when the British first started in the North Sea. I wrote the first instructions in how to mine with what they call a "ground mine." Everybody thinks a mine is something that's got an anchor—a round thing with horns. A modern mine lies on the ground, and looks like a bomb.

I was in command of the Pacific Fleet, so I got in an airplane and I flew all the way back to Washington to try to get them—this was 1965—to give me permission to mine Haiphong Harbor. And it's the same old crap. "Oh, no, the Russians would come down and sweep them up." And I'd say, "The Russians don't know how to sweep these mines. The Russians don't have a vital interest down there." Later on I pointed out that the Russians spent about a billion dollars a year in Vietnam and we were spending twenty-six billion, and that so far as they were concerned it was a hell of a bad investment. They'd just keep it up forever. They weren't going to help us end it. Some of the planners in Washington thought the Russians would help us negotiate with the North Vietnamese. So they said, "Oh, no, we can't let you do that. You'll sink our friends' ships," and so on.

Eight years later, Nixon said to me, "How long will it take you to make a plan to mine Haiphong Harbor?" I said, "Three seconds. I've made the plan. I'll just get it out." So he said, "Maybe we'll do that. Can you guarantee it won't leak? I want to go on TV the minute the mines splash in the water." I said, "I'll guarantee it won't leak, because I know what carrier to use. Only the Navy can guarantee that because I know what ship to use. If reporters happen to be abroad, they can't go ashore, and if some are coming out, they can't come out. It won't leak. We won't let them have a radio circuit to communicate."

Nixon was desperate at that point, because the North Vietnamese had come across the DMZ in Easter of '72. So we did it. At that time we were flying a thousand sorties a day in all of Southeast Asia. The mining took twenty-six airplanes, out of a thousand. They were gone an hour and a half. Not a single person got killed or scratched, and not ship left or entered that harbor again until we went up there and took the mines out. That was seven or eight years after I'd tried to get them to do that.

They were getting most of their support by ship. But our air power was criticized heavily here in the papers for not being able to stop the support on the railroads. The reason for that is that it was seventy miles from Hanoi to the Chinese border and there was a thirty-mile buffer zone on China. They were so afraid we were going to bomb the Chinese. There was ten-mile circle around Hanoi. So ten and thirty is forty. So there were only thirty miles of that seventy-mile railroad they ever let us bomb. And they didn't need the railroad anyway, because they were getting everything by ship.

If you are going to attack transportation, you have to attack all transportation. You can't leave part of the transportation inviolate, as was the case with the ships. It was crazy. These East German, Soviet, South Yemen, and even British ships would steam right through our fleet, and we knew damned well they were loaded with ammunition and machine guns and everything that were going to kill our boys maybe a month later. It was the craziest war I ever heard of. I've been in three of them and this one takes the cake.

What was worrying the hell out of me was when I saw that we didn't have the guts to win the war like we should have at the very outset. We started a troop withdrawal, which made us the only nation in history that was withdrawing troops in the middle of a war. And when we started that I kept saying, "Pretty soon the only Americans in Vietnam are going to be POWs. If that happens we'll never get them out." When I was asked what to do about it, I told the President that these people are nothing more than little revolutionaries and only understand one thing, and that's brute force. After Kissinger made his "Peace is at hand" speech in 1972, the North Vietnamese paid no attention to what we wanted. Like the Soviets, they kept violating what Kissinger agreed to. Therefore we had to do something to get their attention, so to speak.

Then came the Christmas bombing in 1972. It was the President himself who ought to get full credit for the Christmas bombings, because I don't think anyone else in the administration supported it. I was involved in every detail of that. I wrote the whole plan at the President's direction to do it. He didn't get into details, he'd just say, "yes or no; do it or don't do it." People were so worried that we were going to kill some Russians or Chinese when we bombed Hanoi. Well, if you ask me, we didn't kill enough of 'em.

The Christmas bombing was not extremely costly. The President asked me how many sorties we would lose, and I said two percent. We flew seven hundred and forty some-odd sorties, and two percent of that is fifteen, and that's what we lost. That was exactly what I said.

It was a very small number to lose against the heaviest anti-aircraft concentration in the world. And of those fifteen, only five went down in North Vietnam.

There was no carpet bombing of Hanoi at that time. Some people said there was, and that was pure nonsense. In fact, if we had done carpet bombing you wouldn't have been able to find Hanoi afterwards. Today Hanoi would be an archaeological dig. Even old Cronkite went up there and came back and said he was surprised at what wasn't touched. It was not carpet bombing. After all, all the foreign ambassadors stayed there and survived.

During the last two days of the bombing they were out of anti-aircraft missiles. Then we stopped it because of the mindset in Congress. Only one congressman supported us. I did all the testifying on that because everybody was away. Kissinger was in Acapulco. Laird was in Hawaii. And Mr. Nixon was down Key Biscayne—of course he wouldn't testify, anyway. And I had to testify before all the committees on it.

The bombing was stopped because the papers were saying we were carpet bombing and destroying all the hospitals. I got a telephone call asking about a statement that Hanoi put out that we were killing the POWs—we never touched a damned one of them because we knew where they were. And the *Washington Post* called me to talk about this. "Please don't put that in the paper," I said, "because it is not true." And I asked, "Are you an American?" They said, "Yeah, we're Americans." And I said, "Why does one American want to turn a very unhappy Christmas into a miserable Christmas for the wives and fathers and mothers of these POWs? Why do you want to do that? It's a damned lie."

Mrs. Nixon was down in Key Biscayne crying because we were hitting hospitals. Everybody—all the Executive branch, members of the cabinet, were all upset because they thought it was going to ruin the next election. They were yelling, "For Christ's sake, stop! Stop! Stop!" Which was nonsense. We should never have stopped until we made them do everything we wanted them to do, including releasing the POWs and getting the hell out of South Vietnam. We could have killed them all if we'd wanted. And on the last two days we didn't lose any airplanes.

But the North Vietnamese were able to manipulate the American press because most of the press are liberal. They don't want the federal government to function. Oh, the press would quote to provide authenticity. But they never left their bar in Saigon. I went up to talk to the executive board of the *New York Times*, they got so bad. They just said, "You're wasting your time. Don't come up here. We're against the war and we're going to write everything bad about it we can." And they wouldn't even listen to what I had to say. I don't know why. The media never missed a chance to put the United States in a poor light on every detail.

And Congress picks this up. The Congress don't know anything. They're stupid as hell. All they know is what they read in the *Washington Post* and the *New York Times*. They grab that every morning and if they're from Omaha or Seattle, or some place like that, they got to prove to their constituents that they are sophisticated like the Easterners. Where do they get their information? They get it out of the *New York Times*. And 99 percent is a goddamned lie.

General Vo Nguyen Giap, who was the commander of the North Vietnamese, made a public statement that the most effective guerrilla force that he had in his power was the U.S. press. I can cite you so many errors.

I can't explain to you why Americans are so anti-American and why the press is. I wish I knew.

When Congress started cutting off funds to South Vietnam, I said, "That's the end." We had made a commitment to the Vietnamese people. And I think giving it up was a terrible tragedy.

I'll tell you something about those years, I never spent such a terrible time in my life. I was in command of the Seventh Fleet. I was Commander of the Pacific Fleet when Tonkin Gulf incident occurred. Then seven years as a member of the Joint Chiefs of Staff, and four years as Chairman. And it was just absolutely crazy what we went through. We had so much power, and we never used it. Never used it! One thing that's going to mystify historians when they write about this thing fifty years from now, is how in Christ's name did a country with the power we had down there—five aircraft carriers, something like thirteen Air Force bomber squadrons, not counting the B-52s, and fighting against a country that had fewer people than Los Angeles and Orange counties and one of the fifty states, and we let that happen?

Johnson made a speech, I think in Houston, and said, "We seek no wider war." That was a guiding statement in Vietnam. He was trying to tell the Chinese and the Russians to stay out of it, so to speak. The Chinese trawlers hauled supplies like mad down to the Viet Cong. They'd steam right through our fleet. We weren't allowed to touch them. We knew what they were doing. Another thing we said was we would not overthrow Ho Chi Minh. Well, the only reason that you ever go to war is to remove a government that is doing something that you don't like. War is a breakdown of diplomacy, or diplomacy by violence if you want to put it that way. You've tried like hell to get them to do something and they wouldn't do it, so you go to war. But Johnson said we were going to war but we're not going to have an objective. And we never did.

Then he said we were not going to invade North Vietnam. And North Vietnam was the only nation that was ever allowed to deploy every operational division they had outside their country, because they knew they weren't going to get invaded.

When Saigon finally fell I was very sad, because I felt that it had a very negative effect on our credibility and it told the world at large to be careful if you are friendly with the United States. I feel the same way about the people of Taiwan. Once I have a friend, I'm a friend. I don't betray them or throw them to the wolves.

I also recognized, and I think very few people did, the wider impact of the fall of Saigon. First there was this business of deserting a friend. Then it brought about for some reason a major assault on the intelligence community, primarily the CIA. It is still carried out today.

What worried me was Cam Ranh Bay, which is probably the finest seaport in the world. We spent a billion dollars and we dredged it out; it's got oil storage and airfields. It's got hospitals, barracks, and a beautiful runway, you name it. Now, the Russians are there, and you know how much it cost the Russians? Nothing.

The Soviets have a squadron of nuclear submarines there. Two squadrons of search aircraft that can search all the way around. They can easily make our cruise from Tokyo to the Indian Ocean over a thousand miles longer than it is now. They can stop every tanker coming from the Middle East, where the Japanese get most of their oil. And they got all this for nothing. You even hear people today say, "Well, it doesn't have any global importance." It has a terrific global importance. And, Christ, they'll never give it up.

Now the Chinese have a problem they never had before, namely the Soviets. It's a move on the part of the Soviets to establish a strong global position all the way around the world, just like they did in Cuba. And they want to get in position. I can't get it through anybody's head what happens all the time. They establish these positions right on what I call the key maritime gateways of the world. The Panama Canal, they're sitting right there looking down the throat of the Panama Canal. And even getting closer to it in Nicaragua. I was violently opposed to the Panama

Canal treaty. I testified, I think, six or seven times. And I told Frank Church, "Do not be surprised if in less than one year's time troops will be staged out of Panama to overthrow a Central American country." Nine months later the troops were flown from Cuba to Panama in Panamanian aircraft and then into Nicaragua to overthrow the Somoza government. Never mind that Somoza was a son of a bitch. But look at what the result is. But then nobody paid any attention to that. I told Church in my testimony, "All I hear out of you is emotion. You say if we give it away everybody will love us, and if we don't give it away they'll tear it up and they'll hate us. The whole world will hate us." He never comprehended in the slightest what the Panama Canal was all about.

Twelve thousand ships go through there a year, and eight thousand of them are either destined for U.S. ports or leaving them. You can't get that kind of stuff through people's heads.

I've visited the Vietnam memorial and I have mixed emotions about it. I would never have built a memorial like that. I don't like the idea that it was not designed by an American, it was not built of American material, and it's under the ground. I at least get some satisfaction that they they have a memorial, period. And it seems to ease the frustration and pain of those who participated, because many of those boys were ashamed to wear a uniform when they got home. There was no public support because the press saw to it there was no public support.

There were no heroes in Vietnam in the traditional publicity sense. The press saw to that. But there was more heroism. You could write a book about the helicopter pilots who pulled people out of the jungle at night when they couldn't even see them. They had to let their cable down through layers of canopy and pull them out despite gunfire and everything else. They had plenty of heroes. I think that those boys did what they thought they should do, and their parents thought they should do, and their country thought they should do. They were all heroes.

I've had press people tell me that what happened to the POWs served them right, since most of them were pilots and had volunteered. They had no business volunteering, the press said, I don't know why the press were so antagonistic towards their own government.

The whole thing—the whole damned thing—is just a very sad experience in our history. It should never have happened the way it did.

CHAPTER **XII**

Media

Ken Kashiwahara, ABC News
"The Bus Ran Over the Baby"

I was in Vietnam for ABC News during the last six weeks of the war. I was there from the middle of March until the end of April in 1975.

When I arrived I saw the chaos, of course. But I didn't sense that the country was going to fall. I don't really know why I didn't think it would fall, but looking back on it now, I think I was sort of caught up in the optimism of it all—even right at the very end. A lot of people covering the war were optimistic about the chances for a last-minute settlement and perhaps a partitioning of the country.

One of my assignments was to cover the Vietnamese legislature at the end of April. They were haggling over what to do about General Minh taking over. There was enough optimism then that if Minh took over as president, they believed, he would be acceptable to the North Vietnamese, and they would stop their offensive, and there would be a negotiated settlement.

When I first got there I went up to Qui Nhon. When we landed, there were people leaving town by the hundreds, heading south. We stayed overnight in the home of an American and then the next day we filmed people leaving the city. Then we went back to the airport. A charter airplane was supposed to pick us up. But the charter never showed up. Later, we discovered that the people in the control tower had fled, so there was nobody in the control tower and our pilot refused to land because he didn't know who was in control—the North Vietnamese or the South Vietnamese. So we just sat there in the airport, waiting. We were there several hours and finally I thought, "This is ridiculous." I saw an Air Vietnam plane on the runway loading some people, and I thought,

"This is it." So I ran out to the pilot and told him, "Look, we're with ABC News and we need to get back to Saigon. Can you take us?" He said, "Sure, but you'll have to sit on the floor." So we got on the plane and sat on the floor and flew all the way back to Saigon that way. The next day Qui Nhon fell to the Communists.

We had four or five correspondents in Vietnam at the time. We were assigned by ABC to different stories. The stories I was assigned to were mainly outside Saigon covering the panic in the countryside. As people left their towns and headed for the coast or for the south there was just chaos and panic everywhere.

After Qui Nhon fell, I went up to Nha Trang. When we arrived everything was pretty normal. There were not crowds of people in the streets carrying all their belongings or anything like that. We stayed overnight in the city and the next day we drove up to Cam Ranh Bay. We heard that some of the Marines from Danang were landing in Cam Ranh and we wanted to see them. In Danang the Vietnamese Marines had gone on a rampage and they were shooting and killing civilians and raping women. They had just gone completely mad. The South Vietnamese government had loaded many of them on a ship and had sent them down to Cam Ranh. But they landed at a point that was restricted and we couldn't get close enough to see them. The government herded them onto another boat and sent them further south to Vung Tau.

When we got back to Nha Trang that afternoon, there had been a dramatic change. The whole town was in a panic. People were in the streets with all of their belongings loaded up and they were heading out of town, heading south. They were also mobbing the American consulate. The U.S. government had flown in charter planes to take some people out, and thousands of Vietnamese now wanted to get on those flights. We went to the consulate to arrange to get on a plane. Then we went out to the airport, and there were thousands of people out there. Most of the flights out of Nha Trang by commercial airlines had been cancelled and many people were trapped at the airport. We managed to get on an Air America flight chartered by the U.S. government. We got out just in time. Nha Trang fell the next day.

As the North Vietnamese Army came closer to Saigon, our travel was restricted. We went out to Vung Tau a couple of times to report on events there. They were landing boats from the North at Vung Tau and again the Vietnamese were landing there. We filmed them landing and being disarmed by government soldiers.

There was a growing hostility toward the press in those days and we were afraid that at any moment the military might turn on us. So we didn't push our luck in getting stories. From a distance we saw soldiers put the Marines on buses. Then the buses headed for Saigon. We followed them. They were stopped at a roadblock and all the Marines had to get out. They were searched. Then they got back on their bus. The government didn't like us filming any of that. But I had a Vietnamese crew and I was mistaken for Vietnamese lots of times myself. My cameraman could talk our way into situations. He told the soldiers at Vung Tau that we were a government film crew. So they let us film the Marines.

I remember the bombing of the Presidential Palace on April 8. We were in our office in the Caravelle Hotel, standing in front of a window that looked out over Saigon. I saw this plane flying low over the city. And it struck me because you didn't normally see planes flying over the city—especially not fighter planes. And it sort of swooped down, and I saw this object fall from the plane and I heard the explosion and then I saw a big puff of smoke. And I thought, "Oh, my God. What's happening?" We ran down to our cars and then raced over to the Palace. There were all sorts of guns being fired into the air and soldiers had blocked off all the streets leading to the palace. I really didn't know what was going on. I found out later that a South Vietnamese pilot had defected and had flown a plane from the South Vietnamese Air Force to bomb the palace. It was very frightening in that in Vietnam you never worried about planes dropping bombs on you. You always worried about small-arms fire, rockets, or mortars. But now we had to think about planes bombing us. And my fear was that if one plane bombed the palace then certainly other planes would follow. And I didn't want to stand around the palace much anymore. I didn't know what might happen next.

Then ABC started pulling out all of its employees. They got out our Vietnamese employees first. There was an arrangement between the media and the U.S. Embassy. It was all handled very well, and the networks got all of their Vietnamese people out safely and in plenty of time. ABC decided to pull everybody out except for two correspondents and two news crews. I was one of those chosen to stay.

My new assignment was to cover the evacuation. And I had to cover what happened in the government. On the twenty-eighth we went out to cover the inauguration of General Minh, which was late in the afternoon. There was a feeling that he was the only hope for Vietnam, that he alone could save the country. We had gone out to his house on the twenty-seventh to film him and discovered that he had decided not to be inaugurated on that day "because the stars were not right." Here the North Vietnamese were pounding on the door of Saigon, and the swearing in of a new president was the only hope for the country, and he was postponing everything because the stars weren't right. It was just incredible.

After the inauguration we came back to the bureau. We had only been there for a short time when all of a sudden all hell broke loose. It seemed like every single gun in Saigon started firing. And none of us knew why. We later found out that the North Vietnamese had bombed and then shelled Tan Son Nhut. All the soldiers were firing their small arms into the air in the hope of shooting down planes. But from our office it sounded like there was terrific fighting going on right outside in the streets.

So we went out to take a look. I took a cameraman with me. We went down one street and there was a group of South Vietnamese soldiers firing in the air. And when they saw us coming up the street they all turned their weapons toward us. And I said, "Let's get out of here or we're going to be dead." We were maybe a half a block away from the soldiers. So I waved at them and yelled, "Okay, we're leaving." And they watched us race off in another direction.

When we got back to the office, all the phone lines had been cut. We filed a radio report and then went to bed.

The next morning I was awakened by gunfire in the streets. The NVA was rocketing the airport again. And soldiers were firing in the streets again. I took my camera crew out early and we just drove around the city to see what was going on. Saigon was in a panic by this time. Helicopters were flying over the the city, back and forth. And people were being evacuated from the Embassy and from some other buildings. We saw the helicopter loading people on the roof of one building—and a famous picture was taken of that, of people standing on the stairway leading up to the roof, waiting to get into the helicopter.

We drove over to the American PX. And the South Vietnamese were looting it when we got there. They had broken in and it was just an incredible sight. They were carrying out everything they could, from cornflakes to appliances. A South Vietnamese soldier was guarding the entrance to the place. He was letting the looting go on, but he was still guarding the entrance, for some reason. There was a strong anti-Americanism at that point—I clearly sensed it. We started going in and the guard stopped us and said, "Are you Americans?" And my cameraman said that he was Japanese. Then the guard turned to me and said, "Are you Filipino?" And I said, "Yes." So he let us in.

We filmed all the looting. Then we went back to the bureau headquarters. By the time we got there, the evacuation was on. Everyone had been told to go to a predesignated evacuation point to get picked up by a bus. Then the buses were supposed to take us to the airport to be flown out. We were led to believe that everything had been planned and organized and there was no need to worry.

So we gathered all our stuff together from the hotel and went downstairs. On the way out I saw an American at the reception desk checking out of the hotel. He was paying his bill, but he was also arguing loudly with the desk clerk. I thought to myself, "This is ridiculous. The whole country is falling and these two guys are standing here arguing over a few piasters." The whole scene was like an island of one kind of insanity in a world of another kind of insanity. Nothing made sense anymore. Adding to the general insanity was the fact that the signal for the evacuation was the playing of Bing Crosby's "I'm Dreaming of a White Christmas" over the Armed Forces Radio. It was April 29 and they were playing "White Christmas."

We went to our predesignated evacuation point and waited to get picked up by a bus. But by that time everything was breaking down. Panic was gripping the entire city. The Vietnamese were now sensing that the Americans were getting out, because they were gathering at the evacuation points. So the Vietnamese also started congregating at those points, figuring that they could get on the buses, too, and get out with the Americans. And every time a bus would pull up, there was pushing and shoving as the Vietnamese tried to get on with the Americans. I was prevented from getting on my bus because of the chaos. The bus drove away without me. I thought, "This is ridiculous. I am not going to try to fight my way onto a bus." So I waited. Then I got separated from my cameraman and from the guy who was the bureau chief. The two of them pushed their way onto a bus and I didn't.

I got on the next bus. And we drove out to Tan Son Nhut. But by that time the South Vietnamese soldiers guarding the entrance to the airport decided that they didn't want to let any more buses in. I think they were extremely upset that the Americans were leaving. They felt that the Americans were abandoning them and they wanted to do something to stop us.

The driver of our bus was from the Embassy. He got out of the bus to ask the soldiers to let us in. There was an argument, and, to make their point, the soldiers fired their weapons at the feet of the driver and shouted at him, "We are not letting you in." So he got back in the bus, and then we drove around.

The whole evacuation process had now broken down. Our driver didn't know what to do. He also didn't know how to drive. He had never driven a bus before; that became obvious as we drove around. He just drove around town trying to think of some place to go to get us out, and looking for help. And as he drove around he hit cars parked on the street and fruit stands on the corners. When people on the street saw us go by they shouted anti-American epithets like, "Yankee, go home!" and they threw things at the bus.

Finally, our driver decided to take us down to the port to put us on a boat. We got to the port and we got off the bus. But it was the same kind of scene at the port that we had found in other parts of the city. There were thousands of people at the port trying to get on boats and barges to get out of the country. And they were panicked. Seeing the chaos and disorder, we decided it was not a good idea to stay there. So we started to get back on the bus. At that point, the Vietnamese, seeing us getting back on the bus, decided to mob the bus. A riot started and I, unfortunately, happened to be the last one in line outside the bus.

The driver started to pull away. And I was still outside trying to get on.

The crowd, seeing him pull away, got real angry, and grabbed me. And they started pulling on me, trying to bring me back into the mob. I don't know why. I had on some shoulder bags and there were people hanging onto them to hold me back. I tried to shake loose and I couldn't, so I turned around to face the people hanging on me, and I remember looking back into all those angry faces. I saw the hatred in those faces. So I turned toward the bus again and I saw the bus driving away. I finally just threw off the bags, dropped them, and ran for the bus. The driver opened the door and I jumped on. But I had lost everything that I was taking out of Saigon. Everything.

Then, as the bus was pulling away—and I remember this very, very clearly and I will remember it as long as I live—a Vietnamese man came running up alongside the bus. He was carrying a baby. And he held out the baby and he was pleading, "Please take my baby! Please take my baby! Please take my baby!" And the bus kept moving. And the man fell. And the baby fell, too, obviously. And the man dropped the baby. And the rear wheels of the bus ran over the baby. The bus ran over the baby!

All of us in the bus were just stunned. People inside the bus were screaming now, and some of them were hysterical. Somebody at the back of the bus kept yelling over and over again that we had just run over a baby. But the driver just kept on going.

I'll never forget that. Never. By that time I was in a state of shock. I had been riding around on that bus for several hours. And now I was feeling fear—really for the first time since I had been in Vietnam. Suddenly, I realized that I might not get out of the country. None of us on the bus would. There were all kinds of rumors of bloodbaths as the North Vietnamese moved south. Nobody knew what would happen when they got to Saigon. People had been saying that there would be mass executions. As it turned out, there were not any bloodbaths; but at that time there was the eerie feeling of the unknown, approaching quickly. We were all wondering what was going to happen to us if we didn't get out. So there we were, just driving around, going nowhere. And everywhere we went, people were shouting anti-American slogans at us. So now I was thinking, "This is really ridiculous. I am going to tell the driver to stop this bus. I am going to get off. I am going to go back to our office and I am just going to wait for the Communists. I can't take any more of this."

But then, before I could talk to the driver, while we were heading away from the port, I remember looking up in the sky and suddenly seeing several huge Jolly Green Giant helicopters coming in, escorted by Cobra gunships and F-4s. What a beautiful sight. That was some relief to me, because I thought, "That is how we are going to get out of here!" The American helicopters were landing in the city.

Several of us on the bus said at the same time, "Let's go to the Embassy!" And the bus driver then took us to the Embassy. But when we got to the Embassy, it, too, was a complete mob scene. It was surrounded by a huge, frantic crowd of Vietnamese trying to get in, trying to climb over the wall. So we got off the bus and went to the tennis courts across the street from the Embassy to try to decide how to get in. There was a phone by the tennis courts and we decided to try to call the Embassy to ask them what we should do to get in. Incredibly, we got through on the phone line.

Someone in the Embassy said we could get inside but that we could not come in through the doors or the gates, because if they opened the gates they would be mobbed by the Vietnamese. They told us all to go around to the back of the Embassy and to try to make our way through the crowd and then climb over the wall. The Marine guards there would let us in.

Now you have to imagine what was going on. It was just sheer chaos and panic back there. Some South Vietnamese soldiers were outside at a sort of roadblock, but a very ineffective one. And they were firing their weapons into the air to try and calm the crowd. But that just added to the panic. We got through their roadblock and made it to the back of the Embassy, and there was just this mob of people back there trying to climb over the Embassy wall. There were American Marines on top of the wall kicking the people down. We made our way through the crowd, and at that point I got real concerned. Because up until then I had been mistaken for a Vietnamese lots of times in the country and it had always worked to my advantage. But at this point I figured it had finally caught up with me. Now I was sure it was going to work to my disadvantage. I was sure that when I started to climb that wall, the American Marines were going to see me and mistake me for a Vietnamese, and, I figured, "when I get to the top of that wall I'm going to get a great big boot right in the face."

So I had to think of what I should say to the Marines to prove that I'm an American. And in that state of chaos and panic, the only thing I could think of was, "The Dodgers won the pennant!" I know it sounds ridiculously funny today, but that's really what I was planning to say to the Marines when they ran over to kick me off the Embassy wall.

But I never had to use it, because I was with the other American journalists and the Marines recognized us. When they ran over, instead of kicking me off the wall, one of them grabbed me and pulled me over.

Once I was over the wall I understood why they were trying to keep all of the Vietnamese out. The Embassy grounds were just packed. Packed. It was wall-to-wall people inside. There were hundreds of Vietnamese already inside, along with third-country nationals and employees of the American government and of the various news organizations. They were crowded around the swimming pool, waiting for the helicopters to come in and get them out.

When we were safe inside the Embassy I tired to find the film that we had shot that morning. One of the guys on the bus had been carrying our film. We found him now and asked him where the film was. He said he had taken the film bags and thrown them over the wall into the Embassy but now he couldn't find them. That was all of our work for the day—incredible film. We asked around for it and discovered that somebody gave it to a CBS person who had already taken off with it in a helicopter. We didn't know if that was true. And we didn't know if we would ever see the stuff again.

We went into the Embassy building, then, to try to find a phone to file a report on everything that had happened so far that day. But there was only one phone working inside and there was already a journalist using it filing his stuff, and there was absolutely no way he was going to give up the phone. So I had a feeling of frustration, then. All the stuff that happened to us that day—and the film was gone and I couldn't get to a phone.

So we stood in line and waited for a helicopter. About sunset we got one. And I thought that would be the end of it. But it wasn't. The helicopters were landing in the parking lot. The back door would come down and people would rush inside. Then they took off. Ours landed and a bunch of us raced inside, and the door closed. Then the helicopter tried to take off. And he got up to about twenty or thirty feet and stopped and then came crashing back down. There were too many people on board. So they opened the door again and they put some people off. Then they tried to take off again. It got a little higher and then came crashing back down again. Too many people again. This happened three times. And I thought, "Oh, my God. I've made it this far, and here I am, and we're all going to get it right here in the Embassy!"

Finally, they got enough people off and we were light enough to take off. The sun was setting and I was looking out the window as we went up. It looked like the entire countryside was exploding in flames. That's no exaggeration. The ammunition dump at Long Binh, which was just outside Saigon, was exploding, and the sun was setting, and in several parts of the city there were big fires with flames going into the sky. It was just incredible. As we flew out over the South China Sea I could see other fires around Saigon and Vung Tau. It really looked like all of Vietnam was burning.

I was afraid we were going to be shot down—either by the South Vietnamese or the North Vietnamese. The South Vietnamese were extremely angry because we were leaving and abandoning them. So all the way out I kept watching for rockets, wondering when one would come up at us. I was just sure that the South Vietnamese would start shooting at us at any moment.

So it really wasn't until we got over the sea that I felt some relief. And then when we landed on the U.S.S. *Hancock* I thought, "It's all over now."

Still, there was no time to reflect. All of us were still on an extreme high—the adrenaline was really pumping, even though it had been an awfully long day. Once we got off the helicopter my immediate thought was, "Let's try to make some sense of this story. Let's try to write something down." So that's what I did. Also, on the *Hancock,* we finally located our film. Someone from CBS had gotten it out for us.

The next morning, as I recall, there wasn't much time for reflection, because we heard that something was happening and that the Marines on the ship had gone on full alert and had rushed up to the deck. The newsmen rushed up there, too. And we looked up in the sky—and it was filled with helicopters. Just like a big swarm of bees coming at us. On our ship the decision was made to let them land one at a time. The people on the helicopters were all South Vietnamese refugees. When they landed the Marines confiscated all of their weapons and then pushed the helicopters over the side. That was an incredible sight, too. We all went to work on the deck and pushed those helicopters off the carrier deck into the sea, one right after the other. And on our carrier, as on all the other ships out there, the hangar deck was just packed with people.

When the evacuation was completed, our ship headed for Subic Bay in the Philippines. But before we arrived in Subic, some of us got to get off to file our stories. Ed Bradley of CBS got off first and he took our film with him. I was taken by helicopter from the *Hancock* to the *Blue Ridge.* The rest of my crew was on the *Blue Ridge.* And as soon as I landed on the *Blue Ridge,* the guy who served as our bureau chief told me, "You're gonna get on another helicopter right now and get out of here. You're no good to us just sitting on a ship without being able to tell a story. We're not sure we can get you a seat on a plane to get out of here, but we're sure gonna try."

So I was put on another helicopter—and I carried several huge bags of film for the networks. I was flown to the U.S.S. *Coral Sea.* I managed to get on a plane that took off from the *Coral Sea.* And that was another experience. I sat facing the rear of the plane, and when we were shot off the ship, sitting backwards, it felt like my entire face was going to come off. Then, finally, I made it to Clark Field in the Philippines. I took all the film to the television station there and they sent it by satellite to the United States.

Those last days in Vietnam were the most intense and memorable experiences in my life as a reporter. During a period like that you don't tend to think about what is happening at the moment. You are so caught up in reporting the events that you never have time to reflect. But now, looking back, I can see how important those last days in April were. That was history. It was being made right there. Not only were we reporting it, but we were part of it.

It doesn't seem like it all happened fifteen years ago. My memory is not normally very good. But I remember those last two days in Saigon perfectly. How could I ever forget them? How could anybody? Even today, I can close my eyes and see it all again just as it happened—the panic, the shooting, climbing over the Embassy wall. And the man with the baby.

John Degler, USN, Photographer, U.S.S. *Midway*
"To Hell with What You Say, We're Coming In Right Now"

When Operation Frequent Wind commenced on April 29, we were all in a state of controlled excitement. Everything was under control, but we were all somewhat tense because this operation was definitely out of the ordinary. We were part of a gigantic task force. I had never before seen as many ships in one place as I did in the last days of April in the South China Sea.

It was my duty to film the entire operation for the ship's record. At the end of the first day I was exhausted, but thought I had done a pretty good job. On the early morning of April 30 I was up on the O5 level taking some pictures of the ship. (The O5 level is the fifth deck up from the main deck.) The executive officer of the ship was standing next to me while I was filming. I turned the camera up to pan the horizon and I saw what looked like specks of dust on the lens. So I turned the camera around to dust off the lens and I looked up at the horizon. At first I saw what looked like a huge swarm of bees coming across the water toward us. But as they came closer I saw that it was really a cloud of helicopters—Hueys. I stepped back for a moment and bumped into the executive officer. He was looking at those Hueys and he said, "What in the hell is that?" and then he said, "Oh, my God!" and left the O5 deck.

It was really remarkable because all of a sudden all those helicopters converged on the fleet. There had been no radio communication from them— no warning that they were approaching. And for a moment we didn't even know if they were friendlies. As those Hueys came buzzing in, the people on the deck were trying madly to wave them off. Then people started running everywhere. And they started landing. They were landing anywhere they could find a place to set down. There was mass confusion. It was like they were saying, "To hell with what you say, we're coming in right now."

Everything had gone according to plan until that moment. I started to film the Hueys coming in. Then all of a sudden I felt on my back this hot wind and I heard the approaching whup-whup-whup—the sound of the blades of a Huey. So I turned around and here's a helicopter right behind me—the blades are turning only six to ten feet from me! I could look right into the pilot's eyes. The guy was trying to come in for a landing between a huge deck crane and the edge of the ship's island. And because the ship was moving and because the island serves as a windbreak and all of the wind was coming around it, this little chopper was bouncing around in midair trying to land, just like a confused bee. I was ready to hit the deck because I knew he could never make it in that small space with that wind. But he was making one hell of a try.

Finally he backed out. Down below they were madly trying to wave him off because they knew if he crashed when he landed the rest of the operation would be in jeopardy and he would have wiped out a lot of people. So after he backed off and came in from another direction, they loaded up that section of the ship (where he'd tried to land) with our own helicopters, so nobody else would try to land there.

When those Hueys landed it was unbelievable. They were filled with women and children. One particular aircraft, I'll never forget, came in with fifty-three people on board, including a pilot and a copilot.

I took a picture of one of the first Hueys to land and it's kind of comical. The pilot was talking to members of the deck crew and they were all looking at a map—God knows what for. It looked like they were trying to explain to him that he made a wrong turn and would have to go back or something. It was pretty funny.

When the Hueys landed, we had Marines on deck who would disable the helicopter immediately by locking the rotors in place. Then they disarmed all of the passengers. We were very afraid that somebody was going to attempt to sabotage our operation. And there was no good way to stop them. There was so many Hueys coming in that one might have come in with explosives and really done some damage.

We got organized in a hurry to take care of those people. We tried to create some order on the landing deck. Right away, though, we had an unexpected problem. The prop wash from the helicopter rotors was so great, and the Vietnamese were so little, that some of the first ones on board stumbled and fell and were blown across the deck. So for safety we used some ropes to guide them from the helicopters across the deck and down the stairs to a processing center. That way we got them safely across the flight deck, and we kept them from getting hit by the other helicopters and prevented them from massing together in one spot on the deck. When people led them across the deck on a rope they looked like big caterpillars coming out of the Hueys and going to the side of the ship.

Throughout the entire two days of Frequent Wind I was completely into the operation itself. I knew that this was history, and I saw my job as filming something like "Victory at Sea." I hoped that some day my footage would be used for something like that. So I felt a very strong obligation to do a good job and get everything on film.

But I was seeing everything that happened through a camera lens, and thinking about camera angles and lighting. I remember one incident in particular when I had taken all of my cut shots of people doing this or that, and I decided that I would follow one group of people through the process of landing, getting off the flight deck, being processed and examined and fed, and then departing on another helicopter to another ship in the fleet.

So I picked one chopper that was coming in. The second it landed I stepped inside and started filming the people on board. Then I filmed them getting out and giving up any weapons they were carrying and then being led across the flight deck. I followed them through the ship and back up on the other end of the flight deck where another helicopter was waiting to take them to another ship. I got down low and shot them getting on the helicopter ramp and shot the ramp going up and then the chopper taking off. And as it lifted off I was lying on the deck filming and I felt myself being pushed by the prop wash toward the side of the flight deck. I was pushed all the way to the side and ended up with my leg over the walkway along the edge of the ship. And I was still shooting. When the helicopter was gone I put the camera down and I started thinking, "What did I just do?" I had forgotten about my own safety, and the feelings of those people, and I had just taken pictures. It was at that moment that I really started to realize the meaning of all of this. Up until then I was pretty much in a daze—it was constant activity, and excitement, hurrying, the roar of engines, the feel of the prop wash, and the sound of the rotors of the helicopters coming in and going out. But suddenly it hit me what all of this meant. We were saving people. And those people had just been torn from their homeland. You could see the torment in their faces. Many of them had fled from their homes only a few minutes before death would have got them. We had a home to go back to when this was all over. But they didn't. We were the first minutes of a completely new and strange life for all of those poor people.

I took a lot of pride in my work. All of us on board the *Midway* felt proud when the operation was over. We realized that we had saved an ungodly number of people in a hazardous situation. We did something that had never been done before. Every man on that ship, from the flight deck down to the engine room, was proud because we had worked together as a team and we had been successful. That knowledge really brought us together. It's hard to conceive of something like that without actually going through it.

For a few hours our ship became a city taking in thousands of refugees. We had to take care of those people and supply them with food and medical care and sanitation facilities. Crew members gave up their bunks for the refugees so they could rest while they were on board. We gave them the royal treatment. I talked with a few of them to find out where they were coming from. They were very humble and grateful and afraid. They just kept saying over and over again, "Thank you. Thank you." Every time we gave them something or treated them courteously, they just flooded us with thank you's.

I saw a lot of crying among those refugees. And a lot of embracing between people when they found their friends had also made it out to the *Midway*. A lot of emotion was expressed that day.

At the end of the operation we were packed and ready to leave the area, and everything was in order. We had all the helicopters arranged on the ship. Then all of a sudden this lone aircraft showed up. We were sitting out there in the South China Sea when this guy comes out of nowhere. He buzzed the ship several times. We couldn't figure out who he was or what he wanted because we had no radio contact with him. Every time he passed over the ship he dropped something. Three times he missed the deck. Then on the fourth time he dropped a wrench and it hit the deck. There was a note wrapped around it. The note said that he was Major Buong and that he had his wife and five kids on that little plane with him and he wanted to land on our deck. His plane was just a little Cessna O-1 "Bird Dog." Once the captain got that information he put us all to work. In thirty minutes we moved every helicopter and aircraft up to the bow of the ship so Major Buong could have the full flight deck with a landing approach to land on. Everyone on board ship knew how dangerous this was going to be. It was a little plane, overloaded, and we were rolling around in the sea. Everyone pitched in to make it as easy as possible for him, but in the end he had to land that aircraft. I filmed him coming in, fully expecting him to crash. But he just came floating in like a bird, made two bounces and rolled to a stop. And at that moment everybody on that ship just broke out in cheers. We were applauding and jumping up and down, we were so damned happy for that guy. A crowd of people ran out and surrounded his plane, still applauding and laughing. And the group got bigger and bigger. I went out with my camera to film him getting out of the craft. And as he helped his wife and kids out of the plane, somebody yelled, "Where in the hell did you learn to fly, anyway?" And he turned around and said, "Texas!" Well, that just blew us away. We all cheered some more. We were just crazy with joy for that guy.

That was the end of our operation—Major Buong landing. It was a happy note to end on. We couldn't have planned it better. It was a neat little victory at the end.

I was only twenty-four years old at the time. And the experience changed me immensely. I had experienced many things before that time. But those days off the coast of South Vietnam really opened my eyes. I saw what life could be for other people—it woke me up to the fact that terrible things were happening out there in the world. Being an American, I hadn't even imagined things like this happening to people.

I had new strength after that. I think all of us on the *Midway* did. We discovered what we were capable of accomplishing when we were called on to do it. We all did an awful lot of growing up in those days. And best of all, when it was over, we knew we were the good guys and we had come to the rescue. And we did what was right.

When we got home there were no cheers or anything. I wish now there had been. I wish more people knew what we did out there.

Mike Marriott, CBS News
"American Traitor!"

When Ban Me Thuot fell and the withdrawal from the central highlands began, I went out with correspondent Peter Collins and filmed the "Convoy of Tears" coming down Highway 7B from Pleiku. The equivalent of three divisions pulled out of the central highlands without firing a shot. A friend of mine from one of the intelligence agencies called me and said, "Hey, Mike, did you know that the highlands have just fallen?" And I said, "Oh, fuck no!" He said, "Look, I've got a porter"—which is an Air America two-engine aircraft—"and I'm going up to pull some of my people out before they get captured. If you come with us I'll guarantee your seats coming back. I've got an Agency [CIA] helicopter to take you over the area so you can film. There are just thousands of people fleeing. I'll give you a survival radio so we can put you down ahead of them. You can wait for the convoy to get to you, after you do some of the aerials, then you can get off in the fields, away from the convoy, radio for the chopper to come and get you, and we'll pluck you up."

So we went out to the middle of the highlands. Right out in the middle of nowhere, and suddenly, as far as the eye could see, there were a hundred thousand fucking people, and soldiers, and tanks and armored personnel carriers—all coming toward us. I filmed it and then we got out.

I was never really concerned about getting out of Saigon until a Vietnamese police captain tried to shoot me. There had been an incident at the Presidential Palace. A plane had buzzed it or strafed it and there was all this excitement in the streets. We went out to film it. We saw this Vietnamese police captain with a .45 pistol shooting at a taxi that wouldn't move and couldn't move because the engine had died. The captain was shooting at the guy in the taxi. He had just totally freaked out. So I started to film him. And he saw me doing this and he turned and pointed his gun at me and started screaming, "American traitor! American traitor! American traitor!" To which I responded, "Hey, wait a moment. I'm an Australian." I was trying to think of something to distract him and to keep him from killing me. So he ran over and put the gun about a foot from my head. And he pulled the trigger. And nothing happened. So he slid back the breech. I could see the .45 round jammed in it. He tried to put his finger in and pull it out, but he was so panicked and paranoid that he was shaking and he couldn't do it. He pulled the trigger three times, aiming at my head. My camera wasn't running at the time. To this day I don't know why. I didn't dare point the camera at him—I just didn't want to make a move in any way, shape, or form that would make him snap out of what he was doing and realize that if he got that round out he could kill me. So I just stared right into his eyes and kept looking at him. After the third time he pulled the trigger and nothing happened he reversed the weapon, held the barrel, and started smashing me over the skull.

Then and there I decided I was not going to stay in town and film the NVA and the VC when they rolled in. I decided as I was running away from that captain, "No, no, no. I can't do it. I don't mind the Goddamned Communists having a go at me. But these guys are the allies. And if they're prepared to shoot me, then I don't want to hang around here. No way."

I left Saigon early in the evening of April 29 from the Defense Attaché Office at Tan Son Nhut. I flew out on a Jolly Green Giant (CH-53) to the *Blue Ridge*. I felt immense sadness at that time. I had no feeling of being glad to get out. I felt, in one way, a sense of pride that two months earlier, even before Danang fell, I had predicted that the country was about to fall. But my friends just scoffed at me. They insisted, "No, it won't. The army will fight." I told them, "Look, you're wrong." And now I had a feeling of, "Shit, I was right. How sad."

As we left Tan Son Nhut we stayed low. We followed the Saigon River for a short distance. Over the river we picked up a couple of F-4s that were escorting everyone out. I remember looking down at the river. Suddenly, I saw my apartment building. I remembered that my apartment was still full of everything that I owned. And I was thinking, "Jesus, some fucking North Vietnamese colonel is going to get all that. And tomorrow morning he's gonna look just great in my suits." It was a strange thing to think, I know.

Then we started to climb. I was on the back ramp of the CH-53 with my camera rolling. One of the gunners back there with me was looking at me and I had tears rolling down my cheeks. And he stepped over and put his arm around me and patted me on the back. Then he turned away and started popping flares out the back of the chopper. If anyone did fire a SAM at us, those white phosphorus flares on a parachute would take them out, because the missiles were heat-seeking and the flares were hotter and brighter than the engines of the helicopter.

When I ran out of film I put the camera down and I helped the gunner pop flares out the back of the chopper as we rolled out over the countryside toward the South China Sea and the American fleet.

On the *Blue Ridge*, the next morning, I saw all the Vietnamese choppers coming in and then ditching at sea. There were so many of them that they couldn't all land on the deck, so they just hovered around the ship like a swarm of bees. Then they would put the nose up in the air and they would jump out the door, and the chopper would just flop over into the sea.

All of the Embassy people were on the *Blue Ridge*. So were the DAO people and the CIA people. They were embarrassed and insulted because they considered that the press had lost the war. Even at that time they were saying that we lost the war for America. The CIA station chief, Thomas Polgar, was the most vocal about that. He really disliked us. General Ky was on the *Blue Ridge,* too. He was still cocky. He was so sure of himself that he just sickened us. He was a multimillionaire and one of the most corrupt men going. He got out with his favorites, naturally.

Not long ago, I went down to look at the Vietnam memorial with those 57,000 names on it. It was so sad because I realized that all of that sacrifice was for absolutely nothing. Nothing. I abhor war. I hate it.

I think that in the end we television newsmen told the truth about Vietnam. What the military objected to—and I'm not saying that it was all the military, not by any means—was that we brought home to those people who watched the *CBS Evening News* the real horrors of war and the futility of Vietnam. There were some accusations that newsmen had staged some shots. I don't know about that. But I do know that no matter how you look at it, you've got real napalm victims and real young Americans dying in the arms of a comrade. And that's not staged. That's the reality of war. I guess we changed the way America looked at the war. But we didn't do it recklessly or maliciously. We did it because it was there.

Ed Bradley, CBS News
"So It All Comes Down to This"

My last day in Saigon was simply crazy. On the morning of April 29, Armed Forces Radio station was playing its usual Muzak. Then they interrupted their program to announce that "it's a hundred and five degrees in Saigon and the temperature is rising." This was followed by the playing of Bing Crosby's "White Christmas." You've got to remember that this was in late April. It jut shows you the mentality of the military. In fact, all you had to do to know that the evacuation was starting was to look out the hotel window. You saw Americans—"round eyes"—walking down the street carrying suitcases. And when the Vietnamese saw that, they knew the Americans were leaving and they started following the Americans. They wanted to get out, too.

We left our hotel and went to our assigned evacuation pickup point, and no one was there. We waited for a while and then decided to go to a second pickup point. Nobody was there, either. So we went to a third evacuation point. It was a school building and it was locked. We were about ready to leave that one and go to a fourth when I said, "Look, obviously this thing is not well organized. But let's just wait here and eventually a bus will probably come get us." I was right. Eventually three buses arrived. But by that time a crowd of nearly 150 people had gathered to wait for them. I helped get people on the buses in an orderly fashion. Then we drove out to the airport. When we arrived at the gate the guards shot at us and we had to turn around and go back into the city. At that point the buses became spearated from each other.

Our driver didn't know what to do after we were turned away from the airport. He spent the next seven hours driving around Saigon trying to figure out where to go and what to do. He was a real jerk. First, he didn't have any keys for the bus. He had hot-wired the bus to get it started and it kept stalling on him, and every time it stalled we had to jump the wires to get it started again. And he referred to himself (if you can believe it) as "the wagonmaster." And finally, he couldn't drive. Years earlier the government had cut down all the trees on certain streets in Saigon so convoys could get through. So do you think that our driver goes down those big wide streets? Of course not. He took the smallest, narrowest streets he could find in the city. Now you should keep in mind that Saigon had all these little restaurants on the street corners. They were just little soup stalls with a pot boiling over a fire and a canvas cover over the top—that was what they called a restaurant. Well, every time our driver turned a corner with his bus he wiped out about three restaurants. This went on for seven hours!

Finally, he decided that we should go down to the port and wait there for some helicopters to pick us up. So he drove to the port and there were about 10,000 people down there in a total panic, trying to get on boats, jumping and missing boats and falling in the river. I saw that and I said to the driver, "You're going to leave us right here and you're going to go? And you tell us that the helicopters are going to land in the middle of this mob of Vietnamese and pick us up? And we have no security? And you think these people are going to stand by and let us leave them behind? You're crazy!"

But by that time most of the people on the bus had gotten off. I warned them not to. One Vietnamese guy got off with his family. He had no ID or anything. Then we left and he didn't make it back on. I remember looking out the window as we pulled away and I saw him struggling to get through the crowd. He was carrying a suitcase in one hand and holding onto his wife with the other and she was dragging along two little kids. People around him were trying to pull off his watch and steal his suitcase. We just left the whole family there. Even today, I can still see the terror in that guy's face as we pulled away and left him.

Eventually we went to the Embassy and climbed over the wall. I took off that night from the Embassy roof in a helicopter. On the way out I could see fires around the city, and I knew that the North Vietnamese were on their way in. I couldn't see any sign of them, but the whole scene was just very surreal. As I looked down on that city and knew we were leaving for good, all I thought was, "So it all comes down to this."

Those last days in Saigon were really something. It was like being at Waterloo. It was so important, so historical. And today it is still very obvious that we Americans have not recovered from Vietnam. And the Vietnamese have not recovered from Vietnam. And the Cambodians and the

Laotians have not recovered from Vietnam. Nothing else in my lifetime was as important as that—as important as Vietnam. It was such a tragedy. We sent so many good people out there. So many really good people. And for what?

You know, when I first went to Vietnam in the fall of 1972, the American military leaders told me that there was light at the end of the tunnel. I thought of that in 1975—"light at the end of the tunnel"—when we were flying out for the last time.

Fox Butterfield, *New York Times*
"Turn Out the Light at the End of the Tunnel"

I first went to Vietnam in 1962. I went as sort of a tourist/graduate student and stopped for a few weeks to look around. I'd been in Taiwan on a Fulbright scholarship and I stopped and stayed with some Chinese people. There was a war going on. My Chinese friends took me out into the countryside. I was fascinated by it and a little scared because I didn't know what to expect. The American presence was already clear. The American GIs and advisors were sitting around the bars and restaurants. I would have loved to stay; I was really fascinated by it; but my professor at Harvard kept telling me to hurry up and come back, so I went back to graduate school. My field was Chinese history, and I did a fair amount of reading about Vietnam and became very interested in it. I led some of the early antiwar protests at Harvard.

At that time, politically, I was well to the left of center. I helped found a group called TOCSIN, which a couple of years later became SDS [Students for a Democratic Society]. We were an antinuclear group. We were calling for a halt on nuclear testing in the atmosphere. That was in 1960–'61. We were actually successful, because Kennedy signed the agreement with Khrushchev to ban nuclear testing in the atmosphere.

My next direct experience with Vietnam came in 1969. My grandfather was Cyrus Eaton, the Armand Hammer of that time, and he got invitations through his Russian friends to go to Hanoi. By that time I was in Taiwan working on my dissertation and also working as a stringer for the *New York Times* part time. He called up and asked if I wanted to go to Hanoi. So I said, sure, I'd love to go. But I didn't take it all that seriously. Then he called back a week later and said, "It's all arranged, and meet me in Phnom Penh."

The trip affected me the opposite from the way it affected other people. I expected, having read Harrison Salisbury, to find a lot of bomb damage in Hanoi. In fact, I found none. And I became skeptical. I kept asking them to take me to the bomb damage, but they never could. I saw that the bomb damage stopped on the outskirts of the city. And that the American claims about the bombing were basically correct. The little damage they showed me and said was bomb damage actually came from rockets that had been shot up and came down on the city.

I think Salisbury and others were misled. The correspondents who went there at the end of the war said the same thing. In fact, bomb damage wasn't what the North Vietnamese said it was. The Americans were very careful about bombing Hanoi. They bombed the crap out of the rest of the country, but not Hanoi.

The conclusion that I drew in Hanoi was that I was dealing with a very authoritarian regime. I also saw that they were incredibly poor. On the one hand, I could see that as partly a result of the war. On the other hand, one of the things that began to strike me was that they were pursuing the war to the exclusion of any development of their own country. The North Vietnamese leaders were not interested in economic development or the well-being of their people; they were interested only in this nationalist goal of obtaining complete power.

On that trip we became the first people aside from Kissinger to talk to Le Duc Tho, who was then negotiating secretly with Kissinger. We met with Pham Van Dong and half a dozen other leaders of the North. I found them to be rigid and clever at the same time. They were not very interested in people. I had a strong impression of their being interested in achieving their goal, and it was victory in the South and unifying the country. They were determined to pay whatever price was required to do that.

I'll tell you what touched me off. The POW issue had become a big issue by that time. And they had provided no accounting of American POWs—no names or anything. So nobody really knew much about the prisoners. And there was a lot of agitation back in the States about finding out about the POWs. I used the opportunity when I was there to put some questions to them about the prisoners. I didn't want to go and see the prisoners, but I did say that the Americans were sincerely interested in getting a list of prisoners. And if they could provide such a list they could probably win support in the U.S., I said, since they were seen as intransigent on that issue.

I got a lot of blank looks. They asked why the Americans were worried about this. I brought this up with some East European diplomats—East Germans and Hungarians. And we had several sessions with the Russian ambassador about this issue. I remember a Hungarian told us, "You know, the North Vietnamese simply do not understand why the Americans are concerned about their prisoners. Look around. Do you see any wounded soldiers here?" And it struck me—you didn't see any wounded soldiers, no amputees, in Hanoi. He said, "There aren't any." I asked, "Why not?" And he said, "It's a very simple answer when you think about it. The Ho Chi Minh Trail is a one-way street. People who were sent down the pike fight till they die or are just left down there. Nobody ever comes back."

When you were drafted in North Vietnam it was a death sentence. They also told me there was a lot of draft resistance in the North because people figured out that once you were drafted you never came back.

Also, remember, there was virtually no mail service in North Vietnam. So a family never got a letter from a son or father sent South. If they did, they were very lucky. When you went South, you were dead.

There was a lot of draft resistance in the North. A lot. But it was never in the press. Things like that really shook me up. On the one hand, I thought, what a noble sacrifice they were making. But on the other hand, how horrible! I got the impression that on the one hand the North Vietnamese leaders really believed that this was their duty—to unify the country. But on the other, the average person in North Vietnam was never particularly enthusiastic about the war.

Hanoi was terribly, terribly poor. Also, there was a real sadness about the place. The war had gone on so long with such a huge sacrifice that the common people had become terribly lethargic. They were so exhausted and they had so little to eat. I had never seen such poverty before anywhere in the world, and I had traveled a good deal throughout the Third World.

The leaders in the North had many cultural devices to draw on to keep the war going: the sense of loyalty to the country and the Communist party was well organized and really worked on these people.

Later, when I interviewed NVA prisoners in the South, I found that they were very unhappy kids. There was a lot of running away, a lot of desertion in their ranks. Now you see it again in the boat people, and in how screwed up the economy of Vietnam is today.

The journalists who went to North Vietnam were a carefully selected group of people. And they came back with these glowing images, like the people who went to China during the Cultural Revolution.

But the East Europeans who knew the North Vietnamese leaders were asking, "Who's crazy enough to do this?" They saw what was happening.

When I was talking to Le Duc Tho and Pham Van Dong about the POWs they would stare blankly at me as to ask, "What are you talking about? Two or three hundred men? Who gives a shit? We've lost 200,000 men going down South and never seen them again and who cares?" It was a very callous attitude, and at the same time it was breathtaking. You know one of those lightbulbs goes on in your head. I said, "Of course, how can they possibly see why we're interested in a few hundred prisoners, when they have no way of knowing what's happened to millions of their people?" That is what life was like to them.

I said to myself, "My God, this is horrible." So my idea of "the glorious cause" was seriously dented by actually going to Hanoi. You see, I'm the funny person who went to Hanoi being very antiwar and came home very anti–North Vietnamese.

I think that people like Jane Fonda who went to the North just didn't look around. They were either not trained enough or basically they didn't look. They didn't see this. They were mesmerized by the banquets and the good cheer and so on.

I was becoming a reporter at that time. I wrote a series of stories on the visit for the *Times*. When the first one appeared, the publisher of the paper called the managing editor and asked, "Who is this guy Butterfield and what is he doing in Hanoi, and what is his bio? Who is he?"

A short time after that I was working for the *New York Times* in New York. I stopped working on my Ph.D. for a number of reasons. First, the thesis topic I picked out wasn't going anywhere; and second, I had been in graduate school too long; and third, this was literally an activist period. People on American campuses wanted to be participating in the action. The idea of being in graduate school at that time really lost its appeal to me. When I began writing stories for the *Times* and publishing them the next day in the newspaper, well, my God! that was something.

I got called in to help out on the Pentagon Papers* in the spring of 1971. After we published the Pentagon Papers, the *Times* sent me to Newark for about a month and then they sent me to Saigon. So the real reward for working on the Pentagon Papers was getting the assignment in Saigon.

Of the individuals who went to Hanoi as correspondents, none ever came to Saigon except me. They went to Hanoi and that was all they knew about Vietnam. They would say, "We know all we need to know about Vietnam."

Harrison Salisbury is an example of this. He's really pretty bad on Vietnam. Read his book. Read his dispatches. He was wrong on all the important issues on Vietnam.

Saigon was this wealthy city, and they were relatively free, and people were telling me how bad it was and how there were orphans on the street. "Yes," I could tell them, "but go to Hanoi and see how bad it can get."

There were political prisoners in the South but there were major re-education camps in the North for political prisoners. I talked to the Eastern European journalists who were there and had heard about them.

By the time I got to Vietnam the American soldiers had become pretty sloppy and lazy and nobody cared. That was 1971. And I made a big effort to spend as much time as I could with the Vietnamese instead of the Americans.

I came to this from a very specific perspective. Early on, people came to Vietnam believing in the American cause. Later, correspondents came as committed antiwar activists. Very few people came having started out with the antiwar movement and then having had a change in their thinking and concluding, as I had, "It's not so simple."

In Vietnam I wanted, because of my academic training, to find a village

* *United States–Vietnam Relations, 1945–1967* (12 vols., Washington, D.C.: 1971).

that could be a sounding board. I wanted to find a Communist village. I drove to Long An province. I'd read a book by Jeffrey Race called *War Comes to Long An,* a good book that's entirely wrong. The book was 100 percent right up until the time he finished it. And then when he finished it, it had no bearing on anything. He wrote the book only up to Tet in 1968, and after Tet everything changed. All the guerrillas from that area went into Saigon to fight and were all killed. And in the aftermath, the U.S. Ninth Division went through that area and they just cleaned out every Communist that was left there.

So I went into this village and walked around. It had been a solidly pro-Communist village, but when I got there I could walk around and stay overnight. I took my interpreter, Nguyen Ngoc Luong, with me and I went back several times.

My conclusion from the village was that the political causes of the war had disappeared. The years of horrible fighting, sacrificing, and killing had affected the people so that they really didn't care any more. They had become survivors. They were contemptuous of the Saigon government for its corruption and inefficiency, and they were scared of the Communists for their very heavy-handed, ruthless methods and their constant appeals to ideology without any allowance for human nature. To them, the rights and the wrongs of the long conflict had almost been eliminated and the primary problem was simply survival.

This war was no better and no worse than other wars. General Weyand said that the lesson we've got to learn from Vietnam is that war is really hell, and if you go to war you've got to be involved in things that war is. War is about killing and death and terror. It's the absolute worst, and one shouldn't think otherwise. And if you can't accept that, stay out of it.

People who say we were in Vietnam out of some malice or that we were so bad and the Vietnamese were such good people, are just misinformed about the horrible thing that war is. And Vietnam was no less of a war than any other war we were in, but it was a lot longer than the First World War or the Second World War. We should remember that.

These figures about the bombing, for example. I remember talking about the bombing of Vietnam in my antiwar lectures and the tonnage of bombs that we were dropping. Then, when I got to Vietnam, I went first to Hanoi and I started looking for the bomb damage. I was honestly looking for it and it wasn't there. In South Vietnam and I was amazed by the tonnage of bombs they dropped and I didn't see bomb damage. We dropped millions of tons of bombs on the jungle. And maybe we killed a few people, but we didn't destroy cities. The figures on the bombing are irrelevant. They were dropped on the jungle—nowhere.

By 1972 I was not optimistic. After the Paris Agreement, the South Vietnamese needed continuing American economic support to keep South Vietnam alive, and they needed American air support to survive militarily.

In November 1973, I left, and said to the guy who was going to take my place, "Remember, this is a war and it's going to end militarily. Don't forget it. You're going to have to go out and cover it."

In 1973 I went to Tokyo and was there until February 1975 when they asked me to come back to Vietnam.

I went up to Pleiku in February 1975, and I went to see the press officer at the II Corps headquarters. This guy kept a little press book and every time a correspondent came in he had them sign his book. And he brought it out for me and I signed it, and I found that the last correspondent to be there was me in 1972. Nobody had been there since. Nobody had been to the highlands and they had forgotten there was a war.

After 1973 the reporters believed in the Paris Agreement, I think, and they got mesmerized by Saigon and the North Vietnamese who had their little camp out at Tan Son Nhut. Nobody was going out to see the real war.

I went to see a number of Vietnamese in Pleiku; I knew some of them there. I met a Vietnamese CIA contact, a very bright guy, and I visited the DAO intelligence people. The Vietnamese and the Americans there outlined for me exactly what was going to happen. They knew where the North Vietnamese were, their unit numbers, their position, and their objectives, basically. I just went up for the briefing.

I did one story on the North Vietnamese plan for the big offensive. I outlined the impending offensive, and I said that the central highlands would fall and nobody could tell the consequences of that.

I also found that the price of heroin had gone way down after the Americans left. The Chinese merchants who brought drugs in from Thailand were stuck with an enormous oversupply of it. The troops in the central highlands who had nothing much to do were getting hooked on it. This was almost pure heroin, very powerful stuff. Not cut.

The troops were very demoralized and they were so strung out they were completely ineffective. At this one fire base, nobody was doing anything. They were just sitting there stoned all the time. And so I started talking to people, and I found that a very high percentage of the combat troops in the central highlands were drug addicts. This was particularly true in Pleiku where the chief pusher in the area was the son of the province chief. He was operating out of the TOC [Tactical Operations Center]. His heroin price was very low, very affordable.

This area was in terrible shape and the men there were very vulnerable.

I traveled around the highlands and did other stories and then I went to the Delta to do stories there. I kept looking at the basic forces.

The American people had turned against the war. Whatever happened in the war seemed quite irrelevant. We were gone. So, in addition to the logistical consequences of the American pullout there were the psychological consequences. The South Vietnamese troops who went out on patrol would think, "I've got no air support and I've got no artillery fire, and the local commander can only fire two rounds a day."

That was all true. Really crucial things were gone. For example, if you wanted to come to the central highlands, the only way you could get in and out quickly was by air, and when they lost all air support from the U.S., they were down to a couple of helicopter flights a day. How can you support two divisions like that? You can't. And the North Vietnamese had four, five, or six divisions up there.

In the Delta, I saw the consequences of December offensive. The Communists had launched their first major offensive in the Delta since 1968 in December of 1974. And they had succeeded way beyond their expectations. The South Vietnamese lost chunks of the Delta that they hadn't lost since Tet. It was very obvious that the South Vietnamese had neither the will nor the wherewithal to stop the North.

I was in Vietnam for three weeks in February of 1975 and I saw some amazing things. The North made huge inroads in December, and the South Vietnamese morale had declined drastically. In the highlands they were sitting ducks, but they were doing nothing about it; they had no plan. I wrote a story about it. But nobody was paying attention. Nobody paid attention.

I went back to Tokyo. Later I went off on a planned vacation to Austria to go skiing. I was skiing for three days and Ban Me Thuot was attacked. I read about it in the *International Herald Tribune.*

I called my foreign editor and said, "This looks like the beginning of the end, and if you need somebody I'll go back." I wanted to know what was going to happen. I thought I could still do a good job there. A few days later, the withdrawal from the highlands began.

So I called again and this time he said, "All right. Go." I got on a train and went to Zurich, and I got on a plane and got to Saigon. I arrived in Saigon with my skis.

By the time I arrived, Pleiku had fallen and offensive had started to succeed. I found that the bureau chief of the *Times*, Jim Markham, had just left and gone to Bangkok. He never came back to Vietnam. But Markham, in his last act as bureau chief, had chartered a plane, a brilliant stroke. The plane came from Continental Air Services—they were there with a few planes. It was a spy plane flown by a guy who was an ex–Special Forces guy, a big guy who always carried a pistol. And for the last six weeks of the war we had this guy and his plane to take us around.

The first time I flew with him was to Danang on virtually the last day it was in the hands of the South Vietnamese. And I flew to Nha Trang on the last day the South controlled it. Then I went to Phan Rang. We went to a lot of places, and we would always be the last people to get out, since we had our own aircraft.

I became very emotionally involved. The funny thing was that the people in Saigon, in the first few weeks of the offensive, couldn't believe the worst would happen. But the Americans who went up there and saw what happened in Hue or Danang—saw the panic—knew that this was the end. And the panic began to spread. It took a long time to get to Saigon—

about three or four weeks. Soon every Vietnamese you knew came to you and wanted help. In the office we said we'd do what we could.

I didn't worry about my own safety until the very end, when Saigon was surrounded. And having seen the chaos and the panic in Danang and Nha Trang, nobody could safely predict what might happen in Saigon. Maybe the Vietnamese would turn on us, we thought.

There was a clear division between the correspondents who went along with the Embassy view, that there would be a negotiated settlement, and the others who believed there would be no negotiated settlement. I thought the North wouldn't settle for half a loaf when they could get the whole thing. I also did not think the North Vietnamese victory would improve Vietnam or the world.

But there was no choice for Americans. There was no way we were going to make the North Vietnamese pay the price and stop. Once the Americans made that decision, there was no way to change it. And it was tragic that so many Vietnamese would lose so much.

The final evacuation was so screwed up it was almost funny. I had a hotel room on the top floor of the Caravelle. I was the only person who was a guest on the top floor of the hotel. There was a bar up there. It made me a little nervous, because when the North Vietnamese rocketed the city, one rocket landed on a hotel just down the street and blew away the top floor.

That last night, I slept there with some trepidation. Soon after sunup I went to the office, about a block away. I wrote or rewrote my stories from the night before, updating them, saying that two Marnies had been killed out at Tan Son Nhut and that the North Vietnamese were inside the city now.

That took me a while. Then I heard that the North Vietnamese had moved into an area near the Saigon Zoo. Luong and I were going to look at that. So I went downstairs and our office car was gone, but Jim Markham had left his Volkswagen. I got in it, but I couldn't get it to start. I spent about fifteen minutes trying to get this thing to go but it wouldn't go. And finally Mal Browne came down the street and said, "The plug has been pulled. We're going to evacuate. Let's go." I was right outside the office. There was a twenty-four-hour curfew at that time and nobody was supposed to be on the street. I went back into the office and pulled my files out of the drawer, all the papers I had. I thought if there was anything worth saving it had to be those files. Then I went back to the Caravelle and got an airline bag I had. I put the files in the bag and came downstairs and we walked to the assembly point we had been told to go to, down on Tu Do Street. We waited for a bus and there was no bus. We waited there not too long, but it was apparent that nothing was going to happen there. So we walked for a ways to a hospital complex and waited there for a bus and it never came. We stayed there for an hour or two, and by that time there were more Vietnamese there than Americans.

There was a housing complex nearby and the idea was that the helicopters would land on the roof and pick us up. But the doors were locked and there was no way to get inside. So we waited. Keyes Beech and Bob Shaplen were there—a group of us.

I was starting to get a little worried. I was mostly worried about what would happen on the street with these Vietnamese civilians. It was natural that they would panic in this situation; and, in fact, a lot of Vietnamese tried to get aboard the buses and they did.

I got on one of those funny buses to the Embassy. The last bus that went to Tan Son Nhut took us out there. The bus drivers were, well, they were civilians who had never been in Saigon before and they never knew where they were going. Our driver took us down to the port and we told him he was taking us in the wrong direction. People were hot and confused and scared. We just didn't know what was going on. They said they were going to Tan Son Nhut and then went to the port where a lot of Vietnamese wanted to get on the bus.

When we got to Tan Son Nhut and tried to get inside there was firing going on and you could hear it. The gate was barred and there were soldiers there. They were pretty mad. They stopped us there for some time. Finally they let us in. We drove in, and as we were going by the American compound, which was on our left, a rocket came right over the bus—you could hear the whoosh as it went over very close—and it exploded about fifty yards away from the bus in the American compound. The stuff was coming in right over the bus. Very, very close. We could see this helicopter lying on its side, burning.

It was a little bit scary. Finally we pulled into the DAO compound. We went inside and got in line. We got in these groups of fifty—a group was called a "stick" by the Marines. They had machine guns and mortars and they were firing at something. I went outside and asked them what they were shooting at. They said they were shooting the bad guys. But I didn't see anybody out there.

We were waiting in a long line and people were telling jokes as we were moving forward. They were saying, "Will the last one out please turn out the light at the end of the tunnel?"

When we got to the front of the line, the Marine captain said, "Drop everything you have, and run for it." Some people dropped everything and some held their typewriters and so on. I had a little paper sack full of underwear and stuff and I dropped that and kept my notes. And they said run, and we ran. I waited till everybody else in the stick got in the chopper. Then I got in.

I still wasn't sure we would make it out. I wondered if they were going to fire rockets at us. As we drove into Tan Son Nhut, we saw a C-119, a "flying boxcar," a South Vietnamese Air Force plane, and it took off to about 600 to 1,000 feet and a rocket hit it and it just came apart. It was filled with people. And I thought if they could shoot that down, they could shoot us down. I didn't feel really safe until we got out over the South China Sea.

I felt very sad on the way out. I felt very sad for all the people I knew who were losing their country. I had studied China, and I knew what happened there after 1949. Now something like that was sure to happen in South Vietnam. I knew that there would be an end to that entire way of life and that anybody who had had anything to do with us was finished, absolutely.

Keyes Beech, *Chicago Daily News*
"Christ Almighty, How Can They Do This?"

I should preface everything I say about Asia and Vietnam by stating that we are all products of our times and of our environment. I belong to the World War II generation. And I much prefer winning wars to losing them. That includes Vietnam. So maybe I'm a bad loser; but I still don't like the way things turned out there.

I don't like the way things turned out there and I don't think it needed to happen that way. But that is a long, long story and I don't want to fight the Vietnam War all over again.

I was somewhat of an anachronism in Vietnam in that I knew that war was hell long before I got to Vietnam. For most of the correspondents there—they were nice guys and hard-working, sometimes very brave and resourceful, and all of that—this was their first war. I didn't get quite as excited about it. And I wasn't nearly as perturbed about the morality of it all as they were. I think all wars are immoral, but some are less immoral than others, perhaps. And I had been a Marine in the Pacific during World War II, I was a Marine combat correspondent, and I covered the Korean War, and then I'd covered a number of other things, little revolutions and small wars, all in Asia. In East Asia for the most part. The Indo-Pakistani wars, and the last of the French war in Indochina. So I was not exactly a stranger to the scene.

I took up residence in Saigon in 1965. I was writing for the *Chicago Daily News* and the *Chicago Daily News* Foreign Service.

David Halberstam was out there at about that time, and Mal Browne and Neil Sheehan and I. I was commuting between Tokyo, which was my home, and Saigon, up until 1965. That was when we committed combat troops and this was no longer a commuting story and I had to take up residence there. I stayed there, except for brief leaves, up until 1971. Then I moved up to Hong Kong. But I never really left. You never really left Vietnam; it was still the only story, and I kept going back.

When the terms of the Paris Agreement were made public, even the antiwar correspondents, the young ones, said, "Well, this is a sellout." And of course it was. All we were interested in at that time, was getting our prisoners back. We didn't give a damn about anything else. Really. And so in return for getting the prisoners back, we legitimized the North Vietnamese presence in South Vietnam and arranged it so they could defeat the South Vietnamese at their leisure. That was really the beginning of the end. I saw no threat from the U.S. for the North after that.

I don't think anyone was deceived by it. It was clear we were getting out and the war had lasted longer than we wanted it to.

I thought it was not a very nice way to do business. I felt that we treated the South Vietnamese government, which was totally dependent on us, rather shabbily. Thieu was not exactly your statesman type, but he was, in my view, not nearly as bad as he was made out to be. I think that he was doing about as well as he could in the circumstances. But I thought it was a pretty shabby way to treat him.

You see we were imposing our morality and our standards of conduct— our rules for democracy—on a country that wasn't even a country, for God's sake. That was simply the southern half of the peninsula that had never really been united, except for about fifteen years, in its two-thousand-year history. And we were demanding that they shape up, hold elections, do all those nice things like we want all our good little allies to do, and observe civil rights, and Christ, we're doing the same thing now in Central America.

I would never go so far as to say the press lost the war for us. I would say that the press did not lose the war, but they helped. Not because they were trying to, but the relentlessly negative reporting without any regard to perspective, was in my view, something that contributed to an erosion of support of the war. There are many other factors, of course, that were more important than this. Such as the fact that Lyndon Johnson never really tried to tell the American people what the war was all about. He was afraid that people would get all wrought up and it would cost him some of his Great Society program.

I would also say that broadcast journalism had far greater impact than print journalism in Vietnam. A correspondent has no honor in the country that he is covering because you seldom see what your colleagues are doing. It always seemed to me that television, no matter how good the correspondent was, was still show business, essentially. Let me give you an example. I knew a very bright and very able AP [Associated Press] reporter whose name I will not mention, who got fed up with AP. ABC offered him a job. He went to work for them. And I said, "So you're going into show business, are you?" And he said, "No, I'm not. I'm going to do it different, I'm going to do it straight. It can be done, I'm convinced."

So one day there was a little demonstration, a "demo," we used to call them in Saigon, by a couple of Buddhists. Somebody threw a Molotov cocktail to get the obligatory fire going and the police came in and chased them off. They didn't beat anybody up I don't think; I was just passing by and stopped to watch it. It was like a fender-bender in Saigon and it probably didn't involve more than a dozen people. In any event, our man was there, the young ex-AP reporter to record this on film. He shot it and then he panned the whole street, to be objective, to show that people were just going on with their daily lives, it was business as usual on that street in Saigon on that day.

Of course he made the evening news. The flames, the Buddhists [immolating themselves]; but not the other stuff. Now that's the way it goes. That's perfectly understandable. Who the hell wants to see a picture of a lot of cars going back and forth? They want to see the bang-bang.

He put his narrative with the story and he did say that business was going on as usual in Saigon. But during those riots that were going on in Saigon back in the 1960s, you would have thought that all of Saigon was going up in flames. But this involved very few people. And yet there it was, in living color, right on the evening news on television.

I know that Morley Safer is quite proud of the job that television did out there. And he is entitled to his opinion. The story that Morley did at Cam Ne in 1965 [of Marines using Zippo lighters to set fire to villagers' homes]; it's ancient history now, but I think that was highly sensational. As an ex-Marine I am biased. I could be accused of bias, but I don't think I was. The fact is that this village had been a pretty tough village and these people had been warned repeatedly that the village would be torched if they continued to shoot at Marines when they went in there. And I think a Marine battalion commander, I knew out there, whom I had known in Korea years before when he was a young lieutenant, said after the Safer story was shown, "Well, a Marine rifleman under fire is not a goodwill ambassador." But there was none of that in Morley Safer's story.

Shortly after that, Safer came up to Danang and the Marines gave him a hard time. He came to me for help. Or for some information. And I asked him, "What do you expect me to do?" I wasn't very helpful. Anyway, Morley is a Canadian, of course, which is not to be held against him; but I think that probably I resented the Canadian coming in and telling us how to run the fucking war. I think it seemed like that at the time.

I doubt that you can really tell the truth on television. There has to be a complete understanding between the correspondent in the field and the people back in New York where the film is going, I suppose. I guess it could be done. But I know that it wasn't.

On the other hand, I think that it's very difficult to defend some of the Vietnamese officials. It was not difficult to make them look bad; they made themselves look bad.

I think that they were greatly misunderstood. Some of the things that the Vietnamese were most condemned for, in their eyes, were not necessarily bad. For example: a province chief's job was very much sought-after. And all province chiefs were by definition considered corrupt by the Americans. By our standards they were, because they took money, they would charge a village head man so much for that job, and the deputy province chief had to pay the province chief so much for his job, and other people had to pay him. But in Vietnamese eyes there was nothing so terribly offensive about that because the province chief would have been derelict in his duty to his family if he had not looked after them first. We call this nepotism, but they would accept this in the Confucian tradition.

Now, what happened was this. To begin with, the Vietnamese were probably no more corrupt than other ancient societies, but when we came in there with all of our money, and everything that went with the American presence, they were much more corrupt than ever before because there was so much more to be corrupt with. And this was something that you don't get into a three-minute segment on the evening news.

It is so outrageous to even mention these things in a news context. You can't do this story, you can't tell it on television, unless you're going to do a documentary on the manners and morals of the South Vietnamese. I don't think that would have gotten you to first base if you had even suggested it. I used to try to work it into my stories from time to time and I did get a lot of it in the paper, but I don't know if anyone paid any attention to it.

Corruption became a terrible problem in Vietnam when it permeated down to the lowest level. Originally, corruption in Vietnamese society was only among very high-level people. A wealthy merchant might want a special favor done. He could go to see the head mandarin and the mandarin would say, You're disturbing the flow of tranquillity here. It would be understood that he must be compensated for this ripple in the tranquil surface in the stream of history that was flowing by. And it didn't affect many people.

I remember my cook, Nguyen Van Minh, came to me one time. He was very agitated and very angry. He said that the police had picked him up, and despite the fact that he had eight children and was over forty-five, they were going to draft him and put him in the army. He didn't have birth certificates for all of his children. However, they said that they might be able to find birth certificates for them if he found 15,000 piasters. Well, Minh was angry not so much because they wanted a bribe, but because they wanted too much. He thought that 15,000 was entirely too much and he had tried to beat them down and they wouldn't come down. Well, I paid the bribe. And so he got off and he wasn't drafted.

It is a difficult position for me, defending the South Vietnamese, whom I have criticized myself. But still I think that they weren't quite as bad as they were painted. Did they have any redeeming features at all? Well, a lot of them did fight, and some units, as is evident from almost any book you read on the last days of the Vietnam conflict, fought extremely well. And some of the officers, rather than surrender, committed suicide.

It shouldn't be forgotten that when Congress cut back on aid, this had a highly negative effect on the morale of the South Vietnamese troops. Here we were the country that was supposed to have such an abundance of everything to fight with, and it would have seemed that the least we could do was give them that. And yet in the end we cut their throats on that, too. I just don't think it was a very nice thing to do.

When Ban Me Thuot was lost in March of 1975 I felt that that was the beginning of the end. I was in Tokyo at that time, on my way back to the States, coming home on leave. I had left Hong Kong, but I was keeping up with the story, and I suggested to my office several times that I should get back there because it was obviously going to be more than enough for one man—we already had a man there. So I went back. And it was evident to me that it was going. Ban Me Thuot was the beginning of the end.

There were so many delegations coming over in the last days. I didn't cover them because I thought they were revolting, really. Actually, they weren't all that bad. Even Bella Abzug, I suppose, was moved by what she saw in Cambodia. They're not bad people. But I just don't believe in tourists around a war. Those people were exploiting the war, in a way. I remember when Ted Kennedy, for whom I have only contempt—really, I do—he came out, once, and he went up to Binh Dinh province, which was a very tough province. He was talking to some of the AID [Agency for International Development] officials and some of the civilian Americans there and he said, "Well, gentlemen, is there anything I can do for you?" And this one guy, a guy named Krieger, said, "Yes, you can stay home and leave us get on with our work out here." That's not the sort of thing you are supposed to say to a visitor, but that's how he felt.

I never foresaw it ending the way it did, leaving from the roof of the Embassy. I really didn't want to think about losing the war. I suppose intellectually I knew that we were going to lose it, but emotionally I found it very difficult to accept, because we invested so much and we didn't have to lose it, in my opinion. Although by that time we very clearly had lost it. In my view the war was lost here in the United States, not in Vietnam. I know it's a cliché, but it's true; we never lost a battle, but we lost the war. And I did not envisage it ending the way it did. I did not think that I was going to have to climb the Embassy wall to get out of Saigon on April 29, 1975.

I was out at Xuan Loc in mid-April. I never thought that they would hold out for long; I thought they were putting up a good fight, but I didn't think that it could last.

I wrote a story on April 14, which was based on CIA intelligence that we had, that said that Hanoi was going to come in and take the place, that they were not interested in any cosmetic solutions or any face-saving devices for the South Vietnamese. There was to be no political solution; they were coming in to take the place. That is of course what they did.

There were a number of correspondents who stayed, altogether about eighty. I didn't stay for two reasons. One was that I knew that the big story was going to be the fall of Saigon. That story I wanted to get out. I wasn't sure that I was going to be able to get it out if I did stay. That was a practical matter. Secondly, and equally, I did not want to stay. No, thank you. Emotionally, I did not want to see the Communists come in. I didn't think they'd come in and shoot all of the Americans or anything like that. As a matter of fact, after we left Saigon and were aboard a carrier in the South China Sea, it was announced on the ship's loudspeaker that all the correspondents in Saigon had been executed by the Communists. And all the correspondents aboard the ship said, "Oh, bullshit." Nobody believed it, and it wasn't true. I don't know where it came from, but maybe it was just wishful thinking on the part of the military.

I wanted to go to Saigon after the war ended. But they told me, "Oh, Mr. Beech, if you go to Saigon you're likely to run into some bad elements among your old friends down there." And I said, "I don't know why; all the bad elements I knew in Saigon are now in the United States. I thought they all got out. They're safe, unlike you poor bastards who are wondering where your next meal is coming from."

I would have liked to go back to Saigon, professionally speaking. But I was not going to beg them to let me go back. I was a professional foreign correspondent. I had thirty-three years in Asia. I was not some guy who's based in Washington or Los Angeles or somewhere else.

I had known John Murray, the first Defense Attaché, since he was a captain in Korea, and he is a nice guy. Before he left Vietnam, he used to confide in me a lot, because we had known each other for a time, and one day he got so emotional, he just sat there with tears running down his cheeks. And he said, "Christ Almighty, how can they do this?" He knew that they didn't have enough ammunition, some of their units. One might say that in the end they would have been defeated anyway; that to give them more military hardware was simply prolonging the death agonies. But that isn't the way you look at it if you are there.

Brian Ellis, CBS News
"They Were Just Boys"

I was running the CBS bureau in Saigon in the spring of 1975 when I became involved in evacuating the employees of all the news agencies along with their families and dependents. Word got out once the first groups started going. It didn't take long for the word to get around the Vietnamese community that somebody was getting people out. So I started getting all kinds of strange visits from strange people. And toward the end I had four rooms in four different hotels. I would change hotels at night because people were hounding me all day and all night—all this on top of running a bureau.

One night Dai Uy Ahn, who was the translator for the Vietnamese government's press briefings, came to visit me at the Continental Hotel, and said he heard about this little plan, because he knew that my Vietnamese staff were gone and some of the others were gone. I said, "I don't know what you're talking about."

So he said, "Look, I want you to make arrangements to get Colonel Hien and me out." I said, "I don't think I can do that. You're military. I'm not involved. If indeed I know anybody who is, they would only be taking out civilians."

He didn't really buy this, and he came back the next night. This time—you know he wears his pistol—he sat in my room, took out his pistol, and he had his pistol on his lap like this, you know, and he kept tapping this thing talking about the urgency of getting him and his colonel out. The message was very clear—that it would be in my best interests to try to accommodate them.

Now I thought, I've got a real problem, because if I do help either one of these, who knows who else they are going to bring? Am I going to start evacuating the whole bloody South Vietnamese military? So I went to Ambassador Martin and asked for an urgent meeting. I said, "Look, I've got a serious problem. I don't know how we are going to deal with this, but I got a visit from Dai Uy Ahn with Colonel Hien. Now we're getting into your responsibility. These people work for the government, and I think if they disappear it's going to be a dead giveaway. Remember, no one has yet seen that there is an evacuation going on. No one has declared an end to the South. No one has said anybody's going." We're doing all this secretly because Martin is insisting we don't trigger a panic.

Martin said, "I'll take care of it." I don't know what he did about it, but I was never bothered by Dai Uy Ahn or Colonel Hien. I did see them on the Embassy grounds the last day, so I knew Graham Martin had taken care of them.

There were a number of politicians and military types who came around, too—I got offered all kinds of things. I must say I was offered everything from gold to their daughters. It was an awful position to be in, having to decide and pick and wondering if you've done the right thing. Some people could say, "Well, it's an enviable position," because I could have made a lot of money out of it and had a great time by myself for the last bit, but I didn't get in it for that. I remember one time somebody offered me this beautiful chess set of ivory. God knows what it must have been worth. Just a beautiful thing. Offered to give that to me if I'd get them out. First they offered me money. I said, "I don't want money. Money is not what I'm looking for." They took that to mean that I wanted something like antiques, because there were a lot of people collecting antiques.

The next day this person was waiting on my doorstep in front of the hotel at about six-thirty in the morning. He's got this box wrapped in brown paper under his arm. He comes up to me, follows me to the lobby of the Caravelle, and says, "Let me show you this." And he opens this thing up and, God, they're beautiful ivory. I couldn't even have guessed what it was worth. But it was obviously something out of their family, they were a fairly affluent family.

Then I got calls from Americans who had their girlfriends there, American newsmen. I remember one guy called me up because he had a girlfriend and wanted to get her out. I said, "This is tricky." I did get her out. I didn't know who she was. I was also opening a new door. If I start taking girlfriends, word gets around. Well I made an exception here, I made an exception there. I broke my own rules. So it was very complicated. The whole thing was very difficult.

On a couple of occasions, people simply threatened me. One time one fellow who's now in the United States, threatened to kill me. He wanted to take his mother, his father, his mother-in-law, and others—it was an impossible number, like eleven, but it wasn't his immediate family. And I said, "We can't do this. But just give me their names"—and he said, "Well, then, I won't go." And I said, "Why don't you do that? You stay." He was with another agency. I said, "If you decide that, it's up to you, but I can't break these rules. If I do it for you then I've got to do it for everybody else. If you take all your relatives off, then everybody else would be entitled as well. I can't do that." This was a very heated thing.

Then he came back that night, and he told me if he didn't get to take his family, no one else was going to go out, and I wouldn't get out, either. He said he would stop the whole thing by stopping me. And I said, "So what are you saying, that you are going to tell on me?" And he said, "No, I'm going to kill you."

I didn't really take him seriously. The man was upset, he was angry; but I think now he might have done it. I don't know. I didn't want to think about it.

It was getting down to the last day, and Mr. Ba, who was one of our CBS drivers, knew that everybody esle had gone, all the Vietnamese had gone. Mr. Ba said, "You've got to take me." He was one of those who had a family of thirteen, eleven kids and I don't know what else. I said, "Mr. Ba, I would love to help you, but I don't have access; for me to go out and try to get thirteen of you on a plane would just be impossible." But I was trying. Even up to the morning of the day we left I was still trying to get people out. I took one run out in the morning. But Mr. Ba decided I had to take him. So I wasn't quite sure what he would do about this.

I was still going on the bureau, and we were covering this; it was starting to come undone, and they were shelling Tan Son Nhut that night. I went back to my room and I couldn't get in. The door was locked. I thought, I don't remember locking this, so I got my key and I couldn't unlock my door. I called downstairs and said, "I can't get in my room. My door's locked." So they came up and tried and they couldn't get it open either. And they said, "There's somebody in there." So I said, "Who is it?" And they said, "Mr. Ba is in there with his entire family." They were in my room, and he was sitting there refusing to let me get my stuff until I promised to take him.

He got one of the room boys to let him in. I never locked my room. I don't know if he had all thirteen with him, but he was in there with members of his family. When I left he was still in my room. He never came out. He was convinced I would take him, I guess, or that I would have to come in. So I had to leave all my stuff there. He was still in my room when I left Saigon.

When I went back in 1985, I tried to find him, but I never did. Poor guy, I felt sorry for him.

By April 28 I was pretty sure it was a matter of days before the end. I had a pretty strong feeling when I was evacuating that something was going to happen because I'd gone out to Camp Davis at Tan Son Nhut, as had others, and I saw the PRG [Provisional Revolutionary Government] representative at Tan Son Nhut. It was at the weekly briefing before Thieu resigned, I think. When the little briefing was over, some of us stepped aside and we were talking about one thing and another, and one of the PRG people asked me if I had made any plans for a vacation this year. There was enough in his conversation to let me know that if I wanted to leave this would be a good time to leave. We kidded about it and I said, "How soon will the North Vietnamese troops be here?" And he said, "Mr. Ellis, you know there are no North Vietnamese troops in South Vietnam"—still going through this charade, with tongue in cheek, I'm sure. But I came to the conclusion from what he said, if I did get myself in a fix where if I felt unsure, I could always go to Camp Davis.

I had another concern. I wanted to stay when the last day came. I thought that there was still a good story there, and I had no real fear for my life.

I had some worry after hearing about what happened to Ed Bradley and Mike Marriott—being chased by the police. That worried me. And there were times when I went to the airport and was given a hard time by the cops there. It was obvious they were angry. People were leaving. They thought they were being abandoned. It got very awkward. I toyed with the idea of staying, but being a family man, of course I had responsibilities to my family. So I sent a message to New York. By that time phone calls were almost impossible, so you sent by way of the telex machine. And Dick Salant, the president of CBS, ordered everyone out. "I don't want any heroes," he cabled back. "No heroes: this is a decision made by all the networks."

Apparently there was some meeting in New York. They all decided that no one would stay, that everybody would leave. If anybody did stay they would be "pool" material—one of the things I didn't want to get involved in. In other words, all three networks would have use of it. And I wasn't sure that was fair, or even possible.

So it came time to evacuate. Ambassador Martin said that when we heard "White Christmas" on the radio we would know that the time had arrived. But how in the hell do I go back and tell people, "When you hear 'White Christmas,' you'll know it's time to go to your designated evacuation points"?

Here we are in April and they're playing "White Christmas"—who do they think they are going to fool? First of all, the North Vietnamese don't know anything about this, anyway. And it seemed an odd choice of music to say the least. And it was no real secret in Saigon. At that point, everybody in the city knew it. There were people whistling "White Christmas." We were all kidding about it. I do remember hearing it played. I remember sitting in the bureau. And somebody suddenly said, "Well, time to go." Some people did head out, went downstairs. I remember Ed and Mike and Keyes Beech, and Bob Shaplen, and some others tried to get on one of the buses. They rode out to Tan Son Nhut, had a hard time, and went to the port. There was a list put out of designated places and this was for Americans.

I didn't have anywhere to go at that point. The thing was, whatever I was as chairman, since I wasn't an American citizen, I was a third-country national [TCN], so I was not entitled to go on one of the buses. And I could not officially go to the American Embassy. The Americans had no responsibility for me.

So I was sitting there thinking, "What have I done to myself?" I knew the British had long since left. I certainly wouldn't go to the French—although I shouldn't say that because they were kind enough to the boys at Phnom Penh.

I went down to the American Embassy. And I left a fellow Brit in the CBS bureau, Eric Cavalero, bless his heart. He was an eccentric English soul who had lived in Vietnam for many years, had all kinds of strange quirks. He was our night man; used to watch the office. We had this very British farewell and I wished him all the best. I said I was going to go to the Embassy. I was going to try, but I didn't know if I would get in. And he said, "Well, I'll be here when you get back." Just like saying, "The kettle will be on; we'll have a cup of tea."

So I get to the Embassy, thousands of people around the place, and the MP wants to see my passport. I've got my British passport, and he allows as how that doesn't do any good for me and suggests I go to the British Embassy. So just about then I saw somebody going in. I forget who it was, it may have been John Hogan. I called him through the gate and said, "I need to talk to you." And he said, "Okay, okay."

So they opened the gate enough for me to go in. I said, "Look, I've decided it may be smart for me to get out of here." And he said, "They say you can't come here, we've no place for you," and he gave me this routine about there's no provision for the press here. Then I saw Bob Simon with David Green and a camera crew, shooting the last people leaving, and somebody else was there, inside the compound. By this time the helicopters are starting.

The choppers are now landing in the courtyard, and the guys are filming people leaving. And I'm being given the story that I'm not supposed to be here—go to the British Embassy. So I walked around. I guess I was going to look for Graham Martin. I finally got into the Embassy itself by going over the top of the wall. So I was inside and this bag of film came flying over the wall, so instinctively I just reached down, picked it up and carried it. It was supposed to be going somewhere. The bloody thing was a nuisance. I had to keep carrying it around.

It was chaos inside with choppers coming in, people running and trying to climb over the wall.

I finally got up to the sixth floor to see Graham Martin. Of course there was all kinds of chaos in there, people running in and out.

I got to see Martin. We chatted just momentarily. I said, "Look, I don't think I have a way of getting out of here." And he said, "Well, stick around; we'll get you out." So I stuck around, went back down in the courtyard, watched the choppers. It was starting to get a little dark. There were not many people left and the choppers were the last to be coming in. Some Marine said, "Those of you still hoping to get out of here, better be on the roof in the next fifteen minutes or you're not going to go."

So I went inside the Embassy, went up the stairs, got on the roof. I sat there waiting, and nothing was happening. There were still quite a few people there, I guess, and this chopper came in. It was a Huey, an Air America Huey. The pilot was waving his finger, signaling. We couldn't figure this out because there was no radio communication, because this wasn't part of the military. There wasn't any frequency where he could talk to the Marines. The chopper sits down on the Embassy roof. The marine pulls back the door. I'm the only one on the roof now; there's no one else there. There are still others down below waiting to come up.

The Marine grabs me and says, "Get your ass in there if you're going," and he throws me in. Well, as I go in through the door, there are at least three Vietnamese in the back of this thing. The pilot takes off. The three Vietnamese have hijacked the helicopter!

It was an Air America craft and it was about to leave Air America at Tan Son Nhut, and these three ARVN soldiers came out and got in with their pistols. I said, "I manage to get out of this place, and now I'm in a damned chopper that's being hijacked."

We flew out. I'm sitting in between the pilot and these guys, and the pilot turns around and says, "Welcome aboard Flight 707 to Havana. I'm not sure where we're going, but these boys want to go to our ships." He was shouting. I could barely hear what was going on. I was all confused.

We were watching other choppers going because we were dropping flares out, because they were worried about heat-seeking missiles. We flew down the river and started dropping altitude. We crossed over this little beach area, and choppers were sitting on the beach. So we went down to a pretty low altitude and the Vietnamese guy was saying something to the pilot. We circled back over the beach where these choppers were, and the next thing we saw was these choppers coming off the beach. They were looking to follow someone. These guys didn't know where the American ships were. They didn't have the coordinates, I guess. I figured this out later. I didn't know it at the time.

It was still light, we could still see. And we had this convoy of choppers coming in behind us. We headed out there and he spotted a carrier, and it was the U.S.S. *Hancock*. We started heading in for it. The pilot had a conversation with the ship.

So we set down, and as we hit the deck, all these Marines were standing there with their rifles. Because the pilot had told them, "I've got armed men on board." So I get out and these bastards made us all spread-eagle on the deck, and they came over and searched all of us and frisk us all down, and this guy shoved his hand up my butt. I guess he thought I might be carrying something there. It was the most ridiculous thing I've ever seen. I was angry and embarrassed by this whole thing. I kept saying, "I'm not part of this." So they took us off to one side and they were questioning these people.

By this time, of course, the choppers are coming around, and there's no room on the deck for them and they're tipping them over the side. It was an absolute zoo out there. One chopper came down on the nose of the carrier. He just tore everything up at the front end. He sat down among a bunch of choppers; his rotor was just spinning everything to hell.

One chopper had a motorcycle in it. These things were packed to the gills, some of them. Not just on our carrier but on other ships they were just pushing them over the side because there was no room for them. Then when we finally went below decks, the place was packed everywhere with people. I went into the wardroom and that's where some of the other correspondents were. Ken Kashiwahara was sitting there and that's when I walked in with his bag of film.

I have never bought the argument that the press in any way cost or lost America the war. The demonstrations were going on back before I ever went to Vietnam. There was a long protest about the war, and it was growing and growing. I don't know what we could have done to make the war palatable. War is an ugly thing anyway. You say, well, we should have gone out and shown the boys winning? Well we didn't always show the boys losing. There were times we did stories on many of the good things that were done there by Americans, by Vietnamese—the so-called positive story.

But if you are watching the place slowly unravel it's hard to be positive

about it. We saw a lot of the things that were wrong. What are we supposed to do? Look the other way and say it didn't occur?

I don't talk about Vietnam a great deal. All these books that have been
written and where I've been mentioned and quoted, those are not things
that I volunteered to those people. They gleaned it from others. I guess I
do tend to bottle it up. I have troubles with it, sure. There are a lot of
things I wish I had done differently, both personally and professionally.
There was even one period when I looked back and thought the whole
thing was a waste. I don't now. I don't feel like I came away empty at all.

I didn't come back with all the excess baggage that some people do. I
think I've been able to keep it in some perspective. I wasn't carrying a
gun, or out there shooting at anybody. I was not faced with that. But then
I did spend three years there. I lost some good Vietnamese friends, a Vietnamese camera crew that I was very fond of was killed. It's not pleasant
to have to go out and bring their bodies back and tell their families. They
were killed because they were covering for American television. They
were killed in an attack. Their famiiles don't even know what American
television is. They never knew what their husbands really did.

The first time I went down to see the Vietnam memorial, I was with a
Vietnam vet. Most people think Edward Alvarez was the longest-held
POW—but there's another guy who was held a lot longer than he was,
who lived down in Key West. And he suffered a stroke not too long ago.
When I was doing the program in 1985 I was looking around for POWs
to go back to Vietnam, and I had not been to the memorial until then.
Anyway, this fellow came to Washington, and I met him in a restaurant.
It was obvious that I couldn't interview him because he had trouble;
speech was difficult for him. And I said, "Tomorrow would you like to go
out and look at the memorial? . . . Have you ever seen it?" And he said,
"No." I said, "Would you like to go out?" He said, "Yeah."

He was wearing his uniform. He had not worn his uniform in I don't
know how many years, but he felt like he should wear his uniform to the
monument. We walked down there. It just seemed like a wall with names.
I really wasn't struck too much by it. We walked by it and he kept looking at it. He kept shaking his head, saying, "All those names, all those
names." Then we got out to the statue, and he stood there and kept looking at it. And he started crying and said, "They were just boys, good
boys." And then suddenly it hit me what he was saying, *they were just
boys!* You kind of separate soldiers—men who are paid and trained to go
out and kill—from kids. But these were just kids. It was at that moment, I
guess, that it really came home to me and I realized that they were just a
bunch of boys on that wall. It struck me. Here's a guy who spent almost
fourteen years in a prison camp, and he felt sorry for them. The guy stood
there, tears rolling down his cheeks. And since then I've gone back a number of times.

I'm fortunate in some ways that there's no one on that wall that I know personally. But I have an attachment to it, somehow. It's a piece of all of us in a way.

Chuck Neil,
Armed Forces Radio
"I'm Dreaming of a White Christmas"

I had been in Vietnam since 1967 working for various companies. In 1973 I was working for FEC-ITT [Federal Electric Corporation–ITT], and a friend said to me, "Hey, the military are leaving and they're going to have to have civilians take over their radio station. Why don't you apply? I've gone through your records here and I see that you've had radio and TV experience."

And I said, "Yeah, but mostly behind the cameras in TV, and in radio, I've done some announcing but it's been years."

He said, "What the hell, give it a whirl. Call Colonel Hutchison at the radion station." He was the military manager of American Forces Radio.

So I did call the colonel and he set up an appointment for me. I went in and auditioned and interviewed. They had a master sergeant who was one of their program directors. Hell of a nice guy. He got in the engineer's booth and I got in the announcer's booth opposite him. He gave me the material to read—one page with a lot of words, names, place names, including President Nguyen Van Thieu's name, and he had Cairo, Egypt, and Cairo, Illinois. They wanted to see if you knew they were pronounced differently, Then they had a script to read, some type of PSA [public service announcement]. And they had me rip and read some news. They had three teletypes there at that time. AP, UPI [United Press International], and AFRTS [Armed Forces Radio & Television Service] Washington.

I forgot about it, really, for about ten days.

Then I got a phone call saying, "You got the job." So when I went to the station I met E. M. Turvett who had also been with FEC and I recognized him. I was acquainted with him. And they had a young fellow who had been an Army lieutenant there, by the name of Mike Monderer. He was the other announcer who had won the job. A real sharp kid, young guy. And at the University of Colorado, Colorado Springs, he was on the radio station part-time. He majored in communications. Then we had a chief engineer. There were four Americans. As an alternate engineer we had a fellow by the name of Ed Powers, so if our engineer wasn't available for the transmitter, Ed would come in and troubleshoot.

Of course the military was still there when we first came in and they sort of segued us into the job gradually over the period of a couple of weeks. And when the military left in March, they kept one American GI there who'd been at the radio station for several years. They kept him to help in the transition. He was supposed to be invisible, because all the American GIs were supposed to have gone. But he was still there along with several others a month or so after the official exit. They were sort of shadowy figures. Some wore uniforms because they could claim they were attached to DAO; which actually they weren't.

So there we were, four Americans, taking over American radio. In fact, we changed the name. Ian and I got together and said, What can we call it? We can't call it American Forces Radio, or Armed Forces Radio, any more, so we came up, simply enough, with American Radio Service, Vietnam.

We had a regular format—news, music, sports, twenty-four-hour day, one hundred thousand watts, FM radio.

My job title was "news announcer." But when we got there it was expedient that I do everything. The first few weeks we were on the air I did quite a lot of live broadcasting. News, live DJ shows, et cetera. We had Vietnamese personnel who were fluent in English who'd been with Armed Forces Radio and we retained them.

Several things were taped for us. We call them "actualities"; tape with a congressman or senator making a statement. But we got those primarily from the feed that we had, the twenty-four-hour-a-day feed, a satellite shot to the Philippines, and cable over to Vietnam. We were getting shortwave and feed from Washington, D.C., and we had a bank of tape recorders and we'd just take that right off the feed.

The station was Number Nine, Hong Thap Tu. Right in town, only about six blocks from the Embassy. It was a separate entity, a compound, I'd say about half an acre, quarter of an acre.

Well, about '74 we started to feel that Congress was going to take a hands-off approach to Vietnam, which they subsequently did. I wasn't aware how serious that was until just a couple of months before the fall. I kept hoping, most of us did that were there, that Congress would allocate some money to the Vietnamese to subsidize them and keep them going. And they didn't. That's what caused the fall.

It was just the last couple of months when we knew the shit had hit the fan. We knew that Vietnam was going to fall, but we didn't know it was going to be that quick. We thought I Corps would go, and then maybe the deep south and the Delta, but we thought that perhaps a perimeter there of a hundred miles or so around Saigon would hold for some time. Indefinitely, we thought; but that didn't prove to be the case.

We were privy to a lot of news from DAO, and when we heard they were abandoning the central highlands, Jesus Christ, we were flabbergasted. We thought, uh-oh, that's the beginning of the end. I said, "Perhaps they're going to regroup a little further south and make a stand there"—wishful thinking. It just didn't happen. We realized after that that it was just a question of time.

I didn't come up with that idea for the radio notice of the final evacuation. The public affairs officer at the DAO did, Ann Bottorf—the late Ann Bottorf. She was on the orphan airlift C-5A, and when the door opened the suction took her right out.

I don't remember exactly how we got started on this thing of the early warning, but we knew that somehow we were going to have to notify Americans there. A lot of Americans there were not connected with the government. They were working for private, U.S. government–invited contractors and they might not have any means of knowing, "Hey, it's time, get your butt out of here." Just about a hundred percent of the Americans there listened to American radio because it was the only radio station around. There were a couple of Vietnamese stations, but it was all Vietnamese or Chinese music mostly. As a matter of fact, a lot of Vietnamese listened to American radio because we had great music on the station. I could walk down the street by some Vietnamese villa or apartment house and hear my radio station, hear my voice come on.

Ann and some of the security people got together and said we'd have to have an early warning. So Turvett and I were called up to the Embassy to the security office and we tried to figure out what we could do on the radio to alert people to move out to their evacuation point or staging area for immediate evacuation.

So I said, "Why not play a recording of something that every American will recognize in a split second?" Plus the incongruity of the thing being played in the middle of summer would alert them to the fact that they'd have to take a hike. So why not play "I'm Dreaming of a White Christmas"? Of course I was thinking about Bing Crosby's rendition, the biggest seller, but of all the thousands of records and tapes we had at the radio station, I couldn't find Bing Crosby's recording, so I got Tennessee Ernie Ford's. It didn't matter who I had; but I noticed Frank Snepp and several other people said that it was Bing Crosby. It doesn't make that much difference.

Then I announced after the song, "The temperature in Saigon is 105 degrees and rising." That was the signal, then, that the evacuation was on. We recorded that and put it on a tape cartridge.

That was the plan, but by the time it all came down, every Vietnamese in town must have known what was happening. A lot of the younger Vietnamese there spoke some English, and just about all the Vietnamese, naturally, who had worked for the Americans were fluent in English. But the announcement wasn't for the benefit of the Vietnamese. This was for the Americans.

It's difficult to describe those last few days, believe me. It was a carnival. Nobody knew what was going on. People were leaving daily; busloads of Americans were going out to Tan Son Nhut. You'd see guys with Vietnamese families, guys who had gone Asiatic completely and married over there and had three or four kids. You'd see them in these U.S.-sponored buses going out to Tan Son Nhut with bag and baggage.

The night of the twenty-eighth of April, even the twenty-seventh, was bad news. A lot of heavy concussions and explosions. By the twenty-eighth, some of our radio station personnel, most of the young ladies and their families, we had already gotten out, they had gone three or four days prior from Tan Son Nhut. But some of our loyal personnel elected to stay and help us through the final days—about four or five Vietnamese. They got their families to come down to the radio station for the last two days, because we all knew that there was going to be an order to evacuate but we didn't know exactly when. They were so afraid of getting left behind that they were sleeping and living right there at the radio station.

These Vietnamese families are not small. They bring the mother, the grandma, the aunties and uncles. Those six people were responsible for maybe a hundred of their relatives, plus some of their friends, plus some people who just somehow got through the gate.

We must have had two hundred people in there. The toilet facilities were only built for a couple dozen. They were overflowing and inoperable. The place started to stink, and it was just awful, but there wasn't anything we could do about it. You couldn't say, "Clear out."

So on April 29, about 11:30 or 11:40 in the morning, I got the call from DAO, some colonel. I answered the phone and said, "This is Chuck." And he said, "Chuck, how many Americans do you have there right now?" And I said, "Four." And he said, "Well, you're ordered as of right now to evacuate immediately and proceed to the U.S. Embassy for evacuation flight." And I said, "Jesus." I knew the North Vietnamese were at Newport, which is a couple of miles down the road. Okay—this is it, then.

I hung up the phone and went in to Turvett, and said, "Hey Ian, this is it. Evacuate now." So we had a little plan with our Vietnamese employees that we were going to take them first because they had elected to stay and we had assured them that we would get them out. We didn't want to panic the Vietnamese who were there, but we had no means of getting them to the Embassy—two hundred people. We had a van and two pickup trucks there. So we took the van around to the side and alerted our Vietnamese engineers. We said, "Just don't say anything to anybody. Just walk out this side door into the van." Which they did. And I told the Americans, and some merchant marine happened to be there, I don't know how, and he was scared shitless. He didn't know what to do, he didn't have any place to go, so we took him into the station. Also an old Vietnamese-American expatriot by the name of Smitty. Turvett the station manager, me, and a friend of mine by the name of Van Buskirk who happened to be there. We got them in the van, and then I went back inside.

We had a big Gates Automatic Programmer. We programmed most of our day on that machine. And I went back in there and took the cartridge with "105 degrees and rising" and "I'm Dreaming of a White Christmas," and popped it in the slot and punched it up. And that was my final act at the radio station. We didn't just rush out though, because I said, "Hey, maybe we should take a goddamn weapon. At least take the shotgun." The day before that or a couple of days before I had a flak jacket on, a Winchester twelve-gauge shotgun, when all the explosions were going on. I thought we were going to be invaded. They were still right there. I thought about taking them. But I realized that might be fruitless. What am I going to do with a shotgun against the whole North Vietnamese army?

I took the flak jacket off, but we kept the shotgun, thank God. We had to run the gauntlet to get to the Embassy. By this time the ARVN were getting rather surly, jealous, and mad that we were taking off. We were de-de-bopping on out and leaving them there. *De De Mau* is how they say it in Vietnam. Means "take a quick split."

So we kept the shotgun and I had my .38 Colt Cobra. Ian Turvett had his Walther 380 automatic and one of the other guys had a Colt .45 automatic. So we were armed to the teeth. We got into that van. By this time there were hundreds of people outside this radio station. The only thing that kept them back was a big chain-link fence. And we still had a couple of guards there from the PA & E Security, Pacific Architects and Engineers. But we had some Vietnamese guards who were still on the job. I have to hand it to them in that respect. People were trying to climb the fence. Some were succeeding.

But we got out. We had to honk the horn and people had to part for us to get out. They couldn't see that in the back were our Vietnamese engineers and a couple of Americans. And I'm sitting with my revolver tucked in my waistband. We weren't afraid of the North Vietnamese—it was the ARVN. Sometimes they would stop you, in the last couple of days; they would stop Americans from getting through checkpoints, just being contrary.

So we started down the street. It was only about six blocks to the Embassy, but right at the intersection there was a checkpoint and they wanted to see—they didn't want to see any Vietnamese being taken out. These guys had M-16s, locked and loaded. And I don't know if you've heard, but these ARVNs were quick to pull the trigger. Just shooting in the air, even. And they looked mean.

Turvett was driving. I was sitting on the passenger side on his right. So we stopped and said a few words. I reached in the glove compartment where I had a carton of Salems and I just threw the carton of Salems and the guy said "Thank you," and waved us on.

Then coming up the street slowly we could see thousands of people surrounding the U.S. Embassy. And we thought, "Jesus Christ, how are we going to get through this?" Well, we did. We made a left up a side street right by the national police headquarters and then the next gate down was the U.S. Embassy. They had the side entrance and that's where we got in. It was bristling with Embassy security personnel with machine guns, shotguns, you name it.

I think we were one of the last vehicles to be allowed inside. We had a shortwave radio and a big antenna for emergency purposes, and so at first the guards weren't going to let us in. They said, "Just leave the van, and come on in." There were vehicles abandoned all over the place. And we said, "No, we got an emergency radio in here." So they said, "Okay, see if you can squeeze it in." There were a lot of vehicles in there already, but they had to leave the courtyard open for the choppers to get in.

When we got there they were chopping down two trees that happened to be in the middle of the courtyard. So we parked and this guy got out with the shotgun, and I said, "Geez, disarm this shotgun." And I jacked all the shells out of it. He was waving it around and I thought the damned thing was going to go off. You weren't supposed to take any weapons with you. Some guys did. One Air America guy said, "Hey, this .45 automatic has been with me over here for six years and I'm not about to give it up." But my little .38 Cobra I took over to one of the Marine guards whom I knew, and I said, "Hey, here's a present for you." And he said, "Jesus Christ, thanks."

The Marines and the Embassy guards had set up several thirty-caliber machine guns. They had one at the Combined Recreation Association compound, where the swimming pool was. They had this thirty-caliber machine gun set up pointing toward this gate that fronted on Hong Thap Tu Street. And about a week before the final day they had put up extra sheet steel and welded that to the regular gate, which had just bars. They put some reinforcing bars in back of it. And believe me, it was straining even then with the thousands of people leaning up against it. But they had this machine gun trained on that gate. And some of the guys had rolled empty hundred-gallon oil barrels up to the gate and the wall and were looking out over the top and helping pull up some of their buddies— Americans. And a lot of Vietnamese would stretch their hands to be pulled up, too. You couldn't do it. My God, the compound was already loaded. We must have had three thousand evacuees, not only Vietnamese but a lot TCNs from the Philippines and Korea. And, of course, Americans. When we got there about quarter after twelve that afternoon, already that place was jam-packed.

They had all of the evacuees and the refugees back in the CRA compound area. They were well behaved, but it was crowded. A couple of security guys were at the swimming pool. They had collected weapons. They were taking the automatics and popping the clips and dropping them into the pool, and the revolvers they would turn over and empty right into the swimming pool. But the guns they were throwing into these boxes, and they had four or five boxes jammed with all kinds of weapons.

About this time, everybody was going inside the CRA restaurant and just taking over. There was no personnel there to speak of. The manager of the place was still there, but he just opened the refrigerators. Some of the people were frying up steaks on the grill, and the liquor locker was open and hundreds of bottles were consumed until finally there was nothing left. About three or four that afternoon the Vietnamese outside shut off the water to the compound, so we had no water. And everybody was getting thirsty, but I found a bottle of Vichy water, or something, with a cork, and one little Vietnamese girl, about fourteen, asked me for a drink. And I gave her that to drink and she handed it to one of her little brothers or sisters and they had a drink, and then her mama-san had a drink, and then they passed it around, and by the time it got back to me it was empty. Geez, I was thirsty. Didn't get a drink until the Marines finally got there.

The first chopper came in about four o'clock, I guess. Right in the parking lot.

The Americans had number-one priority, but they were lined up around the pool in long lines, just sitting around by this time. What we were looking at were just about the last Americans in country, with the exception of a few scattered. And I can't recall how many were there; not that many, maybe a couple hundred Americans, and the rest of the crowd was all Vietnamese and third-country nationals. Jeez, I can see it now. And it was hotter than hell, naturally.

The explosions started a little later, just before dark, and some of the Marines were yelling—the first time I heard a Marine yelling, "Oh, shit! Incoming!" And by this time I was inside—I could get inside the Embassy compound because I had a pass. There was a gate from the CRA compound to the Embassy compound and a fence separating them.

I saw Martin there, the ambassador, in the halls. I just saw him walking from the office of one of his underlings. As you can imagine, he looked rather hairy. For some reason I had to go up to communications in the Embassy itself on the third or fourth floor. Of course things were in disarray. A lot of the Embassy personnel had already gotten out; not all, but a lot, and they had abandoned their weapons. There were beautiful handguns lying around all over the place, just left there. Probably the Marines gathered them up before they left.

They were trying to take people in rotation from the line that formed outside in the compound. But I really wasn't in that line. I was back and forth between the compound and the Embassy, and I just stuck around to make sure that our Vietnamese engineers got out. We had higher priority than they did, but I wanted to make sure that they got out, and they weren't taking any Vietnamese at first except a select few.

We got on the telephone and called the radio station and told them to use the vehicles to shuttle from there to Newport. I understand they had a hell of a time but they made it. We had tried to get out, Ian and I, to take the van and see if we couldn't shuttle some back and forth, but there was no way. They wouldn't let us out. I don't think we would have been able to make it in the van anyway, because there were too many people out there on the street.

It got dark and then, either artillery or rockets, but heavy explosions started. I don't think they tried to zero in on the Embassy itself, or they would have. I think they were letting us get out. But occasionally some rounds would come in, small-arms fire. I think that was dissident ARVN, but I have no way of knowing. There was one explosion just outside the wall. At first I thought, "They're trying to zero in on us." But to my knowledge they didn't, even after I left.

I didn't get out until about one o'clock. I was one of the last few Americans to be evacuated.

We walked up those damned stairs to the roof and I could look down and see that CRA compound just filled with Vietnamese and TCNs. The chopper was waiting. We had about four of our Vietnamese engineers with us on the same chopper.

I knew that our exodus was permanent, at least for the foreseeable future. I was disgusted with the whole thing, to be honest with you. I felt like we abandoned a lot of people.

After all, I'd been there so many years it was getting to be like home to me. And I thought about some of the young people I knew, some of the young girls that worked—the bar girls, the hostesses. Some of them were nice kids, really. I'm not talking about whores. There was a gal I knew who'd been married to a friend of mine, and I just wondered to myself, What the hell is going to happen to these people? Are they going to survive, or what? I almost decided, "Well, I'll leave the Embassy and just stick around."

We got off okay, but some of the choppers, a couple from the courtyard, just barely made it over the wall. They were heavily laden. They threw baggage off and a couple guys would jump off. Finally the chopper got up and it was laboring, but finally it started to go and just cleared the wall by a foot and then it slowly gained altitude, and then it was okay.

Our chopper didn't seem to have much trouble getting off the roof. We had about forty-three or -four on our chopper. As we flew out you could see they were burning some oil and gas dumps. Long Binh was ablaze. Fires all over the place.

By this time some of the people were anxious to get the hell out and get it over with. We got up to altitude and we only had to fly about a hundred miles out to the ship. Forty or fifty miles to Vung Tau and then about sixty miles east of that to where the *Hancock* was lying off. So I think it only took us maybe an hour and a half.

As we went out, I could look down and see lights in Vung Tau. I could see the ocean, the white surf. And I thought, Jesus Christ. I wasn't ready to leave yet, you know. I felt like we were letting a lot of people down.

At the moment you are confused about the whole situation. I had mixed emotions about it, but I was glad to get out with my butt intact, and yet again I was sorry to leave so hurriedly. All those years I was there and then all of a sudden the place that had been my home for years was gone.

The following day, about eleven in the morning, I heard my voice come on the radio and say, "It's twelve o'clock midnight in Saigon on American radio." Jesus, we thought. We had diesel generators. And the generators must have still been operating because we were still broadcasting. And I thought to myself, "Gee whiz, it's funny they haven't gone to the radio station and shut everything down or blown it up." They didn't want to blow it up; they wanted to keep the equipment.

When we first touched down, the Navy guys took us over to the bridge side of the ship—I was there with these Vietnamese engineers that went with me—and they said, "Okay, drop your trousers." I said, "Hey, no way." But the Vietnamese did and they gave them a finger wave. They were checking for weapons. I thought, What kind of weapon would a guy stick up his rectum? Not a knife. And I said to Ian, "Geez, these Vietnamese must think it's some strange Occidental custom." That was their entrée to the U.S. Navy.

The Vietnamese helicopters came out the next morning. About half a dozen Marines would come out with their M-16s and kneel down and point them at the chopper, and then one Marine, unarmed, would walk up and pull the thirty-caliber machine gun from the cradle and dump that over the side. Then he'd have the guys spraddle up against the chopper and search them for weapons. The Vietnamese pilots. If they had any, they'd pull them out and throw them overboard. They'd take the Hondas out and push those overboard, and you could see the Veitnamese guys just looking aghast at that. Because instead of taking people they had filled up the empty space with Hondas, but the Marines threw those right overboard. And rightfully so. Then they towed the chopper to the stern and pushed it overboard.

A lot of the Vietnamese officers in Vietnam were a conceited lot and could even be a little surly, but their attitude changed real fast after they got on the *Hancock*. And they herded them down below, just like anybody else. Most of them took off their insignia.

I think about Vietnam quite often, still today. I think about it often. It feels like unfinished business, somehow.

CHAPTER XIII

Civilians

John Walburg, "Vietnam Johnny"
"Sweet Jesus, I'm Back in the World"

When Danang fell, I figured we had maybe three or four months left before the North Vietnamese took over. I knew they were coming. But my wife kept telling me that it wasn't going to happen. She thought the U.S. Marines would come running in at the last minute—just like the cavalry in the movies—and save everything. I knew better than that.

I had been living in Vietnam since 1969. I was married there and my wife and I had three kids. We lived between Bien Hoa and Saigon. I actually planned on living there for good. But then the war went bad for the South and everything changed.

Outside Saigon there was this big supply depot where all of the stuff that the Americans gave the Vietnamese was stored. They had a big Cyclone fence around it. And whenever I drove into Saigon I passed the place. And week after week I watched the supplies dwindle, until in mid-April it looked like a big, empty parking lot. As I watched that supply depot get smaller and smaller, I knew what was happening and I knew the end was coming.

It took me two days to get our papers to get out of the country. Two days of standing in line and filling out forms. We were supposed to be on a flight out of Saigon on April 28. But then they bombed and rocketed the base before our plane could take off, and we had to make other plans.

We finally got inside Tan Son Nhut on the morning of April 28. The guards at first didn't want to let us in, but we paid them some money and they let us through. Inside the gate we were told to proceed to the DAO annex, which was to be the departure point for us. We went there and had to get some more papers and wait in line some more. We got our papers stamped and got a number. We had Number 29, I remember, our plane number. And at that time they were up to Plane Number 17. And everybody kept asking, "What plane are they on now?" Everybody seemed worried about getting out and there was a lot of praying going on.

After we got our number we had to sit on the ground and wait. They had parachutes spread overhead to protect us from the sun. Finally, we got on a bus that was supposed to take us out to our plane. And we were all sitting on the bus when all of a sudden a rocket came in and hit the building next to us. It blew the top of the building off—the roof flew over and landed in the DAO swimming pool. We heard that rocket coming in. And I really thought we were going to get it, right there on the bus, on the steps. The door of the bus was closed. I grabbed my son and ran to the front of the bus and pushed the door open and kicked the driver out the door. There was a real panic, and everybody was screaming and running for that door. My wife was right behind me with our two daughters. The three of them ran across the street and lay down in a ditch. I lay down on the street with my son and protected him with my body. Then all of a sudden I thought, "This is really stupid." I was in the middle of the street. So I picked up my son and carried him to the side of the street. We were there the rest of the night. Rockets and artillery fire kept coming in. And everybody around us was screaming and crying and praying. Everybody was trying real hard to become part of the ground. When daylight came we were still taking some incoming fire. With daylight nobody knew what to do. The bus driver had disappeared. So I told everybody to get back in the bus. I saw helicopters landing and taking off at the DAO headquarters right around the corner. I drove the bus full of people to the gate of the DAO headquarters. There were Marine guards posted there. They wouldn't open the gate. They said, "This is a secure post and nobody can come in." I told them that all of our names were on a manifest to go out on a plane and that there weren't any more planes and we wanted to get out. Then they said, "Well, we can let you in because you're an American citizen. But we can't let those other people in." But, damn, there was no way I was going to leave my wife and kids and those other people sitting on the bus. So I just sat down in front of the gate and said, "Well, buddy, we got nowhere to go now. So we're just staying right here."

Finally, an officer came out to the gate. I showed him our papers and he let us come in.

They led us to the communications building in a corner. By this time the people with me hadn't eaten in more than a day. So I walked over to the PX. Nobody was in charge. I loaded up with some apple pies, some sandwiches, and some Twinkies and carried them back to our group. I passed them out to everybody. Then I went back and got some more—candy bars and more sandwiches. There were seventy people in our group and I was taking care of all of them.

We were left alone in the building without any escort. I started looking around the room. I found an army helmet on the floor and put it on. In a desk drawer I found a .38 and I stuck it in my belt. I was in charge now.

After a while I really thought they had forgotten we were there. So I walked over to the main building, which was packed with people. They were processing people there to go out on the helicopters. I found a guy who looked like he knew what he was doing. He was in the library of the DAO, and he had a stack of cards that people were supposed to carry. They were all TWA baggage tickets. He told me to write numbers on the cards, starting with 1–1 and then 1–2. I was to go up to 16 and then start over at 2–1 and 2–2, and so on, up to 16 again. Everybody in my group had to have a card. There would be sixteen people in each helicopter. The first number was the helicopter you would be on.

So I went back to our group with all those tags, and all of a sudden everybody was yelling, "Me first! Me first!" A Vietnamese congressman walked over and offered me $400 for the first tags so he and his family could be the first to leave. I knew all of us were going, so I took his money and gave him the tags. Then I started filling them out for everybody else. There was a priest there and some pregnant women and I put them on the first helicopter, too. It was something like assigning lifeboats seats on the *Titanic*. Everybody was quietly, politely mobbing me. There was this very old man and his wife. They were just scared to death. He came over and offered me five dollars to put them on the first chopper. I told him to keep his money and I put them on the first chopper. My wife and kids and I were on the last helicopter for our group.

Then I lined our group up and led them all over to the main DAO building. There was a long line inside and we stood in that line with our baggage tags. As we got near the front of the line they suddenly told us, "No suitcases." We could only bring one small bag per person. I had a briefcase and my wife had a small travel bag with clothes, and that was all we brought out.

It seemed like forever, standing in that line. In fact, we were there all day long. Finally, very late in the afternoon we got to the front of the line and they led us out to the helicopter—a big Chinook. We got in, but they stopped our group right after my wife. There were two young Vietnamese women behind her and they signaled that the women had to go back inside and wait for the next helicopter. But they were really scared. They apparently didn't think there would be a next helicopter. So they grabbed onto my wife and started crying and wouldn't get go. The ramp started to close and they were still hanging onto my wife. I tried to push them back, but they hung on, screaming, "Help me! Help me!" They were Vietnamese nurses and they had worked for the Americans. Finally, they put the ramp back down and brought them inside. Then we took off.

I stood next to the door gunner as we pulled up. I was thinking, "Man, I'm finally out of here." I was happy to be in a helicopter again. I hadn't been in one since I'd been in the Army. They had me pass cotton balls out to the passengers so they could stick them in their ears because the engine was so loud. We flew over Vung Tau and saw the beautiful beach there. That was our last look at Vietnam.

I was looking ahead to see where we were going. Then I saw the American fleet—the whole Goddamned fleet just sitting out there in the South China Sea. What a beautiful sight.

We came down on a helicopter carrier. I jumped out first and then helped my wife and kids out. There were American photographers, Marines, and sailors all around and everybody was speaking English on the deck. Everything was under control. And I looked around and said to myself, "Sweet Jesus, I'm back in the world."

Dr. Bruce Branson
"A Planned Program of Terrorism"

Around the time when the Peace of Paris was signed and the American military were about to withdraw from Vietnam, the State Department contacted our Adventist hospital, which was in downtown Saigon, and asked them if they would be willing to be responsible for taking care of Americans there at the Embassy. The hospital that we had was taking care of Vietnamese almost exclusively at that time. It was a relatively small place, so the administrator of the hospital said if they had larger quarters and could get more help, they probably could do that. The Third Field Army Hospital there had been pretty well evacuated already. It was about a mile from Tan Son Nhut Airport. So an agreement was reached to transfer the whole hospital over there, and that became the new Saigon Adventist Hospital.

One of the provisos of the Embassy was that they would need to have specialists available in surgery, orthopedics, and internal medicine. Now, there had been specialists there in orthopedics from the United States— there was a lot of trauma, of course—and in anesthesia, but they didn't have regular full-time specialists from the United States in surgery or internal medicine. So the dean of the Loma Linda University School of Medicine flew out and met with the Embassy officials and some of the mission personnel, and they signed an agreement to provide the hospital with staff from the medical school. I was chief of surgical services at Loma Linda University Medical Center at the time, and I went out on a regular rotation along with quite a number of other people in 1973 and put in about a three months' rotation.

The hospital was usually full. And we had very large clinics. We had two or three wards that were reserved for Americans, and the rest of the hospital was for Vietnamese. The Vietnamese government required that forty percent of the people we saw had to be indigents. The others could be part-pay patients or full-pay patients; then the U.S. government reimbursed us at cost for the Americans we took care of. When they got well enough to transfer, if they were close to the time when they needed to go home, the military transport or the medevac team would fly them out to the Philippines.

In '73 things were reasonably stable. In fact, they took me on a trip to Danang and Hue. We had mission hospitals and orphanages up in Danang. Even that far north it was reasonably stable, although there were Viet Cong guerrillas living in the hills and mountains. In the cities the South Vietnamese had control.

In 1975 in March things began to crumble and there was a real panic in Danang when the North Vietnamese began a serious advance. It came my turn again to go out there. There had been some confusion about whether or not the hospital should try to stay open in Saigon. A couple of the Americans who were there decided they'd pull out, and they a left a gap in the surgery coverage. They went to Hong Kong and decided they'd sit it out there for a while to see what would happen. We got an urgent call from the Embassy that they were not being covered, so I decided to go out and fill the gap.

I don't think we were getting completely accurate information. Things were a bit confused. But it seemed to be relatively safe in Saigon. You have to remember that Phnom Penh had been surrounded for about a year; six months to a year, and the city had held out with a siege, and it was possible to carry out an orderly withdrawal from the Embassy there. So people felt, both in Saigon and at Loma Linda, that this fighting in the north was probably going to be contained and that it wasn't really all that serious.

We were able to communicate with home most of the time by telephone, so I could keep in touch with people at Loma Linda and my wife and family. After a while the telephones were difficult to use and we began to use ham radio operators. They'd contact people in California and patch us through into the phone circuit, and we could talk. So I was able to keep some communication open that way.

We had had a nursing school at the hospital. But they let the nursing students go home when things became really unsettled in the countryside. Many of these nurses came from different parts of the country, and they didn't know what had happened to their relatives. They wanted to go home. So they closed down for an extended interval. Then, about two weeks after I had gotten there, we began to receive nursing students back again who had been up-country, in Nha Trang and along the coast. They said that the advance of the Vietcong was much more rapid than the South Vietnamese radio was admitting, and that they had witnessed massacres and had to travel by night and hide out during the day. They told real horror stories. They had witnessed mass executions by the North Vietnamese near Vung Tau.

There was active fighting all up and down the coast. These young women had gone on foot. Twenty of them straggled in over a period of a week or ten days, and the stories they told were so intimidating that it got everybody quite edgy about what was happening. Nobody felt then that they could believe what the government radio was saying anymore.

They would tell stories of the North Vietnamese coming into a village or town and rounding up what they thought were the leaders, and just shooting them or beheading them. Or if they captured South Vietnamese soldiers as prisoners, they would just line them up and shoot them. It was that way all up and down the coast. It seemed to be a planned program of terrorism. It made us rather worried down in Saigon because it was well known that our hospital had previously been an Army hospital, that we were taking care of Americans, and there were a lot of American nurses and physicians. We discovered that quite a number of people who lived in the vicinity and actually some of the employees were Vietcong sympathizers. Yet some of them also had close friends who were working right there in the hospital. The Vietcong let them know that there were certain people on the staff who had been put on a blacklist to be executed as soon as the North Vietnamese came in. On that list were most of our administrative personnel.

It made everybody a little uneasy because you didn't know for sure who was on our side and who was working for the Vietcong. I think some of them just wanted to be on the winning side no matter which way it turned.

So we talked to the Embassy folks about this. And they said, Well, if it really comes to evacuation, we'll do everything we can to help you get some of those people out who would be most vulnerable.

At that time everyone in Saigon seemed to expect that Congress would vote additional funds to beef up the South Vietnamese army. But as I would talk by ham radio with folks back in the United States, it became obvious that what we were hearing over the radio and TV was quite different from what was happening in America. Probably our best, most accurate news came from the BBC overseas broadcast. The local Army radio would just be playing jukebox music most of the time and saying nothing substantive at all about what was happening.

When it became obvious and the folks in Loma Linda saw that Congress was not going to vote any more money, they began urging us to get out while we could.

We stayed on, I guess altogether, about six or eight weeks more. While our own administrative personnel and ministers were up from Singapore trying to assess the situation, in our emergency room we began getting casualties from guerrilla warfare and hand-to-hand fighting out on the periphery of the city. That was the first inkling we had that the Vietcong were that close. So we reviewed that with our leadership, and then they began to practically live down at the Embassy, trying to find out what was going on and what plans were being made for an evacuation if it became necessary. They never could get any really straight answers about it. The ambassador was determined not to let it appear that anything was wrong. He didn't want panic and rioting to break out in the city, so he didn't start an evacuation.

But there was a major general in the Embassy who began dealing directly with the problem. We found out later that back in Washington there was a debate going on between the Defense Department and the State Department, and finally the Defense Department just started taking things into their own hands. At that time they still had about fifteen thousand Americans out there who had been in the military but in civilian clothes and were doing various important jobs in the country. They realized they had to start getting those folks out. Many of those individuals had Vietnamese dependents, wives and children. So they began an airlift about April 15 as I recall, and then things did begin to move.

Large numbers of Vietnamese began to come to the hospital and wanted us to help them get out. We had some Vietnamese friends who were already in this country. We had two Vietnamese students here going to medical school. One was the son of the dean of the School of Medicine of the University of Saigon, and the other was the son of the chief appeals judge of the Appeals Court in Saigon. They desperately wanted to get out and join their families that were in the U.S. So we began a series of trips to the Embassy and then to the airport.

The Embassy at that time had a ruling that the only Vietnamese who could be gotten out were dependents of Americans. This is when they were trying to get this rather large number of Americans evacuated. So some of us started adopting some of these folks. We would take relays when we weren't in surgery or at the hospital or clinics, and go over and stand in line to process all these people to get them out of the country as our dependents. Before it was over, I think the eight Americans that were there each formally adopted fifty or sixty Vietnamese, some of whom were older than we were. We guaranteed we would support them, house them, and take care of them.

All during this time we were trying to get as many American patients out of the hospital as we could, and the medevac flights were still in progress, so we could put these people in the ambulances. We would put in as many Vietnamese (acting as attendants and nurses) as we could with each one of these American patients. When the guards at the airport would see the ambulances coming and the IVs running and the bandages and everything, they would let them go on through. Then the so-called attendants, of course, would not come out. They would stay with the patients and end up in the Philippines. This was illegal at the time because only dependents of Americans were supposed to get out—they agreed, however, that we could send Vietnamese attendants along. But before long we ran out of American patients. And we pleaded with Medevac Headquarters in the Philippines to keep the flights coming so that we could get more people out who were employees and people who were at high risk.

So for several days they were willing to keep up that façade, and that helped us get through the line. But after a while they said, "We can't continue to do this. We don't have authorization any more since there aren't any more American patients there."

So then Ralph Watts, who was the head of that section of the [Seventh-Day Adventist] church's work, came up from Singapore and finally got approval from the Department of Defense representatives at the Embassy to evacuate a certain number of the Vietnamese hospital personnel. They at first gave us just a few slots, because there weren't nearly enough planes for all the people who really needed to get out, including a lot of folks who had worked for the CIA and been promised evacuation if it should come to that. But things began toppling so much more rapidly than any-body anticipated that a lot of people were left behind.

What was frustrating was the total lack of planning by the Embassy for any realistic evacuation and that they fell through on their promises to get the Vietnamese out who were extremely high risk. That left a great deal of sadness and, I'm sure, bitterness in the people they couldn't get out.

Ralph Watts had told the hospital folks that they had to make up their own list of the people, that we couldn't be given the responsibility of de-ciding who should leave and who should stay. So they stayed up all night trying to make up the list. In the middle of the night they called Ralph Watts and said, "We just can't do it. It's just too painful." And he said, "Well, you're the only ones who know these people and know which ones are in the worst danger." So he sent them back to work again and by morning they had the list. But it was a heartbreaking experience for them.

We left on the twenty-fifth and Saigon fell on the thirtieth. We trans-ferred all the remaining patients to other hospitals in the city during the last three days so that we left no patients behind unattended. There was a medical school that had about ten medical students rotating through our hospital, and most of them decided to come with us. The rest helped transfer the patients to other hospitals. Many didn't want to leave be-cause they didn't want to leave their families. A Canadian lab technician decided that he would stay too. As I recall, he felt that he could help protect the remaining workers there and at least look after what was hap-pening in the hospital and maintain some kind of control in case riots should break out. We did have guards assigned by the city police. But there were hundreds of people outside the gate of the hospital trying to get in because they thought they'd be safer inside the hospital than they would in their own homes. So things were beginning to get rather uneasy. Everyone, I think, was concerned that it might turn into a real riot. That never actually happened within the city.

On our last day in Saigon we put one American in each ambulance (we had eight ambulances), and we piled the rest of each ambulance up with Vietnamese civilians who were hospital personnel. We were given blanket approval for this list of names.

Some of our people had to stay because we couldn't get enough names on the list through the Embassy people. They were under a lot of pressure, of course, to get people out from other areas as well, so there was a definite quota. It was a hair-raising exit from the hospital compound, because just at the last, as the sirens began to go and people began to close the doors of the ambulances, there were probably thirty or forty of our own hospital workers who tried to rush the ambulances and get in. It almost turned into a riot. The only thing that the ambulances could do was speed up and go, because if we lingered any longer, we couldn't have gotten anybody out. There was a lot of yelling and screaming, and a lot of crying.

The only ones who were notified that we were going were the ones on the list that we had permission to take out. We instructed them not to tell anybody else. We had about two hours' notice for them to get back home and get their wives and children, or whoever was allowed to come with them. So the rest of the people didn't really know what was happening until we were actually loading up the ambulances. It was very rough on everybody, because some of the people who were left behind were very close friends or relatives of the ones in the ambulances. It was one of the cruelest things to try to decide who should be on the list.

Even though we had approval by the American Defense Department, it was still tough to get through the South Vietnamese guards at Tan Son Nhut airport. There were big carriers, of course, to get into the airport, and there were thousands of people standing outside the airport against the gates, trying to get in. So it was a messy business trying to get the ambulances through. But we did have the advantage of the sirens and the flashing lights.

The staging area at the airport had been set up by Marines and there was very little water and no housing, of course; so that first night we slept out on the sidewalks and the streets inside the airport. The next morning we got our names on the manifest lists. There were long lines of people that would laboriously make their way through to the point that was the actual loading area. And the Marines went through all our luggage and made sure there wasn't anything—firearms or anything. While we were waiting in line, you could hear guns and fighting on the other side of the airport. So we knew the Vietcong were very close.

The Marines kept them at bay, though, while this airlift was going on. We were able to get out on a C-130. They flew us to Guam. We were then able to arrange to get our group out on two 747 flights. Pan Am had donated their planes to go over and pick people up. We landed at Camp Pendleton. Loma Linda University then emptied out their gym and set up cots in it and were able to accommodate everybody there. Then they set up tents outside for a camp-style mess. Altogether I guess we got out about four hundred and twenty-five people.

What happened to those who worked for us who didn't get out before April 30? Well, a lot of them were sent to detention camps out in the jungle for "re-education," as they called it. Some of the relatives were finally able to get letters out to France and then to this country. Some of them were in prison in these re-education camps for two or three years. Quite a few of them began to escape on the boats and flee to Malaysia or to Thailand. For the past ten years there has been a steady stream of Vietnamese showing up in California who have gotten out by boat and then have gotten to the refugee camps and then have waited for quota numbers to get into the United States.

It was all extremely frustrating. I think most Americans felt we'd let them down. And yet we all knew there was an intense amount of feeling back in the U.S. about the Vietnamese War. The feeling of most of the people in Nam was that if we were going to preserve South Vietnam as a democracy in the free world, and if we were going to have to fight a war to do it, then we should have gotten in there and done the job right. But throughout the entire affair we put limits on ourselves. We announced in advance that we would not bomb the border with China, and China kept pouring equipment and ammunition across the border. We kept announcing in advance what we were not going to do. At every point the North Vietnamese took advantage of that.

I think I felt like the others—by fighting a half-baked sort of war, with limits, we made it almost impossible to win. As a result, it dragged out over years and years, and in the end cost far more lives, I think, than if we had gone in with a short, sharp attack and gotten it over with.

If you are not going to do that, you might as well not start out at all.

George Lumm
"Holy Christ, They're Gonna Shoot Us All!"

My family lived in Saigon in the spring of 1975 while I was working in Hong Kong. My children, of course, were U.S. citizens by birth, and the U.S. Embassy did give us passports for them. But in order to leave Vietnam, they had to have visas. Even Americans who left Vietnam had to have an exit visa.

I believed that we would come back and support the government, mainly because I was thinking of the oil. There were those islands off the coast of Vietnam and the Vietnamese had a dispute with China over them. They claimed there was a lot of oil there. And I figured, hell, if there's an energy problem, there's so much oil there that the United States will definitely support Vietnam if only for that. So I wasn't thinking any more in terms of protecting freedom or democracy. By that time I was thinking that the whole war was nothing but a way to make money. I figured there's so much money in oil, surely they're going to protect them for the oil.

I didn't start to get real nervous until about a month before we left. That was when Danang fell.

One of my wife's cousins lived up around Danang. They had six kids and her husband worked on military calls—picking up trash, that stuff. And they were scared to death. She showed up in Saigon alone and said they had killed her husband and her kids. Her husband had told her to go out and get some supplies, because they were going to have to try and get out. He said, "They are coming and they're going to kill me." I don't know how they knew. But that happened. They killed him and the kids. After that she walked all the way to Saigon from some place near Danang. She said that the Vietcong had just gone crazy, shooting people, killing people. I wanted her to come with us when we left but she wouldn't. She said she didn't have anything to live for any more.

But we did get thirty-two Vietnamese out. I flew into Saigon on Air Vietnam. I had return tickets for my wife and my children. But even before that I was worried. I had gone to the American consulate in Hong Kong because I wanted to get my wife's mother, father, brother, and sister out. And they gave me the runaround. They said, "Oh, yeah, there's no problem. You just go to the American Embassy in Saigon; they'll approve it. They'll give you entrance visas to the United States for your wife's family." My wife had become a U.S. citizen. I went to the American Embassy—and this was still in March—and they told me I'd have to go back to the consulate at Hong Kong to get some documents before they could issue the entrance visas for my wife's family. It was back and forth, back and forth. Finally in April I went again to the American Embassy, about a week before the country fell, and I was panicking. I said, "Jesus Christ, what's going on? I got to get my family out of here, my wife and kids. My wife can't leave without her family. She's an American citizen. You're supposed to get the families of American citizens out." And this guy I talked to, the son of a bitch, was vice-consul or something in Saigon. He says, "I'm going to give you this letter and you take it over to the Vietnamese immigration to get your visas. They'll give you visas for your wife's family. No problem."

Well, shit, I went over there, and I waited hours before I could even see the Vietnamese receptionist. In Vietnam you always paid to see who you wanted, so I paid her and I got to see this guy the vice consul told me to go see. I explained what I was there for, and he said, "What are you talking about?" So I gave him the letter they gave me at the Embassy. And he just laughed at me. He said, "I don't know what's wrong with him. He knows damned well that we don't issue exit visas. We have too many things to worry about. I told him personally not to be wasting my time by having any of you people come in here asking for visas for Vietnamese."

I went back to this vice-consul, and he wouldn't see me. So I had to see some new guy. I said "Hell, I need an exit visa and they won't give it to me; they say they've got too many things on their mind. My own son with a U.S. passport, they won't give an exit visa." He said, "There's nothing to worry about. There's no reason to be panicking about getting them out of here." And I said, "There's an evacuation going on and I need an exit visa." And he said, "No, there's no evacuation"—he said that a week before the Goddamned thing fell. I said, "You're telling me there's no evacuation! Jesus Christ, all the American companies are gone; the Bank of America is gone; the construction companies are gone. What do you think all these people are lining up outside the Embassy for? We're U.S. citizens. We have U.S. passports. I want to get my family out of here."

He said, "Well, I'm too busy. There's no big problem; there's no evacuation. You're just overly excited. We're not going to abandon Vietnam."

Then I went back, I think it was the twenty-fourth, and what a mess. There were Vietnamese and Americans and everybody all over the Goddamned place. And I swear—I'm not lying to you—there were at least 400 people lined up at the Embassy. We waited about four hours. They wouldn't let me see anybody but this nice Vietnamese girl who was working there. And she told me that indeed everybody was leaving; that they had promised all the Vietnamese working in the Embassy that when they left they would take them.

I said, "Well, hell, I think they should. I think they should take anybody that's ever worked for the Americans." And I told her I was trying to get my family out of there. She showed me these forms and said, "These are the forms that people are taking down after they're filled out and stamped, and they take them to Tan Son Nhut to be evacuated." So I grabbed a bunch of them. She gave me one completed form with the Embassy stamp on it. I went to a printer and said "I need a stamp right away." He made it in a couple of hours. So I forged the same signature that was on the copy she gave me, and I put down my wife's family, I put down the neighbors, we put down friends: thirty-two Vietnamese altogether.

But then, how do you get into Tan Son Nhut? You had to pay the guards at the gate. You don't get in without paying. I had to take on an additional Vietnamese, a colonel who worked at Tan Son Nhut, and he wanted to get his family out. So he said, "I can get you in if you take my family with you." I said, "Fine, I'll take all I can." So he got us in.

We put thirty-two people in three cars and we drove into Tan Son Nhut. It was hotter than hell. We were all hungry and thirsty, and there was no way to feed everybody. They did give us water when were were inside.

The Embassy was just a bunch of shit. Goddamned politicians. But the

Air Force was terrific. You had to take these forms over to these Air Force personnel processing people for evacuation. This noncommissioned officer says, "All right, Mr. Lumm; do you know that you are only allowed to take immediate family members of American citizens out?" I had a Catholic priest there who was in his eighties, and I had their names and their birthdates all listed. He said, "Are all these people related to you?" I said, "Yeah, either directly or by adoption." He said, "What in the hell is this? Here's this eighty-year-old priest." And I said, "Well, that's my adopted son." He laughed and then he okayed the whole lot—"You guys got in here, we'll do our best to get you out."

Originally I wasn't going to go with the evacuation because I had tickets on Air Vietnam, but I wanted to make sure that my wife's family got out and all these other people. I intended to get them inside, sign the papers for them, and then leave and take my family on Air Vietnam. The Air Force guy tells us that all civilian flights are cancelled. There are no more civilian flights. And I'm saying, "Holy shit, what am I going to do?" I had a job in Hong Kong. At the time I was working for DHL—a courier service—and they had an office in Hong Kong and another in Guam.

We waited there two days. Finally they gave us a bus—just for us—all thirty-two Vietnamese plus my wife and I. The Vietnamese bus driver was also trying to get out. To get to the plane you had to go through the Vietnamese part where they had the Vietnamese guards, and they stopped the bus. The females were no problem, but military-age guys were on the bus. They stopped the bus and opened the doors. I'm trying to get my wife to tell me what the hell's going on, and the stupid driver, he says, "Oh no, I don't want to go, I'm not going. I'm just driving the bus for them." So what do they do? They drag his ass off the bus. Most of the buses had U.S. Air Force personnel driving, but with our luck, we had a Vietnamese. So then this one soldier tries to get onto the bus, and like a fool—I don't know where I got the courage because I about shit my pants—I jump up and grab the bar by the door and say, "You are not allowed access on this bus. This is U.S. Government property and these are U.S. personnel," and all this shit, and the guy doesn't know what I'm talking about. He's talking on the radio and my wife is telling me what he's saying; he's calling some captain and telling him that some American wouldn't let him get on the bus. The captain says, "Well, push him aside." He says, "I tried that but he insists. I'm afraid he's from the Embassy." And he says, "We'll have to talk about it; come here." So he left to go talk to his captain.

I never drove a big vehicle before. I didn't know how to drive stick shift or nothing. This bus is sitting there and the engine is running. Nobody knew how to drive it. An empty bus was coming back and it had an Air Force guy—a black guy. God, I loved the sight of that guy. I'd kiss him today if I could see him. That son of a gun stops his bus; says, "What's going on?" I say, "Holy Christ, they're gonna to shoot us all!" I told him what happened. Meanwhile, here comes the soldier again and he's yelling and screaming "Stop! Stop!" because the Air Force guy is getting on the bus. The Air Force guy says, "Fuck you, buddy!" And he takes off with the bus, and they're shooting at us. They're actually fucking shooting at us!

When we got to the plane—this is funny—the young males were really scared because they figured they were going to get stuck. I don't know what kind of plane it was, but it's where the tail comes down and you can get on that way. And they didn't have seats; you had to sit on the floor. Well, when that bus stopped I never saw anybody run so fast in my life. These young kids left that bus and were on that plane in a split second. All of us were scared, but that was really something.

You know, I really thought we were going to get stuck there and be killed.

They took us to Guam. At first they told us that nobody could leave. And I said, "Hell, I'm a U.S. citizen. Why can't I leave? I'm not military or anything. Here's my passport." So they let me leave and I went to DHL's office in Guam. I asked DHL, "What am I going to do? Here I am on Guam and I don't know what's going to happen to us." They said, "We'll arrange for you to go back to Hong Kong. You can be couriers." So we went as couriers for DHL. And that's how we got back to Hong Kong.

CHAPTER XIV

San Clemente, California

John H. Taylor, Assistant to President Nixon
"The Next–Most Depressing Day"

President Nixon was living in San Clemente at the time of the fall of Saigon. He has told me and others that next to the day he resigned the Presidency, it was the most depressing day in his life. As he pointed out in *No More Vietnams,* it was a war that was not lost by our fighting men, but by the members of Congress who refused to provide the military assistance to our South Vietnamese allies that was permitted under the Paris peace agreements in 1973 to match the aid provided by the Soviet Union to the North. At the time, he predicted that even greater damage would be done to U.S. interests around the world than to the people of Southeast Asia. His prediction, unfortunately, proved to be correct in the period between 1975 and 1980, when over 100 million people were either lost to the Communists or by the West because of Congress's, the media's, and the Carter and Ford Administrations' fear of "another Vietnam."

His distress over the fall of Saigon was magnified by the fact that a major relocation center for Vietnamese refugees was at Camp Pendleton near his residence in San Clemente. He would often drive by the camp areas, and he has vividly described to me seeing the children playing and the women hanging their laundry outside their makeshift quarters.

Part Two

VIETNAMESE

CHAPTER XV

Military

Colonel Le Khac Ly
"Only I Am Left to Tell You the Story"

In 1974 I went to General Pham Van Phu and presented myself. He invited me to his house in Pleiku to sit down and talk about his plans. And the first thing he told me was that he wanted to move the MR 2 headquarters from Pleiku to Nha Trang. He asked me what I thought about it. I said, "I don't think that's a good idea. I have been in this area long enough to understand why we have to have the headquarters in Pleiku. Actually, President Diem created and developed this section and he was right. He wanted to bring the influence of the South Vietnamese army to the high plateau. It is a key area, a very strategic area, very good soil for agriculture. So when you want to make the country rich, this is an area you can use. And when you move away from this area, the people will move with you. When it is empty the Communists will come in here. When they control this area they will use it as a base and we will lose all South Vietnam. So you stay here and the people will stay here with you. The Communists, if they come, will have a tough time taking this away from us. So you cannot ever give it to them."

MR 2 is a big area. We had fourteen provinces in it. And we only had two divisions, the Twenty-second and the Twenty-third. The lowland area is important, too. That is an economic and industrial region also.

But Phu wanted to move. He said, "We are here as a corps headquarters in the front, and we have troops in the rear." And I said, "That much is true. But if you make any movement now of the headquarters, people will know that you are high headquarters and they will become afraid and they will move with you."

After the 1973 Paris Agreement, the people watched the army, and when it moved they moved with it. The people saw that the Paris Agreement was not the agreement to end the war. Something was still cooking—behind our backs. People in Vietnam knew Kissinger's plan. They knew why he signed that Paris Agreement without South Vietnamese authority. And any higher headquarters location always attracted people. When it moved, even if the lower headquarters was still there, the majority of the people would move with the higher headquarters, and the area would be more or less abandoned.

There was a very big population in the highlands, and if they moved, the Communists would have a very good chance to move in. The people did not want to be abandoned to the Communists. They watched General Phu very carefully.

General Phu usually stayed in Nha Trang. Some people told me he was scared. And I think it is probably true. He had been captured at Dien Bien Phu in 1954, and whenever he thought about the Vietcong he was scared. I had no faith in him when we came under fire.

He decided at that time not to move the headquarters, but he personally moved the majority of his belongings to Nha Trang and most of his staff went with him. I ran the show in Pleiku. That is true. I do not mean to boast.

Phu had a personal conflict with two other generals: General Tran Van Cam, who used to be Twenty-third Division commander under General Nguyen Van Toan and when Toan moved, Cam became Phu's assistant for operations); and General Pham Duy Tat, who used to be Twenty-first Division Commander and had became assistant commanding officer for pacification in Nha Trang.

He liked neither of them. And he had no executive officer. Phu then created his own staff. His adjutant general, Lieutenant Colonel Tran Tich, appointed officers to positions on his personal staff and worked with his wife closely. I ran the show for operations, intelligence, and logistics in the highlands.

I heard many rumors about his appointments. Some were true and some were exaggerations. I heard stories about people paying money to Phu's wife to buy their positions. That was very demoralizing, but there was nothing that could be done about it. You could report it to President Thieu. But that did no good, because he was already bought, too.

I told my officers that I kept my mouth shut, I kept my ear cocked, and I just tried to do my job and do my best. I didn't care about the other things.

Now, as for the attack on Ban Me Thuot: We knew it was coming. We didn't know exactly where, and we didn't know the size of the Communist forces. But we knew that something was going to happen. So my intelligence officer who is now in a reeducation camp in Vietnam, Colonel Trinh Tieu, discussed with me the fact that an NVA division was in the highlands area and was on the move. They were going to attack somewhere. But when we reported to Phu, he thought that they would attack Kontum or Pleiku, so he concentrated forces to defend those areas.

General Tat, the Ranger commander in II Corps and my classmate—he, too, is in a re-education camp in Vietnam—defended Kontum and Pleiku. Kontum is easy to attack, and Pleiku is the corps headquarters. An attack there would be very good political propaganda. But my intelligence officer and I had doubts about it. If they wanted to make political propaganda they would attack a province chief's headquarters, and if they attacked in Pleiku they could not attack the province headquarters. If we were attacked we knew we would get reinforcements right away from Saigon. So we put Ban Me Thuot at the top of our list of Communist targets in MR 2.

Phu inspected Ban Me Thuot and thought maybe it would hold if it was attacked. They couldn't get into the city, he believed. And I didn't see any fifth column there. The NVA armor was not too important to us because we had air power and they didn't.

When they finally attacked in Ban Me Thuot, everyone panicked. Phu was in Nha Trang when the attack came. And so I decided to deploy troops to Ban Me Thuot. We had the Fifty-third Regiment there already and we reinforced with Rangers.

There was an air strike by our aircraft, but it hit accidentally on the Advance Command Post of the Twenty-third Division and knocked out all communication. When we had to redeploy, we took half of the city, because the NVA were too strong inside the city. They took the city slowly because they were afraid of an ambush. Then the Twenty-third Division commander took troops to secure a landing zone for a helicopter to pick up his wife and family. That was a shame. He was supposed to command the operation to retake Ban Me Thuot, and because his wife was on the outskirts of Ban Me Thuot, he feared for her security, so he took a landing zone and ordered the attacking troops to turn around and secure that zone first. The NVA observed that. When he did that they sealed the city. He gave them more time. He gave them a good chance for success. Then he advanced only slowly.

That was a punishable offense. He disobeyed an order. But who is going to decide what to do to him? Phu or Cao Van Vien [Chairman of the Joint General Staff]? Later on I came face to face with him again. He said his helicopter was hit by a sniper and he was wounded. He said all the troops got out of the helicopters and went to take care of their own families. He told me he couldn't control them. We had been friends for a long time. I said, "General Tuong, you are division commander; why didn't you shoot some of them?" He had no answer.

Phu then flew back to Pleiku to look at the situation. He was in CTOC [Corps Tactical Operations Center] with me. He got a call from Saigon from President Thieu. Thieu said he wanted to meet with Phu on the next day in Cam Ranh Bay, March 14.

I prepared briefing charts and a situation report for the meeting. I
reported that the situation was a very grave emergency. We thought he
wanted to know what the operations were and how they were going.
Then, next morning, Phu flew down there to meet with him.

After he met with the President, Phu called a meeting that night in
Pleiku. At that meeting were General Phu, General Cam, General Pham
Ngoc Sang, the Sixth Air Force Division commanding general, General
Tat, and myself.

The first thing Phu said when he came in was that he had Thieu's
approval to promote Tat. He pinned the star on and we applauded.

Then he announced, "We were going to withdraw from Pleiku and
Kontum!"

When he said that, I opened my eyes large, large, large. I thought I
wasn't hearing clearly. But he said we would redeploy in order to take
back Ban Me Thuot. Cam, Sang, Tat, and I just sat there. We pinched
each other. And I said to myself, "Do I ask him how do we withdraw this
army?" I asked him. He said then, "You use Route 7B." My first reaction
was, "No sir!" And he said, "It is already decided by President Thieu.
We have no choice, because we have to gain the element of surprise on
the enemy."

I told him, "Sir, I have lived here long enough to know the area. Route
7B has been abandoned for a long time. The U.S. Special Forces, the
Vietnamese Special Forces, and the enemy have all operated in that area,
and they have mined the entire area. And if we withdraw with heavy
equipment we will have to clear the road of mines. Nobody knows where
the mines are. And it has to be repaired. There is no time to repair it.
And when you decide to withdraw from here, everybody will know. There
will be no surprise! I suggest if we move, we use Route 19 and go straight.
We'll have some casualties but we'll make it."

But he said, "No. It's all decided. You have no choice. Tomorrow I will
fly to Nha Trang and you have three days to withdraw the troops." And
I said, "General Phu, it will take at least three weeks of planning. We
have a lot of troops, a lot of supplies, a lot of equipment."

He said, "That is all decided, also." Cam and I asked him about the
Bao An, Popular Forces, and the district and the province administrators
and the people. He said, "You don't have to worry about them. Forget
them."

I asked him if he had told the Americans in the area—the DAO and the
CIA people. And I will never forget this. He looked right at me and said,
"Forget the Americans! Don't tell the Americans anything!" Those were
his exact words. I am ashamed now to tell you the truth of what happened in Pleiku. I couldn't believe it. He was planning to abandon them,
too, without warning them about the withdrawal.

The real orders were coming from Thieu. Everything Phu told me he
said Thieu told him. Among the five people who were at that meeting in

Pleiku, I am the only one alive to tell the story here in America. Phu committed suicide. Sang is a prisoner, Cam is a prisoner, Tat is a prisoner—all in re-education camps in Vietnam today. Only I am left to tell you the story.

Phu said he had to do this because he was following a direct order. "You don't have to worry about this," he said. He was very nervous when he said that. But it appeared he had no disagreement with the order.

I was made commanding officer of the withdrawal. Tat took care of the tactical forces, all communications, and logistics. So I said to myself, "Oh, my God, I'm in trouble."

The next morning, at eight o'clock, Phu left. He flew away. I was left to take care of everything. A short time later, from Saigon, General Dong Van Khuyen, the chief of staff of the JGS, called me and asked, "Where is General Phu?" And I had to laugh, it was so ridiculous. So I had to ask myself, "What should I say? Should I tell him the truth or should I try to cover for Phu?"

I said, "I don't know. I don't have contact with him right now." Khuyen kept calling. Finally I said, "Okay, call Nha Trang, and talk to him there." Khuyen asked, "Why he is there?" I said, "I don't know. Ask him. I have authority to run the show here. And Phu is in our new headquarters in Nha Trang."

More than one battalion commander of armor, artillery, and logistics came to me and yelled, "Why are we withdrawing? We can fight! What is happening?" All I could say was, "I agree with you. But now we have the President and the JGS ordering us. We are professionals. What can we do? Disobey them? Of course not. I know it's wrong. But that is the order. Do you want to start a rebellion?"

I believed at that time that they must have a secret plan that we didn't know about. They couldn't be this stupid. Maybe something is cooking and since we are not at the top levels, we don't know about it. Cam and I were discussing this mad withdrawal from the highlands. We sat and laughed, and Cam told me, "I'll bet you they have an agreement and we will have no more war. I'll bet the war is over." And I told him, "I doubt it." But he said, "I think that we could resist any attack with what we have here for at least three months. And so I'll bet you they've come to an agreement and this time we'll have real peace. I don't know, but I just feel that way."

Cam flew away, too. Tat and I were left in the headquarters, and I said to myself, The Americans have been allied with us for years. And this is a very important development and they don't know. Why don't we have to let them know? That's why I called them and told them that we were withdrawing. They had no idea about it.

I told the CIA people and the consul general of the area that we were withdrawing. When I told them, they didn't believe me. Then they called Saigon and checked around and found out it was true. Then they flew out, and I got credit from the CIA in Saigon and my name was put at the top of their list of people to help if Saigon fell.

The beginning of the withdrawal was successful. At the last minute my helicopter broke down, so I stayed with the convoy out of Pleiku. A withdrawal is always a difficult operation. You need detailed, careful planning. I had three days to withdraw 100,000 people, and I could not abandon anybody. The people who lived around us deserved to be taken care of. Even though I could not protect them, they came with us. In a short time, it was out of my control. My battalion commanders could not control all the people. It all fell apart on the road to Tuy Hoa. We'd had no time to do anything in three days. All you can really decide in that short a period of time is who goes first and who goes next, and so on.

Every night, I still see that convoy. Tanks, the APCs [armored personnel carriers], trucks, and all the troops and their families and dependents just covering them; the old people on top, and mothers and children, sleeping on them and sprawled on them. Sometimes they would fall off, and the convoy kept moving and they screamed and were crushed. I heard that. I saw a half-ton truck loaded with people turn over and people were crushed and their bones broken. I heard their bones breaking. We couldn't help them. I saw them lying there beside the road, dying. It was a nightmare.

East of Cheo Reo we were mistakenly attacked by our own Air Force and many people were killed. My headquarters was at Cheo Reo and when I got there I was surrounded by the NVA and they shelled it. I had one radio to communication with Nha Trang, and I was being shelled.

My communication unit called Phu in Nha Trang and he wasn't around. I talked to the second officer on the radio in English. The enemy was only about one kilometer away from my headquarters. I told him, "You tell the general the situation here is very critical. And you understand what I mean when I say critical. That's it. I don't have time to elaborate. I will try my best here. But the enemy is closing in." He understood and called me back twenty minutes later on the radio, and warned me about the number of enemy troops in Phu Bon province closing in on us. Tat was about three kilometers away from me with his troops. The air commander was ordered to take me out of the area by helicopter. The armor brigade commander was ordered to open the road and go, no matter how many casualties we took, and Tat would support him with his troops. I was to fly to Nha Trang. Phu sent me two helicopters. The enemy's ground fire was intense when they landed. And there were exactly twenty-seven people in my helicopter, a helicopter that was designed for seven at a time. The other one had nineteen. And they took off and flew away to Tuy Hoa. We were just lucky to get away. Phu was still in Nha Trang at that time.

The next morning Phu called me and ordered me to Nha Trang. I flew there and reorganized the staff. I stayed there twelve days, and he abandoned me again—cleaned up his house, moved out his family, and flew away without telling me anything. One day my secretary, a captain, came to my office and knocked on the door and said, "Colonel, there's just you and I here now. Nobody else." And I said, "What are you saying?" I had been working on plans to redeploy troops. That was about noon. I was very tired and I had lain down. I came out of my office and went downstairs. Two of my staff were there working and they reported to me that Phu had left. I went to Phu's house and nobody was there. It was empty. I asked the major there, a battalion commander, where Phu was, and he said, "I don't know what happened. Right now there is nobody in the house, but my troops still keep security around the house. But I don't know what to do now."

I collected the officer and troops in five jeeps. What could we do? Everybody was gone. I was told someone saw Phu in the airport. So we drove to the airport. The MPs [Military Police] there wouldn't let me in at first. Finally, they opened the gate. I was surrounded by Air Force troops and met the Air Force general. He was looking for Phu also. He said, "If Phu is gone and Ly is going, why do we stay here? Let's leave here." But I wasn't leaving. I was looking for my commander.

Then I got a call from Cao Van Vien at the airport. He said, "Where is General Phu?" I said, "I don't know. I am looking for him." And he said, "Well, you stay there and you find him for me." I said, "Fine, I'll stay here."

We waited and waited and heard nothing from Phu. And after seven days of no eating and no sleeping, I finally collapsed. My troops and officers pushed me onto an airplane while the other troops withdrew.

The airplane was supposed to go to Phan Rang to establish a headquarters there. But instead it flew directly to Saigon.

When I got to Saigon, Phu was there. I went home. The next day, I was urinating blood and was not well. I went to my doctor and he gave me some medicine and told me to rest. I went to work.

I tried to communicate with General Phu again about what to do. And the first thing he told me, was, "Ly, we are betrayed!" I said, "By who?" He said, "By Thieu. Thieu has trapped us. He threw everything to us. He says everything is our fault. He ordered us to withdraw and now he says it is all our fault." Phu wanted to prepare a report to prove that it was not our fault and describe how we conducted operations, why we didn't take Ban Me Thuot, and why we withdrew.

So I prepared a very thick report for Phu.

I visited Phu and General Ngo Quang Truong [Commander of MR1], who was now there in the hospital. Truong embraced me and cried. He said, "Ly, we've lost everything." Of course, Truong loved his country, and his troops, and his I Corps. And now it was all gone.

When I saw Phu again he was angry. It was the first time I had ever seen him so angry about the President. After I prepared the report for him, he signed it, and the final day I went to see General Khuyen and had the report sent to Thieu and Cao Van Vien. I never saw or heard of that report again.

I asked General Khuyen, "What should we do next? Have we lost everything?"

He said, "No. We will redeploy and draw the line, and you will have your II Corps back again."

But I said to myself, I think this general is not telling the truth. The truth is now that we cannot do that. If you had said that when I was in Pleiku I could do that. But right now I can't command anybody. There is no army for me. And the enemy is everywhere.

He asked me, "If you were in my position what would you do?" The big shock was that I could not think of any solution now to our problems.

When I went home, my wife and I heard airplanes taking off every night, and we knew that DAO was flying people out, and a lot of information was coming to us every day telling us who was leaving. I went to see a friend of mine, commander of the Second Division. And he and I tried to reorganize the Twenty-second and Twenty-third divisions and collect the men.

Then suddenly we heard all the news of losses. And I visited my good old commanding officer, General Hieu, who was a real honest officer in the Army.

I asked him about the situation in MR 3. He said we had to reorganize and try to block the enemy armor advances. And a couple of days later he was killed.

I went back and forth from Vung Tau to Saigon, and finally I got in touch with my friends in the Embassy to see what was going on. They called me back and told me they had my name on a list of people to leave.

I went to the Embassy, to the back door because it was so crowded, and they let me in. I saw General Charles Timmes, a very good friend of mine. He told me that he had orders from Washington to take out Cao Van Vien and my name was right after Cao Van Vien's, in that order, because I had saved the Americans in the central highlands.

So I got my immediate family, my wife and my children, I took them to a staging area to wait. We were picked up and taken to Tan Son Nhut on an Embassy bus. We waited there until the next day.

We flew out of Vietnam on a C-130. We flew to Guam to a tent city. That was on the twenty-fifth of April.

I knew when we left that everything was lost. I thought if there was an agreement between the Communists and the Americans, then that was wrong. We heard that the Americans had sold us out in order to get other friends.

I thought that when Kissinger went to China and shook hands with Mao Zedong, that was the end of Vietnam. I knew there was no hope for

Vietnam after that. After the Americans had gone to Beijing to shake hands with the Communist Chinese, suddenly they didn't need Vietnam any more.

To me, that was how they sold us out. We had nothing to say about it. I think that President Thieu should have seen that and prepared for a bad time ahead. But he did not. So to me he was not a good leader.

Now, think about it: If you are Vietnamese and you love your country, then you must ask why the Americans did this. This is my question to the Americans—Why did you do that to a friend?

Many people say we were sold out. And, sadly, I have to agree.

Nguyen Truong Toai
"We Died"

I was born in 1943 during the war against the Japanese while my family was fleeing from the fighting. My mother came from the North and my father was from the central part of the country. One day in 1951, during the war against the French, when I returned home from school, I saw my mother crying and she told me that my father was dead in Hanoi, in the North. I was eight years old. Later on we found out that he was killed by the Communists and his body had been dumped in the Red River.

When we got the news that he died, I was young and I was sad, but then I forgot. I continued on with my education. In 1954, I remember, in the era of Prime Minister Nguyen Van Tam, under the Bao Dai regime, there were people whose houses were burned, and some of them stayed with us. I was touched by their plight and I was saddened by the events, but as a young person, I didn't stay sad for very long.

And then came 1963, when President Ngo Dinh Diem was assassinated. I was a university student then. But by that time I did have this concept of a free world and a Communist world. As I read more about the subject I became aware of the situation, and by the time I joined the military in June of 1968, I had formed a clear idea of the difference between the free world and a Communist world. By reading books on Communism I began to get an understanding of who the Communists were and what they did. And the people my age joined the military because we had an ideal and we understood what it was to live in a free world and to live in a Communist world. It was not like people said, that those who joined the military were just conscripted into the service and didn't have any ideas of their own. But the Americans never seemed to understand that.

One of the most painful and sad things that I saw just before I joined the military was when the newspapers carried the pictures of General Nguyen Ngoc Loan, who shot the Vietcong prisoner in the head during the Tet Offensive in 1968. The articles that the Americans wrote, the news reporters, were such that when I read them, I had the feeling that they didn't understand the reality of the war, the truth of what was going on in Vietnam.

And I witnessed the event when General Loan shot the Communist. I was there. And I knew that guy, I knew that Communist and I knew what he did. You know what he did? In 1968 in Saigon, he pushed the children out during the fighting—innocent children—as a wave of people so that his own people could escape from the fighting. During the heaviest fighting he used children as shields, and the soldiers could no longer shoot when he did that. And General Loan could not take that. He got so angry at this despicable act, that when he caught those guys who had escaped by hiding behind children, he shot him. And I felt the same way and I would have done the same thing; I would have shot this monstrous guy if I had caught him that way.

But when General Loan shot that criminal, a photographer took the picture. What that photographer did, what people around the world saw, wasn't all that really happened, it was only a little part of what happened. And all of the negative feelings after that actually destroyed General Loan's whole career and life, and that wasn't right. The Vietcong deserved to be shot for his wicked act, using innocent children in war. He and his kind were putting mines in that neighborhood and burning homes. And when the police force came in and fought them, he forced the children in the neighborhood to become his bulletproof vest.

At that time it was all chaotic. General Loan was the chief of the police force, so when he saw the corpses of the children and he asked, "Why? What happened?" and when he found out why those children died and who was responsible for this act, this tragedy, he shot the man. Did you see the picture in *Time* and in *Newsweek?* I am telling you the real story of what happened. That picture ruined General Loan's life and career. I don't think the American people ever truly knew what was going on in Vietnam.

In the spring of 1975 I was stationed in the area of Ban Me Thuot and Pleiku with the ARVN Twenty-third Division. I was a second lieutenant.

Some time in February, our battalion was marching to the secret zone called Quang Nhieu, which was about seventeen kilometers from Ban Me Thout, and during this operation we encountered a group of North Vietnamese soldiers scouting, and we opened fire and killed seven of them and captured two. One of them was an officer. On our side we sustained four deaths. Along with the captured soldiers we found a lot of information and important documents. Our Battalions 153 and 353 received orders to continue to march into the area, and we sent the documents and prisoners back to headquarters. Then after we marched for about a kilometer, we receiver orders to stop and retreat, because the security people had gotten information from the prisoners that there were many units of the NVA stationed about two walking days from where we were at that time. But the truth is that they were only about two kilometers from where we were, and if we had proceeded we would have been wiped out by them. So we retreated to Quang Nhieu and stayed there to protect it.

So we knew the actual strength of the Northern army and we knew how serious the situation was, but I don't think that the officers back in town or the chief of that region understood how serious the situation was or that there were so many NVA troops in the region.

So the situation then was very complicated. Our battalion was composed of four companies, and my company, which was Company 1, received orders to return to Ban Me Thuot, right in the heart of the city, to offer support to the Eighth Division tankers. Company 2 was stationed in the headquarters of the Twenty-third Division. Another company was sent to offer support to the light headquarters of the corps, but it was wiped out.

The night of March 9–10, my company received orders to secure Bridge No. 14 in order to hold open a road, but that night the North Vietnamese shelled very hard, and we were put on alert. I took my soldiers out and the MPs told us to get back to our position and be ready because of the serious situation. It did not look good. So I think that everybody knew ahead of time that the attack was coming.

The NVA managed to take over in two days. I know the story of the fall of Ban Me Thuot well as a combat soldier. Here is how it happened.

On the night of March 9, there was a convoy of trucks carrying ammunition arriving in Ban Me Thuot, but before that, we had heard news that the road from Nha Trang to Ban Me Thuot was obstructed and there was no traffic. But why did these trucks get through? They came from Nha Trang so we were very reassured. We felt better and we thought that maybe the South Vietnamese Army had fought off the Communists and had reopened the road. It was not until later that we discovered that these trucks belonged to the NVA and not to us. There were many insiders and infiltrators in our ranks.

We never knew where the trucks orginated from. But by the evening of the ninth of March they were there in Ban Me Thuot with all this ammunition, and something happened and some people knew, and that is why when I took my men out I was asked to return. And also that night our battalion headquarters gave the order to our company to go to Bang Dao at about three in the morning, but the shelling started at about two in the morning and there was no way we could move. And at about eight or ten in the morning, an ammunition warehouse that wasn't far away from us exploded. Not too far from that warehouse there was a cemetery and the Rangers' station, but I don't know where they went because it was empty. Then we got news that they had T-54 tanks coming into town. A troop of us went out and we met a group of them coming in, and they screamed at us and started firing the M-72 at us. At that time we heard loud noises, and later on we found that the T-54s weren't really T-54s.

They were actually a kind of truck used in the jungle to carry wood and timber, and they disguised them, and when they came to town with those things, they didn't move them. They raced the engines and let them stand there, and the noise of the engines was the same noise as the engine of a T-54, so the ARVN soldiers became dispirited because we were just a small force compared to what we were facing. But there was panic because of the mistaken belief that the NVA had so many tanks.

They took over the whole place in two days. Later on in our rear camp, about ten kilometers from Ban Me Thuot, at Phung Duc air base, where our Corps Headquarters 53 and 44 was stationed, we fought with them for almost ten days, and the number of casualties for their side was greater than for our side. The ratio was seven deaths on their side to two on our side. We fought until our ammunition ran out. We had helicopters supplying us with ammunition. But under the intense firing our pilots became afraid and they flew too high and didn't aim right. They dropped boxes of ammunition closer to the Communist side than to our side and we were not able to retrieve the ammunition. So we fought to the last bullet, and all of us nearly were wiped out. Near the end, only the corps commander, Lieutenant Colonel An, and two soldiers were able to escape from that massacre. I was one who was able to escape at that time. Later I heard from my soldiers that the Communists decapitated captured ARVN soldiers who were big guys or who had a moustache or beard. I did not witness that action, but many people witnessed it and I heard it later from many soldiers. And actually at Chau Son, this happened also. They decapitated many people, including many Catholic priests.

Right after that, they were after ARVN soldiers who had escaped capture. They captured me for a short time. But I lucked out. I was not big and I did not have a beard or a moustache.

They herded a lot of people into a temple and I was in this big group but I bolted and ran. I wasn't familiar with the town of Ban Me Thuot. Although I was there for a long time I was seldom in the town. I was a combat soldier and I just spent the majority of my time on marches or operations. We didn't go into the town that much.

Ban Me Thuot's loss was inevitable. There was only one battalion to defend it and there were only four companies, and one of the companies was deployed somewhere else, so you had only three companies. There were other soldiers, but the rest of them were just people who worked in the offices. And to say that Ban Me Thuot was lost in two days is not exactly correct. It was lost in one day. However, you must know that there was a bigger fight ten kilometers away from Ban Me Thuot at the air base, and that is where we were really able to fight with them and to hold them off for over a week.

There was an attempt at a counterattack to regain Ban Me Thuot. Remember, I belonged to the Corps 53, and remember the battle that we had, and at that time Corps 53 was pretty much finished. We died. Then the attempt was met by Corps 44, which was stationed in Pleiku. As they reached the Tinh Thuong area, about ten kilometers from Ban Me Thuot, the soldiers themselves met up with their families who were fleeing from Ban Me Thuot. As soon as they saw their families running, they decided to drop their arms and join their families. Even their commanders could not direct them any more. Maybe that is why we lost the battle. The soldiers just didn't want to fight any more and so we lost. There was some fighting by those who stayed, but it was not for long because there was no point in fighting any more. We were small in number and those who stayed to fight didn't believe they could win the city back. The cause was lost.

But you need to know that not all of the soldiers ran away. A number still stayed, and we fought the Vietcong everywhere, at that center and at other places. Just small fights, but fights all the same. Those who fought, fought with enthusiasm; they did not fight just for the sake of fighting. They struggled with the Northerners.

On the tenth of March when they were attacking us, when Ban Me Thuot was not lost yet, there was fighting going on, and by tuning our radio to a certain channel we overheard a conversation between the headquarters of the division and General Phu in Pleiku. Phu was flying in a helicopter and he had a conversation with the vice-commander of the division, Colonel Quang. I have a friend who was a captain in the Signal Corps and he tuned into the same channel and also heard what I heard.

Phu said, "Well, at any price you need to keep Ban Me Thuot. Whatever you need I will give it to you; I will supply it to you, be it ammunition or troops. But you need to keep Ban Me Thuot at all costs." That is what I heard clearly.

But I have to say that this colonel was not a good commander. No, he was not a good commander at all. He lied. He said that we were able to fight on. But look at the reality. We had only two battalions and one was deployed at Phuoc An, and as far as our battalion at Ban Me Thuot was concerned, one company was wiped out already and that was on the tenth of March.

I got caught in Ban Me Thuot. They stopped people from fleeing and isolated certain areas, and they surrounded people and made them stay put. So it was crowded and chaotic and I got stuck there. I was in a sense their prisoner, but not really, since they didn't single me out and I was able to dodge them, and I didn't report to them like a number of military personnel did. And those who reported to the Communists got taken to God knows where, because they just disappeared and nobody ever saw them again. So I dodged them. I didn't give up until the twenty-fifth of March, 1975. I met up with two high school teachers who knew me because they taught at the school where my friend taught, and they took me and offered me refuge and that's how I stayed out of the hands of the Communists and survived.

In early April I was able to escape from Ban Me Thuot and I fled to Nha Trang. By that time Nha Trang had already fallen to the Communists. It was the home of my maternal relatives but by the time I got there my sister and her husband had already fled to Saigon.

Let me tell you about the trek from Ban Me Thuot to Nha Trang. It was unbelievable. On the route the many buses that carried people, like big American Greyhound buses but not as nice, got shot at by the Communists on the way. They didn't care that they were shooting at civilians. To have survived that trip required a tremendous amount of luck.

My bus was stopped by the local guerrillas, and they said, "There must be military men on this bus, and if you don't get off, we will shoot everybody on the bus." The term that they used for us was "Nguy Quan." They threatened to shoot everybody on the bus and so others and I got off the bus. And, lucky for us, at the moment we got off the bus, there were two A-37 bombers that came by and dropped bombs in the area. The local guerrillas ran away and we ran away and the bus drove away. But, bless his heart, the bus driver was so kind that he stopped a short distance away and picked us up again.

One of the most unforgettable scenes that we witnessed was something that really hurt us in our guts. There were two companies of South Vietnamese Airborne men who got captured by the Communists and were ordered to march without any shoes or uniforms, and they looked so pathetic. Those of us in the bus looked out at this scene and we just wanted to cry because it hurt us so much, and we were so angry. Another thing that really hurt us was to see so many corpses of the Airborne troops along the road. Too many corpses. There were many corpses of the Communists, too, but they were removed, so what was left were just the bodies of the Airborne men, especially in the area of Phung Hoang. The Phung Hoang route leads from Ban Me Thuot to Nha Trang and it is very close to Nha Trang.

I got stuck in Nha Trang, and the local militia, the Communist administrative people, made me report to them. If I'd had the chance to go to Saigon, I would have gone there, and I would have left the country. But I got stuck in Nha Trang. At that time, Saigon had not fallen yet and so they treated me in a way that you could say was polite. Somewhat politely. Most of the people who reported themselves to the Communists were treated politely in Nha Trang until Saigon fell.

But as soon as Saigon fell, they switched. They started to treat us differently. Even before Saigon fell we were in re-education camps.

When Saigon fell it was they who told us the news when we were in the camp. Before that we never thought for one minute that Saigon would fall. Not for one minute. I hoped that one day my friends and I could escape from the camp. So at first it was a shock, that it fell so suddenly. But in the beginning, after that news, there was a period of relief, and a feeling that, Oh well, the war is over at least. The Communists were also Vietnamese and we were all Vietnamese, and we thought it would now be all right. We thought, No big loss, and maybe we would be able to live together. But the older people in the camp who had once lived in the North under the Communists, didn't buy that for one minute. They told us, "You guys are too young and you should not be too optimistic about the prospect of being able to live together with them in peace." They warned us about this. So we became sort of suspicious. But the prevailing sentiment of the time was one of intense sadness. We were all very sad.

We realized that our future was very bleak indeed. In the re-education center they made us study the ten lessons about why the Vietnamese people had to fight against the American government and troops, and why the Americans wanted in intervene in Vietnam. Then they made us write out personal histories, like our autobiography. They would make us do that in the morning and then they would ask us to do it again in the afternoon and then in the evening they would ask us to do it again. Most of the day, every day, we had to write out our autobiography—three or four times a day. In the beginning people thought they would have to do it once, but as they made us write it over and over again we just couldn't remember all that we wrote. They would take the different biographies that we wrote and they would ask us about them.

And let me tell you, they started to tell us stuff that was extremely strange and unbelievable and improbable. But as they told us the same things over and over again, I found myself starting to believe what they said. I began to feel that I myself had been a criminal for fighting in the ARVN, as if I was guilty of some charges that they drummed up and they dumped on our heads. But lucky for those of us who were younger officers, in our years as university students we learned how to meditate, and so now we used meditation as the way to keep our sanity.

We otherwise would have been driven insane by the things that they did to us and made us do. And the things that they said, so repetitious and illogical, day and night they would say the same things to us, all the time, and the personal history things that they made us fill out every day several times.

At night, about ten o'clock, under the light of a candle or a small oil lamp, they made us fill out personal histories. Then at about three in the morning they woke us up to again write out our personal history; it was so hard, so terrible.

I was fortunate. I stayed there for a little over three months and I got released. The people who worked in the psychological warfare unit of ARVN were the ones that they really went after. But then again it was just a matter of luck or chance. Because my friends who were of the same rank and combat soldiers also got held by them and I never saw them again.

There was an officer of much higher rank than me, and he was released three days before me, and the Communists used him as propaganda. They said, "Look at this guy, he was a much higher ranking officer and yet he was released. That means that he is re-educated," and they said that it meant that we were unwilling to be re-educated. And to our families that was torture, because they could not understand why he was released before us. They then believed the Communists and believed that we didn't want to be re-educated, and that was a real psychological blow they dealt to us.

Many of my friends had gone into the jungle and joined the resistance forces. But I just went home to my family. I had no idea of leaving the country at that time. I nurtured a hope that I would be able to get in touch with my friends who had not been captured by the Communists. I knew that they were around somewhere, and I wanted to be in touch with them to see what I could do. Soon the Communists became suspicious of my movements and my motives. As they became suspicious of me, I decided to go to work in some fields, and then I had to report to them every week and do more personal history records for them.

I came to the U.S. in 1979. I left Vietnam by boat, a really tiny one. The person who had that boat had been a friend of mine since we were small. I got in touch with him and he let me escape with him. We left a place very near Nha Trang.

I looked back at the palm trees lining the beaches when we left. And I thought about how happy I was to have a seat on that tiny boat. We had only a small military compass to guide us. But we made it to the Philippines.

In the beginning when I was in the U.S. I kept thinking about Vietnam and wanting to return. It was a dream, a hope. Even now I still have that dream, to return in order to fight, and not to take it easy, like other people.

Of course, I dream of Vietnam. A strange dream. I dream about going home and getting near my house. But then, in my dream, I am too afraid to go into it again for some reason. Maybe because I am afraid of the Communists' capturing me again. When I wake up I feel regretful. I think to myself, "I was so close to my home in my dreams, but I couldn't go inside again." Even in my dreams I can't ever really go into my house in Vietnam and live peacefully again.

There were rumors before I left Vietnam, rumors that I believed, that a resistance force had been marshalled. My friends thought if we could escape we would go to the U.S. and join that force and return and fight the Communists. But it wasn't so. And our hopes and ideals were deflated here. That was the thing that hurt us, to get here and find out the reality and the truth. There was no real resistance. The war was over.

I still hope that someday I can return to Vietnam. That is my final hope and today that is what keeps me from going insane. That is my final hope.

"You could almost see it in their eyes, 'Why did you abandon us? Why did the Americans leave us?'" Refugees outside Danang fleeing from the advancing North Vietnamese Army, March 1975.
(*Courtesy of Tran Khiem*)

"Only I am left to tell you the story." Colonel Le Khac Ly.
(*Larry Engelmann*)

"Look at them!
They are angels!"
Tram Tran in 1975.
(*Courtesy of Tram
Tran*)

"Mother, I will make you proud of me."
Nguyen Thi Hoa.
(*Larry Engelmann*)

"When the doors closed I was caring for the children." Refugees boarding a C-130 at Tan Son Nhut, late April, 1975.
(*Author's collection*)

"The Americans looked very beautiful to me and they were now my protectors and I felt I must trust in these people." Crew members carrying children aboard the U.S.S. *Blue Ridge*, April 29, 1975.
(*Courtesy of U.S. Navy*)

"The situation is we got a couple thousand people and where are the helicopters?" The gate of the U.S. Embassy, Saigon, afternoon of April 29, 1975. (*Courtesy of AP/Wide World Photos*)

"Stand back, boys. The war is over."
Nguyen Phuc Thieu, South Vietnamese
helicopter pilot.
(*Courtesy of Gary Parker*)

"You know, even Marine pilots can't fly forever." The first evacuation helicopter
leaves the deck of the U.S.S. *Midway*, April 29, 1975.
(*Courtesy of U.S. Navy*)

"Soon we shall surely be like the caterpillars." Vietnamese refugees on the deck of the U.S.S. *Midway,* April 29, 1975.
(*Courtesy of U.S. Navy*)

"We just loaded them like cargo. They were everywhere. Even the lifeboats were full of people." The U.S.S. *Pioneer Contender* of the Military Sealift Command, loaded with 16,600 refugees, off the coast of Phu Quoc Island.
(*Courtesy of U.S. Navy*)

"We were their saviors." Refugees on the U.S.N.S. *Greenville Victory*, April 30, 1975.
(*Courtesy of U.S. Navy*)

"They were wonderful, these people. I love them." Refugees aboard the U.S.N.S. *Greenville Victory*, April 30, 1975.
(*Courtesy of U.S. Navy*)

"When something presents itself in front of you, you just do it. Maybe later on you think about it. There these people are—let's get them out of here. It's that simple." Bringing refugees aboard the U.S.N.S. *Greenville Victory*, April 30, 1975.
(*Courtesy of U.S. Navy*)

"Drop everything you have and run for it!" The evacuation of the Defense Attaché Office compound at Tan Son Nhut air base, April 29, 1975.
(*Author's collection*)

"In a short time the Vietnamese people themselves would be like the bees."
The swarm of Vietnamese helicopters approaching the U.S.S. *Midway* on the
morning of April 30, 1975.
(*Courtesy of U.S. Navy*)

"My, God, what a mess." Some of the last Vietnamese evacuees at Tan Son Nhut
air base, afternoon of April 29, 1975.
(*Author's collection*)

"What you end up with is deep melancholy. You are damn glad the fire is out." U.S. Marines aboard the U.S.S. *Midway*, preparing to depart for Saigon, morning of April 29, 1975.
(*Courtesy of John Degler*)

"It was, finally, the best thing." Marine colonel George S. Slade on the U.S.S. *Midway* with souvenir from the U.S. Embassy in Saigon, April 30, 1975.
(*Author's collection*)

"I don't buy that peace with honor stuff. We shagged out of there and left them to the North Vietnamese. And you know how kind they are." Marines at the U.S. Embassy compound guarding the gate to prevent unauthorized entry, April 29, 1975.
(*Courtesy of AP/Wide World Photo*)

"I remember watching the last American soldiers leave Vietnam." Colonel Bui Tin (center, holding notebook) counting the last American soldiers leaving Vietnam, March 28, 1973.
(*Courtesy of Colonel Bui Tin*)

"Your power has crumbled. You have nothing in your hands to surrender and so you cannot surrender what you do not possess." Colonel Bui Tin accepts surrender of President Duong Van Minh (dark, short-sleeved shirt) in the Presidential Palace, Saigon, April 30, 1975.
(*Courtesy of Colonel Bui Tin*)

"Then I went to the roof and took pictures with my comrades." Colonel Bui Tin (holding briefcase) and his North Vietnamese Army comrades celebrate their victory, April 30, 1975, on the roof of the U.S. Embassy in Saigon.
(*Courtesy of Colonel Bui Tin*)

"All the things we saw in those days! You would not believe them. You really don't want to know." Boat people arriving in Hong Kong, April, 1989. (*Courtesy of* South China Morning Post)

"The long war is over." Victorious, General Vo Nguyen Giap (next to window), Commander of the North Vietnamese Army, and Colonel Bui Tin (standing, in dark shirt) with a local Communist official, on a helicopter survey, May 7, 1975. They pass over the "ancient battle front" of Operation Junction City where North Vietnamese and Viet Cong units fought the Americans in 1967. Giap observed, "How very beautiful our land is today!"
(*Courtesy of Colonel Bui Tin*)

"Every night I still see that convoy." Refugees along Route 7B, March, 1975.
(*Author's collection*)

"He's a general and he's staying." General Nguyen Lao Ky (right) and General Ngo Quang Truong aboard the U.S.S. *Midway,* April 30, 1975. (*Courtesy of John Degler*)

"We watched them start to push our helicopter over the side." Aboard the U.S.S. *Midway,* disposing of helicopter, April 30, 1975. (*Courtesy of U.S. Navy*)

"Groups of people were clinging to the rope." Refugees being aided by crew members aboard the U.S.S. *Midway*, April 29, 1975.
(*Courtesy of U.S. Navy*)

"They were all looking at a map—God knows what for."
(*Courtesy of John Degler*)

General Ly Tong Ba
"There Was a Kind of Sickness"

I was born in the southern part of Vietnam in 1931. I attended the Dalat Academy and I was commissioned as an officer in the army in 1952. I served one year in the Red River Delta as a second lieutenant.

In 1975 I was a brigadier general and commander of the ARVN Twenty-fifth Division at Cu Chi. I was chief commander of ARVN armor before then. At the end of 1974, they'd asked me to take command of the Twenty-fifth Division and I was five months, then, with the Division.

When the attack came on the Ban Me Thuot, I was directed to the northern part of Tay Ninh Province to stabilize the situation. The Communist forces tried to block us there.

When I heard that the central highlands were being abandoned, I knew that would create a very big problem. I thought that maybe later on they would stabilize and turn around. I know that we had the forces to form a front somewhere. But nothing happened. They never turned around and fought. I don't know what happened.

Meanwhile, we were fighting the Ninth NVA Division near Cu Chi. They were trying to push their way to Saigon down Highway 1. And my men fought them all the way. In late March we caught them at Truong Mit and lost over 400 men in the fierce fighting. Nobody ran away.

I heard that other generals were abandoning their forces. I wasn't surprised at all. But I knew my men, I knew my army, I knew my leaders. I had confidence in my men and they had confidence in me. I knew who the enemy was and what they were trying to do. And where they were.

I tried to contact my chiefs, Nguyen Van Thieu and Cao Van Vien, to tell them what was happening. I wanted to tell them that we finally couldn't do it anymore and that everything was going wrong. The Twenty-fifth Division was fighting one full division, but after several days we were facing three divisions with armor.

The Eighteenth Division was fighting at Xuan Loc with Le Minh Dao to protect the approach to Saigon from the east, and we were blocking Highway 1 from Saigon to Tay Ninh in the west. On the morning of the twenty-ninth I led my last task force in Ben Tre, but I had no more troops, nothing more to do; the rest of my men were spread out. I wanted to regroup my remaining forces and continue to fight. I asked General Toan to let me put my division back together. The Communists continued to attack us. But our ARVN soldiers didn't worry. We continued to fight them as we fell back toward Saigon.

I told my men as we were pushed back, "Don't worry about what's happening now, just fight and make them pay dearly for everything." My men continued to try to maneuver and fight and counterattack. But the soldiers were finally worn down in the fighting.

But there was something else, too, besides the fighting. The soldiers of the ARVN by that time also had a kind of sickness, a mental sickness. There was a kind of sickness that infected them, the sickness of an idea. The soldiers of the ARVN in the end believed that they had been lied to. Look, they were in a bad situation. To fight a good war, they could not be led by a man like Nguyen Van Thieu. The Americans were not helping them any more and their own government was not helping them, either. They were fighting and dying, and for what?

Some of my soldiers finally started to run. The sickness got them. And when I saw that, I could not do anything else. The Army was finally gone. I decided to walk back on foot from Cu Chi to Saigon.

I wanted to find my soldiers and to rally and regroup them at Hoc Mon, and to draw a defense line there. But before I could do that, I was captured by the Communist forces, who had already occupied everywhere between Cu Chi and Saigon.

As to the infected mentality of the Vietnamese Army, you must see that the society of Vietnam had become corrupted and chaotic, and that kind of attitude got into the Vietnamese army and soldiers, too. The commanders' mentality was not a fighting mentality. When the fight became tough, they didn't want to fight any more. They wanted to depend on America, and when they could not depend on America they ran away. That was the sickness that they had caught.

I am a fighter. My leaders had their own problems. But I had been fighting since I was a young soldier. And now I found that the Army leaders weren't doing their job. I was doing my job, but they weren't doing theirs. So I can say that in the higher ranks of the military we had the wrong kind of men to be leaders.

The Northern soldiers overran all of our positions. I was wounded in the leg. They had surrounded me and my remaining men. So many of my soldiers surrendered. I told my aide, who was by my side, "You see me, you do what I do. Everything I do, you do." So when the enemy told us to lay down our weapons, many men just put down their weapons. But when the Communist soldiers told the men to stand together, my aide and I just went into a rice paddy and stayed under the water with our noses up above the water. Then they thought we were dead. We stayed for three hours in the water, from three in the afternoon until six that night. Then we went to a stream that leads to the Hoc Mon bridge, a small stream. I tried to get there in the darkness. I got into the stream. I tried to swim down to the bridge. From there I knew I could get on the road to Saigon. But when I was in the stream, swimming, I heard a lot of noise from men on both sides of the stream. They were all North Vietnamese soldiers. By then it was very dark. So I got out of the stream and tried to make my way back to Cu Chi on the land. In the darkness

I just walked around in a big triangle and I didn't know where I was or where Saigon was because it was dark and it was raining.

So in the morning, I was still with my aide, but I could not move any more. My wounded leg was getting worse. I told my aide to go to try to find a doctor. But before we could find a doctor we walked into the midst of fifty or sixty North Vietnamese soldiers. I thought they were South Vietnamese soldiers from a distance. And so I said to my aide, "I think we will be captured now. We can't run anymore."

My uniform was all muddy by this time and they could not see that I was a general. They did not know who I was. But one old woman saw me and she came over and said, "General, what happened to you? Why are you so dirty?" And several of the soldiers around heard her. Before that, they just thought I was a lieutenant colonel, and they had no idea that I was the Binh Duong province chief.

Then they put me in a room with barbed wire around it. And I just sat there. I was thinking that they would probably kill me when they found out who I was. So my soldiers asked me if I wanted to write a letter to my wife. And I said, "No. I don't want to write a letter to anybody."

Of course, the soldiers who captured me belonged to some of the three divisions that had fought against the Twenty-fifth Division. They said that their commander was coming to see me. They said that he wanted to meet the man he had been fighting against.

I told them, "You can do what you want. I lost my army and you can do what you want now."

When the North Vietnamese commander came to see me I said to him, "You see how I treated your soldiers when I captured them. All I ask of you now is that you treat my soldiers the same way I treated your soldiers. I treated my prisoners better than you treat your prisoners."

So he said, "We have nothing against you, General. But at first our troops were still very excited and maybe they didn't treat you well."

I told him, "They had us sleep on the ground behind the barbed wire. And the treatment they were giving my men I didn't like." I wasn't worried about me. I was concerned about the treatment of my men. I still thought they would kill me.

On the third of May my wife heard a rumor that I had been killed at Cu Chi, so she and our children left Saigon and went to the Delta. There she found a wooden boat and went to Malaysia. There some Americans who knew me found out who she was and brought her to the United States. But I didn't know about that for one year. When my wife left Saigon, she thought I was dead.

I thought I would be killed; that is why I didn't write a letter to her. I thought if I wrote a letter she would stay and wait for me and I thought that they were going to kill me anyway.

The soldiers that they captured they finally released. But they held the officers. All of us.

They took me back to Cu Chi with my staff officers. Again, they kept us behind barbed wire. That was for one month. Then they sent me back to Saigon, where they had me report for "re-education." Then they sent me to a "re-education camp." At that time I thought my life would be spared. I was sent north in July of 1975 and I was not released from the re-education camp until December of 1987. I labored there for twelve years. General Le Minh Dao was in my re-education camp.

I fought for my country. I did my duty. I did the best I could. And I lost. Yet I am proud, still. When I could not perform my job any more I still tried to fight. I lost my army, but I was never defeated. I just did my job for Vietnam. And when the NVA General that I fought against said to me, "What do you think now?" I said, "I am Vietnamese. I want to see Vietnam rich and the people happy and free." But I think that Vietnam is still fighting for freedom. The war isn't over. Still the people want freedom.

From the time I was a second lieutenant until now, I think that is true. We Vietnamese try to decide our problems through war. And what was decided? Now the North has won and we hoped then that Vietnam would be a very good country. Vietnam lost many good citizens in the war and now look at the country. I must say that we got nothing from the war. The war is still on. And I still say to the leaders of the country, "I did my part. You won and I lost. And now you do what you wanted to do. If you do good, if the people become free and prosperous, then I have nothing against you. But now look what has happened to the country. What does your victory mean now? What are you going to do?"

We are a poor country. We are a small country. We need help from outside now. Maybe we need new leaders now.

The Vietnamese people are hard-working and good. And the people are ready for freedom and for prosperity. They are ready to become part of the world again. The potential is there. But, again, they have this sickness, the new regime has it in the way that the old regime had. Corruption—a sickness that eats away at the people. If you don't like someone, or if you don't like what he says, then today they put him in prison.

This society is corrupted. The people become corrupted because the leaders are corrupted.

My soldiers ran away because they had a sickness that they caught from the leaders and from the society. The society was not worth dying for. The sick soul of the society had frightened them. But if you shoot that soldier who runs away, you kill him but you do not kill the sickness. And then when they punish people for corruption, they punish the individual but the sickness continues.

I never thought of committing suicide when the war was lost. Why should I commit suicide? That is very egotistical. Suicide! What good would that do? My duty was to fight. I should fight until I die or am captured. What am I, a Mandarin who is going to die for the Emperor?

I fought with my men. I didn't die. I was just defeated on the battle-field. I was defeated. But I am still alive.

Now I am here in Saigon and I have nothing to do. I have applied to go to the United States to join my wife and my daughter in Nevada. One of my sons is now a student in San Diego at the university. And my youngest boy is now a football star in the United States.

Pham Van Xinh, Security Officer, Second Infantry Division
"We Were Like a Snake Without a Head"

I was in Danang when it fell to the Communists. I was a security officer with the Second Infantry Division. I had been in the Army since early 1968. We had been stationed at Tam Ky, then we were ordered to go to Danang. But when we got off our ship in Danang, we found that our commanding officers had taken another ship and had gone south. We had been abandoned. We didn't know what we were supposed to do or where we were supposed to go. We were like a snake without a head.

Some of the men got on refugee ships going south. I did not. I was afraid because I knew about the Hue massacre of 1968, when the Communists had killed thousands of Vietnamese. We thought they would do that again, we thought they would kill all of the soldiers first. So we threw away our uniforms and put on civilian clothes.

When the Communists arrived in Danang, at first they did not do anything terrible. Nobody was arrested at first and nobody was sent to a prison camp. But then, after a couple of days, we discovered that the Communists had lists of people who had cooperated with the Americans. Those people were called traitors, and the Communists said they were very dangerous. I don't know how many names were on the lists, but I did see many people arrested. Those who were on a special list were shot right away, right there in the street. The Communists said that those people did not deserve to live. It was not like an execution, really. It was more like a murder in the street. They did not even lead them away, as they did in Hue. They just killed them where they found them.

I saw several people shot that way. It was frightening. The Communists had no mercy. None at all. I was afraid because I was a soldier, and I thought that my name was probably on one of their lists.

I felt some safety without my uniform. But Danang was my home and the people in my neighborhood knew that I had been in the army, so I could not hide. I knew that some of them would turn me in to please the Communists. So I moved to another part of the city, where the people didn't know me. But somebody gave my name to the Communists, and they came for me. They had a list with my name on it. I felt very ashamed when they arrested me. I thought that maybe I should have kept my uniform. I thought maybe I should have fought back. But there were no leaders anymore, and there were no orders. So I did not fight back.

The Communists sent me to a New Economic Zone. I was there for six years. I hated it. I knew that I would leave Vietnam as soon as I could. I had no money, though. And to get out on a boat you needed money.

In 1983 I returned to Danang. I found a man with a boat. I told him I would be his navigator if he would take me out of Vietnam. I told him I would get other people who would pay him. He agreed to help me. I found twenty-two people who wanted to leave Vietnam and they paid the man with the boat. We left at night in December, 1983. We sailed to Hainan Island. There the Chinese helped us and gave us food and water. Then we sailed to Hong Kong. We were at sea for twenty-four days. Today I am a free man.

Nguyen Phuc Thieu, Second Lieutenant, South Vietnamese Air Force
"Stand Back, Boys. The War Is Over"

I was a helicopter pilot. I had been in the Air Force for five years by 1975. I had been stationed at Danang and Nha Trang and finally in Saigon at Tan Son Nhut. None of us believed that the country would collapse. We thought that maybe the Communists would make it to Saigon. Maybe they would even get into the city, like they did in 1968, but then we would push them out again. We expected the country to be partitioned again with a new border somewhere near Nha Trang.

Communist airplanes bombed Tan Son Nhut on April 28. We were told that the pilots were defectors from our ranks. That was not surprising. We had a large air force and if two or three pilots defected to the other side, that was just to be expected. The rest of us were loyal.

On April 29 the American Marines landed and surrounded the Defense Attaché Office. From there they began to fly out refugees by helicopter. We stayed in our barracks and waited for orders. We didn't know that our commanding officers had already abandoned us. We had five helicopters standing by and we thought that we would soon go into action. We thought that maybe our commanders were at a secret meeting with the Americans and would soon return with new orders. We never thought our commanders would never return.

When the Americans had completed their evacuation, they blew up the DAO. Then the Marines left. And we were still waiting for our orders. On the night of April 29 we listened to General Ky on our radio. He made a speech in which he said he would stay and fight to the death. He said we should do that, too. Then he left.

On the morning of April 30 we decided we could no longer wait at

Tan Son Nhut. It was 5:00 a.m. when we decided to fly south in our helicopters and to join up with units in the Delta to continue the fight against the Communists. But when we went to our helicopters we found that most of them had been vandalized. Parts were missing and the batteries had been stolen and someone had taken most of our fuel. We took parts from some of the helicopters, and fuel and batteries, and we got two helicopters working. All of us got in those two and flew down to Can Tho. We tried to radio the units at Can Tho but they didn't respond. When we landed there, some of the soldiers came to us and asked, "What are you doing here? Haven't you heard the message from the Americans?" They told us that the Americans had said that all Vietnamese helicopters should fly out to the Seventh Fleet to keep their aircraft from falling into Communist hands. So we talked about what to do. Finally, we decided to fly out to the Seventh Fleet.

We flew out over Vung Tau. We flew low over the city and could see Communist soldiers there. We were low on fuel and we did not know how far away the Seventh Fleet was. When we saw the American ships we only had five minutes' more fuel in our tanks.

We thought that when we landed on the American ships, we would be resupplied and then regroup. Then, we thought, we would go back to Vietnam and fight and the Americans would go with us. We thought they were calling us out in order to make new plans for a counterattack. And that sounded like a good idea. We were still ready to fight.

But as soon as we had landed on the ship, American Marines took away our weapons. We thought that was very strange. Then they led us to another part of the ship. And then we watched them start to push our helicopter over the side. Some of our men started shouting and they tried to run over to stop the Americans. But a Marine stopped our men and said, "Stand back, boys. The war is over."

Some of the men started to cry. And when they saw our helicopter fall into the sea and they knew we would not be going back to Vietnam, some of them tried to jump in the sea. The Marines stopped them. Many of our men had left their families in Saigon and they wanted to go back to their families. But now there was no way.

When I saw our helicopter sink in the sea I felt very sad. When I first saw the American ships I thought everything was going to be okay. But I was wrong. For us, the war was over.

Hai Van Le, South Vietnamese Air Force
"It Was a Very Nice Day. The Sun Was Shining.
And Everyone Was Crying"

My parents moved to the South in 1954, when the country was partitioned and the Communists took over the North. I was just one year old at the time. My parents knew the Communists and did not want to live under their government. So they came south to freedom.

I joined the Air Force and went to flight school. I got out of flight school in early April of 1975. By that time, when pilots flew they never had enough fuel. We had to take some planes apart in order to get parts for other planes. And we never had enough bullets. We had to count the bullets for the planes. We wanted to fight. But how could we fight without weapons?

Some of us in the Air Force talked to each other about the possibility of losing the war. But when we talked like that we were afraid because we thought maybe we had heard too much Communist propaganda. We knew that we had good generals at the top. As long as we had good generals, how could we lose?

I was at Tan Son Nhut on April 28 when North Vietnamese pilots bombed us. They came over in A-37s and dropped bombs on us. It didn't frighten me at all. In 1968 during Tet, the Communists had come into the city, too, and we pushed them out. So this was nothing new to us. But then, on April 29, we heard that our generals had run away. We couldn't believe it. We—the young ones—we expected to continue fighting. But how could we fight when there were no generals to lead us any more?

On the morning of April 30 all of the pilots were talking about a message they had heard on the emergency radio channel. They said that the American fleet had told all Vietnamese pilots to bring their aircraft out to the ships so that they would not fall into Communist hands. Many of the pilots took helicopters filled with people out to the American fleet after they heard that message.

I wasn't yet sure that I wanted to leave. So I didn't go out on a helicopter. I knew that there were still soldiers fighting in the Delta. So I thought maybe I would go south and join them. But then, late in the morning, I heard that the government had already surrendered to the Communists. Only then did I decide to leave.

I went with a friend down to the Saigon River. There was a boat that was just leaving, so we decided to get on it. We were feeling bad about leaving, but when the government surrendered, there was no more hope. People in Saigon were celebrating because thy had been fooled by the Communists. They thought that when the Communists took over there would be no more war. But now they would have to learn.

When our boat went down the Saigon River no one fired at us. There were more than 3,000 people on the boat—men, women and children. We had no food or water on board and we did not know what would happen once we got into the South China Sea. But we believed that we could not stay and live under Communism.

We all looked at Vietnam for the last time as we left. The last thing we saw was the beautiful beach at Vung Tau. It was a nice day. The sun was shining. And everyone was crying.

After we saw Vung Tau for the last time, a soldier on the boat took his own gun and put it under his chin and shot himself to death. And some people jumped over the side of the ship and disappeared in the sea. I watched two men jump over the side.

We were in the South China Sea for three days without food or water. On the third day a Danish ship found us. They took the women and children off and took them to Hong Kong. Then they gave us food and water so we wouldn't die at sea and they told us how to get to Hong Kong. During the rest of the journey we didn't talk to each other because we were so sad about losing our country.

Captain Nguyen Quoc Dinh
"Oh, Man, Get Out of My Boat"

I was an officer in the Vietnamese Navy and was assigned to a small boat with a crew of six people. It was called a PCF—Patrol Craft Fast. We worked only along the seacoast in Vietnam. I patrolled the coastal zone looking for contraband and for Vietcong trying to bring in supplies. We didn't see much action. In the Delta the Communists were strong, but along the coast they weren't.

I was quite young when I was commissioned as a captain in 1969. I attended Officers' Candidate School [OCS] in the United States. By the time I joined the Navy they needed officers, but we had only one training school in Vietnam. So the Americans helped us train officers in OCS in Newport, Rhode Island. I learned English in Vietnam after graduation from basic training. They sent me to an English school taught by an American soldier, eight hours a day.

I don't know much about politics, but the Paris Agreement worried me some. After the American troops were gone they cut off the supplies and we began to run out of fuel and ammunition. On my boat, some parts broke, and some days we had to wait a long time for replacements. Then we had to cut back on patrols because of the fuel. Before the agreement I could patrol all day and all night, but after that I could only patrol a few hours every day.

Then in the spring of 1975 I was in Qui Nhon and I picked up some civilians and some soldiers on the coast after the abandonment of the central highlands. After that I went to Cam Ranh Bay with my boat and withdrew some more people and took them back to Saigon.

I saw that the situation was real bad. There was no good plan and the troops just abandoned everything and ran.

When the withdrawal began, our boat continued to patrol. There were a lot of refugees in a bad situation. Some soldiers who were withdrawn got mad and they turned out to be bad guys. They raped women on the same boat with them.

Refugees went to Phu Quoc. I was there and the situation was bad there, too. I transferred up to Qui Nhon, then. As the theater of war got smaller we stopped patrolling. I did whatever they ordered me to do. They told me to do nothing, so I did nothing. The high-ranking officers didn't seem to know what was going on so they just stopped giving orders. They wanted to keep the people calm so they didn't do anything, but I don't think they knew what was going on. My crew members asked me, "What is going on?" and I said, "I don't know what is going on. Nobody does."

I patrolled a little bit on my own, trying to find frogmen who might try to destroy some of our ships, but I didn't find any.

Then on April 29, I didn't know what was going on anymore at all. My boat was being fixed that day; one of the engines was broken. We were about ten miles from Saigon on the Saigon River. I saw the American helicopters start to come in. I really had not thought earlier about leaving the country. I never even dreamed of it. Then on the twenty-ninth, they said that they were going to reorganize the Navy. They said we would go to Con Son Island to reorganize. My commanding officer commanded about twenty boats, including mine. He told me, about six in the afternoon of the 29th that I should go to Con Son Island. When he told me that I thought maybe we would lose the country. But my family was in Saigon and I didn't want to leave them behind. So I thought I would go to Saigon and pick up my family first. I went back to Saigon. But some of my crew didn't want to do that. So some of the men went in a boat directly to Con Son, and some came with me to the Navy headquarters, about one mile from my home in Saigon. The other Navy ships had already pulled out of Saigon. I didn't really know where the bigger ships were going; they didn't tell anybody. I got into Saigon about midnight. It was really crowded and chaotic and people were trying to get on all the ships. I thought people might try to steal my boat, some people from the Army, maybe. I had a crew of five people, and I left three of the men to guard the boat, and I left with one of my friends and we went home. People were out on the streets. I walked by the American Embassy and saw the people crowded around the front gate. I tried to get a motorcycle there. Cars and motorcycles were abandoned all over the streets. They said there was a curfew, but it wasn't enforced. It was at night and there were fires, and I saw people standing on top of the Embassy, but I didn't see any helicopters landing. Some people were trying to get in, but I think they knew that they couldn't get in anymore. This was about two in the morning on April 30. It took about one hour to walk home. I still had on my uniform and my helmet. I felt that I was ready for combat then.

My family was still at home and they didn't know what was happening. They were scared. My father, who had been a Saigon policeman, was concerned, but he didn't know how to get out of the country. There were

my parents and eight children—ten people in the family that I had to get
out of the country. Earlier the Air Force pilots tried to take some of their
families to Thailand and they were caught and brought back to Vietnam.
They told us that if we tried to leave they would arrest us and put us in
jail.

I brought home a couple of hand grenades and some handguns, and I
told my mom that if the Communists came into the house I would kill
them all and kill myself with them. And my mother said that whatever I
wanted to do I could do. I said that I might kill the whole family, we
would all die together, and she said that was all right, too. I didn't know
if I could do that, but that is what I told the family. Then my father
said that was all right, too.

I didn't know if the country had been lost by that time, for sure. But I
had brought other weapons home a week earlier, because I thought no
matter what happened, sooner or later I would be dying and I wanted my
family to take care of itself if I was gone.

I was the man of the family. My father really couldn't do anything. I
really didn't even know where we would go or what we would do if we
left the city.

But I decided we would go. I said to my mother and father, "If you
want to get out, then come with me." I had a motorcycle, so I took two
children on the motorcycle to the port. I dropped them there and then
came back and got two others. My boat was still there and there was a
big crowd. They didn't take the boat because the soldiers were guarding
it. My boat stayed in the middle of the river and came back and forth
when I brought my family to the river. I called them over each time.

After my second trip I told my friend to go pick up the rest of my
family. Some of the men were scared and they thought if they left the
boat I would leave them. But I assured them I would wait until noon
for them. And still they decided to stay rather than go and get relatives.
Seven members of my family came out. My father and brother and another sister stayed in the house. They wouldn't come. My sister was a
teacher and she and her husband didn't want to leave.

I was getting mad. People and businessmen came to the boat while we
were waiting for my family. They handed me a lot of dollars and gold,
and I said, "Oh man, get out of my boat." I shot up in the air to get them
away. They begged me and cried out, but I didn't have room for them. I
told my men to throw these people out of the boat, and they did. Some
had their wives and children with them and their suitcases. But I had to
bring my own family out; I wanted to take care of my family first.

A lot of people had guns but they didn't come on board because they
didn't think my boat could make it. I had about forty people in my boat
by that time. It was pretty crowded. The boat was about ten meters long
and about three meters wide and had two levels.

We left in the late morning of April 30, about eleven in the morning.

We went down the river to the South China Sea. We had to go past Rungsat where there were a lot of Communists, and the river was very narrow there, and it was dangerous to pass through. Two other boats accompanied us. I was scared because it was a small boat, and one rocket would have killed everyone. We saw a bigger boat coming down the river, a civilian boat, with a lot of rich people on it. It was named the *Vong Hong Ni*. They had about 300 people on board. I pulled up to them, told them to stop. I had a gun in my hand and I told them I would shoot them if they didn't stop. They were scared of me, so they stopped, and they let us come on board. We cut our boat loose and let it float away. We went out past Vung Tau that night. We heard on the radio that Saigon had surrendered. And I said to myself, "Well, that's it."

After we went out from Vung Tau we saw the American Seventh Fleet. We thought they would come to pick us up in the morning. But they had disappeared by then. Then a Vietnamese Navy ship came by us and we followed them for seven days and seven nights.

Finally we came to the Philippines, to Subic Bay, and from there we were taken to Wake Island and then Fort Chaffee. Then we moved to New York City.

I tried to write a letter to my father after that. But I could not write directly to him. So I sent it to a neighbor near our house, and they gave the letter to my father. So my sister knew that we had made it out safely. My father was sent to a re-education camp and he spent five years there. He was just a captain in the police so I don't know why they sent him to the camp for so long.

In 1980 he was released. He tried to come out with my sister and brother. We sent them money to buy gold so they could get out. But my father didn't make it. The boat had too many people on it. It was supposed to have forty people, but they had 120 people on it because the owner of the boat was so greedy. He thought it would take only two days to Malaysia, but it took seven days and nights. They had no pilot and they ran into storms at sea. So my father starved to death during the trip to Malaysia. My sister and her two daughters and my brother survived. But her husband died also. There was water leaking into their boat and he worked so hard to keep the water out and to save his family that he died of exhaustion.

My life is much better here, to tell you the truth. And a lot of my friends say the same thing. If I had a chance to go back there I don't know what I would do, really. Some nights in New York City I had nightmares. I dreamed I was in Vietnam and that the Communists took me to their re-education camp. I had those nightmares for a couple of months. But I don't have them any more.*

* Captain Nyuyen Quoc Dinh died of lung cancer in the summer of 1987, shortly after this interview took place.

CHAPTER **XVI**

Civilians

Nguyen Phuc Hau
"Yes. We Fought"

I was the vice-chairman of the supervisory board of Nha Trang and Khanh Hoa Province. I was elected to that position in 1970 for four years and then was reelected in 1974 for four more years.

Politics is in my blood. I wanted to go into politics to try to help my people. I was born in 1931, so my generation is a generation of war. When I was a boy it was the Second World War. We fought against the Japanese. When I got older we Vietnamese were fighting the Chinese, the French, the United States, and each other. Always fighting.

I would really some day like to talk to Mike Mansfield. After Saigon collapsed I was hiding in Saigon and I listened to the Voice of America, and I heard Mike Mansfield say, "Vietnam is not worth a single American life." It made me feel very sad, because I remembered the courage of my American advisors during the war and I loved them very much. I think the Americans I knew who participated in the Vietnam war thought they were fighting for a noble cause—to preserve freedom. Mike Mansfield didn't know about how many people died in Vietnam fighting against the Communists, and he did not watch television to see how many thousands of people ran away from the towns when the Communists came. He should have known what they were running from. In 1954 more than a million Vietnamese fled from the North to the South. Mike Mansfield must have known why.

I was there the day Nha Trang collapsed. I told my wife she should go to her sister in Phan Rang for safety and I'd stay in my city because of my job. I was the organizer of assistance for the refugees arriving from the other cities. Two days before Nha Trang fell, we sent a letter to the general who commanded troops around the city and we asked to have a meeting with him in order to organize a defense for the city. Then at nine o'clock on the day that it fell, I came to the office and had a meeting with the people in the organization for assistance of the refugees from the other cities and waited for a general to come in. But at eleven o'clock nobody called. Then we called Province headquarters and nobody was there. I called other officers. Nobody there. And then someone came to tell me they all left already. They left without saying anything.

I couldn't believe it. One week before that I went with my boss and the province chief to Khanh Duong on the border between Ban Me Thuot and Khanh Hoa province. The parachutists were over there. We brought them food and supplies to promote their spirits. We talked to them and told them that all the people in the province were behind them and their mission was to keep fighting; to stand, to keep the area out of the hands of Communists. We were proud they were doing a very good job. And we believed we could fight again; but that day, it was very sad.

I heard later that they almost all died. The day the Communists attacked them, they did not know the rear was leaving, so they called and called for assistance from the Air Force and they called for assistance from the supply department, and nobody answered. They kept fighting, and they were surrounded by the Communists and killed. They didn't want to surrender. The Airborne is very good. The best.

I was very stubborn. My wife came to me and said, "Hey, I heard about the Americans leaving and that we are losing the war." She asked me, "What was your plan for the family, to escape or not?" I said, "I don't believe it. That's stupid." That was in early 1975. I said, "We can fight against the Communists." She said many families were moving already to the Saigon. And I said, "Let them move. We stay here."

I believed that even if they lost other provinces, they could keep Nha Trang and we would be safe.

After the commanders and province chiefs left, then we had turmoil in the city. Prisoners got out and broke into the stores and burned the market.

The way we lost the war is very strange. The janitor at the parochial school in Nha Trang was a Communist. He used the school for stocking the arms for the Communists and led the Communists in the city. Later he told us that the Communists of Nha Trang didn't know the ARVN commander was leaving the city. If they had known that, they could have taken over that day and the city would not have been in chaos. He said he went to Tuy Hoa and told the commander of the Gold Star Regiment, "Okay, the city is empty now. The people are leaving; the commanders are leaving. So we should come take over." And the commander of the regiment did not believe him.

He said the commander thought he was telling a lie or something like that. He convinced him he should send some people back with him to

Nha Trang to look at the situation. That group came back to report the ARVN was leaving—and then they came and took over the city. We just quit.

We just quit Vietnam like we quit Nha Trang city. We could have won the war. But we just quit; we just ran away. The collapse and take-over by the Communists of Nha Trang city was typical for the Vietnam war.

I don't know why. When I was in Vung Tau I came to Saigon for a supervisors' meeting and we recalled the situation of every province. I had contact with some political people, and then we decided we wanted to organize and come back: an organization to keep South Vietnam. What did it matter if we won or not? We had a plan to move the government to Can Tho and leave Saigon empty so the Communists could take over there, and we would fight and save the government so we would have a legal voice to talk to the world outside.

I felt very good about this. I said, "We want to send a message to all of the people who want to fight the Communists. They can go to Can Tho and we will organize our front line there to fight against them and keep the government safe."

One week before the total collapse of Saigon I came back to look at the situation and my friend told me, "No more! The Americans don't want it."

I had very many opportunities to get out in 1975. I had many friends coming from Nha Trang with boats; but I was very disappointed with the Americans. I said, "I will stay." That mistake will be with me for the rest of my life because of the death of my first son.

The battle came closer and closer to Vung Tau where I took my family. And the Vietcong sent rockets into the city. We had Vietnamese Marines there and they were fighting and fighting. On the day Vung Tau fell I saw two American soldiers with the Marines and they were captured by the Vietcong. I don't know what happened to them.

My wife and I and our children got together and prayed and cried. The whole nation was collapsing. The worst things were about to happen to us, we thought. The Communists kill the people. I had one friend who was very scared. He went to that center for refugees in Vung Tau. He went to the bathroom and locked it and stayed there the whole day. He was scared of the Communists because he said he was nearly buried alive by them in the Tet Offensive in Hue. I called him to come out and take a little food. He finally came out and ran away, and I don't know what happened to him after that.

There were some machine guns firing from the hotel near us on the morning of April 30. There was still fighting. We listened to the radio as the people in Saigon handed over the power to the Communists.

I want you to tell this story to the American people. After noontime on April 30, after the government handed over the power to the Communists, one location in Vung Tau city fought until two-thirty. It was children. The children went to the military academy; only little kids, the children of soldiers who had been killed in battle, a junior military academy. They kept fighting after everyone else surrendered! They were students at the Truong Thieu Sinh Quan Vung Tau.

Many of them were killed. One day later I met one of them in the chaos of the city. I did not know him but I could recognize him because of his special style of haircut that all of the students at the academy had. I said, "What happened? Did you keep fighting over there?" He said, "Yes. We fought." He was very proud of fighting the Communists. I asked him what happened, and he said that the day before the Vietcong got into the town, the American adviser came to the academy and took the commander, a colonel, on a helicopter with him. So the second in command, a captain, gathered all the students and said, "Okay, now we will go somewhere." And they left with the captain but they didn't know where they were going. The captain did not have formal orders from his colonel so he did not know what to do. So he finally stopped the students and said he wanted to get them out of the city, but didn't know where to go. So everybody now had to disperse and go away. The children did not know where to go either, though. Some were from Vung Tau, some from Danang, some from Can Tho, and they don't have money to go.

So the oldest students gathered all of the other students together in the street and decided that the oldest ones would come back to the center and organize a line for fighting the Communists. They asked the little kids to run away and maybe find some families to keep them. Then about fifty of these oldest guys, who were twelve to thirteen years old, broke into the storage rooms at the academy and took out a machine gun and organized a defense line and a fortress for fighting when the Communists came. And when the Communists came in, the cadets fought them. The Communists could not get into that academy. The cadets were very proud as they told this story. At noon the government handed over the power in Saigon and the cadets kept fighting. At two-thirty in the afternoon, the Communists told them if they did not stop fighting, they would send a rocket into the academy and kill everybody.

I asked what happened when the Communists came in. They said they were gathered in the yard and were told to go home.

I didn't know where to go with my family. So we decided finally to take a truck and go into Saigon. On the way into Saigon we had an accident and my oldest son was killed. Our truck ran into a hole made by the explosion of a rocket. The front wheel was broken. It was a pickup truck with an open back. The truck turned over. My boy was killed.

In Saigon the situation was chaos. Everybody looked like they did not understand anything. Just like you get a shock and you don't feel anything or believe anything.

We buried my boy and the war was over.

Nguyen Thi Lac
"We Are All Going to Die Right Here on the Ground"

I was born in Dalat and raised in Hue and Danang. I went to high school in Danang. My parents helped me open a small business in Nha Trang— a gift shop. It did well and I opened another shop in Saigon. Most of my customers were Americans.

When the Americans pulled out of Vietnam in 1973, many of them told me that South Vietnam would not survive. They said the American public had grown tired of Vietnam and that without American help we would be defeated. There were also rumors in Nha Trang and Saigon during the negotiations in Paris between the Americans and the Communists that the two sides had come to a secret agreement. The Americans would pull out, the rumors said, and then the Communists would take over and nobody would stop them. The rumors said that in a few months we would be invaded. The rumors were right.

Right after the Paris Agreement was signed I went to my parents and said, "The country is going to be defeated. The Americans sold our country to the Communists. Now we don't have a chance. No more Vietnam." I said that we had better start thinking of a way to get out of the country if we did not want to live under the Communists.

In early 1975 I heard the stories about the bees and the caterpillars. But not everybody believed them. People in the countryside tended to believe stories like that more than people in the cities. In the cities we were not as superstitious.

When the refugees from the highlands and the north started showing up in Nha Trang it was very bad. Lots of soldiers showed up with the refugees. And the soldiers were out of control. They would kill people for no reason at all. They used their guns to rob people. They frightened everyone and they raped many of the young girls. There was no one to stop them.

I wanted my parents to leave Nha Trang and come to Saigon, but they did not want to. Nha Trang was their home. I wanted to move my sister from Dalat to Saigon so she would be safe. But she had a boyfriend in Dalat and she would not leave him. She is still there today.

Then Nha Trang fell to the Communists and all the refugees came to Saigon. I knew then that we were in big trouble. The refugees said that the Communists would kill anyone who did business with the Americans. They said the Communists had lists of names of people they wanted to kill. I thought, because I did business with the Americans, that my name was probably on one of their lists, and that if I was still in Saigon when they came in, they would kill me. I had to get out.

I tried to sell my shop. I tried to sell my house. But nobody was buying. All of my money was tied up in my business and my house.

Even at that time, many people in Saigon did not believe that the Communists would come into the city. They said, "Oh, this will pass and the Communists will be defeated. The Americans will come in if we get into too much trouble." But other people said, "That's crazy. The Communists are going to win. We are going to lose." Those people were trying desperately to get out of the country.

But it was really difficult to get out of the country. Americans and foreigners could get out with their families, but not the Vietnamese. You had to have an American friend to get out—a sponsor. And I could not find one. When I asked at the Embassy how I could get out, I was told, "No way!"

But I kept asking around. Then I heard of an American civilian who worked in the Embassy and was married to a Vietnamese woman. I was told that he and his wife had a way to get people out of the country. But they charged a lot of money. I did not have a lot of money, but I thought I might see if there was some way they could get me out.

A Vietnamese woman who worked with the American and his wife came to see me. She said they wanted all the money I had to get out of the country. I said I didn't have much. She told me that some of the top military men in the country had paid as much as $30,000 just to get out. She said if I had the money I could get out. But if I did not have the money, forget it.

I got some money together and I arranged to meet the American. I had a friend drive me to a building where the American was making arrangements to get people out of the country. The building was on Hai Ba Trung Street. I went in and was directed up to the fourth floor. There were no signs on the building, but there were American guards around it in uniform. When I got to the fourth floor there were a lot of people already there. I waited in the hallway with all of the other people for a long time. A woman was interviewing people in a room on the fourth floor. Finally they called me into the room. A woman and a man were there. They asked, "Where is your money?" And I told them that I only had a little money and jewelry. They asked, "How much do you have?" I gave them all the jewelry and money I had. They said, "This is not enough." And I said, "How much do you need?" "We need $10,000. If you do not have that much money you will have to stay here. And if you stay here you will be in all kinds of trouble when the Communists take over. They will probably kill you." I told them I had no more money. I begged them to let me go. They told me to go back out in the hall and wait.

They decided I could go. They told me to stay in the hallway with the other people. A little later they took some of us down to the lobby. We waited there for a little while and then a car came for us. An American was driving the car, but he said nothing to us. We were told to get in the car. I had only one suitcase with me then, but in the rush to get in the car, I left it in the lobby of the building. Then I had only the clothes on my back.

He took us to another building on Hai Ba Trung Street. They took us into a building and up to the second floor to an empty room. They told us to wait there and to be quiet. We stayed in that room all night. People slept on the floor. Everyone was very nervous. Nobody talked because we had been warned not to talk to each other. None of us could say for sure where we were or where we were going. In the morning we talked a little among ourselves and joked a little bit. We had nothing to eat or drink for about twelve hours.

Finally, in the morning, one guy said, "I'm going outside and get some food for us to eat. I'll get some rolls and some coffee." And I said to him, "Maybe you won't make it back here. You had better not go." And then some other people told him, "Don't go." But he said, "Why not? I know the Americans. They are good people. They will wait for me. I'll only be gone for a few minutes." So he went out to buy some rolls and some coffee. He was a very sweet man and very generous. He was going to buy something for everyone. He said it would be our last meal in Vietnam. And only about a minute after he left, some Americans came for us. They told us it was time to go. We told them that we should wait for the one man. But they said no. So we left. And when he came back we were all gone.

The Americans told us that they would now drive us to the airport. We tok an elevator down to the garage. When the elevator door opened there was a van waiting for us. It was like a bakery truck, without windows. We got into the van and they drove us to Tan Son Nhut. Suddenly everyone was sad to be leaving. Some people in the van started crying.

We got to the airport late in the morning. We got out of the van and they directed us to a big barracks building. We saw that all of the people waiting to leave were in different barracks. As one planeload of people left, everyone in one barracks building would move to the next barracks. When we first arrived they put us in the barracks farthest away from the planes.

I went outside to see what was happening. Outside the barracks I saw an American who had been a friend of mine, a Mr. Albertson. He was glad to see me. He asked what I was doing there. I told him I was leaving the country and that I was with the people in the barracks waiting for an airplane. He said, "Those people will never get out. It's too late." That shocked me. I told him I was afraid I would be killed and I started to cry. And then he said, "Don't worry. I'll help you get out." He walked me up to the first barracks. He pointed to an airplane—a big C-130—and told me that was the next plane and that I would be on it. I went into that barracks and waited with the people there.

In a few minutes a bus came for us. The driver told us that we were leaving on the next plane. We got on the bus and the driver took us out to the runway. Then he stopped and we just waited for a long time. Then, while we were sitting on the runway waiting, some airplanes flew over very low and dropped bombs on the runway. It was late afternoon and very hot and the bombs were suddenly hitting all around us. The driver started screaming for us to get off the bus and lie down on the ground. There was confusion and shooting and explosions everywhere. Then rockets started hitting buildings around us. A Marine outside our bus told everyone to lie down flat on the ground and stay flat and not to move. We could hear the bombs and the rockets and could hear stuff flying through the air around us. And as we were all lying there, I started thinking, "Oh, no. We are all going to die right here on the ground." The ground was shaking and everybody was crying. Some of the people started whispering to each other. I heard them say that the Communists had taken Bien Hoa and now they didn't want anybody to leave the country anymore. They said that the Communists were coming to the airport and that when they found us trying to get on planes they would kill us.

Then the bombing and the rocketing stopped. And the American Marine said, "Don't worry. That's just the last reaction from the government of South Vietnam, from the Minh regime." I didn't know what he was talking about and neither did anyone else. He was trying to say that the people who had just attacked the airport were our own government. And we knew that wasn't true. Maybe he was just trying to make us not be afraid. All he did was confuse us. What did he expect us to think when he told us that our own government was trying to kill us?

We had to stay there on the ground for several more minutes. Then the Marine told us, "Get on the bus again. Hurry. Don't bring your baggage." They drove us around a corner to a C-130 that was waiting for us with the back door down. The door of the bus opened and some people started yelling at us, "Hurry up! Hurry up! You just have five seconds to get in. Hurry! You just have five seconds." So everybody started pushing to get out the door and then they ran for the plane. Many of the people were still carrying small packages and they threw them away as they ran for the plane. While we were all running for the plane I saw a towel on the ground that someone had dropped. People were stepping on it and stumbling over it and kicking it as they ran. And just for an instant, I thought I saw the towel move by itself. So I stopped for a second, and I said to a woman running past me, "There is something in that towel." But she paid no attention to me. She just ran into the plane. But I picked up the towel and then ran with it. I felt that there was something in it. It came open at the top when I was running and I saw the top of a baby's head. The baby wasn't moving. Then I felt the baby's foot with my hand,

and the foot was not moving. And I thought to myself, "Oh, no—I just picked up a dead baby. What should I do now?"

I ran into the back of the airplane and the door of the plane started to close. We were packed in very tightly. There were still people out on the runway trying to get in the plane. They didn't make it. As soon as the door closed the plane started moving down the runway.

We were squeezed into the plane so tightly—we were all standing—that I could not move my arms or my legs. I was holding the baby and I thought it was dead. I tried to hold it tightly against me to hear a heartbeat. But my own heart was beating so hard and the engines of the plane were so loud that I couldn't hear anything else. I stood against the side wall of the plane and tried to brace myself so I wouldn't be crushed and the baby wouldn't be crushed against me. Whenever I tried to move my feet I stepped on somebody. I said to myself, "What have you done? Why did you pick up that towel? Now, when you land you will be holding a dead baby and you will be in big trouble. They will probably send you back to Vietnam." I was so scared I started to cry again.

Then I started to think that a rocket would hit us and that we would all be killed—like the people on the C-5A. Then I asked myself, "If I die right now—did I do anything wrong my whole life? Will I go to hell if I die right now?" And after a moment I thought, "No. If I die right now, I will go to heaven. I have been good. God knows that I have been good. So if I die I will go to heaven and I should not be crying." I stopped crying. But I kept thinking, as we were taking off, of the pictures I had seen when I was a little girl, of heaven and hell. They had shown us pictures of people roasting in a fire. They were all screaming and there were fires all around them. Everything was red and the people were terrified. And I thought, "That looks like Tan Son Nhut a few minutes ago." I knew I did not want to go to hell and I did not want to go back to Tan Son Nhut. Then I thought of the pictures I had seen of heaven. And everything in the pictures was all white and there were angels in white. It seemed very nice and everyone was smiling. I thought, "If we get hit by a rocket, that is where I will be in just a few seconds." I had already walked through hell and God had let me out. So now maybe God was taking me to heaven. I was no longer afraid.

It took us several hours to get to Clark Field in the Philippines. I was really uncomfortable and my legs fell asleep but I still could not move. Not even an inch. I felt the wheels go down and I felt us land. Then the airplane came to a stop.

When the back door of the airplane opened we all looked out and there were bright white lights—very bright—and in two rows there were women dressed in white. Everything seemed to be white. The women in white were waiting for us and smiling. And I thought, "I have gone to heaven. I made it. What a nice death. How easy it was to die. What a nice release. I have crossed over into heaven and I know now that God loved me, because these are his angels." I was so happy. I started to smile when I saw the angels.

The angels asked us to come out of the plane, and I saw that they all had Red Crosses on their sleeves. The angels were Red Cross nurses. I was alive. I was not in heaven. I was in the Philippines.

One of the nurses stopped me and asked me if I was hurt. She saw that my whole side was soaking wet. Then she asked me what I had in the towel. I was very frightened. I handed her the towel. She looked inside the towel and then told me to follow her. She walked over to a doctor. They put the towel down on a table and opened it. Inside was a baby—a little boy. He was smiling and he started kicking when they took the towel off. He was less than a day old. Everybody around the table started laughing and looking at me. And I started laughing, too. Then I started crying, I was so happy.

The doctor examined the little boy and he said, "He's all right." And I said, "Really? That can't be. People were walking on him and kicking him. Check him again." And so the doctor checked him again and he said, "Yes, he's all right. He's a tough little boy."

They said he was very hungry and he needed to be fed. They asked me if I wanted to nurse him now. And I said, "How can I nurse him? I have no milk. I am not his mother."

Other people from the plane had gathered around and they were being very nice now and saying, "Make room for the mother and the baby." Earlier they had been stepping on the baby.

The nurses started to look for the baby's mother. They found a young girl—a teenager—who was all colorless and sick. She did not even have any color in her lips. They questioned her for a moment and then they brought her over to me. She looked at me and asked softly, "Did you save my baby?" And I said, "Yes, I did." She told me she had the baby at the airport earlier in the day and she did not think they would let her come on the plane with a new baby so she had put him down on the runway, hoping that somebody would pick him up and take him back inside the barracks. She started to cry and she told me that she was so frightened at Tan Son Nhut that she didn't know what she was doing. She was not married. She was alone and very afraid. She was afraid now that they would not give her the baby. She was afraid that I wanted to keep him.

I picked up the baby and handed him to the girl and said, "Feed him now."

In the Philippines I got a feeling of love and I thought that maybe God still loved the Vietnamese people. I thought that maybe just the way that I held that little baby, now God would hold us. I started to see how wonderful it was to be alive.

I thought that maybe the baby in the towel was a test. I believe that because I picked him up and brought him with me, God decided to let our airplane make it to the Philippines. Had I left him there, God would have let a rocket hit our plane and we would all have been killed. But I picked up that baby and held him and God saved us all. I know that is true.

Everything turned out all right. Life is beautiful again.

Tran Minh Loi
"They Could Not Move So They Could Not Shoot Us"

I was practicing law in Saigon in April, 1975. I was twenty-five years old at the time. I thought that if the Communists took over, I could not live under their regime. I didn't think they would kill me, but I loved freedom and I knew they would take that away from all of us. As they took over parts of the country, people fled because they could not live with them. People from Danang and Nha Trang came to Saigon seeking freedom. Thousands of them came into the city every day.

From the twenty-fourth to the twenty-ninth of April I tried to find a way out of Vietnam. But I could not. You had to have money to get out, and I did not have much money. On April 30 I drove down to the Saigon River with a friend. We had heard that there were ships leaving and we thought we might get on one. There was a big crowd at the port, and there was a ship that was leaving. Earlier, its engines did not work. But early on the morning of April 30 they were able to repair one of its two engines. Then they loaded the boat and left. We had to go very slow with only one engine. Before we left we heard that President Minh had already surrendered to the Communists. So we had to hurry.

As we went down the Saigon River we were afraid of gunfire from the shore. We flew no flag because we knew that would be very dangerous. We were not afraid of airplanes so much as tanks on the shore. As we passed the Majestic Hotel we saw that a Russian T-54 tank had pulled up next to it facing the river. The tank crew was watching us. But people all around the tank were celebrating and they were climbing on the tank and waving flags. And because of all the people on the tank they could not move, so they could not shoot us. The tank crew just sat there looking at us. Had they shot us it would have been all over.

When we approached Vung Tau, most of the people went below deck so we would not look suspicious. We thought if the Communist troops there saw a ship loaded with people they would shoot at it. Only a few people on deck got a last look at Vietnam, at the beach at Vung Tau. There were no ships behind us. We were the last to leave.

When we got out on the South China Sea we met an American Navy ship. We signaled an SOS and they came aboard. They tried to repair our engine for us but they said it couldn't be done. And they said we could not go very far on just one engine. So we all left our ship and went on the American ship. After they had taken us all off our ship, the American ship fired big cannons at our ship. They missed several times, but finally they hit it and it caught fire. When we last saw it, it was on fire, drifting back toward Vietnam.

All of us felt bad that we had lost our country. We felt that the American government let the Communists win. We thought that all we needed to continue the fight was supplies from America. But we ran out of supplies. We did not understand why America let us down.

Many South Vietnamese did not know the Communists. They heard Communist propaganda and many of them believed it. But now that the Communists have taken over the people have learned the truth about them. And they will fight against the Communists. Even today there are people in Vietnam fighting against the Communists.

Nguyen Ngoc Bich
"Absolutely Hell"

I was the acting chancellor of the Mekong University right in Saigon. It was only our third year and we had maybe 600 students.

We relied on the information that we had about American support of Vietnam. Everybody believed that the American presence would be a permanent one. It was unthinkable to many of us that the Americans would someday leave.

My story has a little bit to add, because I was among the very last delegations to visit the United States. There were only two of us, Gregory Hung and myself. We knew that the situation was desperate. It was the nineteenth of April that we came to the U.S., at the very end, the last delegation. We knew that the American Congress was in a bad mood. They were not going to go on giving us aid. But we felt that we still had some trumps in our cards. One was the long-standing promise of Lee Kwan Yew of Singapore that he would help us. He thought that the only way to defeat Communism was through social programs. He promised us half a billion dollars for a housing program. President Thieu sent Hoang Duc Nha to Singapore to see if Lee would be willing to lend us that money to buy weapons and gasoline instead. Nha went to Singapore, and Hung and I came to the U.S. to try to persuade Congress not to make it public that they were not going to help us any more, since that would be too demoralizing. We said that we were willing to stake the oil that was being discovered in Vietnam as security for a loan promised to us in some other form by Saudi Arabia—a half billion to a billion dollars. The same money that they offered us could buy only half the fuel that our armies and our air force needed.

We thought that if we could get the Singapore and Saudi Arabian money and make Congress stay quiet about abandoning us, then maybe we could pull it out.

We left Vietnam on the nineteenth of April, and the first message that we got on arriving in Washington and meeting with Tran Kim Phuong was that there was nothing that we could do to change the situation. It was really a tragic thing. We met Ambassador Phuong right at Dulles Airport, and he told us that the situation was hopeless. We did not want to believe that; we said he was wrong. All three of us were shouting at each other and then we were in tears. After that we went to see some people, they also told us that it was hopeless.

Thieu resigned and the trip became meaningless, because that was why we came to the U.S.—to bargain. Gregory decided to stay here.

I went back to Vietnam. I was on the last civilian plane to go into Tan Son Nhut Airport. We landed at 8:30 on the twenty-sixth of April. I thought that my mission had failed.

So everybody on the plane from Los Angeles was Chinese from Hong Kong! I don't know what they were doing on the plane. I wondered about it. I thought they were either going there to invest and speculate on the fall or they were going there to try to retrieve relatives. Three of us were not Chinese. There was an American going back for his wife and family, Professor Nguyen Manh Hung, and myself.

The first thing I started thinking about was getting back out. I had a passport. There was already a lot of shooting near the airport. So I made my report to the government and the next day we were making our plans to leave Vietnam.

We finally left by the wharf at midnight on the twenty-ninth. We went out past Vung Tau and were finally picked up by a ship, the *American Challenger*. It was absolutely hell. The capacity of the boat was 1,080 people. They picked up something like 7,500 people. They intended to go to Subic Bay and drop us there. But offshore from Vung Tau they picked up more people. That was too many people, so they proceeded directly to Wake Island.

The eeriest thing was at night on the thirtieth of April when they picked up people in boats. The boats came up to us with their lights on and the people came onto our ship. When everyone was off the Vietnamese boat they would set fire to it and push it away. All over the sea there were these eerie fires of boats burning and drifting in the sea. They lit up the water that night, and it looked like the South China Sea was starting to burn.

There was crying and yelling on board the ship. It was all unbelievable. A Catholic priest came on board with a Honda. They would not let him bring it on board. Another boat came, and a dentist wanted to bring his dentist's chair on board. He said, "That is the only way I can make my living." But they would not let him bring it on board.

The whole South China Sea was on fire that night and we watched it burning.

Hue Thu
"He's a General and He's Staying"

I lived in Saigon in 1975. I taught English. Some students I taught at my home. A lot of people came to study English and French.

I am not a political person, so I was surprised by what happened in 1975. I had an American friend, Jim Bradley, and on April 25 he told me I had to get out of Saigon quick. He told me that we would lose. But I didn't believe him.

I saw when they started to take all the orphans and children out. But I wanted to stay. My way of thinking was this: If the Communists came we would still have a house there and money from my family. My father and mother had died and I had a hotel and restaurant in Dalat and two houses in Saigon. I thought, "Well, I have a lot of money in the bank but I have empty hands. How can I get out empty-handed? I'll wait to see what happens; maybe a few months after they come in I can get some money and get out if I don't like it."

Then I remember I heard Mr. Ky speak on the radio. He said, "I will stay here until my last blood, until I'm dying." I told my friend. "He's a general, and he's staying. Why do we have to run?" They all said, "Why do we run away? We have to stay and fight." We all stayed. I said, "I'm a woman, I'm not afraid of Communists. I'll stay and see what they will do to me."

I listened to the radio. Then I heard them say President Thieu and General Ky, all of them, already ran away. I said, "My God, just last night I heard General Ky say on the radio that he would stay to spend his last blood here. How could I have trusted such people?"

On the thirtieth we heard that we'd lost and all of a sudden it was gone. I was very surprised. I was at the front of the Ban Hanh University at the Newport Bridge and we sat there and saw all the Communists come in. The Airborne soldiers were there first and some of them just shot all their bullets into the air to finish them and then held their faces and cried. I saw many of the Airborne soldiers take off their shirts, shoes, and pants and they just wore underwear and ran by. They threw away their weapons. When I saw that I started crying, too.

When the Communists came in, we saw how they looked. And why were some people so afraid of Communists? I'll tell you why. Because they looked just like monkeys to me. And I said, "My God, I don't know how we can lose to those monkeys."

One thing I know. In Vietnam they say if the snake loses its head he will die. With all the soldiers, all the head is gone. The tail has to lose.

But I tell you even though we lost in Vietnam, I still have pride. I don't look at the Communists like I'm scared. I'm not.

I still don't like the way Ky, or Cao Vien,* or Thieu ran like that. They should stay and fight, that would be better. There was no fight at the end at all. I was there. I didn't see any fight at all. I don't know how they lost, but they didn't fight. Duong Van Minh just announced that we lost. I went to Tu Do Street. I went all over. I saw people go on the ships at Vung Tau. I didn't see any fight. Maybe they fought at Pleiku, Ban Me Thuot, or Danang, or Hue, but they don't fight in Saigon. I think some people made a big mistake.

Dr. Nguyen Thi Thanh-Nguyet
"Why Didn't You Bring My Grandson Here?"

In the spring of 1975 I was doing my "externship"—that's like an internship in the United States—for my fifth year of medical school. At the end of March I was doing my rotation in the Seventh-Day Adventist Hospital in Saigon. I sensed, as did everyone else, that we were gradually going downhill. But I never believed, even then, that there would be a collapse and a surrender. The worst thing that could happen, I believed, was that Saigon might fall and there would be a temporary occupation by the North. Then after a short time everything would return to normal again.

Then in mid-April there was a growing concern about getting some of our staff out. General Homer Smith** signed a paper authorizing 175 of our people to leave the country—the paper gave them all blank sponsorship for entry into the United States. But there were many more than 175 who wanted to get out. So we came up with a system for getting everyone out—by medevac. We put casts and bandages on some people who wanted to get out. Then we put them in ambulances and turned the siren on and drove them to the airport. The Vietnamese guards let us through without examining our patients. If they had checked the patients they would have discovered that we were putting on a show and we would never have gotten out. Once we were through the gate we put our patients on medevac planes, and they were then flown to the Philippines.

I remember that one doctor had a wife and three children and they were all very healthy. We put bandages and casts on the children and gave one of them a false IV, and we got through the gate that way. Then we had to wait for the medevac plane. While we were waiting, the chil-

---

* Cao Van Vien was Chairman of the Joint General Staff of the Vietnamese armed forces. He left the country just before the surrender and was succeeded by General Vinh Loc, who also left the country prior to the formal surrender.
** The Defense Attaché.

dren started to run around and play. There were military guards inside
the airport and I was afraid they would see the children running around
when they were supposed to be sick. So I told the doctor's wife to quiet
the children and tell them to act sick or we would never get out.

We would put about twenty people in two or three ambulances and
go out to the airport. Attending nurses and doctors would accompany
them and get out with them. In that way most of our staff who wanted
to get out actually got out. Those who weren't medevacked out were
put on the list of 175 who had sponsors in America.

Of course, as more people got out, the hospital staff got smaller, and
so did the number of patients we could care for. On the twenty-fourth
of April we discharged our last six patients. Until that time I had not
planned to leave. I was talking that day with our senior resident physician and he told me that if I wanted to leave that night on a medevac
flight at 11:00 p.m., then I could. I was to be at the hospital no later
than 5:00 p.m. If I did not show up by that time they would assume that
I did not want to leave. I asked him if I could bring my son with me
and he said that I could, but only my son. I was separated from my
husband at that time. My son was only ten years old then. It was 3:00
p.m. when we talked about leaving, so I had to make up my mind and
get ready in just two hours.

I tried to get in touch with someone who might know what the
situation would be like if the city fell. I needed to talk to someone who
could help me make up my mind to leave or stay. I finally got in touch
with a classmate of mine. And she said that I should leave. I asked her
why she wasn't leaving. She said that she was the oldest of ten children
in her family, and now she had to help support her family. But, she said,
if she were in my situation, she would leave. After talking with her I
decided to go.

I came home and had a brief talk with my mother. She was very sick
at the time. I told her I had decided to leave. She started crying. Then
I went across the street and told my sister and her family that I was
leaving with my son. And they cried also.

I got on my motorcycle and drove to Khanh Hoi, which took about
thirty minutes. I wanted to say goodbye to my father, who was working
there. When I told him, he was just petrified. And he asked me, "Why
didn't you bring my grandson here? If he is leaving with you, maybe
this is the last chance I will have to see him." And that really was the
last chance he had to see his grandson. My father died when we were
here in the United States.

And I said, "Father, I was in such a hurry, I forgot." I had been so
busy getting together my papers, my education records, and some clothes.
I kissed my father goodbye. We were both crying. Then I rode my motorcycle back home. I tried to change some money to take out with me. But

that was impossible. When I left Vietnam I had not a single penny in my pocket.

That night when we left Saigon it was very dark. At the airport there was a big confusion. We did not know for sure that we would be able to take off until the plane actually started to leave. We flew directly to Guam because by then the government of the Philippines was not accepting any more Vietnamese flights.

I was in Guam when Saigon fell on April 30. We heard the news on the radio. We cried and cried. We heard that the North Vietnamese came into the city in tanks, and had driven down Thong Nhat Boulevard and seized Independence Palace. Each of us, in our own minds, could see that happening. We were so sad. We talked about Vietnam that night. We told stories about what we remembered and what we loved most about Vietnam. And we talked about how surprised we were that it had fallen, and how it had happened and what we could do about it. But it was too late to do anything about it. All we had left on that night was hope.

Ho Quang Nhut
"He Was the Last American I Saw in Vietnam"

I was in Saigon when it fell to the Communists on April 30, 1975. I had come to the city from Bien Hoa, where I was a high school teacher. On April 30 I was on Le Loi Boulevard when the surrender took place. I saw a lot of people rushing around trying to find a place to hide from the Communists on that day. Then, on the street, I saw an American. He was the last American I saw in Vietnam. He was standing in front of a restaurant. His eyes were red and I think he was very sad. He was waiting for somebody to come and pick him up, I thought. Or maybe he was waiting for someone to come and help him, to hide him, I thought. But nobody came to help him. I saw him look at his watch several times and then look up and down the street. But it was too late for him.

At 4:45 the Vietcong came along the boulevard in a truck. When they saw him standing there they stopped and jumped out and started to question him. Hundreds of people were watching this. The American said to them, "I am an American citizen." But they hit him and pushed him into the truck. He kept saying, "I am an American citizen." But they weren't listening to him. They didn't want to hear anything like that. They drove away with him and I never heard of him again.

CHAPTER XVII

Children

**Duong Quang Son
"Tears Before the Rain"**

Every night I cry for Vietnam. I remember and I cry. In the darkness my memories turn into tears. There are tears for my dad and my mom and for my brother and my sisters, and for all of the people who ran away from Vietnam and for all of those who could not run away. I don't want my memories to be lost, like tears in the rain. So I will tell you my story. Then you can tell it to others. Maybe if enough people know what happened to Vietnam, then my memories will never be lost. Maybe then they will be like tears before the rain. So listen. This is very important. This is what I remember. This is what happened to me. These are my tears before the rain.

My dad's name was Tran Phong. He was a Buddhist. He was born and raised in Haiphong in the North. He fought against the French. But in 1954, when the Communists took over North Vietnam, my father moved to Saigon in the South. He hated Communism. He loved freedom. All he ever wanted was to live in freedom. So he became a refugee in 1954. He was very sad about his country being cut in half. But he wanted to stay away from the Communists. My mom was born and raised in the North also. And she came South with my father in 1954. Her mother and her brothers and sisters stayed behind in the North.

We had a beautiful life in Saigon. My dad was a boat mechanic and he made good money. I was the youngest child in the family. My father called me Ut, which means in Vietnamese, "the youngest one." I had an older brother and two older sisters. An aunt lived with us also in Saigon. We lived in a big house in Section One of Saigon—Quan Nhut. I attended a public school and my brother was in college.

I was sixteen in the spring of 1975. At that time in school kids were starting to worry about the Communist's taking over. Some of them talked about leaving the country. Some days, on the way home from school, I saw long lines of people trying to get papers or trying to change their money so they could leave the country.

My brother came home from college. My dad told my brother and me that he wanted us to leave the country for a while. "You are young," he said. "You have a future. And when everything is safe again you can come back." He thought we should go to the United States to study. Then when we returned to Vietnam we would have a better future. But it was very difficult to get out of Vietnam, and for a long time we did not believe we would be able to leave.

My best friend's name was Nguyen Quang. His sister, Nguyen Huong, worked as a clerk at the American Embassy. He told us that she might be able to get us out of the country. The Americans told her that they would fly her and her relatives out of Vietnam. All she had to do was type our names on a list. So we said that would be all right. She told her boss—who was also Vietnamese—that she had two young men who wanted to get out of Vietnam and that they were not relatives. But she said she wanted to put the two names on her list. And her boss said that was okay.

After our names were on the list she called us and said that we had to be ready to leave at any time, day or night. She said she would tell us where to go when we were scheduled to leave.

Then at ten in the morning on April 28, she came to our house and said, "Sonny, you had better get ready, because you will be leaving in one hour." She told us where we were supposed to go. A bus was going to pick us up there and take us to the airport. We could only bring one bag each for clothes. We did not have much time to say goodbye. I only had time to say, "Dad, I love you. I have to leave now." Mom and Dad cried a lot that morning. They told my brother, "Take good care of Ut."

Dad then drove us to where a bus was to pick us up. We had no special papers and we really didn't know if we would be asked for any. We drove to a big building that had a fence around it. We knocked on the gate and a man let us in. He had a list of names. Our names were on his list. When we got inside the fence I was surprised because there was a large courtyard and it was filled with people who were waiting. The people had come from all over the country—from central Vietnam and from the northern cities. There were about a thousand people there. I asked some of them, "Where did you come from?" I didn't see anybody I knew. And they told me, "We came from Danang," or, "We came from Nha Trang." So many people from so many different cities. And there seemed to be nobody there from Saigon but my brother and me.

I felt happy at that moment. I was young and I would not have to live under the Communists. I could go to school in the United States and then when the Communists had been driven out I could come back to Saigon.

We had not been in the courtyard of the building very long when they called our names. My brother and I went to the gate again and a bus driver was standing there with a list and he checked off our names. We got on the bus. I could hardly believe it. We were the first ones to leave the courtyard. We were each carrying just one bag. My brother and I had no money. My dad told us to call him when we got to the U.S. and then he would send us some money. We were going to stay with a friend in California.

We were driven to the airport. It was really crowded. We had to get off the bus and stand outside. There was a big field with people in it and the sun was very hot. There were loud-speakers paging people and vendors trying to sell food and drinks and trying to exchange money. Lots of people were crying and lots of them were shocked because they didn't really know what was happening or where they were going.

We really didn't know what would happen. Then all of a sudden they called our names over the loudspeaker. I was very surprised because I had asked some of the other people, "How long have you been waiting here?" and some of them said, "One week already." Others had been waiting two or three days. I thought at first that my brother and I would never get on a plane, but then they called our names. We were taken into the terminal with other people. They searched us there and searched our luggage. Then they asked us to stand in a long line. After a little time they led us out to an airplane. Outside the plane there were two Vietnamese MPs standing and watching the people. They wanted to prevent deserters from leaving the country. The looked at everyone carefully. They didn't stop us or question us and we got on the plane.

I thought it would be a nice airplane. It was a big C-130. We walked up the back ramp. When we got inside we saw that there were no seats. We just had to get in and sit on the floor—like sardines. When I saw that I thought, "Oh, my God, are we going to take this all the way to the United States without seats? And packed so close together?" But nobody was saying anything so I didn't say anything about it, either. I just thought that thought.

As they were loading us—it was very late in the afternoon—all of a sudden I heard a lot of explosions outside, around the plane. And I thought, "Oh, my God, what is happening out there?" The door was still open and I saw an explosion right behind the plane. A big explosion. Then the airplane started to move with the door still open. I was looking out the door and I saw people running around in all directions shooting crazily into the air. They seemed to be in a panic. People all around me on the airplane started screaming and crying. Some of them started praying very loudly. I grabbed my brother and I said, "I hope we don't crash."

They didn't even have time to close the door. They just went down the runway with the door open. As we took off, all of us could see out the back, and on the ground it looked like there were hundreds of explosions and fires and people were running in all directions. It looked like the whole airport was going crazy.

Then right behind us another C-130 came up—it took off on another runway only a few seconds after we did. I think we were the last two planes to take off from Tan Son Nhut. We were very lucky.

As we left Saigon, there was an American soldier standing at the back door of the plane, and he was shooting at the ground. He just kept shooting as we pulled away. And people were still crying inside the plane. I watched the soldier shooting and I wondered what he was shooting at. I think he was just trying to show American power one last time. I think he was trying to say with his gun, "Don't shoot at our airplane. Don't mess around with this airplane. We've got guns on board. We're Americans. Stay away. Leave us alone." But I can only guess. I don't think he knew what was happening, either. We were all confused.

Anyway, that was my last look at my country. I saw Vietnam as we flew away and at the back door of the plane was a soldier with a gun shooting at it.

We landed in the Philippines at Clark Field. We were taken to a big warehouse. The Americans had everything very well organized for us. We were surprised. They put us all in a big waiting area. We had televisions and beds. The next day they told us that the Communists had taken over Saigon. We were shocked. We did not know that would happen. "What about our family?" we asked. "What about Mom and Dad? What will happen to us now when we get to the United States?" We had nothing but questions.

We watched the news on television. We saw the Communists in Saigon. A lot of people cried when they saw that. My brother and I cried, too. Our family was still in Vietnam. And we looked at each other and asked, "What will happen to us tomorrow?"

Nguyen Thi Hoa
"Mom, I'm Leaving Now. I Will Make You Very Proud of Me"

I grew up in Saigon. My dad and mom ran a small cafeteria near Tan Son Nhut that served the Americans. But when the Americans left in 1973, my dad lost the cafeteria. Not enough business. He also said that many of the Americans had left without paying him. He let them pay bills on a monthly basis. And many of them just left the country without paying their bills, and my dad lost his little business. After that he was bitter and he did not like the Americans any more. My dad and mom had to take other jobs and we didn't live very well after that.

In the spring of 1975 my friends and I were very afraid that the Communists would come into Saigon and take over. There were stories that they would kill everybody, like they did in Hue in 1968. In Hue, during Tet, they killed 3,000 people for no reason at all. They tied their hands behind them and then shot them in the head. So we were very afraid.

But my father was not afraid. He said that those were just stories. He said that when the Communists took over nothing would change. But I didn't think so. I wanted to leave the country, and so did my younger sister. But my father said, "No. Nobody is going to leave. Nobody is going to die. Don't you believe what people are saying. The Communists are not going to hurt you."

I decided to go anyway. At first, I planned to go with my brother. But then he changed his mind and decided to stay. Then I decided to go with my sister. I was sixteen. My sister's name is Nguyen Thi Thiet Nghia. She is two years younger than me.

First, we had to find a way to get out. Of course, we did not have any money. But I found that one of my friends, Nguyen Thi Xuan, had parents whose friends owned a boat. And she said that if my sister and I wanted to leave on that boat we could. We would not need any money. So I said that we wanted to go on the boat and she said she would call when it was ready to go.

She called on the morning of April 29. She told us to go to a certain corner and a car would pick us up and take us to the Saigon River. My sister and I each took one bag of clothes. We had to sneak out of the house because my father did not want us to leave. So I did not say good-bye to my father. But we went to the restaurant where my mother was working. She didn't know that we would be going on that day. I said to her, "Mom, I'm leaving now. I will make you very proud of me." She kissed me and she kissed my sister and she said, "Okay. Good luck." She was very strong at that moment. She did not cry. She just said good-bye. If she had cried my sister and I would have stayed. I think she knew that. And she wanted us to go. Her name is Thanh Thi Tran. She made me strong enough to leave.

My sister and I went to the corner where the car was supposed to meet us. We waited, and the car never came. So my sister said, "I'll go back and call them and see when they are coming." She left her bag with me and went to a telephone. While she was gone the car came. It was full of people already. I told the driver that we had to wait for my sister and he said there was no way to do that. "We cannot wait," he said. "If we wait we cannot get out." So I got in the car. I left my sister's bag there on the curb. I was very nervous now and very frightened without my sister.

When we got to the river we had to hurry to get on the boat, and in the confusion I lost my bag. So I left the country without anything but the clothes on my back.

The name of the boat was the *Tan Nam Viet*. It was a big boat and it carried about five or six hundred people. I thought maybe my sister would arrive before the boat left. But she didn't.

I was very scared as we went down the river. Some of the people on the boat stayed on the deck to get a last look at Vietnam. The last thing they saw was the beach at Vung Tau. But I did not look back. I was so sad. I was leaving everything behind. And I didn't know where I was going or what would happen to me.

Later I learned that my sister tried to get out and she got caught. She was sent to jail. When she got out of jail she tried to leave Vietnam again. And again she was caught and put in a special camp. She is still in Vietnam.

Tram Tran
"Look At Them! These Are Angels!"

I've never known my country to be at peace. There were always soldiers around—American or Vietnamese. In my neighborhood in Saigon there were two big buildings with gates around them, and they had swimming pools and recreation facilities. They were called "villas" and that was where the Americans stayed. The gates were always closed and the Americans would come to the gates and let other Americans in and out and then the gates would close again. I remember watching that when I was small. They had big dogs to guard the place. Whenever the gates would open the children would want to get close and look in, but then the dogs always barked and we ran away. It was like a game with us. It was very mysterious. The children were friendly with the GIs. We would wave at them and say, "Hello, Salem!" just like the cigarettes. And then the Americans would usually smile and wave back at us and we would laugh and run away.

I tell you this now because when I finally left Vietnam I had this huge hatred for the Americans. My feelings underwent a dramatic transformation in a short time and I am not really sure exactly why that happened.

My father did some business with the Americans making flags for them. These Americans came to my father one day and they wanted to order a lot of flags for their unit. They wanted a picture of Snoopy on the flag. So they showed my father the picture, and my father said that he thought this was really an ugly dog and that it was drawn by someone who didn't know how to draw a dog. So he said that he would re-draw the dog for the Americans and they, at first, said that was all right. So for the next three or four days my father just drew pictures of dogs, realistic ones and mean-looking ones, all kinds of dogs to put on the flags for the Americans. He was sure that they would like his work because it was all very realistic.

The Americans didn't like what my father did. They said, "No, we want Snoopy." My dad didn't understand why they should want such an unrealistic and funny-looking dog on their flag, but he agreed, although he was disappointed, and made them their Snoopy flag. Later, he said that the Americans didn't like the Vietnamese and did not respect the Vietnamese soldiers who fought under their own flag. The Americans, he believed, were willing to go out and risk their lives and die for their Snoopy flag, but not for the Vietnamese.

Then they asked him to do a big American flag. My father heard that Hawaii and Alaska had been added to the United States and he wanted to make his flag modern and include the new states. So my dad carefully improved on the flag that the Americans gave him to copy. He thought there were fifty-two states and so made a big flag with fifty-two stars. It took him many sleepless nights to arrange the fifty-two stars so they would be balanced. The Americans came to pick it up and they thought that something was wrong with it, but they didn't know what. Then they counted the stars. There were fifty-two but they took it anyway. So somewhere in Vietnam the Americans were flying and saluting a flag with fifty-two stars on it.

My parents had come from the North and they were very anti-Communist. The people from the North knew what the Communists were like, because they had lived with them before. But although I heard about the Communists, I never actually saw one before the end of the war. I heard stories about the VC penetrating the city and doing whispering work, but I never had contact with them. And I never saw dead bodies in Saigon.

My family was musical because they loved music and not because they were talented. So one of the famous musicians in Saigon, Le Van Khoa, was interested in my family because my aunts just loved music so much. He began to use everyone in my family for his productions. He took the kids, my aunts, and my mom and would teach us how to sing some songs and to do some traditional Vietnamese dances, and some dances that we made up ourselves. He would then take us to the hospitals; first in the city, and then later to the countryside where the troops were stationed. We moved further and further from Saigon to entertain the troops. There were hospital sites where tents had been put up in the countryside for the wounded soldiers.

Sometimes we traveled by helicopter and sometimes by jeep. There were wounded soldiers and some doctors there, in uniform, and we were introduced to them. Mostly I saw wounded soldiers. Most were not hurt badly and they were recovering. Those who were in the process of recovering would come to the tent to see us. And sometimes we went to their tents to cheer them up. We sang and performed happy songs. We were always very welcome. I felt that it was very much a romantic period of my life. I felt like a little cherub when I was performing, in student uniform or a white dress. I always liked my white dress because I felt like a little angel when I performed.

But it was shocking. The smell was particularly terrible at times, and it was hot, often. But I was so happy being an angel to the soldiers that I didn't mind that much. Two things I remember from that time. One was sadness at seeing the pain, and the other was that I was acting happy in order to create and receive happiness.

In Vietnam the childhood was thought of as a very happy period. I wanted to fulfill the soldiers' expectations. The soldiers wanted to believe, because of their sacrifice and their great pain, that Vietnamese children were still very happy. So I fulfilled their expectations by ridding myself of all pain and sadness. Although I could feel it inside, I could not show that to the soldiers.

I did not know anything but war when I was small. At one level I told myself, This is life. Because I knew no other way of life. Theoretically I guessed that there was something else. And I always had this inner sadness. I accepted it as though there was no other way. When I came here, and I saw that everyone was not sad, then my own sadness became greatly intensified. So much so, in fact, that I wanted to commit suicide. I have talked with others who thought of suicide after arriving in the U.S. I think many Vietnamese have the same feeling as me, but they have too much pride to talk about it.

One time I stepped on a nail during our travels. And that became infected and then we went on a big trip. I was upset because it hurt so much, but I wanted to make the trip. So I lived with that pain. By the time the trip came and we had to leave, my foot was very infected. So I went with the group, and it was hot, and my feet hurt, and the pain became more obvious. I felt that was the first time I had some of the pain that the soldiers had. I had the pain but I had to pretend like I was all right. That was how many of the soldiers lived their lives, I thought. And so I shared, in a small way as a child, some of the pain of the young soldiers.

It was a very difficult time for me, because I was expected to be a happy child and I felt the pain and the unhappiness around me.

In 1973, I heard that everybody anticipated that the VC would strike again after the Americans left. Nobody seemed to believe that the VC would keep the Paris Agreement. Perhaps the Americans did, but nobody else did.

After the Americans left, the two big villas that they had occupied had activity around them. But it was no longer American soldiers. Now these were American civilians.

I believed that the VC would strike again. I was not afraid. I always believed that good would win over evil. I had faith that the Communists would always lose, and I think now that is the way children look at the world. I was taught that outside was a force, the United States, that was good and would help us, especially since we were attacked and we did not attack anybody—we were being invaded. Even though they won battles I thought that we would win in the end.

In 1975 most of my family, aunts, and uncles had left their homes by the start of April. Their houses were empty. My grandmother began to burn all of her letters and documents that said that we had been associated in any business way with the government. Anything that would tell the Viet Cong of our past, she burned. When she started that, and she did it very quietly, I asked why she was burning the material. But she did not have to speak because I understood her actions. We destroyed all photographs, birth certificates, everything. I can recall now the emptiness of the house, people very close who had left, and then the burning of the letters; all of that changed the atmosphere and the feeling in the home. That is when I realized that we were losing and it was serious.

Many of my relatives had already left the country and had gone to Guam on their way to America. My aunts had worked for the Americans. I was aware that they were going. They did not say goodbye. Just one day they were gone.

I became afraid and I remember crying about it because I wanted so much not to have to face the threat of the Communists coming into Saigon. Then I was afraid because the same thing would happen to us that had happened in the North. People would start to watch each other. And then children would prosecute parents, spy on their parents, and life as we knew it with the concept of freedom, would disintegrate.

School was suspended for us. And there was always a curfew.

I was taught not to say goodbye to anybody in case we could not go; then no one could prosecute us for trying to leave the country. We were very secretive.

I was in church the day we decided to leave. My parents had been looking for me all over and they could not find me. I had gone to church in the morning and I stayed for three masses on Sunday. So my father told my mom to take the children and go on ahead and he would try to leave with me later. Because his logic was that two people would have a better chance than all nine people together.

I was religious then. I almost became a nun. I was afraid, and at Mass I think that I was very connected with my church. The first two Masses I came there to help collect the money and then during mass watched the motorcycles so that nobody would steal them. And in the third Mass I went in. I was sitting there and then suddenly one of my friends came in, and when he came in I suddenly had the feeling that I would not see all of this again. Just some sort of intuition. I knew that he had come for me. But when he came close and talked into my ear, I jumped.

He said, "Your family is looking for you." And I knew that we would leave the country then. It was Sunday, the twenty-seventh of April.

My friend wanted me to get on his moped, but I didn't want to. I just ran all the way home. I jumped on my father's Vespa and we tried to catch up with the rest of the family.

For a month we had always had bags packed, just in case we had to go. We went to where we were supposed to go to catch a bus to the airport. One of my aunts could have left before us but she volunteered to stay because she knew the family had no connections for getting out without her. My family would have had no way to leave the country if she had not stayed and helped.

A few weeks earlier she was told by another aunt to go to her office and clean out the desk, and was told that she could keep whatever was valuable in the desk. So she went to clean out the desk. At the office there was an American who had come into the country. It was his first day there. He thought my aunt was one of the employees, so he ordered her around. And by the middle of the day he asked for some papers and she said she didn't know where they were. He yelled at her and said she should know where they were because she worked there. She said she was just there to clean her sister's desk. He was very apologetic and told her that if she would stay and work with him he would try to get her family out in return.

That was the connection for us to get out of the country. My father's sister came and took the Vespa after we got to the bus stop.

I was both sad and very happy at that moment. Sad because, even if I was thirteen years old, that was old enough to realize how important it was to be leaving your home and your country. But I was also glad because I felt I would survive.

We caught up with the rest of the family at the building where the bus was supposed to pick us up. We were stuck there until the twenty-eighth. We waited inside a building for the bus. It did not come until six o'clock that night. We almost went home before it came. But my father said that we should not go home because of what he went through in the morning just to get us together. He said we would wait until the bus came, even if we had to sleep there that night. But we would stick together, no matter what. Half of the people got discouraged and went home before the bus arrived.

At the airport there was an air attack on the night of the twenty-eighth. People were running to the sand bunkers. But my father said, "We are not going to lose each other now. And if there is a bomb in the bunker it will not make any difference." So we just stayed in an open field together. We did not see the planes, but we saw the explosions and the fire.

For children it was very exciting. I was not as afraid as I was excited at that time. Only after I came to the U.S. and was in peace, did I begin to see that war was abnormal. But back then war was very normal to me, so I was excited by the raid.

One year after we came to the U.S., we were in San Francisco celebrating Chinese New Year, and my sister suddenly started running and crying. She was five years old then. She was crying "Phao Kich! Phao Kich! Phao Kich!" ("Air raid! Air raid! Air raid!") So I knew that for me it had been exciting but not for my sister.

I was not just excited about the air raid. Everything was mixed in those days. Half glad and half scared. Always half this and half that. My feelings were split then.

We stayed in Tan Son Nhut that night, and we finally left by helicopter the next day. We saw the Marines arrive at the airport by helicopter. I must say that the Marines are so good-looking. I just looked at them when I saw them coming in. All I could think at that time was, "Look at them! These are angels!" They looked beautiful to me then because they were coming to save us.

No one in the family spoke English except for my aunt, so we could not talk to them except through my aunt. We were a big group then, all of us together. I observed all the families at the airport. My observation of the families was more interesting than my thoughts about myself at that time.

I saw this pregnant woman, very pregnant, and her husband. Every time they would move us, he would pack their money under her stomach and tape it there. It was so embarrassing to watch, and at the same time it was so interesting. I remember it because it was the very first time I had ever seen a pregnant woman's stomach and this man kept taping his money under the stomach. She must have given birth to her child later on the ship because she was so pregnant.

We were relocated many times during the night because many of the men were of military age, and if the Viet Cong came they would take the men, and if the South Vietnamese came they would take the men. This one American who was my aunt's boss took care of us at the airport wholeheartedly. He was so nice to us; but I do not remember his name because it was so foreign to me.

The children were all quiet because we sensed the seriousness of the situation. The American provided canned American food for us. When the Americans left there was food all over the airport. There was, I remember, one very large piece of cheese left behind. These things were very expensive in Saigon, but now they were suddenly free. So we all ate the cheese. Campbell's chicken noodle soup was there, too. We were so hungry it seemed like a real blessing. They had a commissary line where they were serving the Campbell's soup for us. Again, I don't know who these people were.

I had my own little bag with me. When we left, because the helicopter could take only a certain weight, I had to leave my bag on the ground.

But I was wearing three pairs of pants and three blouses. The main thing was to stay together. My youngest sister was four and the next was only six. When they said, "Run!" and all of us ran together, even my four-year-old sister would run very fast and stay in line; she understood how important that was.

Ours was the last helicopter to leave. We were supposed to leave with the first group, but we were so pessimistic about getting out that when they called our name, we didn't go on the first flight. And then we waited all day and they never called our name again. We began to fear that our name was not on the list. Then an American came over and asked who we were. My aunt told him and he then told us that we had been called first. So we left that evening.

I had been in a helicopter before when I had sung for the soldiers, so this was not my first time. I was aware that this was a very important moment. My family had thirteen people in it, with nine of us in the immediate family, and then my aunt and her friend and my grandparents. We got into the helicopter. We had waited so long by that time. I remember, when the first helicopter came, everybody was on the field and they announced that all the Americans would leave first and then the Vietnamese. So we thought then that we would be left. But they promised; they said, "Don't panic, we will come back and pick you up." We were waiting for about an hour and a half after that and then suddenly all kinds of helicopters were on top of us and people were clapping and waving and crying and praying and standing up, they were so happy.

When my parents saw the food that the Americans had left all over the airport, they were sure that the Americans had abandoned them. Then they came back and everybody was so excited. My parents had a different reaction from mine. I knew the seriousness of the situation and I could not help but be very happy with all of this food around me—this was the first time in my life I had seen so much food. So half of me was with my parents worrying and the other half was very glad because at last we had food to eat.

When the Americans left, the people who worked for them brought the food out, just like manna from heaven.

When the Americans came back it was still daylight. We saw them coming before we heard them, and I had just the happiest feeling. From the moment I left the church until the moment we were on the helicopter, I had this feeling we were going to go. I had that faith all along. So even though my parents were worried and the people around us were worried, I was not worried.

We were held back at first when the helicopter came down. I remember the wind pushed us back. My little sister was holding my hand, fighting against the wind. We ran as fast as we could, leaning forward, to the helicopter. I remember one time when I was a child when a storm came in from the ocean, and it felt just like that once again. There were two or three Americans at the helicopter door to help us in. We ran in between the Americans, and I remember that one of them picked me up and lifted me into the helicopter. I had the chance to be at the window of the helicopter along with my family friend. He said, "Pray!" A thankful prayer is what he wanted. "Say thanks!" he said. And I looked at him and suddenly I felt ashamed, very ashamed. Because, suddenly, that was the first moment that I really hated the Americans.

I felt very hurt. I looked out the window and the helicopter was lifting up. My last view of Saigon was that it was bright red from the sun and from the fires.

I was not excited any more. At that moment I started to hate the Americans. I was becoming traumatized. The moment that the helicopter left the ground then I knew that something very bad was happening. I tried to cry. I did have tears in my eyes, but not as much as I wanted. I wanted to dramatize all of my feelings inside, and I wanted to cry more, but I had only a few tears left. I stayed at the window and looked out as we left. I saw the people as we left Tan Son Nhut, and then they became very small and disappeared.

We went over the beaches and out to the South China Sea. I watched it all from the window. The scenes of Saigon I remember most clearly.

I don't know what the others were doing, crying or not, because I eventually blocked out most other memories of that day. It was very crowded inside the helicopter.

I was not afraid. I had that irrational feeling that everything would be all right. One of my last thoughts was that I did not have a handful of the ground from Vietnam. I read in some romantic story that a person took a handful of the earth from his country with him. I intended to take a handful of earth from the airport, but with all that was happening, I did not get a chance to get it. I dramatized everything, and perhaps I should not have done that—the thought about the earth of Vietnam in my hand as I left.

We landed on the *Midway*. When we were there for about two hours, they handed us ropes to help us walk across the deck of the ship.

On the ship I still had some mixed feelings. I had some resentment, but at the same time the Americans looked very beautiful to me and they were now my protectors. I felt I must trust in these people on the *Midway*, they were so tall and so beautiful to us in their physical appearance, big and strong and healthy.

We were then transferred onto a small ship. I remember a lot of going up and down on the ocean. We did not have food for about three days. One of the theories that people had on the ship was that they did not have enough supplies and the little food they had, they had to keep for the American soldiers on the ship. When the helicopters came to transfer the Americans, though, they still did not have enough food. So the second theory was they wanted us to be hungry so we would not fight with each other or with them.

My mother told my brother to go to sleep and he complained that he had not eaten all day. I was very hungry, too. We had water, but nothing to eat. So finally one day I stole some food. I feel bad about that even today.

The story is significant for my trip. I am of course embarrassed about it today. There was a bucket of fish, canned fish, that I discovered one day. I found it always sitting in the same place, so I picked up some of the fish in the can, then closed the can and ate some of it. It tasted very good to me. It was very fishy and cold, but at that time it tasted so good. I got sick from eating it but I could not tell people that I had stolen food and eaten it.

Our small ship transferred us to the Philippines. I thought on the ship about Tan Son Nhut and all the food there and wished I had brought some with us. On the ship we slept on the floor and it was packed. At Subic it was like paradise because all we did was stay in big tents and we had mattresses and bedding to sleep on the ground. They gave us shots before we could go to Guam. They had us take showers also, so no disease and no lice would be brought to Guam and then to the United States. We all received vaccinations.

My family wanted to go to California because we had heard that there were more Asians there and better weather. So at Guam they said that they were going to fly us to Fort Chaffee, Arkansas, which had a vacancy, instead of Camp Pendleton, and we refused because we wanted to go to California and not Arkansas. So they let us stay longer on Guam. We did not know a lot, so whatever we did know, we hung on to it—and we knew that we wanted to go to California.

Vu Thi Kim Vinh
"We Cried When We Realized That It Was All Over"

My mother gave birth to me in Tay Ninh in 1961 then brought me back to Saigon. We were Catholic. My parents had ten children and I was the middle child. I have six older sisters, two brothers, and one younger sister. But now I have only one older brother. One brother died four years ago from an intestinal infection when he was in a refugee camp in Malaysia. He had an operation there after his escape. Then he came here. After five operations he got an infection and died from it. He was twenty-seven years old.

I remember the war going on when I was small, because I used to go with my mother to visit my dad when he was in the Army. At that time he was in Binh Duong province. And when I was a kid I got sick for a few months and I lived with my dad so the army doctor could take care of me. The things that make me think of the wartime and danger are things from 1968, the year that the Communists attacked during the Tet celebration. My parents and our family had just had lunch, and my father received a phone call from the general and he had to hurry back to his post. So we were really worried because it was the New Year and everybody celebrated and had a good time. But that time we had only Mother with us and we knew nothing of what might have happened to my dad. We lived in fear and we just prayed during the Tet celebration. My mother really worshipped my father. And we prayed that everything would be over soon. My father was a lieutenant colonel.

I am very proud of my dad. He had retired before 1975. After he fought in 1968 he received many certificates and awards from Nixon and Westmoreland, because he was the one who took back Binh Duong province and opened the road for other troops so the Communists were defeated. He was a very brave man. After that he retired. It was too political, he thought. He had traveled a lot. He could speak English and French and he was familiar with America because he had been there for some special training.

When we heard rumors about the Communist victories in 1974 and 1975 my father wasn't concerned, so we didn't worry either. Even when they came close to Saigon, we didn't worry, because my father believed that the Communists would never win.

My sister got married to a guy whose father was rich. His father knew a lot of officers who worked in the Thieu government and he knew what was happening. And this guy told my dad that he had better pack his clothes and collect all his money and leave the country because it was hopeless, because the allies were not going to help us. This was at the beginning of April. Even after the twenty-first we didn't think there was a way we could lose; we had a strong army and a strong military. Even though we did not like the Thieu government, we did not like the Communists, either. And we were confused, too. We heard rumors that the Communists were coming and that they would establish a new government, but we had nothing else to believe in, no middle way to choose to fight for. We fought, though, because we were forced to. But we were tired of the war. We were afraid that if the Communists took over, our family and our lives would be in danger. The problem was, after mid-April, all the important people in the government started to become refugees, and it made everything chaotic at that time. Everybody got scared. After the first wave of refugees left the country, many people panicked.

My uncle worked in the ICCS, and he arranged for people to leave the country and arranged for them to go to the airport and get on the planes to leave. People started to panic when we lost Ban Me Thuot and then Nha Trang. My family started to try to find a way to leave, and it was only because we saw other people going. The Vietnamese extended family is very close. If one family moves, and the others don't go, your life will be empty and sad without relatives around. So when relatives started to leave, our other relatives started to leave, too. But we got stuck because we had too many options and we could not choose one. My sister worked in an American bank. She said her bank would be evacuated and they would take her with them and they would accept one more person with her. So we chose another sister to go with her. And another sister, the one who married the son of a rich man, she wanted to go and to take her baby. She went earlier, and when she got to Tan Son Nhut she found that anybody could go who could get through the gate to the airport—without limit—so she tried to telephone us to come to the airport, but the line at the phone was a long one and she could not get to the phone to call us. Had she gotten through, we could have left with her. She had her own baby of about eight months, and she had another baby from my other sister. And she had to feed them. She flew out that night to Guam. After that my family had tragedy after tragedy. My brother-in-law did not know that his parents had left without him. When he went home nobody was home. He panicked and came to us because he had come back to Saigon without permission. He was in the Air Force. We had to hide him and find a way for him to leave first.

My uncle, who worked in the ICCS, tried to help him and put him on the list. But because most of the people knew that he was the son of a millionaire, they thought that if he left he would bring a lot of gold and American money with him, and somebody told the police at Tan Son Nhut that he was a pilot and there was a law that no soldier could leave Vietnam without permission, and if they caught him they could shoot him without trial. He got caught on April 27. Because of him we got stuck. My mother was a very nice and brave woman with a golden heart. Sometimes she cared for other people more than her own children. She thought that he needed help, and she said that we could not go as long as he was in trouble, unless she saw him walk up to a helicopter to leave the country.

So on the twenty-eighth, my sister (his wife), left the country. Because she was pregnant, she went first. My mother asked me if I wanted to go with my sister to take care of her. I said I would do that; but my younger sister was closer to her and she cried when she saw her sister leaving. So I was stupid and said that I would let her go in my place. That one decision cost me five years of living with the Communists.

The problem was my uncle. He did not want at first to help the relatives, but rather some people who were richer than us. They gave him dollars and gold. So he postponed the time when we would leave, and he put the strangers in our place. I don't blame him, because he needed money. Who knew what would happen the next day? He had to take care of his family. He planned to be one of the last to leave.

When he came home, he said, "Oh, God! I could have put you on the flight today, too. There were three cancellations." My mother was angry and asked why he did that to us. He just said he didn't have time.

He got left behind, too. On the twenty-ninth, the last day. He came home and cried and said, "It's hopeless." My mother was shocked and asked why, and he said that all of the ICCS members left without him. There was a big crowd at Tan Son Nhut and he could not get through the gate. The other ICCS members could not wait and they left without him.

My sister called a friend who worked in the American Embassy but her phone was disconnected. So we all finally went to the Embassy and there was a very big crowd. That was on the twenty-ninth. People were crying and fighting to get into the gate. Other people knew that some families had left and they went into the houses and looted them—refrigerators and furniture, and so on. These looters were almost the only people in the streets.

When we got to the Embassy we knew for sure that there was no way to get in. I was not afraid at the time—I was numb. I just felt angry and supset, but not scared. I kept thinking, "This is not fair!" I could not understand why this was happening to my people. But who said that life is fair?

It was raining, I remember, because my parents said that we could not stand out in the rain, so we went home and tried to find another way out of the country. Also, we wanted to go home because we thought that the looters might go into our house if we were gone for too long. And we didn't want to go home to nothing. But later on, my father didn't want to leave the country because he still had his mother back in North Vietnam and I knew that he wanted to see her. He said that now, if it happened, at least he would have a chance to see his mother and sister. This was an irony because he could not see her; he was in a concentration camp when she died after the war was over.

On the twenty-ninth we turned on the television to watch the last show by the last free government, and we heard Vu Van Mau condemning the Americans and ordering them out of the country. We saw one of the radical students, also, who worked for the Communists secretly. He had got out of jail. He said something like, "Now is the time for the youth and the students to prepare for the new happy things in a reunified Vietnam." At that time I still hoped—I am so naïve—that the people wouldn't betray what they said would happen. I still thought that the others loved my country, too, and that perhaps everything would be all right.

In the early morning of April 30 I didn't see troops in the street. About 9:00 a.m. we turned on the radio and General Minh said that he didn't want the soldiers to fight any more. He announced that the war was over.

About noon I heard the troops and the jeeps as they drove past my house with flags. I went up to the terrace to see them. The first thing we did after seeing them was change clothes. We changed into all-black clothes. We heard a rumor that they didn't like people who dressed nice; that meant that you had money and they would kill you.

General Minh announced that he would not be president anymore, and we knew that was it. We cried when we realized that it was all over. My dad cried, too. I was the one who had to burn all of the papers and the certificates that my father got from the Americans and from the government—from Thieu, Nixon, and Westmoreland, and from all those who thanked my father for what he did. All of the photos that my dad kept as souvenirs I had to burn. And I cried. I went up to the terrace and saw the last plane leaving the country, a DC-3; I watched it trying to take off, and I saw it explode in the sky. I saw a missile hit it and it exploded. We saw the debris and the bodies fall out of the sky and back to the ground. That was on the morning of the thirtieth.

We saw a helicopter that flew to a physician's house. He was a physician in the Army and chairman of the hospital for the wounded soldiers. The helicopter tried to take him, but he could not get onto it because the rope was not long enough. The helicopter stayed over the house but he could not get into it, so it left him behind. Many people had tried to find a way to go, and here was a man who had a way and could not get into the helicopter.

After April 30 you could still leave Vietnam easily. The winners still celebrated their victory and they did not exercise much control over the sea. My parents tried to pay a boat to take our family. But on the way they met some Communist soldiers who were hitchhiking and my parents talked to them, and they said that everything would be all right and there would be no bloodbath. My parents asked them about being sent to concentration camps if you were in the Army, and they said, "No, no! Everything will be all right." They told us about how beautiful the North Vietnamese girls were and how much nicer they dressed than the South Vietnamese girls. They said that there would be no revenge: "Don't make us out to be monsters, because we aren't."

But the first day of May was a very sad day. The day was very heavy and sobering. The electricity was out and the Communists could not fix it. We heard on the radio the voice of a Northerner, very high-pitched and loud, and he condemned America and the people who cooperated with them. He humiliated us by saying that we had been the servants and the dogs of the American government because we had worked with them and against the Communists. We were very hurt to hear that.

It was very dangerous to go outside because the people still broke into houses when they thought people had moved away. It was very chaotic. Many people had guns and took things from other people in the street, so it was frightening.

I went for a ride on my bicycle. I saw some of the South Vietnamese soldiers. They had taken off their uniforms, and they were crying. Some of the people had seen them, and those people, during this transition from the old to the new, were chasing the soldiers and throwing things at them and hitting them to try to make themselves look good to the new government. It was very embarrassing to me, as a child, to see something like that. I felt sick when I saw that. And these same people cheered the Communist soldiers and hugged them like their long-lost brothers. I was surprised when I saw that, and I felt so bad.

At that time if your family had someone who worked for the government in the North, even just a regular soldier, you could feel safe at last, and say, "Oh, we have somebody who fought against South Vietnamese!" That psychology confused me because before that time you dared not say that you knew someone in the North or had a relative fighting in the other army. Nobody told anybody that, but immediately everybody knew what to do. Everybody was suddenly wearing the Vietcong flag. The flag was security or a credit card that could save your life. Everybody had one. It made me scared because the people were so scared that they seemed to lose their sanity, their reason; they could not think any more. I had a blue shirt that I loved but we had to tear it up to make a flag and I cried when we did that, and I remember how silly it was. My brother was athletic and he had a pair of yellow shorts. We cut the star from them and made the flag and hung it in front of the house. Once that flag was up the family felt safe. Everybody seemed to do that, and the atmosphere was a lot different. People seemed suddenly to look at the world a different way.

The liberators used a strange language, even though it was Vietnamese, and some of the people started to imitate that accent. It was so strange.

After a week they divided us into sections and we had a political guy on our block. He told us about Marxism and Leninism and we had to discuss it in a meeting. What was humiliating about this was that they made us criticize ourselves. Even my father at these meetings had to criticize his own behavior. He had to say that he killed innocent people. But I knew he didn't kill innocent people, because if he hadn't killed them they would have killed him. But he said that he was a guilty man and asked for forgiveness for killing what he called "innocent people." And I watched him cry in front of them. It was the first time I had ever seen my father cry. I had to do the same thing but I didn't have to write it down. I said that I didn't want my parents to be the way that they were. This was after listening to the guy who talked about Marxism-Leninism and the sacrifices of the North to liberate the South. So I said that I hated people like my parents who did what they did. I said that to survive.

Tran Thi My Ngoc
"They Are Ants Encircling Us"

My parents were divorced when I was just a baby. My father was going to law school and then he was in the Army. My mother was very dependent on my father and it was hard on him. So when I was born they divorced. My mother was left with two small children. I have a sister three years older than me.

So my mom was broke, didn't have money. We were living in a blue-collar neighborhood. But the people there were really warm. They took care of me. My father remarried soon after that and took my sister with him. So I was alone with my mother until I was about six.

My mother was in business. In Vietnam there was a lottery and she worked for it. She was working in the lower rank at first and then moved up, and finally she got lottery tickets from the government and other people from different parts of South Vietnam would come and get them from her. So she made money that way.

By the time I was six years old my father took me to live with him so I could get an education. My mom was so busy working. I grew up with my dad after that, and every weekend I would come back and visit my mom.

My dad was then working as a judge in the special judicial system, where he tried the merchants and capitalists. Then he was transferred and was working with the military judicial system until the day Saigon fell.

After I went to live with my dad I was very naïve because my life was so protected. No one could get near me. The kind of friends that I had belonged to families of the same standing.

I went to a private school—the Lycée de Marie Curie on Cong Ly Street. You pass it when you drive to Tan Son Nhut from Saigon. I went to French school from the time I was small until the day Saigon fell. I even learned to read and write in French before I learned how to read and write Vietnamese. I couldn't forget the day I was forced to learn Vietnamese. I got criticized so much by the teacher because I was so difficult to teach. The Vietnamese alphabet has extra accents on the letters and I couldn't get it through my head. I got whacked so often that finally I had to learn fast just to protect myself.

I began to see that things were not good early in 1975, during Tet, the lunar New Year. Before Tet we had the custom that you bring gifts to your friends and so on, and they give you gifts. So my father and my stepmother took me with them to visit the minister of finance. He was a good friend of my father. We were visiting him that night to give him gifts for New Year and they were talking a long time. I was kind of small and I didn't pay much attention, but then when we came home I heard my parents discussing that he said that my father had to leave Vietnam soon because the Communists were all around Saigon now. "They are coming in," he said. I remember the term he used—"They are like ants encircling us now."

So that guy resigned and left early. At that time my father had to go south to Can Tho to try people like deserters from the Army, military people, or Vietcong they had captured in the Delta region. My father didn't want to leave. My mother was afraid, and so was my stepmother. They were telling him not to go south because something bad might happen. In the south there was unrest.

He said, "I have to do my duty." So he went there. His last trip down there was in April and he had to fly back, I think, because it was going It was happening. So there I was, still going to school, and I didn't really worry because Saigon never fell before. In 1968 they came in but we fought back.

I was feeling strange, but it didn't scare me because I didn't know what a Communist was. I knew that we fought them, but I didn't know what they were like. At the time there were rumors like they would kill people, people who dressed up nice or people who had fingernails painted—if they caught these people, they would pull out the fingernails. So I was kind of scared, but I didn't use nail polish anyway.

And besides, I was feeling kind of secure. Rumors were flying and actually, by the end of March or so, we started seeing people coming in—my friends and relatives from Nha Trang—but I wasn't too scared. Things were going so fast, and my parents didn't do anything, so I didn't really know. But I heard rumors.

My dad came back from his last trip south and said it was true, the rumor they would pull out the fingernails, because they had come to smaller villages and one of the teachers whose fingernails were painted did get her nails pulled out.

The rumors were just terrifying. They would torture you because you worked for the government, he said. At that time my father's friends started to leave. They had a plan for leaving Vietnam but my dad couldn't leave because there was only the one place for him, and they didn't have room for the family, so my father wouldn't leave.

The government then said, "If you try to leave and get caught you could be shot or be tried in a court martial," and my father was a court martial judge.

I had a cousin who was married to a Filipino. They were ready to leave Vietnam and were waiting at Tan Son Nhut, so we packed and got ready to go out with them. This was the second week of April. And we waited at Tan Son Nhut for three days for our plane to come. But for some reason Tan Son Nhut Airport was crazy at that time. We were waiting because the Filipino embassy was taking people out. My cousin and her husband were on their list. They were going to take us with them as an extended family.

I was very calm. It's my nature. Whenever I am in danger, I am very calm; but I break down afterward.

We got tired of waiting. My family and my parents were worried and took us back. And while they were taking us back, that very night, the airplane came in and my cousin and her husband left. They couldn't get in touch with us and they had to leave, so we were left behind.

Then our next-door neighbor had a daughter who was married to an American engineer and she left Vietnam in 1972. They were living in Iran at that time, in Teheran. She asked her husband to fly back to get her family out. Her family is about as big as my family. So my father got in touch with the neighbor and said, "Can you take these two kids?"

It's so funny. They just let me and my half brother go, and I had an older sister and younger half brothers. I don't know why my brother and I were the ones to go.

So the guy came back. The Americans didn't want to let him take us out. They did say maybe he could, but he had to get the paperwork ready. He told my parents, "If I take your children, later on somebody has to pay me, because how am I going to take care of them?" My father said, "Fine. Okay."

This American guy's name was David and he was thirty-something. I remember he was very nice.

It was just like a game to me then. I wasn't real afraid. I was raised so securely, I wouldn't think about things going wrong. I didn't even think about whether I would leave forever or temporarily. In a way I was dazed.

We had a lot of money in the bank and we were trying to exchange Vietnamese money into dollars. My family could just get out two thousand dollars and then it was stopped, because the bank could not exchange dollars any more; the dollars were all gone. So my mom had to buy dollars in the black market.

David did the paperwork and everything and we were supposed to leave on the twenty-seventh of April, I remember that. He said it was very difficult for him. They wouldn't let him walk around because the order was, no Americans walking around the streets anymore. He said, "You should be ready at all times to go to Tan Son Nhut to leave."

He got all the paperwork done, and he said, "I will come back to get you and we will be leaving very soon." His family, too. He went back out to Tan Son Nhut and then they wouldn't let him out. He called back and he cried. He said, "If I got out they would shoot me." The airport was closed the twenty-fourth or something like that. He told us, "I am stuck and can't leave. What you have to do is wait and maybe I'll have a car come and pick you up. Get ready."

We waited until the twenty-eighth. He couldn't get out; no car was coming, and he had to get out of the country and back to Iran.

Now I think my dad was panicking. I was feeling sadder the closer it got to the end. We didn't know that the country would fall on the thirtieth of April, but everybody was running like crazy by the twenty-eighth. More people were coming—it was so crazy, the whole thing. People were running around the streets. I don't know where they went, but you'd go out and people with bags and suitcases and what-have-you were running around all over the place.

You could hear the bombs now closer to Saigon. Never before had I heard anything like that so close.

Then on the twenty-ninth I looked up and saw two airplanes fighting. It was in the afternoon. We didn't know if they were enemies, or what. I don't know anything about planes, but actually they were shooting at each other.

After Big Minh was sworn in my father said, "That's it. We are lost. We have to leave. Everything is lost."

We were all packed on the twenty-ninth and the phone rang from the morning until one o'clock at night. You hung up and it rang again. People were calling my family, telling us to get out, asking my dad's opinion. People were saying he hadn't left yet, so maybe it's not serious; they were waiting and seeking his opinion. So everyone was asking questions and the phone was ringing off the hook.

I started to feel sad; I had a premonition that something bad was coming. I saw the neighbor who had a husband in Canada. He had left a few months ago. She was so worried, she was running around like crazy with her two children. Finally she packed up and left. I guess she knew of a ship that was leaving.

I saw helicopters flying overhead but I didn't know what was what—who they belonged to or what they were doing.

There was one helicopter I saw trying to land close by where there was a big building of a religious group. The pilot was trying to land but he couldn't because of the antennas and everything. Finally he had to leave. But he was trying to land and people were trying to get to him. If he landed they wanted to get in.

My dad wouldn't let us go out, because soldiers were shooting outside. If you drove a car by they would shoot at you. So we were confined to the area we lived in.

By late on the twenty-ninth we knew for sure that the city was lost. And I remember my father said then that two of our biggest enemies were Thieu and the Communists. He said, "Don't ever forget what they did to us! Thieu and the Communists."

The electricity was out on the twenty-ninth and we used candles. My dad was taking out all the papers and documents and burning and flushing them away. He took out all the guns we had and dumped them in the garbage.

Finally, at night, I think around eleven or so, we got a call from the guy who commanded a Navy ship. He had been calling for some time, and finally he said to my father, "Please make up your mind if you want to go. I'll send the jeeps to come to get your family and then your ex-wife's family, too. And you bring whatever you want to bring with you." So my dad just kept thinking, and finally, almost at midnight, he called one more time to say, "I have to leave now. I can't wait any longer." So my father said, "Go ahead and leave." He had made the decision to stay.

The next morning the Communists came into Saigon in tanks. They drove into the Presidential Palace.

My mother told my dad where we could go—a house—and be safe from the Communists. In the morning my dad packed us up in the car and drove us to that place, because he was afraid we would get killed if we stayed at home. People were hysterical, and they would act crazy. So we were driving in the morning and saw all this stuff. I saw tanks going into the grounds of the Presidential Palace. There was an iron fence and they crashed through it. I couldn't see everything because my dad was driving so fast.

Then I saw soldiers carrying flags with the yellow star. I said, "Oh boy, this is it." By that time fear was building up. We were afraid we were going to get killed. I was afraid more for my dad than for us. Everybody was afraid for my dad.

The streets were so deserted. A few days before it was so bustling; people were running around. In the morning there were more tanks than people.

There were thirty-six houses in the unit we lived in. This one family was so happy. Right away they wore a red armband showing that they were Communists. They came out. The twenty-ninth they weren't really out, but the thirtieth they were out. So that's why my father took us away fast.

My mom told my father to take us to this building close to where she lived, because they were her friends and would help us. The street was deserted. It was like after a war; things were strewn all over, and you could see soldiers' uniforms, and things were burning. There was trash all over the place.

There were cars abandoned everywhere. There were only two or three cars moving around. No roadblocks. No roving groups of soldiers. They were busy going into the palace.

The soldiers passed us but they didn't care about us. We looked at them and they looked at us and we drove away real fast. I always thought that our soldiers were sort of slick, nicely dressed, with uniforms that fit. And here were these Communist guys all in baggy uniforms and they looked about as lost as we were. You know what they looked like? They looked like tourists who were lost.

Well, it ended up that the people who lived in the building we were going to were really Communists—they were fifth-column. And we loved them so much. Two women and one man, business associates of my mother ever since I was born. And we never knew they were Communists.

We asked them if we could stay with them, so they said it was okay. My mom knew it. My father was worried about it, and my mom was worried about him, too. Nobody would get into the house. Other abandoned houses they would get into; the fifth column or looters, or whatever, but they said their place would be very safe for my father and us. Nobody would dare to get in.

The woman's name was Phuong. When she did business it was a way to support those people buying guns or food or whatever. She was in the lottery thing, too.

So they said it would be a very safe place; nobody would come in and harm us. My dad said, "Good." He delivered us inside. And he saw people that he never saw before—they were different. They wore the civilian clothes, but they just looked different. Right away he made a U-turn and got out quick. He said, "You kids stay here; you will be safe, but I have to go right away." We didn't know why he was beating such a hasty retreat. I said, "What's wrong with dad? How come he won't stay? This is a safe place." And he said, "Just be quiet. Stay here. Act normal but don't talk too much and you'll be safe." He didn't say where he was going.

I just had a bag, a little bag that contained necessary things like medication, toothbrush, toothpaste, and some money, I think. So he left seven of us there—my half brothers and half sisters and my sister. We were all there with no father and no mother and just these weird people. They were all acting strange.

They looked so calm and so happy. Here we were, scared to death, and they kept smiling at us. People asked us questions, but my dad had said not to talk too much. They were asking things like, "Well, now the country is liberated, how do you feel? Do you like it? What did you hear the government say about the Vietcong?" And being so naïve I said, "Oh, do you know that if they caught people with nail polish on they would pull their nails out and torture people? And people who are rich who worked for the previous government will be caught and tortured. We heard that." They were just laughing at us

They didn't say anything; just asked us questions about what we heard and felt, and I was telling them what I heard. They said, "Well, you are in here and you are safe. Nothing has happened to you. What do you think now?" And at that point I got suspicious that maybe I'd talked too much. So I said, "Oh well, I think those were lies the government was telling us." I knew something was going on. They didn't advocate the VC; they just said, "Now you see the truth. We don't hurt people." After they said that, I just kept my mouth shut.

We ate there and slept there. It was very strange. After the questioning I knew what was going on already. I knew they weren't us.

I wasn't really afraid. I was just feeling worried. A very strange feeling. There was nothing I could do. We were just biding time. I didn't know what was going to happen to us, how long we should stay in this place and when would our parents come to get us home. We didn't get outside. We looked out the windows.

After the thirtieth it was quiet and deserted. People didn't venture out. No businesses were open—nothing.

My mom finally came three or four days later and took us home. We went to her house, which was only three or four blocks away. Later on, my dad went to Cholon—we have relatives in Cholon. We weren't told that he was there. We asked where he was, but they wouldn't tell us because they were afraid if the Communists got hold of us we would blab. He stayed there into May when it was a bit settled and the government said for people who worked for the previous government to report to the re-education camps. Because of his rank he would be there three weeks to three months. People of lesser rank went from one to three weeks.

So we didn't know about him. I think I was taken with my mom to Cholon to see my dad and I remember him saying about taking us to her friends, "Are you crazy? You were telling me to go right into the den of the tiger." And she said, "I didn't know." My dad said, "Why did you tell me to go there? Didn't you know that was the snake pit? I just came in the door and knew right away that's who they were, so that's why I left the children there and retreated right away." I don't know how he knew.

My dad stayed in Cholon until he was called. I think he debated whether or not he should show up, but he said finally he might as well because he couldn't go into hiding forever. And it was only three months. So he went.

By that time, in early May, we'd gone back to our original house. That Viet Cong family was already organizing, becoming the leader of the unit of thirty-six houses, so we had to follow the new rules.

Actually they didn't have any clear thing. They were checking on us, more or less. We couldn't buy anything. We didn't even go to the market. I don't know what we ate. We must have eaten the reserve, the dry foods.

My dad reported to the place where people were supposed to report. It was right by the zoo. There were long lines of people there and they all had a sack of clothing. They didn't know what they would need, so they just brought some clothing and a few other items. There were long lines and the Communists set up tables to take people. So we were waiting there with him, me and my stepmother and my older sister.

My dad came up to the table. I think he was asked to turn in his watch and some other things like that. So he checked in. We didn't know where they took the people who reported, but he had to stay. We didn't know where they sent him.

CHAPTER **XVIII**

Victors

Colonel Bui Tin
"I Became a Man of War and I Never Wanted That"

When President Diem was assassinated in November of 1963 I didn't think the South would collapse. Not even after the death of Kennedy did I feel that it would collapse. I knew there would have to be a struggle first.

What we did at that time was to increase our efforts in the South. We decided to bring division-size units, one at a time, into the South to fight against the puppet regime. The majority of these men were from the South and had gone North. But then we started to recruit Northerners, also.

Two weeks after the death of Diem I was in the headquarters delegation for an on-the-spot examination in the central highlands to see what was happening, and to open the Ho Chi Minh Trail and to make it better organized. I was also to organize battalions and regiments in the central highlands. In the beginning we could only walk on the Trail, but by 1963 the width and the organization were such that now we could bring bicycles with supplies down the Trail. At that time there were few American or Vietnamese planes bombing on the Trail.

The Americans gave the South Vietnamese armored personnel carriers, [APCs] and we had not confronted them before. We were not sure that we could fight against them. Before the battle of Ap Bac we did not have the right kinds of weapons to destroy those machines. So we alerted headquarters that we had to contact the Russians and the Chinese to provide us with weapons that could destroy these machines, and they began to supply us with rockets to destroy them.

Then General Westmoreland became commander of the Americans, and we had to ask ourselves, "Can we fight successfully against the Americans?" We fought the Americans in the Ia Drang Valley in 1965 and we concluded that we could fight the Americans face to face. But we did not say at that time that we could beat the Americans. We just knew that we could stand and fight them. Winning was something else.

We gained a lot of experience fighting the Americans when they used APCs and then helicopters. Every time they came up with something new, we had to come up with something new. What we learned was the American strength, but also our own weaknesses. So after Ia Drang, where the Americans moved their men with helicopters, we had to retreat and rethink fighting with the Americans and come up with new tactics. We had a problem.

Then there was the additional problem of American bombers, especially B-52 bombers. We had to rethink how to confront them also along the Ho Chi Minh Trail.

I did not lose faith. I was very, very worried. But morale among the troops remained very high in those days for us. We never thought we would lose. We just did not know how we could win. Whatever the American government was dishing out we could take. In the beginning, with the B-52s, it was completely terrifying and it worried me a lot. But we watched them and found out the formation they would fly in. And we knew what pattern they would hit on the ground with, so we would go into shelters in areas that we thought the bombs would not hit.

How did we maintain high morale among ourselves? We were fighting for the independence and unification of our country. And we knew that we could survive the war. We were discouraged somewhat in the beginning from the bombing raids because so many people were killed, and we didn't know for a time if we could survive the punishment that the Americans were giving us. But then we found we could survive their weapons and their technology, and when we knew that, we saw that we could win, also.

Were the Americans and the South Vietnamese a worthy foe on the battlefield? I thought about this issue a long time. My conclusion was that they had a lot of weaknesses. The American soldiers belonged to a rich country and they had all the ammunition they needed, but they had so many weaknesses it was not difficult to fight against them. Supplies alone did not overcome their weaknesses.

The greatest weakness of the American soldiers was their attitude. They did not really know what they were fighting for. They were fighting for a country that wasn't theirs and they missed their families. Although they were fulfilling a duty to their own country, they didn't care much for the fight, so they had weak morale. And they depended far too much on their air power and on their artillery. When it came to fighting at close quarters with our soldiers without air or artillery, just us and them face to face, they often freaked out.

The Northerners, now, they were fighting for something. They really wanted to free their country. The Americans fought because it was their job, and most of all they wanted to return home. Their hearts were not in the fight. But ours were. That was the major difference.

Following the signing of the Paris Agreement, I was sent to the South to attend the Four Party Commission (Joint Miliary Commission) for the settlement of the provisions of the Agreement. I went to Camp Davis as a member of the delegation from the North. I was the spokesman. I was there for sixty days. And there, for the first time, I met with Americans. I met with Major General Gilbert H. Woodward and his wife. General Woodward was the chief of the U.S. delegation to the Joint Military Commission. We had many meetings in Saigon, in My Tho, and in Danang, working with the Commission.

Then I headed a team to supervise the last withdrawal of American troops on the twenty-ninth of March, 1973. I was in uniform at that time. I remember watching the last American soldiers leave Vietnam. I shook hands with the last American to leave the country. I remember his name— Sergeant Bienco.* I shook his hand and said goodbye to him. I gave him a small framed picture of the lake, Ho Hoan Kiem in Hanoi, "Return of the Sword" Lake. I wished Bienco happiness when he was reunited with his country, and I wished him good health, and I hoped that he would never come back to Vietnam again. After that I returned to Hanoi just at the end of March.

I came South again in 1975 with General Van Tien Dung. This time I was a journalist. I was with the headquarters unit and came into Saigon with the first NVA troops into the city.

There was no high-ranking official with us when we went into Saigon. So the duty fell to me to take the unconditional surrender of South Vietnam. I was with the first three tanks that came into the city.

Since I had been in Saigon in 1973 already and I had been around the city sightseeing, I was the only officer in the tanks who knew the way through the city streets. In 1973 I had taken a picture of the Presidential Palace, so I knew what we were looking for. I was on my way to Tan Son Nhut to meet with the Hungarian delegation and I had taken a picture of the Presidential Palace and kept it with me.

I guided our tanks through the streets to the Palace. It was a great feeling to be back in Saigon again and then to enter the Palace Grounds. I had always worried about having the war in Saigon and fighting for the city. I thought that we might have to fight in the city for a week or so. Then I heard the firing when we came into the city and figured there

* The North Vietnamese newspaper *Thong Nhat* reported the episode in its March 23, 1974, issue, this way: "The last American soldier to board the airplane was named Bienco. The victors shook his hand, wished him well, and presented him with a post card depicting Hanoi's single-pedestal pogoda. The shocked Bienco gaped at them for a moment, stammered his thanks, and boarded the plane. Its doors closed, and MAC DC–9 #40169 taxied away, lifting off and disappearing into the heavens."

would be a big fight, but it was just soldiers firing their weapons into the air, signifying that the war was over.

We drove on to the Presidential Palace to take the surrender.

I didn't really plan on being the one to take the final surrender of the South. It just happened that way. I just happened to be with the first tanks to enter the city and so directed them toward the Palace because I knew where it was. None of this was planned. It just happened.

I was directed to General Duong Van Minh by the chief of the guard of the armored unit. I went to General Minh's office. He was standing there, and he said he had been waiting for someone to come in and take the surrender. I looked around and I saw that all of the people in the room were very, very worried. General Minh was dressed in a short-sleeved shirt and his face looked tired. He looked like he had not slept in a long time and he had not shaved for several days. He said he wanted to surrender the government of South Vietnam to me. "I have been waiting since early this morning to transfer power to you," he said. And, of course, I said the now-famous line, "There is no question of your transferring power. Your power has crumbled. You have nothing in your hands to surrender and so you cannot surrender what you do not possess."

Everyone from the South Vietnamese government seemed very worried, and so I looked around at them and told them, "This should be a happy day for our country because the war is over. If you love your country, then you should be happy." When I said that, they seemed to relax and not to worry so much. Then, to lighten up the atmosphere of the room, I asked Vu Van Mau about his family and tried to make some jokes and small talk. I asked General Minh how his tennis game was. Minh grew orchids and I knew that, so I talked to him about that. I surprised them because I knew all about them. Everything. And they knew nothing about me! Ha!

I went to the U.S. Embassy then. I took a picture of the large tree outside the Embassy that the Americans had chopped down. Then I went to the roof and took pictures with my comrades. There were lots of helmets, guns, and supplies all over the roof. They left so much behind on the roof. I also looked into the place where the Americans destroyed their documents. Then I went out to the Tan Son Nhut airport and saw the place where they kept their documents. It was still burning.

I was very happy. The thing I enjoyed the most was that the Southerners came up and talked to us. Young people came out to talk to us to find out about us and what we intended to do, so they could go back and report to their homes. People seemed to be welcoming us, but they were worried. And I was so excited about talking with the people and seeing Saigon that I forgot about my journalistic duties and I didn't until that evening sit down and try to write an article about the events of the day.

Then that evening I found myself sitting at a desk on the second floor of the Presidential Palace in Saigon, and in one stroke I wrote four pages about our victory. I didn't know how to get it to Hanoi. Then I remembered the American DAO office at Tan Son Nhut airport where I thought I could telex it. So I went out there, but the Americans had destroyed the telex. Then I went to Camp Davis and told them to try to send my message out to Hanoi. That was the first news that came out of Saigon that day about the victory.

The opening line of my message was, "I am writing this article while sitting at a desk on the second floor of the Presidential Palace in Saigon. The long war is over."

Americans must remember today that the war was regrettable, and it was preventable, and it should never have been fought. It was the most regrettable war in America's history. The American people, and especially the American government, have always been slow in perceiving the real nature of things in Asia. Right now, of course, the Americans have diplomatic relations with China and with Russia, but they do not have diplomatic relations with us. Why not? We were once friends, at the end of World War II. Americans taught those of us who were in the Vietminh how to fight and they supplied us with arms. We should have remained friends and this war should never have been fought. It is tragic.

The Vietnamese are not bitter about the war today. And why not? The reason is that we never did what was morally wrong. We never dropped bombs on America. We never shot prisoners or civilians. What the American soldiers did, we know, was what they were required to do for their country. I spoke with more than 100 American pilots in Hanoi after they were shot down. We had more than 500 of them here in prison during the war. They should never have been our enemies.

Today I am very tired of war. If you have ever been to war you can appreciate peace. All the people of the world want peace.

I became a man of war and I never wanted that. All I ever wanted was friendship and peace. All of our wars were forced onto us. The Vietnamese people hate war. And we love peace. I love peace.

Major General Tran Cong Man
"Everything Takes Time"

Phuoc Long province was liberated in early 1975. The attack on Phuoc Long left us with two possible results after its liberation. Either it would be retaken or it would be forever in our hands. And it was the first experiment by our Army to see what the situation was in the South.

In order to regain Phuoc Long the South Vietnamese government would have to have intensive military aid from the American government. But we were not afraid that would happen, because the attack took place after the Watergate business and there were clear signs that the American public was fed up with the war and the American Congress was becoming dispassionate toward the South Vietnamese.

If you want to win a war, you have to understand the other side, their government. Maybe the planners in Hanoi could not get the finer details of how the Americans operated, but the general patterns we saw and understood, so we had a pretty good idea of how Americans behaved and what we could expect from them.

The morale of the South Vietnamese soldiers was attached to the air power of the American government, and when that decreased, so did their morale. The common soldiers were tired of the war; going on with fighting when the war didn't go anywhere. But the war meant something for the officers in the South Vietnamese Army and their morale was higher, because they knew that if the war should end, their careers would be over.

The Phuoc Long attack was a carefully calculated experiment. We wanted to test the American and the South Vietnamese governments. If we struck Quang Tri, for example, or Danang, that would be too far away and we could not test their response. If we struck in Saigon that would be too close. So Phuoc Long was just about the right distance from Saigon, we felt. And, of course, there was no response. That was what we wanted to find out—would they respond or were they ready to let go? They were ready to let go.

I was in Ban Me Thuot prior to the attack there, but I was in Hanoi when the attack actually took place. I stayed in Hanoi for the remainder of the war.

In the attack in Ban Me Thuot we surprised the South Vietnamese. On the other hand, the South Vietnamese troops surprised us, too, because they became so disorganized so quickly. We did not expect that to happen. We thought that after the attack on Ban Me Thuot the South Vietnamese troops would draw the line there and fight back. We had expected a very intense and long battle with the South around Ban Me Thuot. But the way Mr. Thieu responded to the attack was not even within our imagination.

In fact, his response created a great question in our minds as to whether or not this was a trap, a brilliant tactic to lure us in. We could not believe he was doing what he did. Because of Thieu's action, we thought we might confront a very creative defensive tactic; therefore, our commanders moved ahead very cautiously at first, looking for the trap.

The first few days, we thought the South was planning some big surprise. But when Thieu withdrew his troops from Pleiku, we realized suddenly that there was no trap, and there was no plan, and the South was not up to fighting anymore. That is when we decided to chase them as fast as we could.

In the beginning, in the 1970s, the American government had used

B-52s to fight us, and we were wary of that; but in 1975 that was not an issue anymore because the Americans were not successful in 1972 in bombing us out of South Vietnam, so we knew that there was only the remotest chance that the Americans would try that again.

After we had liberated the central area of Vietnam, there was some diplomatic work between the U.S. government and Hanoi in order to slow down the movement of Northern troops.

But this was not done directly between us, but between a number of other countries and intermediaries. The Americans were asking us to slow down our armies in order to give the Americans time to complete the withdrawal from Saigon. They warned us that if we did not do that, they would intervene again in Vietnam and make the offensive a very costly one for us. That is what we were told.

But we didn't take that seriously any more. It was just a meaningless threat in 1975, and we knew it. The Americans were not coming back again.

So despite the warnings there was no slowdown of movement. On the contrary, we quickened our steps so we would not have to fight during the monsoon season. We wanted to be in Saigon before the rain started. If there had been any moment when it seemed that there was a slowdown, it was due only to the need for a tactical deployment of our troops.

I wasn't in the few privileged to know about this, but it was my opinion that the offensive was managed exclusively by us and there was absolutely no outside planning with the Russians or the Chinese.

After the Paris Agreement there was a diminishing in arms supplies from other socialist countries. But for China it was different, because prior to the Paris Agreement, China and the U.S. had the Shanghai Agreement, and judging by the announcement it was clear that China would not support us and did not really want to have an end to the war in Vietnam. China wasn't really that pleased or happy about the war finally being resolved or about our Great Spring Victory.

The high-ranking officers in South Vietnam were trying to get an agreement to end the war. When they saw that they were going to lose, they suddenly decided that they wanted a coalition government. But we ordered our troops to press on and end the war with a complete victory as soon as possible. We were not interested in any coalition government in Saigon. It was too late.

Our fight was only with the Vietnamese troops and we didn't want to do anything that would involve Americans in the fight. Therefore, we did not touch the Americans or shoot at them at all. We just wanted the Americans to leave the country as soon as possible so that we could focus all of our energy on the Southern army.

We thought that the U.S. Embassy was an arm of the Pentagon, so we thought it was best that all of the Americans leave from the Embassy and go home. We had no agreement with the South about anything. We made no agreement about their Air Force staying in Saigon: of course not. That's funny!

Even though I was in Hanoi, I was briefed hourly on what was happening around Saigon. The news of the fall of Saigon came to a high-ranking cadre here first. And I wasn't the only one to hear it. Everybody heard it, and by noon on the thirtieth everybody was out on the streets and very happy. The war was over.

We celebrated the liberation of Saigon. We really thought it would be more difficult, but it was easy. We were surprised.

Vietnam was at war for a long time, and everybody hoped for an end to the war, but nobody knew when it would end. So the victory at the end of April was a big surprise for everybody. We were all happy. People came into the streets shouting, singing slogans and songs, dancing.

I could not go home at that time. I was too busy. I was editor-in-chief of *Nhan Dan* newspaper. I had to get the story written for the newspaper.

It was a mistake for the American government to be involved in this war. They failed to recognize that or to see the real strength of the people who wanted to unify and liberate their country.

We do not hold American civilians responsible at all for what happened in Vietnam. The young American soldiers who were sent here to fight were deceived by their own government into doing something that was wrong. When these people came to Vietnam to kill they were not really aware of what they were doing.

Now the war is over. There should be no hatred between the people of your country and our country. There is no reason now why we should not be friends.

The American government instigated the war, so they have a moral and financial obligation to the Vietnamese people today. But the Vietnamese people are not going after anything like this. But it would be better for the American government to proceed with establishing normal relations with Vietnam now. We ask for nothing more than that.

This war was the longest one in American history. This war is the longest war in the history of Vietnam, too. It brought thirty years of suffering, grief, and pain for the people of Vietnam. Yet in the end, it brought good, because at last the country is unified and independent. So this was a war that brought about mixed results and mixed emotions. You lose a lot of lives and a lot of materials but you get independence and unification. And peace. So in the end it was worth it.

Remember this is a small country and a poor country, and yet we overcame a big, rich power. So the victory was worth it.

Perhaps this is a Vietnamese trait, but we bear no bitterness now toward Americans. We have had many wars with foreign powers that wanted to take over Vietnam. But when the war is over there is no reason to bear grudges.

As to the American protestors who refused to cooperate in the war against Vietnam, people like Jane Fonda and Tom Hayden and Harrison Salisbury, they did what was right and Americans should bear no grudge against them.

If the Americans had maintained the policy that they themselves had established in 1945 with Mr. Archimedes Patti of the O.S.S. toward the Vietnamese, there would never have been this war. If the American public had been informed of the Vietnamese goals and wishes, then they would have been in support of the efforts by us to reunify our country.

In a way, if the American government was more relaxed in its policies of letting news flow freely and not biased against the government of Vietnam, then people would know more about the people and problems and issues in this country today.

I understand the American discomfort with the Russians being here. But there is a problem in the way information is presented from Vietnam. The American public has been told that Vietnam is a Russian colony now, and if there were accuracy and understanding in the news you would see that we are independent. We belong to no one but ourselves.

The American government is more afraid of the Russian people than of the Chinese people. I don't know why this is. They are both Communist. I don't understand this.

It is going to take time to get the American government out of its anti-Vietnam feeling.

Everything takes time.

General Tran Bach Dang
"We Believe in Forgiving and Forgetting"

I was in the leadership of the National Liberation Front [NLF] in Tay Ninh province in the spring of 1975, working in the high command planning the spring offensive against the government of South Vietnam. Of course I was in close touch with General Van Tien Dung, who was commanding the People's Army of Vietnam (PAVN).

The Cao Dai religion is centered in Tay Ninh. And the Cao Dai, although mainly a religion, did have a militant part with their own soldiers. But they split into two sides. One functioned as a supplementary force for the South Vietnamese government, but the other part worked with the NLF people.

The Montagnards were in Ban Me Thuot and the central highlands in 1975. Some of them were in FULRO,* an organization that was formed by the CIA. But there was another group of Montagnards led by Ibid Aleo. That group had been working with the NLF for a long, long time.

* Front Unifié pour la Libération des Races Opprimées—a Montagnard separatist group in the central highlands.

And other Montagnards joined the Army of General Van Tien Dung when the battle of Ban Me Thuot began. They turned on the South Vietnamese soldiers and joined us. There was also another group that had been working with us in the central highlands all along.

We had also infiltrated the highest ranks of the government of Nguyen Van Thieu. There was some infiltration of our staff, too, but only at the lower levels.

I want to clarify an important point. General Dung was only a part in a big system. He was the front battle commander. He had nothing at all to do with tactics and with timing. He had other duties at the front. The chief commander at that time was General Vo Nguyen Giap.

The main concern was how to get rid of the intervention of the American government in Vietnam. We were focusing in the Paris Agreement on how to get rid of the American presence in the South. Once that force was gone, the plan for taking over the South was an easily calculated step.

Once the Americans were gone it was easy, because then at last it was just Vietnamese against Vietnamese.

By the beginning of 1975 when we took Phuoc Long we knew that we could advance faster than we had planned because there would be no American intervention. And the South Vietnamese army did not strike back successfully in Phuoc Long Province. Before, they had always fought back. But the ARVN did nothing to take back the town of Phuoc Binh, so we believed that this time we could move, and move fast.

After the fall of Phuoc Long, the South Vietnamese president Thieu sent a congressional delegation to the U.S. to ask for more ammunition and supplies. The delegation was led by Mr. Dinh Văn Dê, the chairman of the military committee in the Congress. He asked President Ford for $300 million in military aid and represented the picture of South Vietnam, and when President Ford listened to what he had to say, Ford knew there was nothing that he could do to prevent defeat in the South. When the delegation came back to Vietnam, Mr. Dê prepared a report and sent it to the revolutionary force in Hanoi to let them know what happened. Mr. Dê, you see, was a South Vietnamese congressman, but he was also working for the NLF. So he kept us posted on what was happening.

That is the degree to which we had infiltrated the government of South Vietnam—at the very highest levels. Dê presented his case in such a way that the U.S. government said no, that aid would do no good. When we got Dê's report we knew that there was no way that the U.S. government would intervene again in Vietnam.

We didn't have to infiltrate the American Embassy or the American Central Intelligence Agency in Saigon at low levels like secretaries. We actually maintained very high posts within those organizations. Absolutely the highest positions. We sent in a colonel from the NLF who was also a colonel in the South, and then he worked with the American military intelligence system. Another one of our infiltrators, Mr. Phan Xuan

An, wrote stories for *Time* magazine a lot. The special advisor to Mr. Thieu was also one of us—Huynh Van Trong. As a special advisor for Mr. Thieu, he met with Kissinger and Nixon and spoke with them, but all the time he was working with the NLF. Ha-ha!

We did not use women who were sleeping with American officials or intelligence officers. You see why we did not have to work that way. We did find that our infiltrations of the American Embassy and the Central Intelligence Agency were not that important, because they really didn't know much about what was going on.

I had been in Saigon many times and was in Saigon in 1975. I was not afraid of being betrayed by anyone. The system was very tight, and I had organized everything there, so I knew that our security system was good. I was the first Secetary of the Party in the South stationed in Saigon, and in the 1960s I was here. Then in 1975 I was in Tay Ninh province until I moved with the revolutionary forces back into Saigon once more.

I came into Saigon with the headquarters unit on the morning of April 30. I did not go to the Presidential Palace. That was not my assignment. I was delegated to oversee the receiving of all the mass media within the city. I was in charge of the looking after the ideological and psychological aspects of the city.

Were the Southerners afraid of a bloodbath when the NVA arrived? I don't believe so. Remember, I came from the city, and in 1968 I organized and directed the Tet Offensive in Saigon. I knew the people of the city and knew what they were thinking. They came out to the street to welcome the incoming army, so I knew that they were not afraid.

This place where we are talking now was the home of the former deputy U.S. ambassador, William Porter. When Mr. McGeorge Bundy and other high American government officials were visiting him here, who do you think was living next door to this house? I was! Porter and high American officials were right here in this courtyard talking, and I lived next door. Right over there. I could see them and hear them. There was nothing for me to fear in Saigon. I was protected by the populace. The people knew who I was and what I was doing.

If the U.S. had left behind some lower-level people in the Embassy when they left in 1975 it would have been very beneficial for both sides. Ambassador Graham Martin did not have to leave. Vu Van Mau demanded that the Americans leave because, he said, the National Liberation Front demanded it. The directive was not meant for the Embassy or the diplomatic people, though, it was meant to get the Defense Attaché Office military people—we wanted them out of the country. So that was a very big mistake. The Americans misunderstood that and withdrew the Embassy people.

Before we attacked Phuoc Long Province at the end of 1974, our plan was to capture the South by 1976. That is true. It was out of our hands, though. We hit Phuoc Long and then Ban Me Thuot. We intended then

to go to Kontum and Pleiku or east. What happened after that was all
the fault of the South Vietnamese troops. They just took off and ran
away. So the rapid emergency replanning of events had to take place.
Suddenly we did not have to wait until 1976 to complete our plans. We
were aware that Brigadier Ted Serong had proposed a withdrawal plan
to President Thieu, but we just did not think that Thieu would ever
order it to happen. The plan of Serong (we were aware of the details of
the plan at the same time that they were presented to President Thieu,
and we analyzed them, too) was to take groups from the central highlands
and protect the South. But President Thieu ordered a withdrawal, and
it was a chaotic withdrawal, and that was the end of the story. After taking over Ban Me Thuot, we had a meeting of high-ranking officials to
ponder the possibility of American intervention. It was attended by Le
Duan. The conclusion was that there was no way that the Americans
would intervene in the fighting to save the South. So we decided to
achieve the final victory in 1975, a year early.

I slept over there in the high-rise on the night of April 30. I was too
busy with my new duties, overseeing the mass media, working twenty-four
hours a day, and I didn't have any personal or private thoughts that day.
We had 400 reporters in Saigon, so it was important to keep the news
going out to the foreign reporters. For the first week of May, I was very
busy keeping the news going out.

There were some Western reporters here. Not all of them had run
away. Alan Dawson was here and I met with him, I recall.

As to Ambassador Graham Martin's account of why we shelled Tan
Son Nhut airport on the night of April 28, 1975—because the South Vietnamese Air Force had been allowed to fly its planes to Thailand—well,
that is just a made-up story. There never was any agreement with the
Russians about a time for the Americans to get out. Somebody made that
up. The Russians controlled nothing in Vietnam at that time. The Russian government was not even informed of what we planned or what was
happening.

The real reason we shelled the runway of Tan Son Nhut was not
because the Air Force had withdrawn their airplanes. We shelled the
airport simply because that is when the artillery units arrived within
shelling distance of Tan Son Nhut.

We did not shell the Americans during their withdrawal, because there
was a delegation from the South Vietnamese who came to Tan Son Nhut
to negotiate with people at our base at Camp Davis. General Minh took
power on the twenty-eighth and directed that people come to the air base
and talk to us. Because of that we stopped all of our plans to attack the
city. We had planned to shell the city with 150,000 artillery shells, but
because of appeals from a delegation from Minh, we stopped shelling the
city after the night of April 28. Father Chan Tin and Mr. Trung Ngoc
Lieng came to Tan Son Nhut to negotiate with the NLF.

Minh directed these people to come and talk to our side. We had a representative group from the North stationed in Tan Son Nhut, and there was communication going on at that time.

As for the security of the flight path from the U.S. Embassy to the sea, if you wanted to hit the helicopters, you had to position yourself where you could hit them. But our guns would be stationed in a marshy area, so we could not hit those planes. And there was no reason to do that since there were only civilians on board and not military personnel. We had nothing against them.

Two points. First, because this side was victorious, we are happy and not hateful. Second, we believe in forgiving and forgetting. When the two sides were enemies we had to fight, but once the war was over there was no more reason to be hateful. That is a cultural trait of the Vietnamese.

In 1954, when we tried to liberate the whole country and only got half of it, at that time we felt bitterness and hatred. But now we are victorious and so bear no hatred.

Of course the American government now owes the Vietnamese a moral obligation. There is no doubt about it. Whether or not that obligation is a financial one, that depends on how one believes. That is in dispute. There are differences of opinion on that. However, I believe that the American government should just contribute to the rebuilding of Vietnam, but not by paying a wartime reparation.

I have met with a number of journalists and researchers during the past months. Some of them were Americans. They have the same question: What should the Americans do in Vietnam now that the war is over?

The past is over. We can label the past anything we want to—mistake, evil, miscalculation. Whatever you want, you can call it. Personally, I believe it was something that was regrettable. I want to stop at that. But what was done was done. We cannot bring back the dead. And so now we have to try to go on, because we all live on the same planet, and if we carry on hatred it will not do anyone any good at all.

Nguyen Son
"There Is No Choice But to Stand Up"

When I was nineteen years old I had this tattoo put on my arm. It says "Born in the North to Die in the South." I was in school then. But after I got the tattoo I changed my mind. I didn't want to die in the South. And when it came my time to go into the military, I tried very hard to stay out of the Army. I was able to stay out until the war in the South was over. I wasn't in the military until 1977. I became a soldier, finally, because I was forced to. I was conscripted.

I was living in Hanoi in 1972 when I got the tattoo. I was in the tenth grade. That year the war became more intense and the school I went to had to be relocated outside Hanoi. Then I didn't go with the school at all any more. I stayed behind. I was in Hanoi when the bombings took place at Christmas in 1972.

As I recall it, from the fifteenth of December to the twenty-seventh, the bombers came. Prior to the fifteenth there had been bombings around Hanoi in the suburbs, and from the fifteenth to the twenty-seventh they bombed in Hanoi itself.

The first thing they hit was the broadcasting station. After the radio station was hit, they started to bomb everywhere in and around Hanoi. The An Duong area was the first area to receive very heavy bombings. Basically they bombed Hanoi only at night. I couldn't see anything at night but flashes of light. But I remember in the early morning once I saw planes dropping bombs. Another thing I saw was on the night of the twenty-fourth, near the morning of the twenty-fifth, there was another B-52 bombing in the Kham Thien area. A hospital was hit there, the Bach Mai hospital.

We weren't afraid of being killed by the Americans. I thought, "If I have to die, then I have to die." Of course we stayed away from important targets and many people were evacuated from the city. But also a lot of people died.

You need to understand this. In the beginning, in 1964, the people of the North were afraid of war and of the American planes. But as the war went on, people became sort of toughened; they were not afraid of the bombings and they would not give in. Instead of being afraid, they wanted to stop the bombers.

We received no explanation of the bombings from the government.

I didn't have any deep thoughts on the issue of the bombing. I saw some pilots escorted around Hanoi, but that was in 1967, not later. My house was near a generator building, and since that was the building that gave electricity for the city of Hanoi, it became an important target for bombing; so I got to see pilots who were shot down, taken prisoner, and being paraded. The people were not allowed to get close to the prisoners or talk with them. I only saw them from the distance. I didn't know anything about them, but I wondered why they had bombed us.

At that time I didn't have any feelings about the war or about the Americans. I just wanted to go to school, and I was not paying attention to political news or war reports from the South. But other people in the North were very interested in the fighting and in finding out what was happening with the war. They were really avid listeners and readers on the progress or nonprogress of the war.

I remember in 1972, Le Duc Tho and Henry Kissinger were involved in some sort of meeting preparing for the Paris treaty. Hanoi was bombed—while the meeting for the peace treaty was going on.

The Northerners, the civilians, wanted to not have war any more. And so they were really interested in the development of the negotiations and anything that had to do about discountinuing the war.

Many people died for the ideal of reunification. In my thinking, North or South are both Vietnam, so they should be one country. As I grew older I read more, and I became aware that the time came in 1956 when they were supposed to have a general election and there would then be peace for Vietnam through politics—peaceful measures—not through fighting with weapons. But I know that they didn't agree on what was supposed to happen and that is why we had the war.

I think that Ho Chi Minh was a hero. I really admire and respect him, as he was a very talented and astute leader. Like the way that Hitler was in Germany. He started out as a regular citizen, yet he traveled all over the world to try to find a way to regain independence for Vietnam from the French government. He also fought against the Japanese occupation. And that is why I have great respect for him.

I also respect General Vo Nguyen Giap. Let me tell you of his positions. He was a general. He was a member of the Politburo. He was the minister of the Defense Department. He is a talented person. He can speak many languages. He did not have as much respect as Ho Chi Minh did. Ho Chi Minh was a great national hero. Even after 1975 when there were a lot of important people whose names should be remembered in history, people didn't bother to know those people. They remember first Ho Chi Minh, second Pham Van Dong, and third Vo Nguyen Giap.

When I was around eighteen or nineteen, I thought that if the war was ever to end, it would not be until 1979 or 1980. I never thought it would come so soon. Not in 1975. Yet I never had any doubt that we would win the war.

Unless you live in a Communist state you would not understand why I think this way. You see the South *thought* that it would win and the North *knew* that it would win. There is a famous proverb in Vietnam regarding military tactics: "Know yourself, know your enemy, and then if you do that, you will always win." The South did not know anything about how it was in the North. But the North knew everything about the South.

The Northerners were never afraid of the American military forces. Why? A long time ago, when I was still a small kid, I heard this declaration from somebody in the American government—some general—who said they would "bomb North Vietnam into the Stone Age." They told us that in school. And then I remember how the Northerners were being made enthusiastic and patriotic by Ho Chi Minh, and he said that the war could last five, ten, or fifty years, and therefore we had to be prepared all the time. I remember being asked to analyze those statements in school. Then we became aware of our position and our standing in the war. And from that understanding, we became no longer afraid of the war.

You see, when people are pushed into a corner, there is no choice but to stand up and to meet trouble head on. And so there was no more fear, because we *had* to go on. We were forced into accepting our situation and our fate. We looked above us and there were the Americans dropping bombs on us, and we could only shoot back at them from the ground. If we could restrict the number of bombings, that was good. But what could we do and where could we go? There was no way for us to do anything but to accept the situation and do the best we could and not be afraid any more. And if we wanted to stop the bombing, we had to go to the South and push the Americans out of the country. That is the only way, we believed, that we could protect ourselves.

Life in the North was not normal because of the constant bombings and the strain of the war. People tried to do what they had to do, and everybody went about his business every day. The way things were produced, they were not of good quality because of the status of the country. Good quality would have come if we were at peace.

When Saigon surrendered, everybody celebrated and everybody was happy. I think there were four reasons why we celebrated.

First, the families that had members who were sent South to fight were happy and they celebrated because the country was reunited and there would be no more fighting, and their loved ones would come back to them.

Second was the new emotional and mental status of the Northerners. Before, life was always hard and people worried; and now with the war finished, people didn't have to be worrying about things like bombers and living or dying all the time any more.

The third reason had to do with the ability to reunite with the loved ones. Remember, in 1954, there were lots of people relocated to the South, and during the years that the war was going on, they lost touch, and they didn't know what had happened, who had lived and who had died. Now, with the country being one again, they could renew their relationships.

Fourth, the younger generation wanted to visit the South and make comparisons and see what life was really like there.

Was life any better after 1975 in Hanoi? Yes and no. As far as material life went, it got even worse after 1975. But it was better if you are talking about spiritual, psychological, or inner life. We had a more relaxed mental state after 1975, I would say, and that was good.

But prior to 1975 the Northern government received foreign aid from the European bloc of friendly nations and from China and Russia. Before the end of the war, those countries gave us aid so we could regain control of the South and reunify the country. They had a reason then to give us assistance. But with the victory in 1975, they started to take away aid, so we did not have anything to go on with. Another factor is that after so many years of war the rice fields were destroyed and the roads were destroyed and the pipes—everything was totally or partially destroyed. How would you expect us to recover right after the war, after so many years of bombing and destruction?

So life was harder for people starting in 1975. Even up to now there has been suffering and hardship in the North. In some cases it is even worse than during the war. But there was no longer that general and constant state of fear in people's minds. That was the best part about the end of the war.

Let me use an analogy. In the North, my friends and I used to talk about our lives, and we compared ourselves to leaves in a river. Life was a river, we said, and we were but leaves floating in that river. We had no control over our lives, or over our fates. Like the leaves propelled by the stream, we moved along, and like the leaves we had no way to choose where we would stop. The leaves could be stuck in clear water or they could be stuck in murky water when they moved along in the stream, but they had no control. We had no choice but to live the sort of life that was given to us. When we thought of our fate and our lives in that way, there was always part of me that wanted to break away from that kind of life.

Like my friends, I wanted to be able to be myself and to be able to do things that I chose to do and not what someone else chose for me. I am just a regular, normal person and that is all I ever wanted to be.

The war was planned and carried out by others. We normal citizens had nothing to do with that. We were like regular people anywhere in the world. We worked every day and we had to try to live a normal life.

Part Three

AFTERMATH

CHAPTER **XIX**

*Bui Doi**
"Dust of the Earth"

Lily
"I Have Seen So Many Bad Things in My Life"

My name is Huong, but people call me Lily. Only Lily. I am seventeen. I don't know who my father is. I need to go to America. I don't go to school here. I went to school in Vietnam only three years. Then I went to work.

Every day people say to me on the street, "Hello, American." People see my face. They know I have an American father. I have to go to school and some children they don't like me. They say "Amerasian no good." I'm sad when I hear that.

I listen to people who come here and who speak English and so now I can speak English. I work for tourists when they come here; I translate for them and show them the city. I want to go to America and I want to go to school, and then I want to become a painter. I cannot paint now because I must work all the time. My father in America is a Christian and my mother is a Buddhist. I want to paint religious pictures because it gives me something good to think about and I have seen so many bad things in life. I have suffered so much, so I don't want to think about that.

I like American music. I listen to it and I learn English.

I know something about the war. I've read about it. But I don't want anybody to think bad of my father, though, because of the war. Now I

* The Vietnamese term "Bui Doi" can be translated as "Dust of Life" and refers generally to anyone who belongs to no one. Specifically, the term is used today to refer to the Amerasian children who live on the streets of Ho Chi Minh City.

want a picture of my father so I can see what he looks like. I don't want to live with him. I just want to see what he looks like so I can know. I don't know anything about him now.

In the future I might want to have some children. But I want to do it in a way so that my children will not suffer the same fate that I suffered. Not without a father.

I would want to share my life experiences with my children so they will understand how hard life can be and they can be better people, so they will never be in a situation like I am in.

I am not happy. I smile and I laugh because I am talking to you. But there is nothing here to be happy about.

I listen to the song, "We Are the World." And I get very happy. People from many countries without problems singing. I want people to be like that. I don't want to see anything like war. Just happy people singing.

My Linh
"It's a Hard Life"

My father's name was Isaac. My mother showed me pictures of him. I have a Vietnamese husband now. I am going to have a baby so Isaac will be a grandfather. I wish I could tell him that.

I went to school until the sixth grade. Then I stayed home and helped my mother sell things on the street in Ho Chi Minh City. I want to go to America because my father is over there, and I want to learn to be a dressmaker. My father writes to me in English and he tells me about America.

It's a hard life. I have no religion. What is that?

I hope I can go to America this year. I have been trying to leave for the United States since 1981. But they won't let me go.

Nguyen Diep Doan Trang
"It Is Difficult for Me Here"

I am nineteen years old. I know nothing about my father. He was an American. I have no information on him, but I have a picture of my father's friend. My father's friend was a go-between for my mother and my father.

I finished my high school education last year. I help my mother in her job as a midwife now. My mother makes my clothes for me and makes them like American clothes.

I want to go to the U.S. because I look different from the people here and I think I look more like Americans, so it would better for me to live in America. I feel self-conscious because I am taller than my friends. I feel different and it is difficult for me here.

I know Americans through the picture of my father's friend, and through visitors. I have learned through magazines also. I want to go to the U.S. and go to the university there and become a chemist.

I don't know anything about the war. Nothing.

I think my father is a big, tall guy because of my size. If he knew that I was here he would love me. My mother told me in the past that my father really loved her. But they lost contact.

I want some day to tell my children about my life and about how I came to the United States of America.

Some day I want to get married and have two children. But first I want to go with my mother and two half-sisters to America.

Minh
"Half-Breed"

I have no other name. Just Minh. I am sixteen. I lived in Tay Ninh. I was looking after the cattle for my family. I was with those people since I was small. I called them Aunt and Uncle. I moved to Saigon and now I work in a coffee shop.

Somebody brought me to Saigon. I don't know who it was. I live with a family that runs a coffee shop and I live and eat there. I have never gone to school. I cannot read words.

When I lived in the countryside they did not treat me well. Here people call me names because I am half American. They call me "half-breed." But I am treated well in the coffee shop.

I know nothing about my father. I have no idea who my parents are. I have never known them. I think I love my parents, even though I don't know who they are or where they are. That, I think, is what love is, what I feel inside myself about my parents.

I want to go to the United States to find my father now. I have seen other people leaving for the U.S. and I want to go now. I don't know anything about America. Only what I hear people say about America.

I don't know anything about the war.

When I get to America I will do what I can do for work. I don't have any religion. I don't even know what that is.

I am an American. The people here say I am an American. So I am an American.

Vo Thi Quan Yen
"I Know I Am an American"

I am fifteen. In the beginning, I thought I was a Vietnamese. Then my father contacted me. Now I know I am an American. I don't know his name. I never knew him until now. I went to school until the seventh grade and then stopped. Then I started selling bananas on the street. Now I live with my aunt and uncle. They raised me. My mother is in contact with me also. But I feel no bond to my mother because she deserted me when I was six years old.

My father wants me to be in America now so I want to be there. I want to go to school again. Here life is hard. I want to become a doctor like my father, some day. He was a resident doctor at the Grall Hospital here, the French hospital. He left here in 1973.

I don't know anything about the war. But I watched movies and now I think the American government did not treat the Vietnamese people right. They did terrible things to the Vietnamese.

Up to six years of age, I had a normal childhood and did things that children do. But now I live with my aunt and uncle and they are poor. So now I work. I am a Buddhist because my aunt and uncle are Buddhist. My father is a Christian so when I get to America I will be a Christian. I could not imagine my father's face for a long time, but then I got his picture and now I think I look like my father.

I work every day. What I like to do is play ball or swim, but I cannot do those things because I have to go to work. Now I am looking forward to seeing my father and I hope that life will be better then.

I want to go, but I feel bad because I have to leave my aunt and uncle behind and I will miss my half sister. But I don't care what happens to my mother here. When I get to America I will bring my aunt and uncle and half sister to America.

Nguyen Ngoc Linh
"Life Will Be Better"

My parents abandoned me when I was a baby. Then they came back to get me in 1972. But I didn't want to leave then. My dad's name is John Small.

My parents were in contact with me and then Saigon fell and they got in touch with me again. I was in school until the sixth grade. Then I stopped going because I didn't like it any more. Now I don't do anything. I stay home. My parents in America send me money. I don't speak any English. I'll learn English in the U.S. when I get there. I don't know what

I want to be when I get to America. I think maybe I want to become a soccer player.

I don't know anything about the war.

I want to go to America because my parents and brothers and sisters are there, and if I go there life will be better.

CHAPTER **XX**

Vietnamese

Ly Thuy Ngoc
"What Do You Think It Means to Be Raped?"

I was born May 5, 1967. I came to the United States in 1981. We have six children in our family. My father was a businessman in Vietnam. We actually did well for a while under the Communists in a small town near Qui Nhon. We sold cassettes and music. We still could do that under the Communists. But before we left they said that some members of our family had been to the United States, so we could not sell cassettes anymore. I remember now my mother telling me to get ready to leave. I cried and didn't want to go, but she told me that she would join us soon. I was unhappy about leaving because I would be leaving my friends and my mother behind. I was afraid also of leaving. Maybe something was warning me about what would happen.

We left on a boat at night. The first time we escaped, the weather was so bad on the ocean we came back. And the second time we went, we came back, too. The second time I told my friends that I was going away to the U.S. And they told other friends, so we had to cancel that trip because too many people knew about it, and my parents were angry that I had told people. We were supposed to say that I was going to visit my aunt.

The next time there were forty-eight people on the boat with us. We ran out of water on the first day. And so after the first day we drank ocean water. Everyone got sick. I got sick and vomited.

Then the Thai pirates stopped our boat. We were out of food and water. We tried to signal them an SOS with some white fabric that we had. We didn't know they were pirates. And they raped one lady on our boat after they came to us. The first time they were all right and they just wanted gold. But then on the second and the third day they stopped us also. They took us all off the boat except for one woman. They went on the boat and all of them raped her.

Then they took us to an island. Nobody else was on the island. There was no water on the island, either. It was all dry.

They made us sit in a circle. They picked out the women and took some of them into the bushes to rape them. That was terrible.

I was just a skinny little kid then. Just a kid. And I didn't know anything. But they came and took me away and I was crying. I said I didn't want to go with them. I cried. But they took me. And they ripped my clothes off. I was so little and I didn't know what they were doing to me. I was skinny and I had no hair on my body even, I was so young. They grabbed me and took me into the bushes and then they hurt me. I wasn't just thinking of rape because I didn't really know what that was. But I thought they were trying to kill me. They didn't like me because my body was so skinny.

The men who were with us just had to stay in a circle and look at the ground when they did this to the women and the girls. And to me. But they knew what was happening. I was just so scared at that time.

They didn't kill any of us and they didn't beat up on the men. When they were finished they left us alone on the island. I just had my underpants on after that. They took our clothes when they left.

We then had to find something to eat and it was hard to live on the island. Then a few days later a Thai Navy ship came by with sailors on it. They picked us up and they treated us well. We were starving. They took us to Song Khla.

I was in Song Khla then for many months. My uncle then sponsored us to come to California. I was surprised when we arrived because everyone here is so rich.

I spoke some English because I had learned it in Song Khla. In school I didn't do well at first. I didn't know how to dress and I didn't have nice clothes. The other students picked on me. There was one girl on the bus who always beat up on me because I dressed so badly, I guess. I told the bus driver but she said she couldn't help me. You know, they pushed me and pulled my hair because I was so little, I guess. I was only about eighty pounds at the time.

Then after the eighth grade and I went to high school and everything was better. I did well in school then. Now I am in the university. My mother is still in Vietnam and I write to her.

I am not that happy here, really, after what happened. It was just too much for me. Last year I tried to kill myself again. I took too many pills and tried to kill myself.

My father does not treat me well. He never looked at me in the eye again after what the Thai pirates did to me. So we are not very close.

Very few men understand a woman being raped. Very few. I ask men,

"What do you think it means to be raped?" And they don't know. They don't understand. They don't know.

If I had a chance to do everything all over again I would never leave Vietnam. Such bad things happened after I left.

I remember those pirates and I dream about them sometimes. I remember them today even.

I cannot be affectionate. I cannot hold hands with someone or even be romantic now.

I don't know about the future. I don't know if I'll try to kill myself again. Who can tell?

Melissa Pham
"I Was Young Then"

When we left Saigon in April of 1975 we went directly to the Philippines. We stayed overnight and then went to Guam. We were there only a couple of days. Then we came to Fort Chaffee, Arkansas. Then we were sponsored by a church in Milwaukee, Wisconsin.

My dad didn't speak English. He communicated with the Americans only through a translator. Only my sister spoke any English.

Our whole family lived in an attic of the church annex with mattresses on the floor. Then they got us a house with three bedrooms and one bath, but our family is really large and so we were really crowded.

School was different and scary for me. Four of us went to the same school. They hired an American teacher who spoke Vietnamese, and he spent an hour with us every day after lunch. We were with the other students except for that one hour. We learned English quickly. We were especially good at math since that didn't take much English.

We lived there three years. I went to three different schools during that time and we were always the only Vietnamese there. On special occasions the Vietnamese in the region would get together. We found each other at those times.

In Chicago there was a Vietnamese priest, and he helped us, too. My father got a job in a welding shop. It was hard work for him because he hadn't done anything like that before.

My aunt went to Los Angeles. Another aunt who was with us on the ship lived first in Nebraska and then moved to San Jose. She wrote that things were better there because there were so many Vietnamese and they could help each other out. It was hard for us in Wisconsin because we all had jobs to support the family. And the oldest kids wanted to go to school as well as to work.

So we all came to California. But before we went my oldest sister married and moved to Texas, and my oldest brother married and stayed in Wisconsin. Then the rest of us moved to California.

I was in sixth grade when I arrived in San Jose. I went to a junior high school the next year. That was hard to adjust to, because living in the Midwest I found people were different. Here in California I found much more prejudice. And the children in the class had gone to school together for many years, and so it was hard to make friends since everyone was in groups at the time.

Most of the kids also were physically bigger than me. They made fun of me sometimes because I was Vietnamese, imitating my voice and language. And when you're young that hurts, probably more than it should.

My sister and brother were in a different school but they noticed it, too. And sometimes on the street strangers would say mean things or imitate your voice.

Then I went to a high school. The teachers treated me well and I did well in school. I was the valedictorian of my class in high school. I had also been at the top of the class in junior high school. Now I am in college and am studying computer engineering.

I want some day to marry and have maybe two children. I don't want a big family like my parents. Here it is just too expensive to have many children. I will probably marry a Vietnamese. I would prefer that. It has to do with the culture and getting along with someone.

I am between two worlds right now. I am not sure which one I belong to any longer. The problem is in communication and in thinking. I am a stranger often when I am with all Vietnamese. But when I am with Americans I am a stranger, too.

I cannot speak the Vietnamese language all that well anymore. But I am not really an American either because of my experience. My friends feel that way, too. I even dream in both languages. Isn't that strange?

Now and then I dream of Vietnam and remember my friends there. I miss the feeling that we had there on special occasions: celebrations, the lights, and going out to other people's homes. I miss that.

I was young then. So young. I look at the pictures of myself in Vietnam and I don't seem to recognize myself. It was like moving to another world when I came to America and leaving that world behind. And that was hard because I was just a kid.

Thao Mong Nguyen
"I Always Loved Abraham Lincoln"

We went to Guam for a couple of weeks after we left Saigon, and then we went to Fort Chaffee. My father left there first. A church in Connecticut sponsored us. He went ahead and got a job, and the sponsors got us a place to stay.

The teachers in Connecticut all called me by my sister's name and put me in the wrong grade. They called her by my name. We stayed there for one year. In school everyone fought to be our friends. They argued so they could sit with us at the table. And they were always giving me presents. Jewelry and things. A little girl named Tiffany always drew horse pictures and gave them to me.

I had two birthdays and that confused the American children, because we followed the lunar calendar. I gave the kids both dates in school for my birthdays. I found it hard to explain to them.

I was way ahead of all the kids in math and the teacher kept slowing me down. And I could speak French then, but not English, and the kids were amazed by that. I had no English at all. I communicated generally in sign language at the time.

My aunt moved to Washington with her husband. I remember the morning she called and told us that her daughter had shot herself with a gun they had in the house. They had all been downstairs talking, and the children were playing upstairs. The little girls found a gun and they were playing with it and it went off and shot her through the head. At the hospital she was still crying, "Mommy, Mommy." But she died there. And my aunt called us and I remember telling my class about it in school. I had to use a lot of sign language and French and Vietnamese to tell my classmates what had happened. And I was crying.

I knew my cousin. It was strange because when the phone rang at three in the morning, and my mom answered it, I got up and went into her room.

After she talked on the phone my mom and I went outside. It was snowing then, at night. It was the first time I had ever seen snow. It was a bright night outside and everything was white that night. It was just before Christmas. And it affected me deeply, her death.

I remember that I cried that night. So did my mom. Several months later, in the summer, we moved to Washington. We drove from Connecticut to the state of Washington. We drove across the U.S. in this fifty-dollar car that my dad bought. He's a good mechanic and he kept it in good running condition. We drove across the country in this Oldsmobile, all of us in the back with three in the front. We saw all of the parks and monuments of America. We saw Mount Rushmore with Abraham Lincoln on it. I always loved Abraham Lincoln.

It took us a month to cross the country and to learn about it as we crossed it. We stayed with friends or in motels. We met all sorts of Americans at rest areas along the highway and talked with them. It was another big adventure and we all loved it.

Then we went to my cousin's grave in Washington. I remember feeling a lot of anger. What was the gun doing in the house? And why should she die in the United States after all we went through in Vietnam? But I didn't dwell on it because I thought I would crack if I did. I knew that. So I didn't dare dwell on my cousin's death.

At the cemetery they had these trees, and they had little nuts growing on them and I picked one and kept it. I don't know why I keep it. But I do.

We moved to Seattle. My mom's sister married an American, a white American, and my dad thought that might be a bad influence. My dad worked with the Americans, spoke their language, got along with them just fine, and he didn't want any of us to marry one. I thought that was strange.

In Seattle there were more Asians than in Connecticut. I was still in the ESL* program at that time. I started to do well in classes, too. I had still had this drive to be number one; that stayed with me since I was in Vietnam.

We were in Washington from third to seventh grade. My dad then had friends down here in California and he got a job here, so we came down.

I feel bad for saying it, but there are too many Vietnamese here. I feel like I shouldn't say it. But I wonder who they are. Are they traitors, or who are they? There are so many of them.

I'd like to go back to Vietnam to visit. I have this identity thing. I sometimes forget that I'm Vietnamese. And then I'll look in the mirror and think, "Oh-oh, you're Vietnamese, Thao. Don't forget it." It's really hard. At the Olympics or on the Fourth of July, I feel completely American. And I am curious. If Vietnam was in the Olympics, I would cheer for America. This is my country now. I think that's why I don't like to be around too many Vietnamese.

I don't dream about Vietnam. I look at pictures of Vietnam and can't remember things. I remember some things, a few, but with no real details. The older children remember more.

I resent the fact now that people label me something. I don't fit in with the whites that well, or with the Vietnamese, either. In Washington all of my friends were white Americans. Once I picked up English I fit in really well. And when people hear us but don't see us, they think we are white Americans. Yet they find it very hard to accept that we are really Americans now.

My older sister now lives in San Francisco. She's an artist. She's very creative. Right now she is writing a book. But I try to stay away from conversations about her. You see, she lives with her boyfriend. My dad has disowned her now and never mentions her name.

I go into depressions sometime. It's family-rooted. I don't handle stress too well. My sister put my parents through some rough times, and I resent that. I go out. I have more male friends than female friends. Of all nationalities.

I want kids, but only after I've done my own thing. After I figure out what I want to do.

I go to the university, but I pay for my own schooling now. I work as

* English as a Second Language.

a secretary. At home I'm like the other kids. I don't have to pay for rent or food. But I am responsible for my younger brothers and sisters.

I've always dreamed of having a big kitchen to cook in. But I've always worried that my dad would not like my cooking. I love my dad, with all my heart. But I detest all the things he stands for, almost as much as I love him. I understand his side and his past. But at the same time I believe he should try to understand my side and my sister's side. Our side and our life. We don't live in Vietnam any more, and he doesn't seem to realize that. We just don't talk at home. I'm always the only person who talks at home. I talk, but he doesn't. He gets upset and he sends me to my room. Whenever we have a problem, when my brothers or sisters want something, I end up asking for them and taking the blame.

Lately, I sort of want to move out. My dad said, "If any of you marry a white boy I'll disown you." And my Mom said, "Did you all hear that?" I understand why he says it, but it really hurts me. If we all just marry Americans, we'll lose something, of course. But he doesn't understand.

Van Thuy Mac
"I Am a Half-and-Half"

I was born in 1967 in Saigon. My father is an American. My sister is fifteen and she has a different father. My mother never married my father. She helped my grandparents run a restaurant in Saigon.

They ran a small restaurant down in the Delta. My father left Vietnam in 1973, and then he came back and asked my mom to come with him to America. She didn't want to. In 1975 he wrote to her again and asked her to come to America. She refused again and he wrote back and said then he would marry someone else. And now he has another family.

I lived in Saigon until 1975 and then moved to the Delta to a village between My Tho and Ben Tre. I went to school there. Some of the people looked at me because I was different, part American. They didn't like that.

I lived there until 1979. Then I left Vietnam. My aunt and her husband and two sons wanted to leave the country. We went to them to say goodbye. And on that day my grandparents said that they should send me with them because in America I would have a better future. So my mother decided to send me.

We took a big boat out of My Tho. We were on the boat eight days and nine nights. We stopped in Malaysia. They didn't want us to come in, so they shot at us. Some of the people on the boat got wounded. So the captain said that all we needed was water. They gave us water and we sailed to Indonesia.

I was sick during most of the voyage. I was too young to be aware of most of what was happening. I was happy in Vietnam. But I don't think

I had much of a future. In school we had to do labor on the weekends. I didn't learn much in school. Some of the grades depended on just how hard you worked.

I lived in three different places in Indonesia. The first place was completely abandoned. We had to take a boat for water, and there were no people but us. Some of the people were wealthy and brought gold when we left Vietnam. But they spent their money for food in areas around us when we were in Indonesia. We had to pay for a boat to take us to another island to buy food.

Then there was another camp, with Americans to help us. And they moved us there. We lived in the second camp for one year. Many people died. About every day someone would die because of the water, which was not clean. The mosquitos also got people sick.

I had two cousins in America. We wrote them letters and they sponsored us to come to America. We had nobody else to sponsor us.

I arrived in San Francisco in 1981. I spoke no English at that time. I was happy, but I was afraid because everyone was white. I didn't know what I would do in America.

I lived with relatives in a house. I started in seventh grade and I spoke no English, so I was in the ESL program. I learned English during that year and then started to do well in school. After one year I could keep a conversation going.

I went to a junior high school and then to Independence High School in San Jose. I had a 3.3 average in school. I am in business accounting at San Jose State University now. I want to go into business in America. I work in a store now to pay my way through college.

I am Vietnamese. That's what I am because that is where I grew up. Culturally, that's what I am. Usually, when I meet someone new they ask me if I am a "half-and-half." They recognize that.

Some day I will marry and have two children. It is too expensive to have more children than that in America.

Once when I was young I wanted to meet my father. But I am no longer very curious about my father. I know that he has another family. And I might bring some problems to him if I see him. It is better that I not see him. And so I don't think I ever will.

Nguyen Thi Kim-Anh
"We Tried to Forget Most of the Bad Things"

The day after the fall of Saigon my sister and I tried to leave by boat from Vung Tau. We dressed as peasants in black pajamas and conical hats and went to Vung Tau, and we paid 150,000 piasters each to get on a small boat to leave. We got out only about a kilometer, however, when a patrol boat caught us and brought us back in. They locked us up in an open area next to a school for one night. We were laughing because we lied to them, saying that we wanted to go back to our own village because we ran away during the war and now we wanted to start our new life, and so on. It was only the first day after they took over and they didn't have any kind of policy to treat the people who tried to run away, so they just locked us in for one night. We talked all night without being afraid. The next day they gave us some corn and let us go.

We took the bus back to Saigon. We'd lost all our money, and we were still in Vietnam. That was my first trip. Not until the sixth time did I succeed in escaping, and that was when I disguised myself as a Chinese, in July, 1979.

Back in Saigon people were still running around. There were a lot of people on the street. From that day on we started to see a lot more North Vietnamese soldiers on the street.

The schools reopened and they asked all the teachers to go to one school to study the new policy and the new kind of discipline and the new curriculum. We had to study for twenty days. Then they gave us our certificate saying that we had completed the required course. We had to write a paper every day on a topic like "Why We Like Ho Chi Minh," and every other kind of lie, too.

The lecturers were from both the North and the South, and they talked about Communism and how they won the war and complained that the American government had destroyed the country. We just copied everything down and made it into a very nice paper to turn it back in. If you said exactly what they said, agreed with them one hundred percent, you got a perfect score.

The first session we attended had around five or six hundred teachers from our one area. Among ourselves, when we were with friends, we'd talk honestly to each other. But whenever they saw a group sitting and talking together they would send another person over to sit in the middle, and the discussion would either change or stop completely. They tried to control everything, but especially private conversations. They thought those were very dangerous because they didn't know what was said.

The new semester started in July of 1975. They kept the same administrators as the previous semester because they didn't have enough people to replace them. For every school they sent in Party members to be the group leaders. They divided the school into a social studies and language group and a social science group. The two leaders would be the Party members. In some schools they'd select one person who they thought would be a good Party supervisor. I was picked as one of them—a leader of the foreign language group. They didn't have anybody else, and I wrote what they wanted on the examinations, so they picked me as a group leader.

In my group we had nine members, so three of us were teaching French and English, and the others had literature and social studies; but we'd known each other for two or three years already. Once a week we had the meeting and the other group leader would come and visit and share in the discussions. But once he left, we'd talk immediately about leaving and how to get out. We even convinced one of the Party members who was very young that the Party was bad, and she wanted to leave—when I left the country she wrote to me here. She came to my home and asked my sister for my address and she wrote to me. She said that because her father was a Party member for years, she'd gotten into it. She had been treated well and lived well in the North because of her father, but when she came to the South and worked with us, she liked us a lot. She knew that my family left Saigon in '75 and she knew we were ready to go, so she protected us. She even lied for us. On the day that I left and didn't make it, I told her that I was going to visit my parents. So she was my excuse if anybody asked, even though she knew that my parents were already gone. A lot of people, you see, thought I was going to be a Party member. I tried to be friends with her so she could cover me when something happened.

In November 1975 I left again, and I left her a note saying I was going to visit my parents. If after ten days of teaching leave I didn't come back and report to her, I wanted her to say that something may have happened to me. And so she said I was visiting my parents. Then after three on four days I couldn't make it, so I came back and she just smiled at me. She kept covering up for me. She was great.

Every single time I tried to leave, I lost money. I went to a friend's in Nha Trang the second time, and they said that at five o'clock we were going to leave Nha Trang to go to this special area. So we all gathered at the station area to wait for the Lambretta to pick us up. We waited—five, five-thirty, six, six-thirty, seven, seven-thirty—and nobody came to pick us up. They had just taken our money and abandoned us.

At the end of 1975 my aunt came down to visit us from the North. She had been living there when we left in 1954, and I was very small and didn't remember her at all. She brought us rice and some eggs and things because she heard that the people of Saigon were really poor and she wanted to help us. My uncle came with her and told us that they were told that the South was so poor that the North had to fight against the Americans to save the South. That's why the Northern people had a very strong faith in trying to save their brothers and sisters in the South.

The Communists kept changing the money system in those days; I don't know why. After two times a lot of people committed suicide because they couldn't get enough money to support themselves—some of the wealthy people, especially some of the Chinese. If they had gold they could hide it somewhere, and that is why everyone wanted to get gold. But the money became worthless again and again.

The Communists let the Chinese out very easily; first for money, and second to avoid problems. They didn't want problems with China. And they didn't want any Chinese in Vietnam.

So I learned some Chinese and got some Chinese clothes, and so did my sister. Then we paid our money and went down to the Delta and got on a boat to Malaysia. It took us three days and four nights to get there.

On the way to Malaysia we were stopped and robbed six different times by Thai pirates. We lost everything on the way to Malaysia. Everything but our lives.

The first moment we saw the Thai pirate ship we thought that it was some foreign ship coming to rescue us and we were all jumping and shouting because we thought we were safe at last. But we used our binoculars and saw the flag and we knew what was going to happen. Some of the people already knew about the pirates so they asked us to change our clothes and darken our faces and bodies with charcoal to make us look ugly—all the women. So we did it. We changed to men's clothes. And we darkened our bodies. We had time because we saw the boat from far away.

When we were first stopped by Thai pirates they beat up our pilot. They almost beat him to death. When they asked him for all of our gold, instead of saying, "We don't have it," he said that we used the gold to buy the oil and gas. But they didn't speak our language and so they thought he said it was in the oil and the gas. So they took all the gas and oil and drained it to look for gold in the bottom of the containers. When they couldn't find it they beat him so badly they tried to kill him. They had him lie face down on the deck, and then in front of us they jumped up and down on his back and legs and head.

The sixth time we got stopped wasn't that bad, because when they came to our boat everything was gone. There was not even a piece of cloth. They took everything. They left some fish sauce and some rice. But the last ones, when they saw they couldn't get anything from us, gave us some fish and milk for the children and even towed our boat to Malaysia. Kind pirates, I guess.

After the first pirates left us we had no fuel and the pilot was unconscious, so we just drifted. We got scared because it was night and there was no light anywhere. They had even thrown our compass into the sea.

We all thought we would die then. One day we saw some ships passing by, and we raised the flag and waved and nobody stopped. The next morning we met a second one, and they came over and robbed us again. These pirates were so young, I guess sixteen or seventeen. They'd shaved their heads and whitened their hands. Each of them had a very long knife and held it to the throat of every person on the boat asking for money. They knew only a few Vietnamese words: money, dollars, gold, watch— that's it. We were so terrified. You never knew what they were going to do.

When we go to Malaysia, we saw a small boat with Vietnamese people fishing, wearing colorful dress, because they got it from the Red Cross.

Some of them stayed there for two or three years, so their skin color also changed—their skin got so dark. When we saw them, two boats fishing, we thought they were Malaysian and would do the same as the Thais. We told the pilot to try to get away. The Vietnamese kept coming after us, saying, "Over here! Over here!" Finally we recognized the Vietnamese sound and we stopped.

They told us to go straight to the refugee area. And they said just before we got there we had to try some way to sink our boat. If not, the Malaysians would make us leave. So we did that. And we jumped into the sea. They used the hammer and broke the bottom of the boat out. And we ran up across the beach into the camp and hid.

A German group came and asked us to identify ourselves. And they asked us to climb into the wrecked boat again and jump out so they could film us!

We laughed. We couldn't believe it. They wanted us to swim back out to our boat, get into it and then jump out and swim back to shore so they could make a movie! Strange. But we did it for them and we got to stay.

So our first moment of freedom was spent being movie stars. And in time we tried to forget most of the bad things that happened to us because we knew now that we were free.

Nguyen Son
"We Would Leave and We Would Forget"

I had the idea of coming to the U.S. since I was only twelve years old. Even during the war years, I was curious and wanted to come to the U.S. and so did many of my friends. I had no means to achieve that goal at an early age. My friends and I, during the war, we had talked about trying to come to America. And we thought we would even like very much to leave the North and go to the South. We had to face bombings and shellings in the North and just trying to keep ourselves safe. We were young and had no plans and no directions, and we didn't know how we would be treated once we got to the South.

Finally, we didn't know if we would be condemned if we finally got to the South. We didn't want to go to jail in the South just for going there from the North. But of course during the war it was just not possible to do that.

I was conscripted into the army to fight against the Chinese or the Cambodians. I deserted after seven months in the military and I returned to Hanoi. My mother then said that the best thing for me now was to learn how to navigate a boat. So I took a six-month course on navigating a boat in the river waterways of the North.

When I was taking that course, friends asked me if I was planning to escape, and I told them yes. After that, a bunch of us bought a boat.

Then during the period of 1979 and 1980, the government was deporting Vietnamese of Chinese descent. By listening to the radio, we became aware that the U.N. was now involved in the issue of refugees.

I left with my brother and sister. After we were stopped and checked at Haiphong port, I drove the boat on the riverways out to the sea, and there the other people joined us. There were fifty people at that time in that boat.

So we took a boat from Hanoi to Hong Kong. Our decision was that we would leave and we would forget and we would not ever come back to Hanoi.

By leaving we made the statement that we rejected the kind of society that we had and we would rather make a life for ourselves elsewhere. We also accepted the fact that we might live or die. If we lived through it, then we would not ever return to Hanoi, because that would mean imprisonment or a very bleak existence. If we escaped from the country they would never forget nor forgive us.

We thought that taking a trip at sea was not as dangerous as it turned out to be, and so we were really positive in our thinking. We were thinking that we would survive. And we would then be able to build a better future for ourselves and for our children in a free country.

When we arrived in Hong Kong we were treated very nicely. We were allowed to select the country where we wished to be resettled.

Many people in the North feel like me, and wanted to do the things that I did. During the war years we were all subjected to the same conditions, so life went on. If I went against the stream at that time, then I would be dead for sure. So I had to wait until the war was over.

Had I stayed in Hanoi, my life would be different from what it is now here in the United States. First, I would probably be married and have children. Here I am still single. And second, my hair would not be as white as it is here, because here in America now I have too many worries. Probably my life there would be more settled.

I worry a lot now. I lost my job and I am unemployed, and I have to live with my friends and my sister.

Sometimes I think maybe I should return to Vietnam. No, no, that is just a joke! Just a joke we sometimes use.

Seriously speaking, I have often pondered the issue at night and I have always come to the answer to the question in the same way: leaving the country was the right decision for me. I always say to myself, at the end, I have made the right move. I have nothing to regret, really.

My mind is open here and I am always learning. I feel that I am growing now intellectually and I enjoy that. I meet different kinds of people all the time with different ideas and we talk. Nobody has the big fear here. I enjoy that, too.

I made the right decision to leave the country and what I have chosen is what I wanted. And it is worth it here.

The day that I left Vietnam, I left with the clear-cut idea that I just wanted to leave as fast as I could and never look back. Then when our boat got into international waters with the strong waves beating on it, we started to feel uneasy, and there was a tremendous urge to turn around and go back. It was only seven or eight hours after we left. We already missed the country and we missed our homes, and we realized what we had done and we started to cry. All of us looked back at Vietnam and we just cried.

I left with just a set of clothing with me. I knew that life would not be easy and there would be difficulties and obstacles, and we would have to exchange blood and tears for a living. But we wanted to go ahead and go. And yet when we were in safe waters, we just wanted to go home, and we cried and cried.

Now never a day or a night goes by that I don't think about Vietnam. In my memories I see my family members, I see my relatives, my neighbors, my parents. I remember everything, even a corner of the neighborhood, the trees. Vietnam is totally with me, within my mind. But you must understand, I lived for twenty-five years in Vietnam; that is where I grew up; that is where I had all the bittersweet memories of childhood, teenage years, and early adult years. I lived there for a quarter of a century, and I soaked up a lot of memories there. I cannot just throw them away. They are always with me.

To turn to reality here in the U.S.—I do want an education. Since my mind is full of memories and images of Vietnam, I can't study and I can't learn any more here. Things that the teacher says go in one ear and out the other ear. Except for common pleasantries that one needs to know in order to live here—those things I remember. But other things, I just can't retain, because my mind is so full of Vietnam.

The first day that I settled in the U.S. I made up my mind that I had to mix in and adjust and accept this life. I accepted that. But then again, you would have to give me some time so I can think about Vietnam, too. If I work for eight hours then I won't think of Vietnam but about my job. But when I am not on the job then I think about my home. Then after dinner I turn on the television and I start watching it, and not fully understanding it. I am not good with the language. So then my mind drifts back to Vietnam every night. On the weekends I am with my friends and we naturally talk about home. It is always with me. If I was without other Vietnamese around me, then I might be able to nourish the feeling less for Vietnam, because then I would deal with Americans all the time. But here I am surrounded by other Vietnamese. And we remember. It is in our bones.

I think that even though the older leaders will one day die off in Vietnam, the younger men will come to power and they will see the way of the older generation, and they will copy them. I see no happy future for Vietnam until perhaps after the year 2000. The people are not being enlightened there. Some students go to the East European bloc countries and go to school, but when they go home they can do nothing because the country is poor and there are few educated people, and they are not allowed to see what is really going on in the world. In this way you cannot expect to have an improvement in the standard of living. In order for the country to progress, the leaders of the government should make a change in the way that they do things. They should act according to the people's needs and wishes. If people want to work only eight hours a day, they should then get to work eight hours a day. If they do not want corruption, then there should not be corruption. The leaders of the country should walk along with the people, and try to understand them more if they are going to improve the country. But right now they are not doing that. The leaders force on the people what they want done. And the people do what is demanded of them. But they are poor and they suffer. The people work hard now, and the harder they work, the worse off they are.

Vu Thi Kim Vinh
"A Picture We Could Look At and Dream"

After April 30, when Saigon fell, people were forced to make public confessions and denounce their parents or their children or their friends. And they did it. People didn't care about what they said any more. Everybody was simply worried about making a good impression and surviving. You had to say those things in order for the new order to treat you nicely. I was saying that I hated people like my parents because of what they said and what they expected from us. I wanted to survive, and I didn't care what I said.

Every morning at six they woke us up with two large loudspeakers. We then had to go out in the street for what I eventually called "Jane Fonda Time." We went out in the street and they took roll, and we did exercises. No matter how old you were or what condition you were in you had to do the exercises. They had some funny music and a voice that shouted "One, two, three," just like in the book *1984*. It was ridiculous. I looked at many of the old women who had to do this and I thought, "What kind of new society, what kind of regime has no respect for anybody like this?"

After that, we were forced to volunteer to go out to the countryside to build the houses and repair the roofs in the New Economic Zones. They said we were volunteers but we were not volunteers at all. If you did not want to go, they would cut off your food and your other rations. My mother she could buy things on the black market even if they took away our food and our rations, but still they did not let us alone. They said that if one of your children did not volunteer to go to the countryside, then your whole family would have to go to the new economic zone. So I volunteered.

They really tricked us. At that time only my mom was at home because my father was in jail. And that, too, was because of a trick they played on us.

At first they said that the lowest rank in the military would only have to go for two days for studying and re-education. Then the higher ranks saw that and thought that the Communists had kept their promise. So my father and my brother-in-law voluntarily signed up for a mandatory "six-week term" of re-education. And they left Saigon with the others.

After that time was up we expected my brother-in-law and my father to come home, and they didn't. I remember well that day when the men were supposed to return from re-education. I remember seeing the faces of the sisters, brothers, wives, and children of the men who were supposed to be coming home, of those who had parents or fathers or husbands or brothers in the concentration camps. Even if I were very liberal, very neutral, I could never forgive the Communists for what they did at that time, since I saw the eyes of the people who were waiting, who had believed the Communists.

Everything was bright on that day and everyone put on bright clothes because they believed that on this day their fathers and loved ones would come home, and they cooked and decorated their homes, and they all talked about good memories. They then were disappointed and upset because the men never came home. So the women went to the capitol to ask the head guy when the men would come home. Of course the Communist leader didn't show up to see them. Even with the Nguyen Van Thieu government, you could deal with them through the press or through someone in the government, but with the Communists you have no right to do that. The soldiers outside would not let them in.

My friends and my mother asked one Communist official, "Why did you say that today was the day our husbands could come home, after six weeks?" And he said, "Six weeks is six weeks for transportation, not the six weeks that they will spend in the camp. Those guys who are there thought they were too big, and they owe a lot of blood to the people of Vietnam, so they cannot come home this easily." They did not let anybody know where they kept the people.

In 1984 my father finally came back from the concentration camp. Six weeks became nine years!

During those days we lived in terror because we never knew what was going to happen. On the night before my father was supposed to come home, six weeks or so after he left, a big group of soldiers came to our house and they wanted to search our house. It was two in the morning. They rang the bell, and rang and rang. We were so scared because my father was gone. When we asked who it was, they yelled with a high voice, "It is the liberators! It is the National Liberation Front!" They said it very sternly, and we opened the door and here was this kid. He addressed my mother as "Sister," and he said, "Did your husband go to the camp?" And she said "Yes," but they searched anyway. The real reason they were searching was for money, for gold.

At that time we still had a calendar on the wall with a very nice, healthy, and very physical Japanese girl on it, and she had a shirt on over a bikini and she was looking out to the sea and was very happy. He said, "You have to take this down; it is obscene and it is not a nice thing! It is a hangover from the former regime. It is bad. You have to take it down. Right now!" We almost cried because it was something, a picture that we could look at and dream, and see the sea and the blue sky and a happy woman, and we knew that we would never, ever be like that girl in that picture anymore. And now he wanted us to tear it up in front of him right away.

Saigon was really hot in June, and my brother just had on a pair of shorts, and the soldier who was the same age as my brother said, "The way that you are dressed shows no respect!" He yelled at my brother at two in the morning. My brother said he was not wearing a shirt because it was so hot, and this soldier screamed, "Don't talk back to me. Don't talk back to me, okay!?" My mother apologized and my brother then apologized. The soldier then looked at my sisters. Perhaps he had to act like that to try to impress them. My sisters, when they slept, wore light clothes. And he looked at them and said, "This house is a stinking place, the way you dress and the calendar like that. You have to be more open and study a lot from the new life. Our life is decent and your life is filthy." Then the soldiers left.

One reason I will never forget about this is because I saw the look on my brother's face that night. And you see, my brother later died. He was a graduate of high school, and he took the tests to get into the medical school and engineering school. He was a very smart young man, very smart. And he was very kind and gentle. He knew that he could not get into the school because of his background; because of my father. We were Catholic and we were not poor, and my father had been a colonel in the South Vietnamese Army. My brother got a very high score. We knew that, because on my father's side there were a lot of people who worked in the system. My uncle controlled the medical school temporarily, and he was the one who saw all of the examinations. The teachers who scored the exams and the doctors were still the former ones at that time. And the teachers and the doctors gave my brother the very highest score in the medical school test at that time. Then they looked at his background and simply threw his score out. We knew that he did well, and it hurt deeply when he did not get admitted to medical school. He had the highest score in Saigon.

He then had to get a job, because if you did not have a job they would send you to a new economic zone. My mother did not want him to waste his life in a new economic zone, and so she searched for a way to get him out of the country. At that time, they forced him into the Youth Volunteers to build roads and to go work in the jungle. He had to sign a paper saying that he volunteered.

Finally, we had to do a trick. We lived in a society in which the government tricked and cheated the people. And so to live we now had to learn to trick and to cheat, also. We had to learn the rules of the game. My mom bribed a nurse to say that my brother had an accident and broke his arm and that he had to have a cast on for months. The nurse signed a paper saying he broke his arm, and my mother gave her a two-wheeled Honda for it. We paid a man to come to our house and yell loudly so all in the area would hear, yelling that my brother got in an accident and that the vehicle drove away. Then we brought him home with his arm in a cast. The neighbors came to see him, along with the block monitor and the councilman. The councilman used to work for my mom, and his family had been poor. He was a bricklayer and now he was the councilman. My mom had been kind to him always. Now he was a very important man. He asked what had happened. We were all crying, and my mom said that tomorrow my brother was supposed to go to the new economic zone and he wanted to contribute to the country, and now he could no longer do that and we were all so disappointed. And the councilman said it was all right and that he could go later after his arm healed. Every three months they sent people, so my brother was now safe for three months.

Our living room was now a place where people worked. My mother could knit very well and was very creative. Nobody could do it as nice as her, so they made her a director of a small knitting business in our home. The women knitted in our home each day. They got the wool from the East Germans and they earned around 50 cents for each sweater that the women knitted in the house. The women whose husbands were in the concentration camps came to our house to work on these projects. In the evening, when everybody went home and we closed the windows, my brother would take off his cast.

After six months we found a way for him to go. He always said that if he was lucky he would be free; if he was not, he would die because he was not. But if he stayed he would die anyway in Vietnam.

We found a way for him to go on a boat to Malaysia. He got a stomachache during the boat trip. They took him to a hospital and found an intestinal infection. It was getting serious. They said that if he had spent one more day on the sea he would have died. So they saved his life in Malaysia.

We thought he would go to America and go to medical school and become a doctor. But when he finally got to America he had to work. He then studied English and studied for admission to an American medical school. Yet he got very ill there again, and he died before he could go to medical school.

My mother bought a false name for me in Vietnam. I was able then to go to school again at a lesser grade. If you graduated with a background like mine you could not get a job or get into a college. So I stayed in high school after we got the proper documentation. I spent two years in eleventh grade.

I became one of the boat people. I left the country in 1979 on a boat and went to Singapore. But the people there didn't want us, so they used a big ship to pull us out. They hit us with their ship and our boat almost sank.

I was laughing. Only my friend and I laughed. I saw all the other people on the boat crying and praying. But we said, "There is nothing to cry about now." I don't know why I had that attitude. Maybe because I was single and by myself and had no goal and no money and no nothing. I had to sit at the bottom of the boat for six days. I was no longer a human being down there. People urinated on my head. I had to sit underneath the people for six days. I could not stretch my legs. My legs became numb. At that time the people were not people anymore. They could kill you easily. I thought if people made me mad and I was stronger I would have killed somebody, because life meant nothing. Finally, I was so tired. Every time someone urinated on my head I said, "Oh, hot tea, hot tea! It's tea time."

I got sick and did not have enough water. I was dehydrated, yet I was still so polite. They had a plastic bag for people to urinate in. They transferred it to the top deck and emptied it into the sea. But if someone didn't pass it along right, it would spill and run through the deck and down on us at the bottom of the boat.

But in a way I was lucky because we did not see Thai pirates. Our captain chose to go to Singapore so we didn't see the Thais. In Singapore they gave us water and some rations, some C-rations, which we called "Carnations." We called them that after the Americans came there. When I was little that is what we called the American soldiers—Carnations. They were the only American flowers that we ever had. Carnations reminded me of my father and made me sad because when I was with my father he also ate the American carnations.

We left Singapore and went to Malaysia. I was in Malaysia almost a year. I was unlucky when I was there. But I still think today I am lucky. The people at the village near where we tried to land in Malaysia used M-16s to shoot at us to get us to go away. They fired into the water and over the top of us.

But the captain decided to sink the boat, and he destroyed the engine. So we had to land in Malaysia. Everybody escaped and went ashore. We grabbed something that would float on the water. They kept us afloat in the sea for two hours, and finally they got bored with that game and let us walk up on the beach.

My brother sponsored me to San Francisco. It was hard to adjust, because everything seemed so new to me, especially after living in Malaysia for a year without contact with modern life. I had too many shocks and was almost numb when I came to America. I almost died so many times. In Malaysia I had to live on a soccer field, sleeping on the ground. Three thousand people slept on a soccer field. All the things we saw in those days! You would not believe them. You really don't want to know.

When I came to America I hoped very much at that time that I could some day get back my dignity. That is what I hoped for—to get back my dignity with the passage of time.

Most people say, I know, that they love freedom. But freedom is not enough for me. I want back my dignity, my spirit, my soul. I cannot really tell you how I felt being a boat person on the sea because I had lost my spirit and I could not find myself. I didn't know who I was. I just felt numb. Now I don't know what will happen. I have been through a lot. I cannot lie and say that I am very happy and that I found freedom. You see, I felt free when I was on the sea or in Malaysia or Singapore. That was free. But freedom of the human spirit involves also human dignity. I had been living in the war and left my country. I was a victim of the war. We had no real freedom. Compared with some other people in the world, yes. But *real* freedom for a human being we never had.

This country, some people like and others don't. I know I am thankful for the American people and for this country. Because at least here I have the chance to find my spirit, and dream, and be free.

I always remember the words from Martin Luther King: "I have a dream." My dream may not be the same as his or yours. My dream may be just very simple. But in this country I can do it if I try. I have the opportunity to fulfill my dreams, even though I might just daydream.

I want to be a writer, idealistically speaking. I would also like to become an educator and use my knowledge in science and in life, or whatever, to help people, because I see the people as an end and not as a means. I always see people as an end. Everything I do for me is for people.

If I love and care for me again, first, then I can love others. And I don't mean by "others" just the Vietnamese people. I mean all people. The Vietnamese people did the most suffering, of course. And I will serve them because they suffered. But I am against Communists or racists or governments that oppress or destroy human beings and the human spirit. They see human beings just for production, just as means to an end. And the Communists unfortunately treat people like that.

We are born into the world to make the world a better place to live, not to destroy it. By helping each other we can make the world a better place. I believe that all things have God in them. I believe that humans are created by heaven and the earth. I don't believe in an "-ism," and I never did. I just believe in the human spirit.

Tram Tranh
"I Am Going to Be Happy"

After arriving in Camp Pendleton my family was sponsored by a church in San Jose, California, and we moved there.

I gradually lost my faith after arriving in America. I began to have doubts after arriving here, and my depression became greater and greater until it almost overwhelmed me. There were many factors. There was culture shock, and the memory of Vietnam, and the fact that we could not go back. Also I had a lot of hatred toward the Americans because I did not understand enough about American foreign policy and politics. I was at the same time very happy to be here, but I was also very guilty about being here.

When I was in Vietnam, whenever I talked about peacetime I would see grass everywhere. That is the image I have always had of peace—green grass. Sometimes we would sit by the sea and my father would say that on the other side of the ocean was America. I heard that there was peace over there. So I dreamed of America as a place with grass everywhere. And in California there was green grass everywhere, so I thought that this was peacetime. But somehow, inside me, everything was very turbulent. The image that I saw and the feeling inside me did not correlate.

The peace in my mind and the peace outside me caused me problems. It took ten years before I finally solved it. I went through a long period when I was constantly suicidal. I would find myself in the closet or the bathroom with a knife, thinking about killing myself. I thought then about the train also, because I did not want to embarrass my family, and falling in front of a train would be the best way of making it look like an accident. But the knife would be my second resort in this effort.

Finally, when I managed to overcome my desire to kill myself and straightened out my thinking, I had gone from straight A's in college to almost flunking out. I did not allow myself to be happy in those years. Whenever I found myself happy I would feel guilty and then would get very depressed for several days. So I started to avoid happiness. The problems accumulated and became worse and worse in those years.

Finally, I decided to live only because to kill myself would be an embarrassment to my family, especially to my youngest sister. I was afraid that if I killed myself my youngest sister one day would do the same thing, and I did not want that. So when it became clear that very soon I was going to kill myself, I finally sought out professioanl help. First I saw a priest, and then a therapist. I also read extensively on Eastern religions and in philosophy. One thing led to another, and finally I became convinced that there was no God and the determination to be happy regardless of guilt was something that I had to achieve alone. Verbally I said often I did not want to commit suicide, but every now and then I thought of it and it seemed almost romantic. But I believe now it is more romantic to stay alive than to die, especially since now I believe that there is no life after death.

After I came to America I looked in my heart for God and did not find him. That was the emotional stage. I came back to God even more fervently than before for a time, but still somewhere somehow I think that was merely emotional. Finally, I became more rational and believed that God did not exist.

I went through a stage of hating God also for what he had allowed to happen to my country and my family. But now I am indifferent to God. I have no hatred. You cannot live with so much hatred. So in the end I stopped hating myself and God and the Americans.

I love the Vietnamese people very much. I love them in action, too, as well as ideally. I work with the community. Individually I love many people in America, but generally, I don't feel at home here. I still feel that this is not my country. I don't know where my country is right now, but that question is not as important to me now as it once was.

Patriotism was stressed in Vietnam. Any career plans I had were for my country. I would become a teacher for my country. But when I came here I lost my ambition, because if I became successful it would not be for my country, but for myself. Life was not quite as noble as it was before. I don't think it ever will be again. I have become Americanized and now I pursue a career because it makes me happy, and there is little else that one can aim for here.

I have a fantasy about going back to Vietnam and doing good things for my country—bringing them knowledge about all of the things that I learned about the world. It is my fantasy. It is not as strong as the faith I had a long time ago when I had a different vision of the future.

I began to feel American about four years ago. I began to feel that talking to "you" is talking to another human being. I began to feel "you." Before that time I spoke to Americans in patterns. You see, for a time, looking at Americans I could not feel them. Now I am more a person than a Vietnamese, more a human being in my feeling.

I feel sorry for the Vietnamese who are here in the United States today. It took me a lot to change, and I know that many Vietnamese today don't want to change. They want to punish themselves. They still feel guilty about leaving their country.

The country is still there; it is just a different government. We have not lost Vietnam. It is not wiped out on the map. They should ask themselves why they wipe it out on the map when it is not wiped out. It is because there is a shame in leaving.

We have so much catching up to do, spiritually and intellectually and culturally. We let the feelings from Vietnam drag us down, and we are going often in the wrong direction. We have so many problems here because of our desire to look backward. That emotion I believe is not healthy. Up to a point it is, but if you let it control your life, then things never get cleared up. I hope no one misunderstands me when I say this. I love the Vietnamese people. But many do not have the courage to be happy. I know that. For a long time I punished myself when I felt happy. It took a lot of courage to determine that I am going to be happy no matter what.

No matter who controls my country, I am going to be happy.

Tran Thi My Ngoc
"Just Let Me Die in the Sunlight"

On the twenty-fifth of December in 1979, I was supposed to leave Saigon to go to Can Tho. So on the twenty-fourth my Mom bought Christmas food, like we usually would have. Vietnamese celebrate everything. More so because we are more Westernized than other people. So at Christmas we would have a tree and go partying and come back and eat at midnight. We didn't go partying after 1975, though, because of the Communists. So my mom made Christmas dinner early because I would be leaving on the twenty-fifth. We had sweet bread, ham, and chicken and everything. All the goodies we usually ate.

I was so cross with my mom. It hurt me deeply that I had to leave and I didn't know how to express it. The big Christmas dinner just made it all that harder for me. And I couldn't say it. I knew she did it for me, but I couldn't eat a thing, nor could anybody. Everybody knew that once I was gone there would be no return, and it might be the last time that I saw them or they saw me. The Christmas dinner that year was more like a funeral than a celebration.

To prepare me for the trip my mom gave me an American one-hundred-dollar bill and some jewels. We knew that in the refugee camps jewels were good. Every kid in the family always has jewels, so I took three rings; one of them was twenty-four karat gold. The one hundred dollars was for when I got to America.

My mom sewed the money and the rings into the seams of my clothes. Then I had to disguise myself. Can Tho is the countryside, not a cosmopolitan town. People there are different from people in Saigon. I was to dress as a laborer, wearing black pajamas and a conical hat.

On the next morning I was trying not to cry, but you show grief even if not tears. My mom was crying. She hid behind a door. My mom hugged me and my sisters hugged me and they had to act normal because the Fifth Column people were watching. Then I just walked out the door and never looked back. I got on the bus going south to Can Tho. I was supposed to wait in the bus station in Can Tho for someone to come for me. But night came and nobody came for me. I had to sleep on the floor of the bus station on a piece of newspaper. The night was so long.

Finally, along with other people who came to Can Tho to get on the boat, someone took us to a house that belonged to the man who had the boat. They fed us and we waited for dark again. That night we went to the port where there were these little boats. We got onto the little boats—the first time in my life I had been on one. I was so scared I would fall off. There were ten of us in each of these small boats. They carried us out to another boat. So we got from the little boat onto a bigger boat, which had then maybe twenty some people in there. We were packed in like sardines. We waited that night. I don't know if you have ever been on the river at night. It was my first time. The moon was shining. We were keeping so quiet. A baby on the boat cried and her voice carried up and down the river and all over the place. People were terrified because they thought the baby would attract the Communists who patrolled the rivers at night looking for people like us, people trying to escape.

So we whispered, "Please do something about the baby. Give it something." The baby was lucky it didn't get killed at that moment. Finally they gave him something to drink to sleep; cough syrup.

The boat took us to another boat and in that boat there were about fifty of us, still like sardines. They piled up coconuts and watermelons on the other side to look like they were merchants, and we were all crowded in the middle. We didn't have water to drink. We waited all day on that boat. In the morning it was so hot. We couldn't go to the toilet and there was nothing to eat.

Finally on the night of the twenty-ninth the boat was ready, so we were taken further down the river. I tell you it was awful sitting in that boat. It was so hot and crowded and we were all hungry and uncomfortable.

We got into another, bigger boat. It was worse. The river breaks into tributaries. That night we were really quiet because we were ready to go, and a patrol boat came over and said, "Who's in there?" And the two guys acted like fishermen and said, "Nobody, just us fisherman waiting for morning." They said, "Are you sure, just the two of you?" And they used the lamp to look. They finally went away. The boat started to move to the bigger tributary that was closer to the river mouth at the sea.

My heart was beating so fast. Finally we got close to the mouth of the river, to another big boat. We went to that boat and got on board.

Now the crew on this boat didn't know anything about navigating their stupid boat. There was only one guy who had gone out on the sea before—he was a Navy man and was the only one who knew how to read a compass; the only one who knew anything, really. The rest of the crew did not know anything. We did not know about this until we were in deep trouble. If my mother knew about this before, she wouldn't have let me go.

The engine was running so loud, and the night was so still. Too much noise would attract the patrol. Finally the boat got out safely to the sea.

I stayed in the bottom of the boat. There were people on the top. I was so seasick. They looked back and suddenly there was the patrol boat coming after us. We said, "Oh, my God, those special police are coming for us. We have to stop or they'll fire." So we stopped. They came over and said, "Okay, you guys are going to escape, right?" There was no way to say no. We said "Yes." And then the guy said, "Well, what do you guys have?" I said, "Would you like some money?" They said, "Lucky for you there were only two of us on this boat." We collected gold and gave them the gold. Also there was a radio on board and they took that, too. Then they left us alone. I guess that was my farewell to Vietnam, bribing Communist officials one last time.

Now we were at sea and the stupid crew didn't know where we were going. They didn't know what international waters were, or where Malaysia was. There were high seas. I was so seasick.

Then we saw a big ship and the stupid crew members said, "Now we are in the international waters; now we are safe. Here is a ship. We will ask them to help." They threw up two flares. At that time I was moving up to the upper part of the boat because I was so sick. They threw up the flare attracting that ship and they came closer and closer, and it was a Vietnamese boat coming back to Vietnam! I couldn't believe it.

Everybody was so scared. We saw that this was a large ship with guards from one end to another with guns. We were so mad at the crew because they threw up the flares.

They were a government fishing ship on an expedition and they just happened to come back and see us because we threw up the flares. They said through the louspeaker to stop our engines and stay there. They got closer and said, "Okay, you guys are escaping, right?" And we said "Yes." What else could we say? I said, "Please let us go, we are only fifty people. And we have children here, too." So they said, "Well, we'll let you go if you give us all the gold and money you have." And we said, "But we were just robbed by somebody else!"

Well, some stupid guy on our boat was bringing Vietnamese money with him. I don't know why. But we gave them everything he had. Finally people did have gold, so we chipped in one more time, and gave the whole collection to them. They didn't believe us, and they sent out a small boy about twelve years old to go into our boat to check and see if people had hidden any gold.

I was so tired and seasick that I was just lying there. My rings were all gone and I finally had to break the bracelet and say, "Okay, just give this to them so they let us go." But I still had the hundred dollars. I gave it to the guy next to me to hide.

I had to act again. I think I'm going to be proficient in acting some day just from having lived in a Communist country. This boy was feeling all over all the people to find the gold. He came close to me, and if he found gold, he would find my necklace, which was hidden. So I started to act real sick. I was sick but not that sick. I acted real miserable. People spoke up for me and said, "Oh, leave her alone, she is so sick." The boy came so close to me—at that time I had not had a drop to eat or drink except for a drop of lemon juice to keep me from dying of thirst, and so I was kind of miserable. He looked at me and I looked miserable to him. So he left me alone and didn't touch me. Had he touched me, he would have found it for sure.

Finally they were satisfied. They told us, "You got only one boat, us. So you were very lucky. Had you gone the other way further south there are like sixteen ships coming back, and you wouldn't have enough money to pay them off and they would have to take you back. We were only one ship, so we will let you go." And the stupid crew people—you won't believe this—asked them, "Can you tell us how we get from here to Malaysia?"

They said, "You guys don't know how to get to Malaysia?" And we said, "No." And they showed us how to set up our compass and gave us fish to eat, two big fish.

When they sailed away they yelled goodbye, and said, "Don't feel bad because you got robbed twice. You were lucky it was only twice!"

At that moment I was thinking one thought: How did I get into this? It was not enough that I was scared. After all, I had *paid* for this. And here the crew didn't know anything. Now we knew they didn't know how the hell to get to the place we wanted to go.

Well, anyway, the other boat showed us how to set our compass and so we did that. And I thought they were all right. Except for the fact that they robbed us, they were pretty nice.

We went the way they told us. By the time I got out to the high seas I wasn't sick any more. I got used to it. And besides, I didn't eat anything. So I had with me a small bag where I had an extra pair of jeans and a T-shirt and some underwear. I had lost the conical hat and even my shoes. I was barefoot. I didn't care. I just wanted to get out of Vietnam by that time.

Finally we were in the international waters. That meant we wouldn't be afraid of Vietnamese boats or ships any more. We were on our way, going to who knows where, and on the night of January 1 we sailed into Malaysian waters.

There were sharks swimming all around us, and I kept thinking, "This is it; with this crew, I am going to die for sure." I was feeling so bad for my mother for spending all her money on me. If I died, I wouldn't mind, because I had chosen to leave, but if I died at sea, my mother would not know. That thought was running in my mind constantly.

We didn't see land for I don't know how long. We ran out of water and food. I was eating lime juice all the time. I couldn't tolerate any food any more.

Many ships passed us but they didn't come near to rescue us, even though we tried to flag them down. Then one evening, around six o'clock, we flagged down a ship and it came over to us—and guess what we got this time? Thai pirates! Would you believe it? Our stupid crew did it again!

I wasn't seasick anymore and I was up on the deck breathing fresh air. I watched this ship come over to us, a big metal boat about five times bigger than our rickety boat. When they came over they were wearing knives and guns and I thought, I know a pirate when I see one and believe me, these guys were pirates.

They ordered that we put our boat closer to their boat and they threw a rope over to our boat to stabilize it. Then they made us jump from our boat to their boat. The sea was stormy that night. The waves were so big. The two boats were smashing together and apart. Three of them jumped into our boat and made us jump into theirs. One of them was a young guy, about seventeen, who was smiling at me. He held me back. I was worried.

Actually, we really didn't know that they were going to rob us. They didn't act like they were going to. We were thinking that they would rescue us. So we were jumping. For some reason, I was praying all the time, so I didn't know why this guy was smiling at me and trying to hold me back. I was so worried. I was nineteen then, remember. And I was innocent.

Well, people were jumping onto the other boat so I just jumped with them. I hit something sharp and my toe was bleeding. I didn't feel pain, the cut was so deep. The little bag I had with one extra pair of pants of jeans and shirt, I threw over to their boat first. One girl jumped and missed and fell into the water and the boats were coming together. If she didn't get up in time she would be smashed, so we pulled her up. I don't know how I jumped that far even to this day. You couldn't calculate it. It was hit or miss. I saw that girl fall into the ocean and said, "Oh, my God." It was getting dark now and there was only the light from the big ship. We pulled her up and she was wet like a little mouse.

But we weren't all so lucky. One of the men jumped and the boats separated and he fell into the water. The boats came back so quick we couldn't get him out, and he was crushed and he died. We were feeling so bad. They made us line up and sit down in the front of the boat. Then they started robbing us. They went around and fumbled around in our clothes, trying to get money and gold.

Three of them stayed on our boat. There was a little girl still there who was so sick she was staying in the bottom of the boat, so they raped her—all three of them. The boat was being pushed and pulled back and forth by the waves and we could hear the water and the boats creaking, and we could hear her crying for help, just crying, and we couldn't do anything. So we just cried for her and for ourselves.

There were girls on their boat, too, and they could rape us at any time. It was so awful. It was the first time in my life I was exposed to any such

violent behavior or events. I sat next to some young men and some of
them talked of fighting back. I said, "This is not good. We do not have
guns or anything. We could all get killed if you try to overcome them.
There are three of them in our boat and five of them with us, and we
don't know how many more they have below. So don't fight back."

We had to give them what we had. One thing, though; they were fishermen turned pirates, so they fed us. They gave us dried fish and some rice
to eat and some hot ointment while we were in their boat and they were
raping that girl. Savages! Simply savages! They acted so barbaric. The
way they were dressed, wearing almost nothing. Dirty. Foul. Mean.

I said to myself, "This is it. I don't know what's going to happen. But
if they touch me, I'm going to kill myself." I was scared, but I was calm
then. If they tried to rape me I would kill myself by jumping into the sea
and drowning, I decided.

Suddenly I looked down and saw my right foot was bleeding. I didn't
feel pain. Usually I feel pain. But I was so scared and trying so much to
survive that I didn't feel any physical pain. I looked down and saw my
big toe was bleeding so much, and I couldn't do anything. There was a
little purse I always kept with me, I didn't put in the bag. My mom put
in some antibiotic pills because we didn't know how life was in the camp
and I might need them. I kept that purse and I think those pills kept me
alive.

After they finished robbing us and raping the little girl, they pushed us
back to our boat. They made us jump back. They made holes in the boat,
broke everything, took the compass, took the map, the flashlight, and everything. We were happy because they made us jump back, because that
meant they were not going to kill us.

When we got into the boat water was coming into the boat and we were
sinking. It was night. It was raining. It was storming. And they left us
there to die.

We had big bamboo shoots, and we were searched for the guy who fell
down in the sea earlier. It couldn't have been more than an hour, but it
seemed like an eternity to me. We called his name and dropped those
things in in case he was there. I think deep down we knew he had died,
but we called his name and dropped things that floated so in case he came
back up he could hold on.

The boat was sinking, so we had to divide the people up to distribute
the weight evenly and stabilize the boat. Funny how scared we were, yet
we had the sense to do that—the survival instinct of human beings is incredible. The boat was tipping over and water was coming in, and this
guy said, "stabilize," and we ran to the sides, divided evenly so the boat
stabilized. The men started to take the water out. Lucky for us they didn't
take the patching material, so the crew for once did something good and
found that stuff.

After they started getting the water out, there were no lights. Somebody happened to have a match, and we'd light up and find out where the holes were that they had made. We worked real fast in concerted effort. It was unbelievable. To this day I can't believe how we did it that night.

We were still alive but we didn't see land. We didn't even know whether we were in Malaysian or Thai waters. We said by morning if we did not see land we would be dying because there was no water or food. The boat's condition was terrible. It wouldn't hold for too long. It would come apart in the water and we would all die. It was really raining and we were in the middle of the sea somewhere with no navigator. The only Navy man who knew how to use the compass and where to go had died— he was the one who fell into the sea and drowned—and the crew said, "We don't know where to go. How do we go?" And we said, "You mean you guys don't know where to go?" My God, I thought I was dying ten times over.

Finally, everybody was so tired they said forget it, and the boat just drifted and we all waited to die. The engine didn't work because water got into the engine. Lucky for us there was no big typhoon, just heavy rain.

We just let the boat drift and tried to go the way the Navy guy told us to go. He had set the compass, but now they just guessed. So we drifted through the whole night, the longest night in my life. I didn't sleep.

Have you ever felt that the night has been so long and you are so scared and so alone and you want to see the light, just any light? The darkness itself is so overwhelming. That night I couldn't wait to see a ray of light. I said, "Just let me die in the sunlight."

And morning finally came.

It was such a warm and comforting feeling to see the sun come up. Finally we saw a grey thing in the distance—land. Just a mountainous area, but we had been almost five days on the sea. An island? Who cares?

The crew finally got the engine to work. It was working like it was half dead, but it was working.

There were two Malaysian Navy ships and they were looking at us. We were feeling good now we were going to get rescued. High time, because we had run out of food and water. People were smiling. I said, "Get down. You have to act real sick and real terrible for them to help you. You can't be so happy. Who would help you then?"

The Malaysian Navy men saw us. They told us to stay away from their ships and they would get somebody to come over. They said, Don't get closer. One guy came out and examined us. I was the only one in the boat who could speak up for anything. I knew English, and next to me there was a guy who knew a little bit of English, so I was telling him what happened to our boat, that we were robbed and everything and now we're out of water and we have children and don't have food and so on, and the engine would not work.

We asked that they help us. So he went back to tell the commander of the ship. And he came back and said we could put our boat close to theirs. I was invited up to the big ship and the other guy who knew some English went with me. I went in to see the captain, and explained exactly what happened. He had been in Saigon once. He was asking me about places like the Caravelle Hotel, those big places, and I was telling them that yes, I was from Saigon and I knew them. They were checking me out.

While I was up there they started feeding the people on the boat, giving them water and food to eat. I was barefooted and I had not had a shower since the twenty-seventh, and I had not had the time to comb my hair. I was a total mess. I was vain, being a girl, so after I talked to the captain, I requested that I be able to go to a restroom. I looked at myself in the mirror and I looked like a bum. I said, "Oh, my God, is this me," I had been transformed into a street urchin.

The captain wanted us to go to Singapore because Malaysia had said, No more refugees. But our engine had stopped working again and that meant they would have to pull us out to the open sea again and set us adrift, and we might die. But they could not take us to a refugee camp. He was trying to explain to me that it was hard because he had to follow orders. I kept pleading with him.

I remember distinctly one thing I said to him. "This is a small boat. We have only fifty people. One has died and we have children. Our engine was broken. We cannot go to Singapore. We would if we could. But we can't. So please help us."

He said he would have to think about it. In the meantime, before I went back to our boat—it was New Year's Day, January 1—the captain gave me a whole package of cookies, wafers with filling inside, and he said it was for me only. And he gave me fruit and other goodies to eat, for me only. Meanwhile, people got fed and when I came back to the boat I got something to eat, too. But this was mine, in a little bag, cookies and fruit and something else. It was like a dream, suddenly.

It was the afternoon now, so they let us rest for a while. In the evening, they said, "You have to come with us." So they attached a cable to our boat and pulled us out to the open sea because they couldn't take us. The captain was doing this and I couldn't believe it.

They pulled us out near to an island that was uninhabited. They anchored there because it was night and the sea was getting rough again. We were like an elephant and a mouse—the elephant pulling the mouse. They were a big ship and we were just a small and rickety raft. We were stationed that night near the empty island and they said our women and children could come aboard the ship to spend the night, but the men had to stay in the boat. The captain came out and talked a little bit. We got food to eat, and we camped outside on the deck.

That night we were sort of scared because we didn't know what would happen. The captain was nice, but how about the sailors? One of them got drunk and wanted a woman to go to bed with him. He was making such a terrible noise about it. Luckily he wanted somebody else and not me. He made all kinds of noise, and finally other sailors got him back into order.

In the morning the captain came out and said he talked to headquarters and it was okay to take us to the refugee camp.

I was so happy. That was a very good thing that he did. There was no way for me to repay him. I can't even remember his face clearly today, and I am sorry about that. He said since we were only forty-nine people they would send us to a refugee camp.

So now men and women got on the ship and they pulled the boat to Pulau Bidong camp.

Let me tell you, after being at sea for so long I was really happy. It was about noon when we came to the island where the camp was.

The shore was full of people. It was so crowded I couldn't believe my eyes. I didn't know if this was a good thing happening or what. I never knew what a refugee camp was before. But we were safe after all.

I was the only one talking (talking too much), on the ship, and they said to me, You will be able to leave the camp fast because you speak English. I remember that. At that moment I really didn't care what speaking English mattered. Why would that help me?

Before they let us go, we sang for them. We stood on their deck and sang a Vietnamese song for them, all of us. It was all we could do. It was all we had left to give them—a song. It was a well-known Vietnamese song, so all of us knew it. It was about free Vietnam. A proud song.

Then they said goodbye to us, and we said goodbye and thank you to them.

We were discharged onto smaller boats, because the ship couldn't go closer to the island because of the coral. At that time I only had a pair of black pants and a shirt. I didn't have anything else. The other bag was lost with the pirates.

The refugees who were there before, every time there was a boat coming in they would go down to see if any of their relatives were there. So I was treading water to go in, and the coral was sharp. We didn't even have shoes on. Our boat was towed close to shore and onto shore to be broken, because they didn't want us to have a boat to go around somewhere in Malaysian waters. They wanted us to be confined there.

I waded ashore. It was just a sea of people. It was pathetic. I was standing at the shore on the beach, not knowing anything and trying to find out what was going on.

Among the people was my brother who had left before me. He came down to see if there was anybody he knew. There he was, wearing only a pair of shorts. And I was so beat up. I looked so bad.

There were 46,000 people on the island—all refugees. There was little food and little water. Life was very hard and I was working all the time. I didn't have any other clothes to wear. People lived like animals. There was no hygiene, no sanitary facilities. People had to dig holes for an outhouse. It was awful, awful, awful.

The Malaysians tried to prevent boats from landing there. They would tow them out to sea. The boats would sink and the people would drown. In the morning, we would go down to the beach and there would be bodies everywhere—men, women, and children. All Vietnamese. We would bury them every morning. They were the unlucky ones.

I was so deficient in vitamins that I got bloated. My face was all blown up and watery.

I was on Pulau Bidong for three and a half months. And it's there I learned how people behave when they are desperate. People could kill for a little food or for a little money. Friends turned into enemies in a matter of seconds. I cried so often. I couldn't sleep. I just slept two or three hours a night. I just stared at the sky. I was feeling so bad for myself, for everything, for people.

All of my energy was put into living, surviving, and getting out. I didn't care where I would go, I just wanted to get out of the camp. I had to stay alive.

CBS News came to the island and filmed a program there. I think Ed Bradley was there filming. And you know what happened after that? I think the Malaysian government was criticized about what was going on. Because of that CBS program we started getting better rations. CBS let the world know what the refugee camp was like and what was happening to the boat people. After that we got enough to eat. It came in a package: rice and tea and food. From the United Nations. God bless the United Nations! Each person got a small bag of food every three days. It actually came faster than we could eat it because we were so used to starving for so long.

My brother and I found sponsors and were cleared to go to the United States. We were supposed to leave on the nineteenth of April.

At last I was leaving. I didn't even know then where I was going. I knew I was going to the United States of America, but I didn't know where in the United States.

When I was in the transit camp, they told me I was going to Iowa. I didn't know where Iowa was. They took out a map and pointed to a place and said, "Here's Iowa, in the Midwest." I didn't really understand, but I said, "Okay, Iowa. Fine."

I was sponsored by a church. I landed in Des Moines with about three hundred other Vietnamese. The governor of the state was there to welcome us. Then they matched each of us up to the place we were supposed to go, and they drove us to our new homes. They drove us across Iowa. I remember going through this town on a Sunday evening and there was not a soul in the streets. It was beautiful. It was cold and gray, too. I wondered where we were going and why there were no people in Iowa.

They put me in an apartment that night. I couldn't sleep. I had nightmares. Every time there was a noise outside I would panic. All noises scared me. I remembered the noise of the motor of the Thai pirates on the sea—and I would wake up immediately and be paralyzed with fear and be sweating. That happened to me every night for about three months.

Well, I am coming to my happy ending. The young girl who was raped by the Thai pirates is now living in Canada. She is married now and happy. She was such a sweet little girl. I was so glad things turned out all right.

My brother graduated from the university in Iowa and is now an engineer. I graduated from the university there and earned my master's degree in social work in California. Then I returned to Pulau Bidong and worked with the new refugees and boat people after I earned my degree.

Looking back today, it seems unreal. That's why I had to go back to work in a refugee camp. It was a way not only to help other people, but to let them know that there is a future in the free world for them.

But also I had to go back to heal myself. In that period of time I was living but I was really like a dead person. I just functioned with no emotions. After I survived, I still needed healing. Helping others who went through what I went through and worse has provided that healing.

So today I am not only a survivor. I am also alive.

Duong Canh Son
"My Father"

One day in 1979 I was home watching television. I was watching *60 Minutes* because they were doing a show on the boat people coming to Malaysia from Vietnam. Ed Bradley was interviewing some of the people. They told him they had come from Vietnam in a boat and the Malaysian government would not let them land. And their boat sank and many of the people on the boat drowned. All of the people who had survived were crying.

One of the people Ed Bradley interviewed I recognized. He was my brother's best friend in Vietnam. His name is Phuoc Hong Dang. So I telephoned my brother right away, and I asked him, "Are you watching *60 Minutes?*" And he said, "Yes. Did you just see Phuoc Hong Dang?" And I said, "Yes." So we decided to try to get in touch with him and to sponsor him so he could come to the United States. We wrote to the Red Cross and tried to reach him.

After we got in touch with him he wrote to us. He told us that one of the people on his boat who had drowned was our father. He said that our father had paid the boat owner to take him out of Vietnam. But then the boat sank off the coast of Malaysia and my father was lost.

All my father ever wanted was freedom. He just wanted to be a free man. That was all. He sent my brother and me to America so we could be free. And then he tried to run away from the Communists. But it was too late for him. Too late.

Acknowledgments

Shortly after Thanksgiving in 1984 I began to write an article on the fall of Saigon. The original idea for my article was simply to profile an American who had been aboard the aircraft carrier *Midway* in the spring of 1975 and then to profile one of the Vietnamese refugees who came out to the *Midway* from Tan Son Nhut air base. John Degler, a photographer aboard the *Midway*, was to be one of my subjects, and Miss Nguyen Nhat the other.

Degler, however, after telling me his story of the evacuation, suggested that I seek out additional Americans who had been involved in the operation, and Miss Nhat introduced me to some of her friends who also had stories to tell. I listened. And I began to seek others whose stories, I thought, should be told.

Helene Hicks introduced me to her father, Henry Hicks, who then contacted several of his friends from the Defense Attaché Office in Saigon and set up interviews for me. General John Murray and General Homer Smith, the two American defense attachés, granted me interviews and in turn called friends and arranged other interviews. And so my article became a book.

In California I met Tran Thi My Ngoc, who became my research assistant and translator. My accompanied me to Bangkok, Ho Chi Minh City, Hanoi, and Hong Kong for interviews and told me her own dramatic story about life under the Communists in Vietnam and escaping to Malaysia by boat. My is a tireless worker, an intelligent, sensitive, and energetic young woman who believed in this book from the moment she heard about it and who helped shape its content. Nguyen Thi Lac, Nguyen Thi Kim Anh, Nguyen Thi Hoa, and Bui Le Ha all worked for me as translators and interviewers and did a superb job of locating subjects.

Peggy Adams introduced me to her brother-in-law, Captain Allen Broussard, who told me his story of the evacuation and gave me several photographs he had taken during Operation Frequent Wind. Allen graciously introduced me to Colonel George Slade, who invited me to his home in Virginia to meet and interview a dozen Marines who had participated in the evacuation of the U.S. Embassy and Tan Son Nhut air base.

Fox Butterfield not only granted me a lengthy interview, but helped me arrange interviews with several other Vietnam correspondents.

Peter Kama also helped me by serving as a translator and by introducing me to many Vietnamese in California, and convincing them that by telling their stories to me they would be making a contribution toward understanding what really happened in Indochina in the spring of 1975.

Eventually I interviewed more than three hundred individuals who were associated in one way or another with the fall of Saigon in 1975. In the end, however, the limitations of space meant that many of the stories I gathered with My could not be used in this book. I want to thank all those I interviewed for their generosity, their trust, and their help.

Thanks are due to the following individuals interviewed in the United States: General William Westmoreland, Colonel William E. Le Gro, General Richard Baughn, Lieutenant Colonel Dennis Traynor, General Cao Van Vien, Dr. Nguyen Van Canh, Linda Nguyen, General Bui Dinh Dam, Senator Nhuan Tran, Ngo Dinh Chuong, Y-klong Adrong, Colonel Vu Van Loc, Colonel Tran Tien, Colonel Ngo Thi Linh, Hai Van Le, Tran Minh Loi, Calvin Mehlert, Edward G. Lansdale, Kenneth Moorefield, Anthony Hicks, James Barker, Lieutenant Colonel Jim Bolton, Nguyen Ngoc Nha, Le Manh Duong, Tran Thach Thuy, Lina Lim, Thiro Lim, Rathnary Eng, Vilay Lim, Bui Diem, Tran Thi Lien Huong, Tran Thi Kiet, Ha Ngoc Kim-Loan, Hue Vu, Nguyen Minh, Nguyen Quan Binh, Josiah Bennett, Marvin Garrett, Bach Dieu Hoa, Moncrieff Spear, Joseph Nguyen Van Tinh, Father Joe Devlin, General Nguyen Van Toan, Thai Tan Tran, Melissa Pham, Nguyen Thao, Alphonse Tran Duc Phuong, Nguyen Van Manh, Charles Patterson, Lieutenant Colonel Ngo Le Tinh, Lieutenant Colonel Nguyen Vinh, Captain Quan Dao, Pham Vinh, Sam Chu Linh, Charles Stewart, Ken Healy, Don Berney, Captain Edwin Herring, Charlotte Daly, Mai Van Duc, Bruce Dunning, General Nguyen Cao Ky, Daniel Gamelin, Bill Plante, Tom Sailer, Jennifer Bissett, Oliver Stone, Phil Caputo, Nguyen Xuan Phac, Morley Safer, Rose Tran, Mimi Tran, Daniel Ellsberg, Tom Hayden, Alexander Haig, General Charles Timmes, Tommy Rowe, Gene Hasenfus, Bruce Burns, Uk Siphan, Kamchong Luangpraseut, Malcolm Browne, Jim Markham, Anne Mariano, Jim Bennett, Tran Van An, Sengthong Ta Keophanh, Pham Quang Trinh, Dr. Bruce Branson, Lien Mai, Dat Tran, Mai Thi Tuyet Nguyen, Hue Duong, Ha Thao, Trinh Tran Huyen, Debbie Huynh, Tiffany Chiao, Hieu Trung Nguyen, Pham Hong, Tran Kim Loan, Anh Pham, Phan Hanh Bich, Colonel John Madison, Bill Johnson, Frank Snepp, Ha Ly, Shep Lowman, Phil McCombs, Lucien Conien, George McArthur, Jean Sauvageot, Julia Taft, Bill Laurie, Doug Dearth, George Jacobson, Lucy Parsons, Al Santoli, Norman Lloyd, General Vinh Loc, David C. Simmons, Captain Edward Flink, Hanh

Pham, Richard Armitage, Denny Ellerman, Arnold Isaacs, Nguyen Dat Tinh, Paul Horton, Steve Stewart, Colonel Harry Summers, Captain William R. Melton, Major Thomas Ochala, Major Mike Clough, Lieutenant Thomas Linn, Lieutenant Bruce Duderstadt, Lieutenant Thomas O'Hara, Ha C. Tam, Nguyen Thuy Nhu, Sichan Siv, Lacy Wright, General Richard Carey, Captain Nguyen Phu Lam, Captain Gerry Berry, Philip Habib, Millicent Fenwick, Donald Fraser, Pham Thi Kim-Hoang, Tran Kim Phuong, Brent Scowcroft, Nguyen Gia Hien, Joe Welsch, General Ngo Quang Truong, Major Truong Quan Si, Hue Thu, Vu Cong Duong, Pham Hue, Eugene McCarthy, Pham Duy, Douglas Pike, Yvette Do, Anh Do, Mary Nelle Gage, Captain Ray Iacobacci, General Ralph Maglione, and Neal O'Leary.

In Hong Kong: Helen Tran, Sister Christine Truong My Hanh, Nguyen Dieu Huong, Yukari Sawada, and Arthur Kobler.

In Thailand: Bill Bell and Suphan Sathorn.

In Vietnam: General Ly Tong Ba, Tran Cong Man, Colonel Nguyen Phuong Nam, Nguyen Thanh Long, Bui Huu Nhan, Colonel Bui Tin, Vu Tuat Viet, Nguyen Xuan Oanh, Dang Thi Ngoc Hiep, Le Thuy Duong, Akira Suwa, and "Raymond" and his fellow "Bui Doi."

In England: Robert Elegant.

In Australia: Ted Serong.

Thanks also to my friends and students in Nanjing, China, who listened to parts of this manuscript during the 1988–89 academic year and suggested additional questions and subjects for research. They are: Charlotte Ku, Richard Pomfret, Rosemary Pomfret, Sam Crane, Hall Gardner, Isabel Gardner, Denise Carolan, Ruth Kling, Dick Gaulton, Doug Reed, Jeffrey Reed, Eddie Ou, Eric Tippett, Guo Haini, Xiao Ling, Thao Xiaoying, Li Yuanchao, Ha Fayu, Fang Wa, Feng Weinian, and Liu Liyan.

Thanks also to Kathy Briggs, Barbara Briggs, John Snetsinger, Paul Campbell, Jim Darby, Jean Hamm, Diana Killian, Qi-wei Li, Jia Li, Kasie Cheung, June Yee, Vincent Leung, Daisy Ng, Emilie Chim, Sonia Chim, Peter Lau, Michael Malone, Bill Bellows, Kathy Rebello, Robert Bernell, and Ge Bernell.

James Walsh, dean of the School of Social Sciences at San Jose State University, gave me important encouragement and support while I was writing this book; as did my agent, Emilie Jacobson. Joan Block transcribed nearly all of the English-language interviews for this book and proved herself, once again, to be a reliable and good-humored associate and friend. My daughters, Marya and Erika, lived with many of these harrowing stories for the past five years and accompanied me on some of the interviews. Their company and comments were a constant source of delight and encouragement.

This book would not have been possible without the cooperation of my Vietnamese, Cambodian, and Laotian students at San Jose State University. I was invited into their homes, met and interviewed their parents and other relatives, and, above all else, was trusted by them to tell the truth. I hope that this book lives up to their expectations.

Finally, thank you to Xu Meihong, who helped me organize and transcribe much of this material during my stay in China. Our long conversations concerning the stories in this book, the nature of Asian Communism, American foreign policy, China's role in Southeast Asia, and the future of that region provided me with many hours of provocative and enlightening dialogue. Meihong eventually paid a high price for our friendship. Her dreams and fears and her fate helped me understand some of the bitterness and the behavior of those who won and lost in Vietnam, and why they fought.

San Jose, California   Larry Engelmann

Glossary of Abbreviations and Acronyms

AFRTS	Armed Forces Radio and Television Service
AID	Agency for International Development
APC	Armored personnel carrier
ARVN	Army of the Republic of Vietnam (South)
AP	Associated Press
AWS	Amphibious Warfare School
BLT	Battalion landing team
BOQ	Bachelor officers' quarters
CTOC	Corps Tactical Operations Center
CIA	Central Intelligence Agency
CINCPAC	Commander in Chief, Pacific
CO	Commanding officer
COSVN	Central Office for South Vietnam
CRA	Combined Recreation Area
DAO	Defense Attaché Office
DMZ	Demilitarized Zone between North and South Vietnam
DOD	Department of Defense
ECC	Evacuation Control Center
FAA	Federal Aviation Agency
FULRO	Front Unifié pour la Libération des Races Oprimées
GVN	Government of Vietnam (South)
ICCS	International Commission of Control and Supervision
JAG	Judge Advocate General
JCS	Joint Chiefs of Staff
JGS	Joint General Staff (South Vietnamese)
JMT	Joint Military Team

KIA	Killed in action
LZ	Landing zone
MACV	Military Assistance Command, Vietnam
MIA	Missing in action
MIG	Soviet fighter plane (*Mikoyan i Gurevich*)
MISTA	Monthly intelligence summary and threat analysis
MP	Military Police
MR	Military Region
MSC	Military Sealift Command
NCO	Noncommissioned officer
NLF	National Liberation Front
NSC	National Security Council
NVA	North Vietnamese Army
OCS	Officer Candidate School
PFC	Private, First Class
POW	Prisoner of War
PRG	Provisional Revolutionary Government
RVN	Republic of Vietnam (South)
SAM	Surface-to-air missile
SDS	Students for a Democratic Society
TCN	Third-country national
TOC	Tactical Operations Center
UPI	United Press International
USAID	U.S. Agency for International Development
USIA	U.S. Information Agency
VC	Vietcong (South Vietnamese Communists)
VOQ	Visiting officers' quarters